Barrier-Free
Environments

COMMUNITY DEVELOPMENT SERIES

Series Editor: Richard P. Dober, AIP

CDS/33

Barrier-Free Environments

Edited by
Michael J. Bednar
University of Virginia

Dowden, Hutchinson & Ross, Inc.
Stroudsburg, Pennsylvania

Copyright © 1977 by *Dowden, Hutchinson & Ross, Inc.*
Community Development Series, Volume 33
Library of Congress Catalog Card Number: 76-54798
ISBN: 0-87933-277-8

77 78 79 5 4 3 2 1
Manufactured in the United States of America.

LIBRARY OF CONGRESS CATALOGING IN PUBLICATION DATA

Main entry under title:
Barrier-free environments.
   (Community development series ; 33)
   Includes index.
   1. Architecture and the handicapped—Addresses, essays, lectures. I. Bednar,
Michael J.
NA2545.A1B36   720   76-54798
ISBN 0-87933-277-8

To the memory of Betty Jane Yoder for the lessons that she taught us about the value of life.

Mentally retarded are human beings who are more like other people than they differ from them, no matter the degree of retardation. Their happiness—exactly as that of other people—depends greatly on the houses they live in.

N. E. Bank-Mikkelson

Series Editor's Foreword

CDS publications include state-of-the-art books, handbooks and manuals. They are offered to planners, architects, landscape architects and others who would benefit in having such knowledge in readily convenient format. Philosophically, the books are not bound by traditional theory nor do they presume to establish a philosophic framework for all professional practice. There are themes that identify the series, however, and those who read this foreword should note the conceptual framework within which Michael Bednar's book fits.

CDS books are concerned with active user and client involvement in problem defining and problem solving; systematic searching out of patterns, relationships, and behavioral settings as a prelude to design. They express a high regard for physical interdependence of communities; ecological ethics; an interest in not just finding appropriate solutions, but also in establishing ways and means for having those solutions implemented.

On all these grounds, *Barrier-Free Environments* is a welcomed book—but more than that it is an unusually important reference work. Bednar systematically explores ways in which we can make the physical environment accessible and usable for those who are temporarily or permanently physically or mentally handicapped. His book is intended to help people for whom we feel much but actually do little. And if that last sentence seems too strong, look a little closer at your immediate environs. For all our good intentions, there is much to be done.

Fortunately, there are emerging laws and regulations which will push us further along in responding to the issues implicit in *Barrier-Free Environments*. What once rose from good intentions is now rooted in legal requirements. With a presidential wife active in this area, we can expect further moral leadership and action from the White House. Accordingly, Bednar's well motivated book is also timely and should prove useful to all planners, designers, and their clients.

Richard P. Dober, AIP

Preface

This is an era of growing national concern for the problems of physically and mentally handicapped persons—a concern that in itself is aiding the progress of resolving these problems. Education is improving in quality through increased emphasis on special education programs in most states. Rehabilitation programs and facilities are increasing in sophistication to offer improved rehabilitative prognoses to persons with handicapping conditions. The trend towards de-institutionalization is leading to improved housing opportunities in the community. Work opportunities are growing in scope and number along with training programs.

Many improvements in programs and services for the handicapped require concomitant facility improvements for implementation. Moreover, the normalization movement requires removal of environmental barriers to facilitate the integration of the handicapped with the rest of society. Consequently, planners, architects, and environmental designers are currently taking an active interest in improving facility planning and design for the disabled. Several major research projects are underway to generate new design knowledge and to develop new facility standards. Creative efforts are being undertaken in the planning, design, and construction of new buildings and transportation systems that are responsive to the needs of the handicapped.

The primary objective of this book is to aid in formulating a policy toward physical planning and design for the physically and mentally handicapped. This collection of papers has been gathered together in order to establish an overall philosophical direction that would aid in coordinating various research, planning, design, administrative, and legislative efforts. The book focusses on the larger issues of developing communities in which the handicapped have equal opportunities and a society in which the handicapped have an integral role as citizens.

Planning and designing facilities for the handicapped is a very complex problem with serious political, social, economic, and cultural overtones. In order to solve this problem, planners and designers must understand it and develop a philosophical approach towards it. This understanding and approach form a basis for decision making in the absence of definitive research, design standards, or guidelines. In unique situations, wherein guidelines are not available, a thorough understanding of the problem can form a sound basis for creative problem solving.

The approach to planning and design set forth by the collective chapters in this book is performance based rather than prescriptive. It endeavors to identify environmental barriers and to provide case study examples of their removal. It does not prescribe planning and design solutions for creating a barrier-free environment. It seeks a creative response from the planner and designer that is pertinent to the circumstances of the problem and sensitive to the handicapping conditions of the environmental users.

The structure of the book is in four parts. Parts I and II on physical barriers deal with the environmental problems of the physically handicapped. Parts III and IV on social barriers deal with the environmental problems of the mentally handicapped. The environmental problems are considered as barriers that need to be recognized, analyzed, and removed or countered so as not to restrict the handicapped person from participating in life's opportunities. The two broad classes of barriers correspond to two distinct sets of handicapping conditions that require separate consideration due to their difference. When both kinds of handicapping conditions occur in the same population group, the planning and design responses can be combined accordingly, because they are usually exclusive in their effect.

Within this book, the first of the two parts devoted to each type of barrier deals with theoretical perspectives while the second sets forth case studies and design guidelines. The contributed chapters that comprise the book have been organized into these sections based on their primary content, whereas secondary content does overlap the divisions. Part I, Physical Barriers: Theoretical Perspectives, contains three chapters, each of which has a unique point of view regarding barrier-free access. In Chapter 1,

"Toward a Responsive Environment: The Psychosocial Effects of Inaccessibility," Steinfield, Duncan, and Cardell make a clear statement of a proposition that becomes a recurring theme throughout the book: The built environment as it exists today communicates to the disabled messages of deviancy, incompetence, and inferiority. In their view, "If our society should change its attitudes towards disabled people, without corresponding changes in the built environment, a truly responsive life space will not exist." In Chapter 2, Templer and Jones view the urban environment from the perspective of the handicapped pedestrian. They classify and analyze functional requirements for pedestrian travel, causes of vehicle-pedestrian accidents, and pedestrian mobility impediments; they then discuss systemwide mobility barriers and proposed countermeasures. Their chapter is based upon research being conducted for the Federal Highway Administration of the Department of Transportation. In Chapter 3, James Jeffers presents another point of view with his legislative history of the barrier-free design movement. As Executive Director of the Architectural and Transportation Barriers Compliance Board, he discusses the goals, objectives, and activities of that organization.

Part II, Physical Barriers: Towards a Barrier-Free Environment, contains four chapters that deal with specific efforts in eliminating those environmental barriers that affect the physically handicapped. The Fokus Housing System in Sweden is perhaps the best organized and planned program of providing housing opportunities for the severely disabled in existence today. It has been in operation since 1964, and one of its originators, Dr. Sven-Olof Brattgård, provides us with insights into the philosophy, planning, organization, and operation of the Fokus Housing System as well as illustrations of the apartment unit designs in Chapter 4. Edward Steinfeld at Syracuse University has been directing the project sponsored by the U.S. Department of Housing and Urban Development that is intended to both revise and extend the existing ANSI Standard A-117.1, Specifications for Making

Buildings and Facilities Accessible to and Usable by the Physically Handicapped. In Chapter 5, "Developing Standards of Accessibility," he discusses the problems with the existing standard as well as the issues and processes related to developing and using a new standard of barrier-free access.

The remaining two chapters in Part II deal with the problems of urban and site access. Much more work has been done on the problems of building access and use than on the problems of access and use of shopping areas, business centers, streets, plazas, parking facilities, parks, and transportation stations. In Chapter 6, Alan Winslow takes a detailed look at the design criteria and requirements involved in overcoming functional barriers in the exterior environment. His discussion on policy preparation and implementation procedures is particularly valuable to community planners and local governmental administrators. In Chapter 7, Gunduz Ast presents a case study of planning and designing a barrier-free access system in Downtown Moline, Illinois. Her process model sets forth a methodology for conducting user research related to an elderly or handicapped population group and for applying the results of that research in developing a specific design proposal. Although the design proposal has not yet been implemented or tested, it is an integrated solution available for evaluation and critique.

In the two parts on social barriers, the social consequences of ideologically inappropriate environmental design are explored. Social barriers created by the built environment are equal to physical barriers in import in that they are no less real, although often less obvious.

Part III, Social Barriers: Theoretical Perspectives, opens with a powerful ideological statement of the normalization principle and its architectural–environmental consequences by Wolf Wolfensberger. He points out the various ways that groups of persons have been perceived or characterized as deviant with the resultant design implications. His discussion of the various ways in which buildings serve to devalue handicapped groups or persons is frank and to the

point. This provocative chapter sets the tone for Part III of the book in presenting the highest ideological goals for striving to eliminate social barriers.

The other two chapters in Part III delve into more detailed considerations of the psychosocial effects of the environment on the lives of the mentally handicapped. In Chapter 9, Maxine Wolfe deals with environmental stimulation as a concept that mediates the relationship between people's goals, needs, and expectations and the physical setting. She reports on research into the variables of location, size, and design of bedrooms as barriers to interaction choice, privacy, and activity choice. Authors Knight, Zimring and Kent discuss the behavioral hypothesis implicit in the normalization concept in Chapter 10 and conclude that any concept of "normal" behavior is meaningless outside the context in which it occurs. To be "normalized," environments must support a wide range of personal needs, including arousal, information, and privacy. Their chapter reports on research being conducted at a state school for the mentally retarded in Massachusetts.

Part IV, Social Barriers: Towards a Barrier-Free Environment, begins with a chapter by myself. It presents the national efforts undertaken to implement the normalization principle in the two countries where it originated: Denmark and Sweden. This chapter, illustrated with examples from Scandinavia, discusses the planning of service systems, facility programming, design guidelines, and educational facilities. The Scandinavian experience with normalization provides many lessons to be learned by this country and others in implementing this ideology. In Chapter 12, David Sokoloff takes a look at the new planning processes that are requisite if we are to meet the normalization goal of deinstitutionalization. A successful community-based facility system will only result from carefully structured participatory processes. One of the key community facilities needed to implement deinstitutionalization is group homes. In Chapter 13, Arnold Gangnes, the first architect to be appointed to the President's Committee on Mental Retardation, presents a detailed discussion of program and design requirements for various kinds of group homes. One of the initial needs in implementing any new program of barrier removal is information that is relevant, accurate, and readily available to planners, architects, administrators, programmers, community leaders, and so forth. In Chapter 14, Bayes and Levison present an historical account of the development of such an information center in England with lessons to be learned for a similar endeavor in the United States. This book is truly a collective effort. It would

This book is truly a collective effort. It would not exist without the outstanding individual efforts of each of the contributing authors. They brought to it their long experience, deep knowledge, and clear insight. May this book be a momento of their thoughtful endeavors.

Richard Dober first suggested the volume, and he was instrumental in its inception. Charles Hutchinson made the publishing effort a truly memorable experience. Mrs. Janet Cutright at the University of Virginia School of Architecture was dilligent in providing clerical and secretarial assistance. Frances Crabill, graduate student in architecture, produced much of the graphic material. My wife, Mary, provided much needed support, patience, and encouragement. My sincere gratitude is extended to all of these people for their roles in making this book possible.

Michael J. Bednar

Contents

xiii

Barrier-Free Environments

Introduction: On Barriers

Michael J. Bednar

One dictionary definition of *barrier* is "anything that restrains or obstructs progress, access, etc." (*The Random House Dictionary of the English Language*, Random House, New York, 1966). Under the root word *bar*, we find in the noun form "anything which obstructs, hinders, or impedes" and in the verb form "to exclude or except." Therefore, the meaning of the term *barrier* has both a literal form, as in a fence or railing, and a figurative form, as in a restriction to membership in a club.

This book explores both kinds of barriers, literal and figurative, as they relate to the built environment. The literal barriers are herein termed *physical barriers* and refer to those problems of handicapped people relative to access and use of buildings and mobility in the environment. The figurative barriers are termed *social barriers* and refer to the restrictions to full societal participation imposed upon the handicapped through the built environment.

Physical barriers are direct in their influence and explicit in their effect primarily upon the physically handicapped. They are more easily recognized than social barriers, and therefore, they are more easily changed. Significant progress is now being made in the removal of physical barriers, and efforts are underway for even greater advancements. The topics of identification of physical barriers and the progress being made to insure their removal from the built environment constitute Parts I and II of this book.

Physical barriers deny the full use of the environment primarily to the physically handicapped. They are pervasive in their influence in that they reach to all aspects of the built environment, including all building types and the spaces between buildings. Common physical barriers are found in pedestrian walkways, building entrances, building corridors, stairs, elevators, toilets, and all forms of public transportation.

The reason for this long list of physical barriers lies in the norm that is used as the basis for all environmental design. This norm is based upon the mobility, size, strength, and capabilities of the average-sized, healthy, thirty-year old male. Most of the available anthropometric data commonly used in environmental design are based upon this norm. Stairs, elevators, door hardware, toilets, plumbing fixtures, telephone booths, drinking fountains, and other facilities are designed on this basis. Women, children, the aged, the injured or frail, and the physically handicapped do not fit this norm and are therefore asked to make adaptations in using the environment. Through the development of new kinds of anthropometric data, these norms can change so that environmental design can become more inclusive of the population that it serves.

Social barriers, on the other hand, are more subtle and implicit. They are more difficult to recognize, and therefore, more difficult to change. They are so bound up with the everyday appearance and functioning of our culture so as to be totally accepted. Moreover, they have been in existence for so long that they will require exceptional effort to change. Both the recognition of social barriers and the plans for their elimination are dealt with in Parts III and IV of this book.

Social barriers to full participation primarily of the mentally handicapped in society are evident in many laws, institutions, and opportunities. Classification as mentally retarded is a stigma that acts as a barrier to a normalized life. Institutionalization is a usual concomitant that denies rights to life in a normal community. Opportunities in housing, education, and employment are further denied through barriers to acceptance of the mentally handicapped as full citizens.

Each of these social barriers has environmental factors that give them support and longevity. Many mentally handicapped persons have traditionally been housed in large-scale institutions in isolated, rural locations. They have been denied educational opportunities through the lack of special education facilities, and they have been denied employment through the lack of training and workshop facilities. When given the opportunity to live in the community, their house

often has a sign on it labelling it as a "home for the retarded."

The built environment has a physical inertia that resists change. The capital investment in public facilities insures their long-term utilization. This resistance to change is in itself a barrier to shifts in societal attitudes. On the other hand, changes in the built environment can induce both society and government to change their attitudes towards the mentally handicapped and to grant them more opportunities for a normalized life.

Apart from the physical and/or social nature of barriers, some of their general characteristics need to be discussed. First of all, barriers are always external to the handicapped persons they effect; they are not a concomitant of the disability. They were created by others, both knowingly and unknowingly, to restrict the lives of the handicapped. As such, they can be changed by the creators (society and government) without the handicapped persons involvement or knowledge. For the most part, the handicapped have had little control, if any, over the imposition of barriers, and they are only now becoming active in promoting their removal.

The second general characteristic of barriers is their transparency to those unaffected—that is, only the handicapped are directly aware of the existence of barriers. The handicapped conditions that they have accepted without choice enable them to identify barriers. Thus, a "vicious circle" has been created whereby those cognizant of the barriers and affected by them have had no role in their creation and have little power in implementing their removal.

The key that unlocks the "vicious circle" is the *advocate*, or that person or group who through research and sensitivity discovers barriers and works for their removal. The advocate acts on behalf of the handicapped. Effectuating barrier removal requires both an awareness of the existence of barriers and advocates who are willing to work for a barrier-free environment.

It is with the attitude of the advocate that this book is written. Our intention is to allow the reader to explore the nature of environmental barriers, to understand those barriers already identified, to search for additional hidden barriers, and to study past and future efforts at barrier removal. Hopefully, this book will increase the reader's interest in becoming an advocate—that is, one who is sympathetic to the needs of the handicapped and works for improving their rights to a normalized life.

Some barriers can be removed by the handicapped person through education, training, medical aid, and prosthetic devices. The development of these efforts is quite well advanced for some handicaps and continues to develop for others. Those who espouse the position of handicapped self-cure argue that the environment must be designed to serve the majority, whereas the minority members (the handicapped) must learn to cope with this majority environment. The argument continues that by having to cope with a majority environment, the handicapped will be challenged to overcome their handicaps and/or compensate for them. Furthermore, this challenge is viewed as a positive factor in motivating the handicapped to greater efforts in education and training. Likewise, it will encourage the educators and therapists to develop new training techniques and the doctors to develop better prosthetic devices.

A couple of fallacies existing in this argument must be identified. First of all, the environment does not have to be designed only to suit the majority of its users. There can be pluralism in environmental design. Since barriers are often transparent or unnoticed by those who are unaffected, the removal of these barriers is likewise often unnoticed by the majority. As an example, the inclusion of curb-cuts in sidewalks has little if any effect upon the ambulatory but greatly aids the wheelchair-bound person. Secondly, while the effects of many handicapping conditions can be ameliorated through training and prosthetic devices, they cannot be completely overcome. There is a limit to the results of training and prostheses, thus necessitating environmental changes to compensate for these limits.

An interesting result often occurs when environmental barriers are removed. Not only the capability of the handicapped to use the environment but also the functional capability of the nonhandicapped is improved. As an example, curb-cuts for wheelchairs also benefit bicyclists and mothers with baby carriages. Grab bars in toilet stalls also help the elderly and injured to use the toilet. Group homes for mentally retarded persons enable them to become useful members of society instead of wards of the state.

These "side effects" of barrier-free design suggest a redefinition of this concept as a much broader and more universal one that involves the environmental needs of all users, not only the disabled. James Jeffers, in this volume, redefines barrier-free design to mean ". . . the incorporation and utilization of design principles that result in the construction and creation of functional, safe, and convenient environments responsive to user needs." We all pass through stages in our lives with varying degrees of ability and disability. An environmental design that is responsive to life's stages and the capabilities of all users can truly be termed *barrier-free*.

The design of the built environment is ripe for a great deal of improvement that will make it more suitable to and usable by more members of society. Housing needs to be designed to support and enhance a greater variety of lifestyles. Schools need to be designed in accordance with the scale of children and their aesthetic needs as well as those of the teachers. Public buildings and facilities must be made accessible and usable by all members of the public. All means of public transportation must be readily available to be used by persons of widely varying capabilities.

The goal set forth by this book is to undertake an overall user-oriented improvement in the built environment by first making the environment barrier-free for the handicapped. This goal is set forth for several reasons. The handicapped have received little attention from designers of the built environment in the past. More environmental barriers have been imposed upon this group than any other, and their environmental rights require the greatest amount of improvement. Furthermore, the needs of the mentally and physically handicapped can be more readily identified than the needs of the total population. They are a limited population group whose environmental needs can be satisfied with a manageable amount of resources. Thus, the goal to improve the built environment in accordance with the needs of the mentally and physically handicapped is not only socially opportune but also realistic in terms of national capability. Moreover, by so doing, the environment will be improved for society at large.

Part I

Physical Barriers: Theoretical Perspectives

1

Toward a Responsive Environment: The Psychosocial Effects of Inaccessibility

Edward Steinfeld, James Duncan, and Paul Cardell

Edward Steinfeld is Assistant Professor of Architecture at Syracuse University and a Faculty Associate at the All-University Gerontology Center. He previously was Research Architect at the National Bureau of Standards. His past research includes studies of preferences for age-integration in housing, housing consumer information needs, and the development of self-instructional learning materials on barrier-free design. Currently, he is Project Director of the New ANSI 117 Standards Project and Secretary of the ANSI 117 Standards Committee.

James Duncan is Assistant Professor in the Department of Geography at the University of British Columbia. His previous research includes studies of territoriality on public streets in India and the way in which housing in both the United States and India reflects social identity. He served as Research Assistant to the New ANSI 117 Standards Project.

Paul Cardell holds a master's degree in Regional Planning from the Maxwell School at Syracuse University. He previously worked with the Regional Plan Association on studies of pedestrian behavior in New York City. He also served as Research Assistant to the New ANSI 117 Standards Project.

INTRODUCTION

The study of accessibility for people who are disabled has focused on barriers to movement and to use of buildings, equipment, and landscape. Certainly barriers deter people from pursuing certain activities, but action is not the only facet of behavior. There are many psychological and social implications of inaccessibility. This section explores contemporary knowledge of the relationship between human behavior and physical environment to identify those implications. Specifically, it is concerned with how barriers affect the development of maximum human potential.

Before reviewing knowledge areas, it will be useful to present a model of how people relate to the physical world. The scientific study of behavior and environment is fairly new and there is not yet an accepted paradigm for this relationship. Generally models that have been proposed are based on theoretical orientations from the behavioral sciences, particularly psychology.[1] The model proposed here is based on the work of George Herbert Mead and Kurt Lewin.[2]

Mead's theoretical orientation proposes that a person develop a "self" (self-image) through his or her transactions with other people. A person's sense of self is determined by what he or she does and by the reflections of those actions as transmitted in the responses of others. Thus, a person may do things that are considered deviant by others who, in turn, will "tell" the doer that he or she is deviant by treating them as such; for example, by shaming, punishing, and so forth. The result is that the person develops a sense of self as deviant from others. A person constantly validates his or her "self" through transactions

7

with others and subsequent adjustments to certain commonly held beliefs or norms about how people should relate to one another in a culture or other social system.

Lewin's field theory proposes that human behavior is based on the "continuing interaction of factors within the person . . . with other external factors as they are perceived in a given situation."[3] His concept of "life space" proposes that the environment, which may be social or physical, provides positive or negative forces to influence behavior. The effect of the life space depends to a great extent on how this space is perceived and the state of individual factors at a particular time. Lewin's theory developed out of gestalt psychology, which has as its central focus the concept that perception of the world is based on its total gestalt, or form as experienced, either consciously or unconsciously, by the individual person. People with different experiences may perceive the same object, activity, or other person's actions differently. Depending on an individual's needs, feelings, values and predispositions, the effect of the life space as a field of forces always influences people as a gestalt rather than as individual forces.

Our model proposes that the transactionalist "self" can be formed through transactions with any element of the life space as defined by Lewin. We propose that the feelings of people toward one another can be reflected through the design and management of physical elements in the life space, as well as through social actions. Design, space management, social organization, and social interaction are, in fact, all ways in which individuals and groups tell how they value others and how they value themselves. As proposed in gestalt theory, the perception of these transactions may be different for each person, depending on his or her previous experience. For example, a person raised in a culture with no written language would not experience a sign that stated "no unauthorized persons permitted beyond this point; violators will be shot on sight" as an important "force" in his or her life space. On the other hand, a person with the required authorization would not

either; however, someone who had lost the authorization would.

The theories discussed above deserve more detailed attention as does the model of environment-behavior relationships we ourselves have proposed. But this is not the main purpose of this chapter. Interested readers are referred to the references for further information.

One other assumption guides the following review. A person with a disability may be very competent and talented in all attributes of behavior other than that dictated by the disability. Clearly, a broad spectrum of abilities exists among disabled people. However, an environment that is designed in such a way as to preclude use by a person only because of a disability does not allow that person to pursue life to the fullest potential. One common and current way in which society views each disabled person is as a personification of disability. Their abilities are ignored. Our view is that each person should be viewed as a normal person and is thus entitled to normal use of the environment. Design, then, should insure that a disability is not a handicap in the development of one's abilities. Normal use should not be conceived as normal in the descriptive sense. Obviously, a person in a wheelchair will look different than a person walking when moving from point A to point B. We propose that normal use be perceived from the point of view of personal competence. If the environment allows all people to use it normally, all people will have a normal chance to be competent in it.

The remainder of this chapter reviews several relevant knowledge areas of environmental behavior to identify the psychosocial effects of inaccessible environments. The knowledge areas are:

Environment as language,
Environmental cognition,
Territoriality,
Exploration and the development of competence,
Adaptation careers.

Some of the implications have a strong basis in

empirical research. Others are based on theoretical perspectives and empirical research in other than environmental concerns. Hopefully, the identification of validated and hypothetical implications will help to create an understanding of the costs of inaccessibility beyond the dollars and cents of cost–benefit analyses. Hopefully, designers, planners, and policymakers also will reflect on what they are "telling" some users of the places they control when they allow barriers to access to be built.

ENVIRONMENT AS LANGUAGE

How does the physical environment communicate to people? The study of *proxemics*, the use of space in face-to-face social interaction, has demonstrated how the physical structure of the environment provides "sets" for certain types of behavior. For example, activities normally considered as private do not take place unless conditions are acceptable for private activity.

Osmond and Sommer have identified spatial characteristics that encourage or discourage social interaction.[4] Hall has identified interaction sets for different types of social interaction.[5] These physical conditions are based on physiological characteristics—for example, the maximum distance at which facial expressions cannot be perceived—and on culturally held assumptions of appropriateness—for example, when a person is allowed to touch another. They are modified by participant characteristics such as sex, age, and stigma of the interacting individuals.

Crosscultural studies have made apparent that cultures shape the physical environment according to culturally held attitudes about the uses of space.[6] Environments shaped by people, then, tell an observer something about how a place should be used, since spatial characteristics are associated with space use. For example, monumental stairs tell us that we should have a sense of awe and respect for that which is above. Stairs have been used traditionally to set one person above another. The meaning of building

form, however, is perceived through a cultural screen, since different cultures have different attitudes about the use of space.

Objects can have a social meaning. Clarke, basing her thinking on studies of language, proposes that socioeconomic classes have differences in the vocabulary they use to describe the physical environment.[7]

Studies comparing architect's descriptions of spaces and buildings with those of nonarchitects have shown that different reference groups describe the same environment differently.[8] This backs up Clarke's thesis and lends weight to her untested proposition that social groups code the environment differently—that is, their relationship to it is structured in different ways.

Clearly, the physical environment does send messages to people who use it, and people "read" these messages in different languages. People with disabilities may use different dialects in reading messages from the environment. DeLong has demonstrated that a physiological screen, as well as a cultural screen, can exist in interpreting the meaning of proxemic sets.[9] He demonstrates how elderly people who share sensory disabilities, use physically different social sets than young people of the same culture. They must be closer and have tactile contact in order to maintain communication with another person.

DeLong also demonstrates how incongruence between two different social interaction sets leads to misunderstanding and affective reaction. As noted in his research, doctors who maintain very close interaction distances, which are commonly thought of as intimate, put on a cold technical manner in order to examine patients without getting "intimate" or emotionally involved. The older people associated this set with less intimate social interaction. They felt that the doctors were therefore being unfriendly and treating them as inanimate objects.

Such incongruence in meaning may also exist in interpreting the physical world. For example, a person confined to a wheelchair cannot negotiate monumental stairs. Rather than having a sense of awe and respect, such a person is likely to feel angry at that which is above. If the culturally held meaning of whatever is at the top of the stairs is good—for example, a place of worship—the person may also feel that they themselves are bad as a reflection of the denial of their access to "goodness."

Environmental language that does not treat all people as spatially normal renders them illiterate. Thus, blind persons who cannot find enough auditory and tactile cues to interpret what is around them, may find themselves acting in inappropriate ways for the setting. This behavior in turn, leads to social reactions that reflect the deviance back to the actors. From another perspective, environmental language that creates misinterpretations or other forms of incongruence between cultural attitudes and personal experiences may cause negative feelings of self-worth.

ENVIRONMENTAL COGNITION

Piaget has investigated the development of spatial cognition in childhood.[10] As children progress through infancy, preschool period, middle childhood, and adolescence, they organize space first from an egocentric orientation and then develop coordinated systems of reference based on fixed objects. Piaget has enumerated levels of spatial intelligence: sensorimotor, intuitive, concrete, operational, and formal operational. Apparently, spatial cognition is neither only accumulation nor only innate; it stems from a complex system of cognitive ordering.[11]

The process of ordering space has been called *cognitive mapping*. It is defined as a coping mechanism through which the person answers two basic questions quickly and efficiently: Where certain valued things are, and how to get where they are from where one is. Cognitive mapping is a function of space negotiation abilities, sensory reception abilities, storage capacity, and time spent in an environment.

How can we account for the fact that different groups appear to have different cognitions of the world? In our everyday environment there are an infinitely greater number of discrete objects or parts

of discrete objects than can be identified. We can only notice a small number of these objects; we do choose to notice things that have special usefulness and meaning to us. For example, people with different disabilities select different objects in the environment to use as placemarkers. Since the meaning of objects,therefore, is created through interaction with one's fellows—and since people form discrete interaction groups with different purposes, values, and ways of interacting with objects—it is only natural that people should cognize the world differently. People with certain disabilities, therefore, may have different cognitive maps than do people with other disabilities or the nondisabled. They have these different maps for the simple reason that they use the environment differently.

In all likelihood, a person to whom the community is relatively inaccessible will have a cognitive map with much less detail and accuracy than a person to whom the community is accessible. A cognitive map is basically a representation of what a person knows about a place. An accessible physical environment allows people to develop detailed and accurate images of the community. Without such images, one cannot use the community effectively.

TERRITORIALITY

Territory is the "area which is first rendered distinctive by its owner in a particular way, and secondly, is defended by the owner."[12] Not only does each person and/or group perceive and map space, but persons and groups also attach rights of ownership to spaces they use. Territorial instincts are so strong that sanctions against spatial invasions of territory are often backed up by law.

The study of territoriality began with animals and has extended to human use of space.[13] Humans have a greater scope of territorial behavior than animals. Their territorial ownership extends from geographic space to people, objects, and ideas. As animals mark by defecation and urination, people use nameplates, fences, walls, and so forth as environmental props to mark their territories. Defense of space by humans is seldom characterized by full-scale aggression as it is in animals.

Both in animals[14] and in humans,[15] studies have demonstrated that the possession of territory is intimately related to hierarchies of social dominance: The most powerful obtain and maintain the best territories.

For people who are disabled, barriers to access are territorial markers, just as surely as trespass signs are. That exclusion from valued places leaves one with feelings of helplessness is evident. What is less explicit is the behavioral implication of exclusion. The fact that the able-bodied population has full use of public places means that they have a socially dominant position in respect to those with disabilities. By building inaccessible buildings and transportation systems, they have effectively claimed territorial possession of them. Perhaps the most humiliating aspect of territorial dominance has been the building of special environments, primarily institutional, for those that do not pass the test for entry into the able-bodied world.

EXPLORATION AND THE DEVELOPMENT OF COMPETENCE

White argues that environmental competence is achieved through exploratory behavior.[16] He proposes that as children explore the environment, they manipulate it; and the skill that they develop through manipulating is what we call environmental competence. He argues that at any given time a person has adapted to a certain level of environmental competence and that in order to avoid boredom he or she must constantly explore the edges of this competence. People are constantly seeking a mild state of disequilibrium in order to extend their mastery. If there is too great a discrepancy between our competence and our attempts to deal with the environment, then we become frustrated. What each person seeks is a slow,

continuous adaptation to his or her environment. As White states:

Dealing with the environment means carrying on a continuing transaction which gradually changes one's relation to the environment.[17]

A very great amount of each person's environmental competence is learned as a child; however, each person goes on exploring continuously, and hence this relationship to the environment is continually evolving.

Let us now consider exploration and the development of environmental competence among disabled people. Disabled persons, for the most part, find that a huge gap exists between their level of environmental competence and what is necessary for them to deal effectively with the environment. As White indicates, when there is too much of a gap, exploration is discouraged.[18] Since disabled persons are frustrated in their efforts to explore, there is little chance that they will be able to undergo the adaptation processes that nondisabled people undergo continually. We do not mean that they will experience no adaptation, but that the level will be so low that change in mastery will be minimal. The disabled person, therefore, does not develop an acceptable level of competence in regard to the environment. The gap between existing competence and the demands of the environment will be directly related to a person's dependency on others to meet the needs of everyday life or to a person's unfulfilled needs.

A failure to develop environmental competence has strong consequences for the self. The self or identity is not something that is static; rather it is something that one must continually act out and reaffirm both to oneself and to others.[19] Put simply, the self is created and sustained through action. The type of action, therefore, determines what kind of a self one is to be. The disabled person who is unable to develop environmental competence and who is dependent on others is regarded by others as an *incompetent self*. A person with a disability often finds that their personal identity (the fact that he/she, John or Joan Doe, who lives on such and such a street, is twenty-nine years old, has blond hair and blue eyes and is bad-tempered when he/she wakes up) tends to be overshadowed by his/her social identity (the fact of disability). In the eyes of the nondisabled, the personal and competent aspects of his or her self are, therefore, submerged by the social and incompetent aspects of the self. Since, as Mead points out, we count on others to confirm our identity, the disabled person may share the view of the incompetent ascribed to them by the nondisabled or at least will have to deal with it.[20] Often a person with a disability must work especially hard to assert their competence against the prejudice of others' perceptions. This overcompensation is not required of those without disabilities. Those who cannot overcompensate in some way must accept other people's perceptions as valid. A self-concept of incompetence discourages the disabled person from exploring the environment and, therefore, gaining competence. This process creates a vicious circle: Inability to develop environmental competence leads to self-conception as incompetent, which in turn discourages the exploration needed to develop competence. Even those who overcompensate in some way must face this issue in public amongst strangers who do not know of the competent aspects of their self.

ADAPTATION CAREERS

The question arises, how does one escape from this circle? The answer may lie in the notion of adaptation careers. Ordinarily, the term *career* refers exclusively to a person's passage through an institution, or more specifically, it refers to a person's working life. Glaser and Strauss[21] and Goffman[22] have expanded the notion of career. They use it as an analytical tool to describe the *shared* movement of individual people through a variety of diverse social contexts. This movement allows them to compare such seemingly different phenomena as the careers of academics, patients dying of cancer in hospitals, and husbands and wives as their marriage evolves. Examining these

things as careers has the advantage of revealing the underlying temporal regularity of any given person's status passage. Each type of career has a timetable, which dictates the normal time for passage, and bench-marks along the way, which inform the person who is passing, and others, as to how they are faring. This regularized temporal passage that constitutes the normal career is widely recognized by society. Hence we find doctors expressing surprise that a given patient is recuperating sooner than expected or conversely dying faster. Similarly, we find exceptionally successful young people being defined as precocious because they are ahead of the normal timetable. These careers, which are by definition shared with others, become institutionalized; hence the participants develop a shared perspective. They assess things in terms of their career and more particularly in terms of the particular stage of the career in which they find themselves at any given time.

The kinds of careers in which we are especially interested are those of disabled persons. For any given disability there exist a number of separate careers that overlap and effect the ability of the affected person to achieve varying degrees of environmental competence.

The first career is that of the physiological disability. We can describe the progression of any given disease from its inception to its termination should it be allowed to run its course. Often the career of the disease is aborted, and the person embarks on the career of a person who is well, or the person is left stranded in midcareer with the effects of the disease neither advancing or retreating.

The second career is what we shall term a person's *adaptation career*. Physical therapists and others try to provide patients with skills to deal with their disabilities. Learning these skills can be viewed as a career in that there are certain standard ways in which people with certain types of disabilities can deal with them. There is also a normal timetable for acquiring these skills. Just as a person may or may not have a successful business career so he may or may not have a successful adaptation career.

The third career—one that is relevant to this inquiry and that crosscuts the other two—is age. Clearly, a person's life can be seen as a career. Age impacts on the other two careers in that at certain times within the life cycle a person is more likely to have certain diseases. Similarly, at certain times in the life cycle (notably old age), having a successful adaptation career becomes much more difficult.

The fourth and final career is that of the environment's response to the person. There are certain limits to the extent to which an individual can adapt; these limits are physiologically set. The environment, on the other hand, can be changed in an infinite number of ways and hence is potentially much more adaptable than the human body.[23] By manipulating the environment, we can achieve a much higher level of success in the adaptation career of the disabled.[24] The environment, then, must be constructed in such a way that it can easily accommodate the changing needs of disabled people as they move through their disability careers. Although *flexible* is a term often used to describe such environments, the key variable is actually responsiveness. An environment need not be flexible to be experienced differently. The adaptation career of a building, therefore, consists of changes in the way it can be used. Thus, instead of simply having life-cycle careers (environments get old and fall apart), buildings ought to have adaptation careers that are congruent with the adaptation career of disabled people. Such environments can be built once we know what a successful environment adaptation career is like.

Let us now turn to a brief consideration of styles of adaptation. This crosscuts some of the careers that we have just described. Style of adaptation might be thought of as analagous to the type of professional career that a person chooses. Certain people are, or at least feel that they are, more suited to certain types of work than others. Similarly, some types of people are more likely to respond successfully to one type of adaptation career than to another. Lowenthal and Chiriboga state that different adaptation styles are suitable at different times in the life cycle, as there

is interlocking of the person's adaptation career with his or her life-cycle career.[25] Lowenthal and Chiriboga go on to make the point that there are a variety of possible adaptation styles and that the significant choice factor is stress.[26] A person should choose the style that causes the least stress, in a negative sense. Making the choice in this fasion, as they point out, is a function of a person's reference group, which of course is intimately linked to his or her image of former self.[27] If there are a variety of adaptation styles that are efficacious, are there also a variety of environmental contexts in which this adaptation can take place?

To foster exploration and the development of competence, an environment must be explorable and manipulable by a disabled person to such an extent that it encourages further exploration. The environment must present a challenge but not frustrate the disabled person's attempts to develop skill at manipulation. The process of developing a competent self has similarities with the process mentioned earlier of developing an incompetent self. Just as failure reinforces incompetence, success reinforces competence. The ideal environment for any person ought to be responsive enough so that a progressive spiraling of achievement can take place. Success leads to confidence, which leads to further exploration and manipulation, and hence the acquisition of skills and the positive self-image of being competent. This process is further reinforced by others whose image of the disabled person changes as they see visible signs of increased environmental competence. At least, the environment should allow maintenance of competence levels already reached.

CONCLUSION

The built environment communicates to those who use it. It speaks a kind of "silent language" that transmits messages about appropriate behavior and meanings.[28] These messages also can have an affective component that reflects back to the user. People who because of disabilities are illiterate in the language of environment, or who interpret messages through a physiological screen, may not receive important information or may interpret messages differently than the nondisabled. Illiteracy and interpretation problems can result in inappropriate behavior, confusion, or negative feelings of self-worth.

The way each person organizes space as a mental image is based on how he or she experiences it. Although further research is needed in environmental cognition, evidence indicates that people with disabilities may image space differently than able-bodied people, since they have different kinds of experiences. Differences in experience lead to differences in value on parts of the environment and in systems of orientation. Lack of ability to experience the environment results in poor cognition of it, which in turn, hampers efforts to use the community.

Territorial behavior is closely associated with social dominance. Exclusion through environmental barriers can be viewed as a form of territorial behavior whereby the able-bodied claim the best space. The disabled act out their lowly position in the dominance hierarchy by occupying stigmatized, and often institutional, space.

The development of competence-building settings can improve the adaptive capacity of disabled people. The relationship between these two may be viewed as a set of interlocking careers; the adaptation career of the person and the adaptation career of the environment. If the environment is responsive enough to meet the needs of a person, then opportunities are created for increased competence and the resulting greater adaptation to the circumstances of a disability. Environments must be designed so that they can respond to the physiological and adaptation careers of the individual person.

Although we have identified several discrete psychosocial implications of inaccessibility, they do not act independently to affect a person's behavior: The entire social and physical world impacts on a person. Individual forces in the life space cannot be added together as simple sums; rather they work as a whole and as a function of the individual person as well. For example, all disabled people probably do not experience the negative effects of territorial exclusion as social dominance. Moreover, attitudes and action of other people that send positive messages to the disabled person may counteract negative messages from an inaccessible building.

It is important to remember that while a society may act supportively in many ways through the interpersonal actions of its members, social actions that shape the physical environment may be unsupportive—not because of society's attitudes, but because of its traditional ways of building and lack of alternative responses. If our society should change its attitudes toward disabled people, without corresponding changes in the built environment, a truly responsive life space will not exist.

OUTLOOK FOR THE FUTURE

The task that faces us is to design truly responsive environments where all people have opportunities to develop competence. As we have seen, we cannot speak of competence as being a quality that lies exclusively within individual people. Rather, it is a relationship between each of us and the object that we are attempting to manipulate. Environments are constructed to fit average physiological norms—that is, to allow the average person to display an average amount of environmental competence. Moreover, few environments are designed to respond to disability careers. If the design of the environment gets out of line with the physiological norms of people, then the people, of course, become less competent. The term often applied to an environment where such a discrepancy exists is *nonfunctional*—that is, a person cannot function (be competent) within it. When such a condition exists, the blame for the misfit is placed upon the environment and it is subsequently changed. Since the disabled person has different physiological norms, that his relationship to the environment is different from that of the able-bodied person is only natural. He or she can no more be expected to adapt and develop competence in a misfit environment than can the able-bodied person. However, when such a misfit occurs for the disabled person, the blame is placed on the person rather than on the environment.

This shifting of blame from the environment to the person is an ideological position based on the value assigned to disabled people. Once this position is changed so that the environment is blamed, then responsive environments can be created in which disabled people can display competence and, by extension, overcome much of the dependency and stigma that stems from being environmentally incompetent.

NOTES AND REFERENCES

The research and studies forming the basis for this report were conducted by Syracuse University pursuant to a contract with the U. S. Department of Housing and Urban Development (HUD) Office of Policy Development and Research. The statements and conclusions contained herein are those of the contractor and do not necessarily reflect the views of the U. S. Government in general or HUD in particular. Neither the United States nor HUD makes any warranty, expressed or implied, or assumes responsibility for the accuracy or completeness of the information herein.

1. Proshansky, Harold M., William Ittelson, Leanne G. Rivlin, and Gary H. Winkel, *An Introduction to Environmental Psychology* (New York: Holt, Rinehart and Winston, 1974).
2. Mead, G. H., *Mind, Self and Society* (Chicago: University of Chicago Press, 1934); and Lewin, Kurt, *Principles of Topological Psychology* (New York: McGraw-Hill, 1936).
3. Ittelson et al., *An Introduction*, p. 69.
4. Sommer, Robert, *Personal Space: The Behavioral Basis of Design* (Englewood Cliffs, N. J.: Prentice-Hall, 1969).
5. Hall, Edward T., *The Silent Language* (Greenwich, Conn.: Doubleday, 1959).
6. Hall, Edward T., *The Hidden Dimension* (Garden City, N. Y.: Anchor, 1969); and Rapoport, Amos, *House, Form and Culture* (Englewood Cliffs, N. J.: Prentice-Hall, 1969).
7. Clarke, Linda, "Explorations into the Nature of Environmental Codes," *Journal of Architectural Research*, January 1974, p. 34.
8. Hershberger, Robert, "A Study of Meaning and Architecture," in Henry Sanoff and Sidney Cohn (eds.), *EDRA 1* (Chapel Hill, N. C.: Environmental Design Research Association, 1970).
9. DeLong, Alton J., "The Micro-Spatial Structure of the Older Person: Some Implications for Planning the Social and Spatial Environment," in L. Pastalan and D. Carson (eds.), *Spatial Behavior of Older People* (Ann Arbor: University of Michigan Press, 1970).
10. Piaget, J., and B. Inhelder, *The Child's Conception of Space* (New York: W. W. Norton, 1966).
11. Hart, R. A., and G. T. Moore, "The Development of Spatial Cognition: A review," in R. M. Downs and D. Stea (eds.), *Image and Environment: Cognitive Mapping and Spatial Behavior* (Chicago: Aldine, 1973), p. 286.
12. Sommer, *Personal Space*.
13. Lyman, Stanford, and Marrin Scott, "Territoriality: A Neglected Social Dimension," *Social Problems*, 1967.
14. Hall, *The Hidden Dimension*.
15. Esser, Arstide H., Amparo S. Chamberlain, Eliot D. Chapple, and Nathan S. Kline, "Territoriality of Patients on a Research Ward," *Recent Advances in Sociological Psychiatry*, vol. 7, 1965, pp. 37–44.
16. White, R. W., "Motivation Reconsidered: The Concept of Competence." in H. M. Proshansky, W. H. Ittleson and L. G. Rivlin (eds.), *Environmental Psychology* (New York: Holt, Rinehart and Winston, 1970), pp. 125–33.
17. Ibid., p. 132.
18. Ibid., p. 127.
19. Mead, *Mind, Self and Society*, and Strauss, A. L., *Mirrors and Masks: The Search for Identity* (San Francisco: Sociology Press, 1969).
20. Mead, *Mind, Self and Society*.
21. Glaser, B. G., and A. L. Strauss, *Awareness of Dying* (Chicago: Aldine, 1965), and *Time for Dying* (Chicago: Aldine, 1968).
22. Goffman, E., *Asylums* (New York: Anchor, 1961), and *Stigma: Notes on the Management of Spoiled Identity* (Englewood Cliffs, N. J.: Prentice-Hall, 1963).
23. Lawton, M. P., and L. Nahemow, "Ecology and the Aging Process," in C. Eisdorfer and M. P. Lawton (eds.), *The Psychology of Adult Development in Aging* (Washington, D.C.: American Psychological Association, 1973), pp. 619–74.
24. Ibid., and also Perrin, C., *With Man in Mind* (Cambridge, Mass.: MIT Press, 1970).
25. Lowenthal, M. F., and O. Chiriboga, "Social Stress and

Adaptation: Toward a Life-Course Perspective," in C. Eisdorfer and M. P. Lawton (eds.), *The Psychology of Adult Development in Aging* (Washington, D.C.: American Psychological Association, 1973), pp. 281–310.
26. Ibid.
27. Ibid., p. 287.
28. Hall, *The Silent Language*.

Additional Readings

Altman, Irwin. "Territorial Behavior in Humans: An Analysis of the Concept." In L. Pastalan and D. Carson (eds.), *Spatial Behavior of Older People*. Ann Arbor: The Institute of Gerontology, University of Michigan, 1970.

Suttles, Gerald. *The Social Order of the Slum*. Chicago: University of Chicago Press, 1968.

Wright, B. A. *Physical Disability: A Psychological Approach*. New York: Harper, 1960.

2

Pedestrian Mobility: The Accessible City

John Templer and Michael Jones

John Templer is Director of the Pedestrian Research Laboratory and Associate Professor of Architecture at the Georgia Institute of Technology. He is an architect and urban planner, and his doctoral work is in the field of pedestrianism. Currently, he is principal investigator for a research contract entitled "Provisions for Elderly and Handicapped Pedestrians" funded by the Federal Highway Administration, Department of Transportation. Dr. Templer was born in Oxford, England, and holds architecture and planning degrees from the University of Pretoria, South Africa, and the University of Witwatersrand, South Africa, respectively. He also holds a M.S. in architecture and a Ph.D. from Columbia University. His previous teaching experience has been at Natal University and Columbia University. Since 1961, he has conducted research work into the objective use of color in hospitals, housing needs of the elderly, regional health service planning, and physiological and behavioral responses to staircases and ramps. The latter research was recently completed for the National Bureau of Standards in a project entitled "An Analysis of the Behavior of Stair Users."

Michael A. Jones is currently Research Architect for the Handicapped for the state of Illinois. Previously, at Georgia Tech he was with the Pedestrian Research Laboratory project entitled "Provisions for Elderly and Handicapped Pedestrians" sponsored by the Department of Transportation. His other research includes the development of a Wilderness Camp for Handicapped and Elderly Veterans, modular plastic housing, a building system for educational facilities on sites subject to mining subsidence. He has practiced and taught architecture widely in the United States and England. He also serves on the Council of Technical Advisers for the International Federation of Pedestrians and various committees serving the needs of the handicapped.

INTRODUCTION

Contrary to popular myth, the medieval town offered little to the pedestrian. Certainly, most activities were within walking distance, but this convenience was outweighed by the many discomforts and dangers. The streets were dark and tortuous for night use. The surfaces were rarely paved, and what paving that did exist was rough, irregular, and slippery from mud, water, and offal and was laid with a degree of unevenness that required the traveler to take every step with care.

There were no storm water drains, and the people had little concern for runoff. Sewers did not exist, and dirt, excrement, and sweepings of all kinds were tossed into the streets from the houses and businesses that flanked the thoroughfares. For defensive reasons, many of the towns had been built on hills that mandated the use of stepped or steep, ramping streets that were made even more treacherous by slime and garbage. And the larger towns certainly were not free from the hazards and pollution generated by wheeled vehicles. We know that as far back as Roman times, limiting vehicular traffic movement was necessary during the day.

17

The industrial city of the late nineteenth century and early twentieth century improved the pedestrian's lot on one hand, but made it worse on the other. The level of hygiene was improved by the construction of sewerage systems, and streets and sidewalks were fully paved. But the development of the motorized vehicle reduced concern for the pedestrian. The primary function of the street was to provide passage and storage for vehicles. Traffic engineering was born with the principle aim of improving the city by improving vehicular access to it. As vehicular densities grew, streets were widened, sidewalks narrowed, trees along avenues cut down, and traffic signals installed.

If workers in traditionally dangerous and unpleasant industries were asked to accept the accident rates and conditions of discomfort and inconvenience that are the common lot of pedestrians in cities today, then certainly the picket lines would soon be manned. The workers would demand immediate change, and they would have the support of the courts and the power of federal legislation behind them. But pedestrians have no unions or collective bargaining power, and our cities have so little in the way of codes or standards that we can almost discount them. The few applicable laws that regulate pedestrian conduct pay scant attention to human motivations, and pedestrian rights in practice are seldom guaranteed by enforcement.

Through their codes, cities mandate levels of safety and comfort for buildings, but not for sidewalks and pedestrian ways. We have standards that act to limit the incidence of accidents related to mechanical movement systems in buildings, but a much lower standard exists for mechanical systems in the streets. No elevator manufacturer would be licensed if he were to offer such poor guarantees of safety, and no designer would stay in business if his buildings provided such an abysmal record of safety and performance. They would soon be uninsurable from malpractice suits, and clients would refuse to accept such a casual attitude towards the users and such careless attention to the design of the whole system.

The National Safety Council estimates that 400,000 pedestrians are struck by vehicles every year.[1] Many thousands more are injured in nonvehicular accidents, most of which are falls. We have no reliable estimates of these latter accidents because few of them are ever recorded in police records, which provide us with most of our statistics.

The absolute number of pedestrian accidents does not reveal the full dimensions of the problem. Consideration must also be given to the severity of these accidents. Collisions between pedestrians and vehicles result in approximately 10,500 deaths per year.[2] Most pedestrians are killed in urban areas. In the largest cities, pedestrian fatalities accounted for more than half of all motor vehicle related deaths and for one-third in middle-sized cities.[3]

While people of all ages have pedestrian accidents, some age groups are disproportionately represented. Studies of pedestrian accident statistics reveal two important facts: the greatest number of pedestrian accidents involve children and the most severe pedestrian accidents involve elderly and handicapped people.[4] One out of ten deaths of children between the ages of five and fourteen is a pedestrian traffic fatality, and primary-grade children have three times the death and injury rate of children twice that age.

The research that is described herein was initiated by the Federal Highway Administration of the Department of Transportation. The aim of the project is to identify the hazards and problems of elderly and handicapped pedestrians and to propose and evaluate countermeasures to improve their situation.

The project is divided into seven phases. In Phase I, the literature was surveyed in order to determine the state-of-the-art. As a subtask we focussed on federal and state laws and regulations and codes directed at removing or reducing barriers to mobility. In Phase II, we scrutinized the target population in order to devise an appropriate definitional and classificatory system. Phase III was a study of the nature and causes of accidents involving the lederly and handicapped. Phase IV was a data-collection period directed at developing a taxonomy of impediments to pedestrian mobility—that is, the mobility problems that face the subgroups of the population we have identified. In Phase V we went through a methodical process for establishing priorities for selecting the most pressing problems for the development of countermeasures. In Phase VI we developed strategies and countermeasures as well as ways of evaluating the solutions. We are currently in the process of testing these countermeasures in five cities. Our final task is to develop a "User's Guide" for agencies that are concerned with the problems of elderly and handicapped pedestrians. In this chapter we discuss in some detail the processes we have followed and the general findings of the study.

THE ELDERLY AND HANDICAPPED PEDESTRIAN: CLASSIFICATION AND DEFINITION

The terminology and criteria used in the literature to identify the elderly and the handicapped tend to be inconsistent and impermanent and often reflect the objectives of whoever is promoting the definitions. Those groups or agencies that are primarily concerned with compensation or benefits for the handicapped tend to rely on medical diagnoses and definitions. For our purposes, this method is not satisfactory for several reasons. First, any given medical condition may result in a variety of functional disabilities, each of which may or may not handicap the patient as a pedestrian. Second, the medical condition may have various degrees of severity, some of which may handicap the patient.

A different direction is taken by those primarily concerned with rehabilitation. Since their objectives are aimed at restoring or retraining their clients for vocational, educational, or at least home-related activities, the degree of handicap is often based on an ability to perform in these settings. Once again, these criteria are inadequate for this study.

A somewhat similar approach was chosen by ABT Associates for their investigation of transit travel

barriers.[5] They listed the activities that people would need to be capable of performing in order to be able to use various transit modes. People should be able to: "walk more than one block," "move in crowds," "stand or wait," and "climb steep or long stairs," and so forth. For our purposes, an attempt to set out a compendium of functional requirements in this fashion would be to make assumptions on factors that are central to the research. It is our responsibility to seek out and identify these functional imperatives in terms of the problems and hazards they present to the target population.

For these reasons, we have chosen to avoid using the causes (congenital, traumatic, or medical) as criteria, and we have avoided the attempt to define functional requirements for pedestrian travel.

We are probably reasonable in our assumption that the pedestrian environment is intended for normal, healthy adults in their prime—that is, for people of normal stature and dimensions, with normal perceptions and reactions, with normal agility and stamina, and with physical equipment that can cope with pedestrian activities without unusual difficulty. The remainder of the population is, by this definition, handicapped as pedestrians. Their dimensions, agility, reactions, and bodily equipment are impaired or inadequately developed to traverse the "normal" pedestrian environment without difficulty or greater than usual danger.

We can then specify the performance levels of the main physical and mental attributes necessary for normal pedestrian movement and conclude that unless those levels are reached, the person is handicapped. Reasonable estimates can be obtained of the number of people who are unable to reach the specified performance levels. We can classify them into the following handicapped groups relating to the use of their (a) size and maturity, (b) agility, stamina, and reaction time, (c) legs, (d) arms and shoulders, (e) hearing, (f) sight, and (g) mental equilibrium. Statistical information is available to enable us to further subdivide the people with lower extremity impairments into three groups and those with developmental restrictions into two groups. Using this method, we have a classification of ten subgroups, as shown in Table 2-1.

Estimates by Categories

The U.S. Department of Health, Education and Welfare (DHEW) conducts periodical surveys of non-institutional populations through random samples of households in order to estimate the composition of the population by various disabling conditions and other associated variables, some of which are used for crossclassification. Tables with short reports are published in *Vital and Health Statistics*. Data from the National Health Survey of DHEW, Series 10, deal mostly with the disabling conditions. These DHEW reports (for subgroups 4–9) and the 1970 census report (for subgroups 1–3) and other publications (for subgroup 10) were used to generate estimates of subgroup totals shown in Table 2-2.

The estimates in column 2 of Table 2-2 refer to different time periods and therefore correspond to different base populations. Estimates for the calendar year 1975 (column 3) have been obtained by assuming that the respective disability rates have remained the same during this period. In other words, the figures in column 2 are multiplied by the ratios of population size in 1975 to those in the base periods of respective estimates, to generate column 3.

At the risk of double counting, the disabled population in 1975 can thus be estimated as over twelve million. In percentage terms, the figure is on the order of 6 percent, and surprising as it may seem, the data make apparent that one out of every sixteen or seventeen persons in the U.S. has a major handicap that acts as a deterrent to locomotion.

If we make the appropriate adjustment for multiple handicaps, then 12.5 million can be regarded as an estimate of the size of the disabled population in the United States in 1975. To this can be added a large number of people who are young or old, but not physically handicapped in other ways. For the purpose of our study, then, we estimate that about one hundred million people are ill-equipped to function in the normal pedestrian environment, and this figure does not include those in subgroup 10 who are confused or disoriented from alcohol, drugs, medication, psychological disorders, mental retardation, and so forth. With the addition of this latter group, the handicapped pedestrian "minority" probably amounts to more than half the population; thus, to be "normal" is to be abnormal.

THE CAUSES OF VEHICLE-PEDESTRIAN ACCIDENTS

A review of the literature shows that one can separate vehicle-pedestrian accidents into three causal categories: those that are the fault of the driver, those that result from the pedestrian's behavior, and those for which the environment can be blamed. This separation is somewhat artificial, because there would be fewer incidents of maladaptive behavior if the environment was less demanding on the pedestrian. However, these categories are perhaps useful when we must examine the extant pedestrian systems in the city, where risk-taking is inevitable and pandemic.

Pedestrian accidents that are entirely the fault of the driver or for which the pedestrian and the environment cannot be held responsible lie outside the scope of our investigation.

Snyder and Knoblauch[6] have identified two types of accidents that are caused by pedestrian behavior:

1. The dart-out: The pedestrian makes a sudden appearance from the roadside (not at an intersection) and is struck by the vehicle which could not avoid the incident.
2. The intersection dash: The pedestrian makes a sudden appearance in an intersection or crosswalk and is struck by the vehicle.

They have further identified two types of accidents caused by the environment:

1. The multiple threat: The driver does not see the

TABLE 2-1
Proposed Subgroup Classification System

Attribute	Handicap	Subgroup[a]
Size and maturity	Developmental restrictions	1. Preschool children[b] 2. School-age children[b]
Agility, stamina, and reaction time	Chronic restrictive conditions related to agility, stamina and reaction time.	3. Persons over 65[b]
Legs	Lower extremity impairment	4. Confined to wheelchair[c] 5. Walk with special aids[c] 6. Walk with difficulty without the use of special aids[c]
Arms and shoulders	Chronic impairment of upper extremities and shoulders.	7. Chronic impairment of upper extremities and shoulders[c]
Hearing	Severe auditory impairment	8. Severe auditory impairment[c]
Sight	Severe visual impairment	9. Severe visual impairment[c]
Mental equilibrium	Obvious confusion, and/or disorientation	10. Obvious confusion and/or disorientation[d]

Note: The comprehensiveness of the classification system is of course limited in that not all people with any particular handicap will be counted. For example, people with chronic restrictive conditions related to agility, stamina, and reaction time will not appear in subgroup 7 unless they are over sixty-five. And similarly, not all those over sixty-five will have these restrictions. Adults of very small stature and those that are obese are not represented at all in the first two subgroups.

[a]The subgroups are not mutually exclusive, and a person may suffer from more than one disabling condition with the exception of age categories. However, appropriate correlations can be made, as discussed later, to avoid double counting.

[b]Data can be obtained from U.S. census figures.

[c]Statistical data can be obtained from DHEW, *Vital and Health Statistics*; the level of impairment selected has been chosen on the basis of medical opinion.

[d]Data can only be estimated within very wide limits or related to known studies of alcoholism, mental retardation, drug abuse and mental disorders. Although various researchers have studied these problem areas, reliable estimates of the population corresponding to these conditions are not available. In round numbers, a figure of twenty million has been accepted, without any attempt at further decomposition.

TABLE 2-2
Distribution of U.S. Risk Population by Subgroups, About 1970 and 1975

Subgroup (col. 1)	Estimated Population (000) About 1970 (col. 2)	About 1975 (col. 3)	Number per 1,000 Population (col. 4)
1. Preschool children (under 6)	20,965[a]	20,926	97.50
2. School-age children (6–17)	48,679[a]	46,482	216.57
3. Persons over 65	20,065[a]	22,170	103.30
4. Confined to wheelchair	409[b]	445	2.07
5. Walk with special aids	4,638[b]	5,042	23.49
6. Walking with difficulty	2,156[b]	2,344	10.92
7. Chronic impairment of upper extremities and shoulders	2,440[c]	2,588	12.06
8. Severe auditory impairment	1,592[d]	1,867	8.70
9. Severe visual impairment	475[e]	482	2.25
10. Obvious confusion and/or disorientation	20,000[f]	20,000	93.19

[a] See U.S. Bureau of the Census, *U.S. Summary: General Population Characteristics*, Vol. 1, Pt. 1, Tables 50, 52 and 53, Washington, D.C., 1970.
[b] See DHEW, *Vital and Health Statistics*, Series 10, No. 78, Washington, D.C., 1969.
[c] See DHEW, Series 10, No. 87, 1971.
[d] See DHEW, Series 10, No. 35, 1964.
[e] See DHEW, Series 10, No. 46, 1963–64; and Hatfield, E. M. "Estimates of Blindness in the United States." *The Sight-Saving Review*, vol. 43, no. 2, 1973, pp. 69–80. Also see unpublished report of the National Society for the Prevention of Blindness, Inc., January, 1975.
[f] Partial reference list includes (1) Mudford, H. A., "Drinking and Deviant Drinking, U.S.A., 1963," *Quarterly Journal of Studies on Alcohol*, vol. 25, 1964; (2) Eddy, Nathan, H. Halbach, I. H. Isbel, and M. E. Seevers, "Drug Dependence: Its Significance and Characteristics," Bulletin *WHO*, vol. 32, 1965; and (3) Martindale, D., and E. Martindale, *The Social Dimension of Mental Illness, Alcoholism and Drug Dependence* (Glenwood Publishing Co., 1973).

pedestrian because of some visual obstruction, usually a car in the adjacent lane.

2. Vehicle turn/merge with attention conflict: The driver's attention is focused on the conflicting vehicular traffic and he fails to consider the pedestrian's location and safety.

Accidents and the Elderly and Handicapped

If we isolate the statistics of vehicle–pedestrian accidents that affect the target group of our research, then a somewhat modified pattern of causality appears.

We find that the primary cause of child pedestrian accidents is the child running into the street while playing. Many of these accidents are caused by drivers expecting children to exercise the physical and psychological maturity of adults.

The elderly, on the other hand, walk a lot, so their exposure to the risks is greater. Many of them cannot drive, and many have low incomes that limit their ability to use public transportation. But at the same time, the physical and psychological impairments that come with age make it difficult for them to react skillfully and with caution. They are no longer able to make quick decisions such as when to cross, when to wait, when to stop, and when to go.

The literature that deals with pedestrian accidents experienced by other categories of handicapped people is very limited, in part because most reporting systems do not record whether a victim is handicapped. For this reason, we carried out a limited study to investigate the causes of vehicular pedestrian accidents experienced by this subgroup. We interviewed elderly and handicapped victims of pedestrian accidents who had been admitted to emergency rooms at some Atlanta hospitals. From our findings, the causes of accidents can be grouped into five categories:

Environmental design failures,
Pedestrian behavioral errors,
Driver behavioral failures,
Failures to educate and supervise,
Failure to keep the pedestrian environment clean and free from debris.

Environmental design failures are of four types:

1. Unsafe equipment: Examples include no handrails on stairs, uneven sidewalks and curbs, and so forth. Most of the accidents we studied were falls.
2. Failure to consider the pedestrian adequately in the design of vehicular traffic facilities: Examples include streets without sidewalks, bus stops at busy intersections without crosswalks, crosswalks in busy streets without traffic control devices, insufficient time permitted for crossing at traffic signals, crosswalks at busy intersections without concurrent stop lines, crosswalk markings that are not kept visible, nonfunctioning pedestrian actuated buttons for traffic control devices, and so forth. These are a few examples, but the real failure is systemic and ubiquitous.
3. The lack of adequate separation or delineation between pedestrian and vehicular areas: Children, the elderly, and the visually handicapped wander off the pedestrian space into the vehicular way and are struck. Examples include the lack of delineation between a busy street and a parking lot, between a busy street and a sidewalk, and between a pedestrian way and a railroad right of way.
4. Failure to ensure that streets are used for their intended purpose: Pedestrians expect expressways to be used for high speed through traffic, arterials for medium speed through traffic, and local streets for low-speed local traffic. When these expectations are violated, the pedestrian is vulnerable.

Pedestrian behavioral errors are typically:

1. The failure to consider traffic prior to entry into a street: Children run into the street or into the path of a vehicle in a parking lot. The problem may be compounded by a visual obstruction such as a telephone pole or a moving bus.
2. The failure to consider conflicting vehicular traffic while crossing the street: The pedestrian observes the traffic before starting to cross, but fails to look for traffic while crossing. Slow-moving elderly people were involved in the accidents we studied. Examples include pedestrians mistakenly assuming that drivers will yield the right of way in crosswalks; pedestrians' failure to consider the second or third lane of traffic in a multilane street; and the inability of the pedestrian to move quickly out of the street when a vehicle is sighted.
3. The failure of the pedestrian to use the available street-crossing facilities: The victim follows a path of convenience and crosses away from a

crosswalk. Both elderly people and children are involved in accidents of this type.

4. The failure of the elderly to realize and adapt to their decreased mobility: Examples include their failure to realize that they walk more slowly than they used to and that they take longer to cross the street and their failure to avoid busy streets, slippery pavements, irregular pavements, drainage gratings, and so forth, all of which make walking hazardous.

Drivers' behavioral errors include a failure to yield the right of way to a pedestrian in a crosswalk, stopping a vehicle in a crosswalk, speeding, failure to observe a stop sign, and so forth.

The failure of adults to supervise and educate their children is typified by children who are ignorant of safe pedestrian practices such as how to cross a busy street, and so forth.

The failure to keep the pedestrian environment clear and free from debris includes slippery conditions caused by water or a greasy and oily pavement, grass and weeds growing on the surface, cracked and irregular sidewalk paving, and so forth.

PEDESTRIAN MOBILITY IMPEDIMENTS

The studies of accidents provide us with a taxonomy and a general perspective of the major hazards—that is, those that are severe enough to hospitalize the victims. But to understand the full range of mishaps and risks, as well as the apprehensions that the target group feel, much more information is required. In addition, we must identify the many impediments to normal travel that restrict the elderly and the handicapped as pedestrians.

The literature on barriers is voluminous and repetitious, but few studies have been directed at generating a catalogue of impediments to mobility. Most of the published material (and codes based on the work) have started with the assumption that the problems are well known. Furthermore, the bulk of

the literature treats architectural barriers in the sense of buildings, and the only relevant national standard has been specifically directed at buildings.[7] The barriers to pedestrian mobility in the city have received scant attention.

To investigate the risks and problems that are presented to the elderly and handicapped as pedestrians, we used three different but complementary techniques—focused but unstructured interviews, panel discussions, and field observations. These techniques were used in five cities—Atlanta, San Francisco, Seattle, Chicago, and St. Petersburg—which were chosen for their topographic, climatic, urban, regional, social, and economic differences.

About three hundred interviews with members of the target group were conducted. These focused on trip information, mechanical and nonmechanical means of negotiating changes of level, stamina, the effect of the weather, walkway surfaces, pedestrian behavior, street furniture, illumination, crime, signage, crossing streets, street and sidewalk layout and geometry, education, the law, barriers, transportation, and so forth, as well as any pedestrian accidents that may have been experienced.

Thirty panel discussion were held on essentially the same topics with groups of people who were themselves elderly or handicapped or people who work with the elderly and handicapped in rehabilitation, therapy, and training programs.

The interviews and panel discussions provided us with a very detailed tabulation of the range of problems that these groups experience and their ways of avoiding or overcoming them. Field observations were then carried out to verify this information and to discover obstacles or responses that may not have been verbalized. About six hundred people were tracked as they moved around these cities. The observer followed randomly selected subgroup members as unobtrusively as possible and recorded abnormal behavior or maladaptive or dysfunctional responses—for example, a person in a wheelchair riding along the street in the traffic; an elderly person using a parking meter as a handrail to climb a curb; a blind man wandering unknowingly out of a marked crosswalk at an oblique-angled intersection. The observer then interviewed about 10 percent of these people to obtain their explanations for their behavior.

Mobility Problems

From the surveys, we have been able to construct a catalog of about six hundred statements. We have grouped these into four types of problems attributable to the following:

1. *Systemwide mobility barriers,* such as an absence of usable pedestrian ways, an inaccessible transit system, and so forth.
2. *The component segments of the pedestrian system,* such as walkways, street crossings, vehicular terminals, recreation areas, and other motor portions of the system. These segments are composed of several elements.
3. *Elements of the pedestrian system,* such as steps, ramps, handrails, elevators, surface materials, street furniture, planting material, and so forth. These elements are the building blocks of the pedestrian system.
4. *Other affective factors,* such as traffic laws, public awareness, crime, and so forth.

Systemwide mobility barriers

Many of the elderly and handicapped complain that the existing transportation systems do not permit easy, safe, and comfortable travel. Vehicles—buses, trains, subways, planes, cars, cabs—and their terminals are ill designed for their needs, and they are often inaccessible. Without an accessible transportation system, the usefulness of the remainder of the pedestrain system is greatly restricted, and the pedestrian system is usually equally unsuitable. Therefore, regular trips to work, or for any other purpose, are often impossible or at least much more complicated

and hazardous than for most people. A survey of these systemwide problems is provided in Table 2–3.

Cities generally have no plans for pedestrian movement. Traffic plans tend to be directed at vehicular traffic, and optimizing vehicular movement is the primary objective. In many new suburban areas, the pedestrian is not provided for at all. There are no sidewalks and little consideration for pedestrian access to shopping centers and community facilities.

During the interviews, people made remarks such as:

> "I would go out more often or make more trips if public transportation was made accessible."

TABLE 2–3
Examples of Systemwide Problems and Countermeasures

Measure	*Countermeasure*
Public transportaton inaccessible	A barrier-free system A special transportation system
Public transportation too expensive	Subsidies for low-income groups
No continuous pedestrian routes	Citywide planning for pedestrians Funding for pedestrian systems
Insurmountable barriers universally in city streets	A sytematic barrier removal plan
No sidewalks or pedestrian provision in the new suburbs and shopping centers	Zoning law requirement to provide for pedestrians Retrofitting provisions
Inaccessible parking downtown	Special parking provision
Inadequate legal protection for pedestrians	Standard code for pedestrian rights and laws Enforcement of existing laws
General hazards from moving vehicles	Time or spatial separation of vehicles and pedestrians Systemwide plans for pedestrian safety Enforcement of laws

"I would go out more often if I had a suitable vehicle."

"I plan my route in advance to avoid obstacles, to avoid heavily trafficked streets, to avoid hazardous situations, and so on."

For this group the problem is not whether there should be a curb ramp on a particular street or an accessible toilet in the subway station. For them the failure is systemwide, and nothing less than systemwide plans can be of material assistance.

Component segments of the pedestrian system

The pedestrian system can be uncoupled into its component segments. A summary of these is shown in Table 2–4.

In generalizing from the survey findings, we see that the component subsystems of the pedestrian network often fail to provide adequately for the needs of the elderly and handicapped. Some of the components may be altogether absent from the pedestrian systems—no places to stop and rest for people with little stamina (Figure 2–1), no accessible public toilets for those troubled with weak bladders, or the subsystem may be difficult or impossible to use because certain of its constituent elements form

Table 2–4
Examples of Problems of Component Segments of the Pedestrian System

Measure	Countermeasure
Walkways:	
Handicapped are apprehensive about being knocked off balance on congested walkways.	Provide for platoons at intersection Provide appropriate walkway capacity design.
Cars parked on sidewalks	Enforce laws Barriers to prevent vehicular access

Table 2–4 (Continued)

Measure	Countermeasure
No sidewalks provided	Zoning laws required to ensure pedestrian provision Pedestrian plan required.
Street Crosswalks:	
Vehicles stop on crosswalk, restrict pedestrian movement	Widen crosswalk Provide stop line
Vehicles park on crosswalk	Law enforcement Widen sidewalk at intersection to width of parking lane
Difficult to cross streets during signal interval.	Increase signal interval time Reduce distance to be crossed by providing a center island Reduce distance to be crossed by widening sidewalks to edge of parking lane Provide pedestrian crossing interval
Rest and Waiting Areas:	
No place to rest for those with little stamina	Plan for rest areas and benches as part of city plans.
Wide streets are too tiring to cross	Provide center islands on wide streets
Toilet Provisions:	
Need accessible public toilets related to public walkway system	Develop city directory to accessible toilets. Require public-use buildings to provide accessible toilets
Walkway Illumination:	
Too dark to see curbs and surface irregularities	Greater emphasis on walkway illumination
Reflected glare from light colored sidewalks, ramps, stairs, etc., makes walkway hazardous	Attention to visibility and appropriate reflectance
Signage:	
Cannot see visual signs	Provide audible signals as well
Cannot hear audible signals	Use visible as well as audible signals

Figure 2–1
San Diego is one of the small number of cities that have some well-conceived resting places for pedestrians.

barriers to movement (curbs, uneven surfaces, and so forth). In the survey, people said such things as:

"There are too few resting places for me."
"I am apprehensive about crossing busy streets even at crosswalks."
"I am frequently forced to travel on roads because of sidewalk barriers."

In order to optimize these subsystems, it is not sufficient to consider the individual elements only. Providing curb ramps does not make a crosswalk barrier-free for all pedestrians. For the more severely handicapped at least, the pedestrian system and its component subsystems are not practical routes to use until there is a systematic and systemwide modification.

Elements of the pedestrian system

The systemwide failures are attributable to an aggregation of elements that cause difficulties either because they exist or because of the way they are designed. The surveys identified a large number of these elements. We have grouped them for classification and provided a summary of the problems that are associated with them in Table 2–5.

Figures 2–2 and 2–3 illustrate some of the typical statements made during the survey, such as:

"I am afraid of bumping into low overhanging projections."

TABLE 2–5
Examples of Problem Elements of the Pedestrian System

Measure	Countermeasure
Steps, Stairs, Curbs:	
Unable to negotiate any step	Provide alternative routes with ramps, elevators, etc. Eliminate level changes where possible.
Visually handicapped may fall into stairs	Provide warnings of presence of stairs
Hills, Ramps, Curb-Cuts:	
Cannot negotiate steep ramps	Provide steps as an alternative
Apprehensive of falling over a curb-cut	Avoid sudden changes of gradient Locate curb-cuts out of traffic stream
Curb-cut directs users into moving traffic	Locate curb-cuts in crosswalk.
For the blind, ramps and curb-cuts provide inadequate location cue of sidewalk edge	Provide curbs as alternatives Provide textural indicator of top and bottom of ramps.
Flooring and Surface Materials:	
Joints in paving cause physical discomfort or falls	Provide alternative routes that are relatively jointless
Walkway surfaces broken by tree roots	Plan for appropriate tree growth Provide maintenance for walkways
Walkway surfaces are slick from oil, water, ice, etc.	Ensure proper drainage Select nonslip materials Prevent cars from parking on walkways and thus leaving oil drips

TABLE 2–5 (Continued)

Measure	Countermeasure
Gutters, Gratings, Etc.:	
Gratings will snag shoes, canes, and crutches	Avoid gratings in walkways Make gratings more visible by painting
Manhole covers cause trips and slips	Replace manhole covers with trafficable surface. Make covers more visible by painting Avoid covers in walkway systems
Street Furniture:	
Will not detect overhanging projections and may bump into them.	Projections should be no lower than 7'–0" Avoid use of guard rails, etc. that cannot be detected by cane until too late
Street furniture obstructs pedestrian movement	Restrict street furniture to strip adjoining the curb Avoid furniture close to intersections.
Street furniture used to rest against	Provide rest areas
Street furniture used as handrail to pull up from the curb	Provide an appropriate post at crosswalks
Seating:	
Cannot get up from benches easily	Provide arm rests for public seating
Seats are too low to get up from	Public seating to be designed to suit elderly and handicapped
Handrails, Guardrails, Protective Barriers:	
Handrails difficult to grasp	Provide anthropometrically designed rails
Cannot see protection barriers before walking into them	Provide audible warnings where possible in addition to visual signs Avoid barriers that are too high for the cane of the blind

Many of the elements of the pedestrian system not only give trouble to many of the subgroups, but to "normal" pedestrians as well. Brick paved surfaces and cobblestones become slippery and irregular with age, street furniture and equipment are located without consideration of pedestrian flow, sidewalks are often too narrow, traffic signals give too short an interval for pedestrians, and so forth.

To sum up, many of the elements of the pedestrian system can be obstructive and even hazardous to the elderly and handicapped, and these elements

Figure 2-2
Street furniture is seldom designed with pedestrians in mind.

"Traffic signals often don't allow me sufficient time to cross the street."

"I am concerned that I may not notice curb ramps and fall over them."

The survey makes clear that each elderly and handicapped subgroup is affected by every one of these elements in a different way. Some cannot mount even a low step and must use ramps; others find ramps too hazardous and must use steps. For some, a hard smooth floor surface is ideal; for others it may be too slippery, particularly when wet.

Figure 2-3
Overhanging projections are a hazard to the blind.

are often used with little consideration for their functional impact. Alternatives that may be more appropriate are seldom considered.

Other affective factors

The survey shows that a number of other factors, either individually or in consort with those already described, adversely affect the handicapped pedestrian's ability to use the pedestrian system. These are not failures of the physical environment as built, but they may effectively bar the handicapped user from the system or make usage more difficult and hazardous for him or her. We have summarized the problems related to this group of factors in Table 2–6.

Typical remarks in this category are:

"I would go out more and make more trips if walkways were kept clear of snow and ice."

"I would go out more, but I am afraid of being mugged if I stop to rest."

"I am afraid of being bumped [in crowds]."

Many of these affective factors seem to be ubiquitous. Sidewalks are seldom kept in good repair, pedestrian rights of way are seldom enforced, turning vehicles are a constant problem to pedestrians, and parked and stopped vehicles block sidewalks and crosswalks. City and state moneys are expended for streets and highways, but seldom for pedestrian ways.

ESTABLISHING PRIORITIES

The results of the accident and problem studies make clear that the pedestrian system more often than not serves all users poorly and the target group worse. Where interventions have been introduced in an attempt to improve the lot of one group of disadvantaged people, these devices have often exascerbated the problems for others. Interventions have been very limited in kind. They have addressed only a few types of problems, perhaps because only a few have been identified or because some subgroup organizations have been more effective in lobbying than others.

Our research task is to look for solutions to the problems and to test them. Within our budget and time frame, however, fulfilling this task is not feasible for all the problems that have been identified; thus we necessarily focus on the most pressing problems.

The traditional way to establish priorities is in terms of the greatest good for the greatest number of people, to determine how many people are affected by each problem, and then to select for action those with the largest constituency. But this approach is ineffective for our purposes, because it tends to select the problems common to the majority to the exclusion of those acute problems that are peculiar to each minority group. Often the pressing problems of one subgroup are of no consequence to another. In absolute magnitude there are few blind people, for exam-

TABLE 2–6
Examples of Factors Affecting the Use of the Physical Pedestrian Environment

Measure	Countermeasure
Pedestrian rights not protected by law enforcement	Enforcement of laws
Apprehensive of crime in the streets	Defensible street design to discourage criminal behavior Law enforcement
Gutters and curbs not negotiable when snow ploughs have cleared the streets	Keep sidewalks and gutters clear of snow at bus stops and intersectons
Garbage and litter on walkways is hazardous	Careful sidewalk cleaning program
Walkways with potholes and broken or cracked surfaces are hazardous	Continuous maintenance of walkways
Turning vehicles fail to give way to pedestrians	Enforcement of laws Pedestrian interval in signal cycle

ple, so the problems that are unique to the blind will be poorly represented in a vote.

On the other hand, if we only address the most pressing problems of each minority subgroup, as has occurred in the past, we run the danger of suboptimization—and still fail to provide a system that works well for all. An alternative strategy is to try to reach a consensus on priorities that will address the most pressing problems of each subgroup also. This approach is the one that we have chosen.

Since resource limitation prevented us from sampling the opinions of representatives of elderly and handicapped people throughout the country, we sought the opinions of an expert panel that we convened to enable us to set priorities. Each panelist selected was an expert in the mobility problems of one of the subgroups. Whenever possible, we chose panelists who are themselves handicapped and could therefore speak for their own subgroups with confidence. In advance of the meeting, each panelist, as representative of a subgroup, was asked to estimate the percentage of his or her subgroup population that would be affected by each of the stated problems. Secondly, they were asked to estimate the precision of their responses. Finally, they were asked to indicate the most pressing problems for which countermeasures should be developed.

At the panel meeting that followed, the results of these subgroup responses were presented and used as a discussion base to seek agreement on priorities. A list of eighteen problem areas was developed and rank-ordered by the panel. From this ranking emerged the three most serious street-related problems for which appropriate countermeasures will be sought:

1. The difficulty in crossing streets safely,
2. The difficulty arising at curbs,
3. The difficulty arising from sidewalks and walkway design or maintenance failures.

Countermeasures will be directed at resolving these difficulties for each of the subgroups in terms of their particular problems. In addition, certain other press-

ing problems unique to particular subgroups—resting places for those with little stamina, for example—will be addressed.

STRATEGIES AND COUNTERMEASURES

Discussing all the countermeasures that we have proposed in detail is not feasible here, but our general approach may be of interest. First, let us discuss the general countermeasures that could be termed strategies.

Priority Accessible Network Strategy

To achieve substantial improvements, proposals for new as well as existing environments are needed, and the aggregate of these improvements must eventually lead to an accessible and safer pedestrian system. The aggregation must be planned in order to husband scarce resources and to give the system some continuity. Money to make the necessary changes is not likely to fund more than a relatively few changes every year. The urban systems that need to be improved are more or less the whole stock of cities, and the resources to do the job will have to be won in the arena of city priorities. Therefore, each location where an improvement is to be made must be carefully evaluated before the appropriate change is made and money expended. The evaluation should ensure that the proposed improvement will act to extend a system that is accessible. Obviously, peppering the city with improvements is of limited value: While each improvement is effective individually, in the aggregate they are ineffective because they are not connected. Typical of this approach is where a curb ramp is installed at only one corner of an intersection. It achieves very little, and it may be years before the others are installed to make the first ramp effective.

This example suggests that probably the single most important countermeasure for any city or district is the generation of a strategy or what we call a *priority accessible network*. This strategy would be a time-resources-implementation plan with the purpose of achieving its objectives in a stepwise fashion. The planners—perhaps a mix of consumers, advocates, and design professionals—would work to identify a limited number of high-priority routes that, if the barriers were removed, would be most beneficial to the elderly and handicapped.

These routes would form an interlocked and continuous system. However, the system would initially be limited in extent, and this extent would be related to the resources available at that time. After completion of this first segment of the network, priorities would be established for the next portion, and so on. The process would be a continuous one responsive to changing priorities and resources. Its systematic and systemic objectives would ensure an expanding, uninterrupted, barrier-free sequence of routes.

Strategies for New Construction

A second important but general countermeasure is the strategy to ensure that the mistakes of the past are not repeated in new construction—that is, to ensure that new towns, new suburbs, and areas of cities that are being renewed will be accessible and usable with a reasonable degree of safety and comfort. This strategy, of course, suggests the need for a pedestrian plan that is as well conceived and implemented as most vehicular plans. It does not mean merely the provision of sidewalks beside the road, although in many new subdivisions this addition would be an innovation. It means making the same sorts of decisions that are routine in vehicular traffic planning—that is, ensuring that pedestrian routes connect major activity areas and that the routes are adequate in terms of layout and detailed design.

Just as the highway system's predominant function is to optimize flow and safety, so should be the pedestrian system's. It should be a system in its own

right, and not an adjunct to the vehicular system. Therefore, its path should not necessarily parallel those of vehicles. And wherever the pedestrian route must cross that of the vehicular system, the choices must be examined carefully. If there is no reasonable alternative to the two systems crossing each other at grade, then the two systems should be separated in time. No vehicular movement should be permitted during a pedestrian signal phase, and vice versa. If this plan will seriously impede traffic flow, then the planners may have a good reason to select a grade-separated crossing. In all likelihood, few situations will require this alternative—that is, if the vehicular plan has been designed with an appropriate hierarchy of highways, arterials, and feeders and with no major roads passing through pedestrian areas.

These provisions simply reiterate some good planning practices. For the elderly and handicapped (and for most pedestrians), a number of other planning concerns should be considered in new work. These are set out in Tables 2–3, 2–4, 2–5, and 2–6 as a series of general recommendations drawn up as countermeasures to problems.

Retrofitting Strategy

The major problem for the forseeable future is reformation of pedestrian provisions that already exist in cities across the country. Many cities have begun to reassess their priorities and their concerns for pedestrians. This interest has been manifested in experiments ranging from temporary closing of streets to the development of pedestrian malls to the production of plans for pedestrian networks.

These assays are rare and are not really representative of a major thrust. Plans for pedestrianism are still so much of a curiosity that they become the focus of discussion at national conferences. The designers seem to be fascinated by the past. A pervasive nostalgia for the seductive qualities of Mykonos and San Gimignano is evident. Bollards, cobblestones, granite seats, and brick paving are the standard vocabulary;

Figure 2-4
A nostalgia for our medieval past may reproduce surfaces that have always been difficult to walk on.

materials that provide the pedestrian with the visual delights of textural richness, but the haptic discomforts of textural irregularity (Figure 2-4). Our ancestors had no choice but to use these materials that were quite inappropriate for wheeled traffic and always hazardous to those on foot. Either the pedestrian waded through the muck or accepted a surface that fit the fundamentally unstable human gait poorly. With the use of these materials, today or then, the probabilities of a slip or a trip are high. Joints fill with water and ice, and adjacent units move differentially over time.

In most parts of most cities, provisions for pedestrians remain as primitive, dangerous, and inadequate as ever, and they continue to be secondary to the vehicular system in design priorities. The politics of planning ensure that vehicular flow takes precedent over pedestrian safety.

Countermeasures for Safer Street Crossings

It is with this backdrop that our specific countermeasure proposals must be made. The proposals must be simultaneously idealistic and pragmatic, which is a somewhat improbable mix. We must try to make it easier and safer, for example, for the elderly and handicapped to cross the street, but if our proposals are to enjoy any acceptance, they must interfere with vehicular traffic as little as possible. Consider, for example, the single most important problem: how to cross the road in safety. A solution is needed that will either keep the pedestrians and vehicles apart or, if this is impossible, that will reduce the time in which they must share the same space. Even with the ubiquitous grade crossing, several solutions can reduce pedestrian–vehicular exposure and confrontation. But most of them will significantly reduce vehicular flow and therefore add to vehicular congestion in peak periods. We can introduce the "scramble" system, for instance, which is a signal cycle that stops all vehicular traffic while permitting pedestrians to cross in any direction and forbids pedestrian movement at all other times. Of course, not only is the

vehicle delayed by this system, but so is the pedestrian. These delays are the price of complete vehicular–pedestrian separation through time.

Because of these difficulties with the scramble system, we have looked for alternative proposals that reduce the traffic exposure time by other means. One way is to reduce the total width of the crossing. For example, on streets where parking is permitted, if we widen the sidewalks out to the edge of the parking lane, as in Figure 2–5, then we have reduced the total width to be crossed by two lanes, or by about one-third on a six-lane street.

There are other gains from this enlarged sidewalk. It enables those who are forming a "platoon," preparatory to crossing, to stand out of the stream of other pedestrian traffic. It permits those with little stamina to rest after the effort of hurrying across the street; benches can be provided. And it allows a gen-

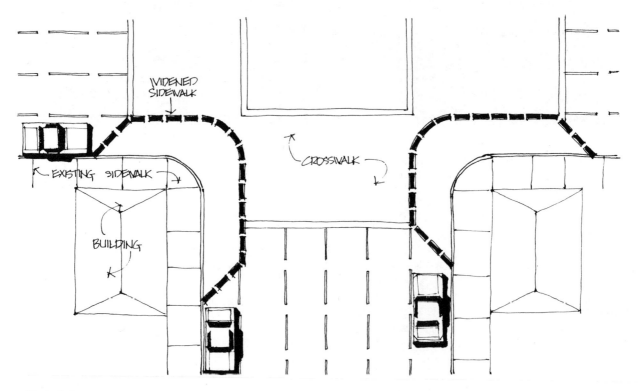

Figure 2–5
Widened sidewalks at corner crosswalks.

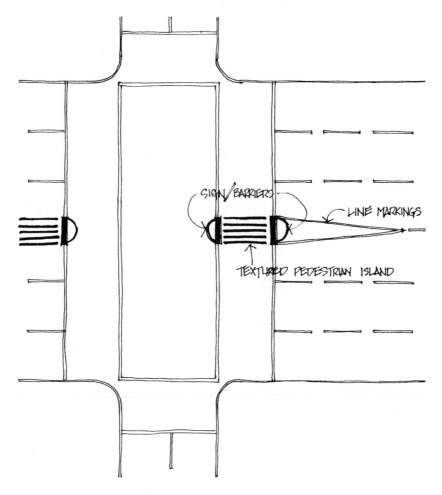

Figure 2–6
Pedestrian island.

erous amount of space for ramping down to the level
of the crosswalk. It also prevents vehicles from stopping and parking in the crosswalk. Finally, it permits
street furniture to be located close to the corner without hindering the flow of traffic.

This countermeasure has costs as well as benefits.
The sidewalk addition must be paid for. If the addition is applied to both sides of the street, the storm
water drains and gutters that are so often found at
the corner, must be reformed.

In the centers of most cities, in the main streets,

parking and stopping are either prohibited or restricted to certain hours. In these cases, the enlarged
curb may be unacceptable or usable on the minor
streets only. However, aiding the pedestrian, and
particularly the pedestrian who has difficulty in crossing before the lights change, is still possible. The next
proposed countermeasure is a pedestrian island as
indicated in Figure 2-6. The island would have to be
at least five feet wide to permit a wheelchair and
attendant to stop there in safety. And, of course, it
would have no curbs. To inform the blind that they

have reached a haven, the surface would have to have a texture that is detectably different from that of the roadway. It would have to be safe for the pedestrian, particularly from turning traffic. It would also have to be safe for vehicles that lose control.

Again, there are costs to be incurred. First there is the cost of building and maintaining the island. The street must lose five feet, or nearly one foot per lane for a six-lane street. But the financial costs are certainly less than those of enlarging sidewalks.

In considering these two countermeasures, we must bear in mind that they are only applicable in certain situations. There are few, if any, countermeasures that will work efficiently in all situations.

Countermeasures for Improving Sidewalks

We have found that usually there is a set of alternative solutions to the problem of curbs. Each alternative is appropriate in some circumstances and inappropriate in others. This situation is typical of most of the problems and hazards that we have identified. Therefore, where the alternatives are limited, we propose to develop a decision matrix to enable the appropriate countermeasure to be selected for each environmental situation. Such a matrix would list the environmental conditions down one side of the table (curb heights, width of sidewalk, width of street, and so forth) and solutions across the other side of the table (various ways of providing transitions from sidewalk to street, for example). The designer would then check off the environmental conditions at the location and quickly be able to see the design options that are available.

Where there are many alternative countermeasures, it is better to set out performance specifications. These are less inhibiting to the designer than prescriptive specifications and therefore are more likely to generate improved solutions. For example, setting out the various relationships between ramp length and ramp gradient that the elderly and handicapped can negotiate is better than prescribing a maximum slope of 1:12 for all purposes and locations. While prescrip-

tive solutions are easier to administer in regulations and codes, they tend to limit the development of good alternatives.

Street furniture is a special concern to the elderly and handicapped. For some, parking meters, mail boxes, litter boxes, lamp posts, and so forth provide a series of impediments to be patiently avoided. For others, they provide something to lean against or something to pull on when climbing a curb. For still others, they may provide a refuge from traffic or locations cues (for the blind).

Most of the disadvantages can be eliminated if street furniture location is more carefully considered, but at present there are no guiding principles. Each utility organization sites its equipment for its own convenience (Figure 2–7). Lamp standards and other poles are moved back from the curb so that they will not be knocked down by high vehicles that are leaning outwards in response to the camber of the road. Parking meters are located close to the curb. Newspaper vending machines are usually set down close to a corner, with no apparent design or concern. Mail boxes, litter boxes, pay telephones, and news vendor booths are located for ease of maintenance and service.

Nevertheless, we usually find some degree of standardization of location, even if it is accidental. Most street furniture is located within a strip that stretches about thirty inches from the curb. If this furniture strip was adopted as an agreed upon location for all equipment that is subsidiary to the pedestrian and vehicular environment, the walkways could be kept reasonably clear. We have proposed indicating the boundaries of this strip by a surface texture change (see Figure 2–8) or at least a continuous joint or marker. This indicator would give notice to the utility installers of where installations are permitted. In some places utilizing the strip for planting, both for beautification and to discourage crossing away from crosswalks, would be possible. With careful design it may serve to provide the blind with a shoreline that is denied them by barriers at the curb and by uneven shopfront lines on the other side.

It should be noted here that we have found many

Figure 2-7
A pedestrian obstacle race: Bump against the canopy, slip on the manhole cover, bruise yourself on the fire hydrant, go into the street to avoid the parked cars.

organizations and instructors for the blind resistant to countermeasures aimed at assisting the blind. Their philosophy is that with good training, the blind can move with little difficulty and that unless clues or cues are installed everywhere in the same way, which is unlikely, they will simply be confusing.

This philosophy is simple pragmatism, but denies the possibility of avoiding some of the worst problems experienced by this group. This situation is demonstrated by the complaints that organizations for the blind have raised about many types of curb ramps. The blind have found that some of these ramps, with their steep slopes, are an additional sur-

face hazard. The ramps do not provide the blind with an edge or curb on which to stand while waiting to cross the road. Clearly, if the environment can be made worse for the blind, it can also be made better. Most of our proposals for the blind have been directed at eliminating things from walkways that they can bump into, trip over, or fail to detect with canes before it is too late. Included in this group are telephone boxes that cantilever from a pole, for example, and barriers that use chains, and so forth.

For many of the blind that we interviewed, large open spaces such as parking lots present particular problems because pedestrian walkways are seldom

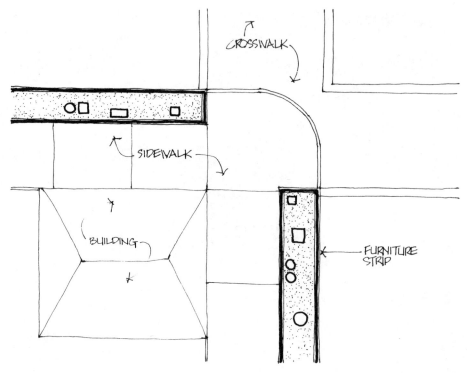

Figure 2-8
Street furniture strip.

provided. They are difficult to navigate through. Where parking areas, gas stations, and so forth are adjacent to sidewalks and streets and the surfaces are continuous, there is a real danger of wandering into the path of vehicular traffic. A blind person with highly developed mobility skills may have little difficulty, but of course the blind vary in skills and abilities.

Devising layouts that avoid these continuous surfaces is not difficult, nor is providing walkways that feel different from asphalt, or separating walkway routes of concrete from other large concrete paved areas. Separation strips of a different texture are easy for the blind to feel and to be warned that some change is imminent.

Curb Avoidance Countermeasures

Some sort of detectable separation is particularly necessary where curb avoidance countermeasures are under consideration. Some of the blind told us that they prefer to have the traditional curbs as this gives them an unambiguous edge at which to wait before crossing the road. Other blind people, particularly those who are elderly or who have other mobility handicaps, were less equivocal. For them the curb is a mixed blessing. The edge is useful but the step is difficult.

For some of those in wheelchairs, a step of even half an inch is insurmountable. And some people who walk with difficulty, or who use crutches, or whose balance is insecure, choose to avoid ramps wherever possible. This leaves few alternative solutions; if ramps are difficult for some, and the curb for others, then we have the following choices:

1. Crosswalk raised to the level of the sidewalk,
2. Ramp for some and a curb for others,
3. Sidewalk brought down to the level of the crosswalk,
4. Some combination of these.

Each of these alternatives has disadvantages as well as advantages.

The best plan for raising the crosswalk at an intersection is to raise the whole intersection so that the vehicles ramp up before entering the box and then ramp down when leaving as shown in Figure 2-9. Apart from the initial cost, which must probably include the relocation of the storm water drains, there are some dangers that people with visual handicaps may stray into the road. But then, this group may also fall into the road over the curb if they do not approach the street with the necessary caution. Clearly, the edge of the sidewalk and the raised crosswalk must be demarcated in a way that can be sensed by the blind, but yet will not obstruct wheelchairs nor trip other pedestrians. A detectable texture strip seems to be an answer.

There are many ways of providing a mixture of

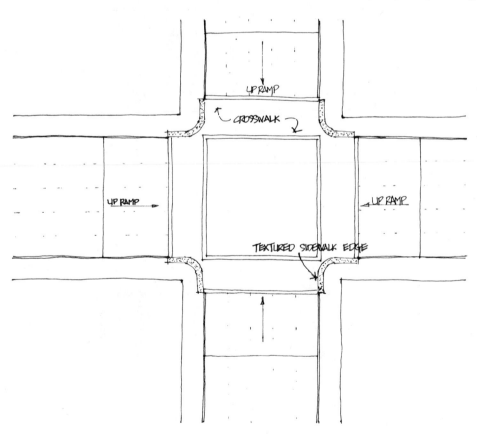

Figure 2-9
Ramped vehicular intersection.

curb and curb ramps (which is the approach favored by most cities), but none of these seem to be problem free. A favorite solution is to locate a curb ramp in the center of the curb at the corner as in Figure 2–10. In this location it is out of the way of most people who wish to use curbs. But it must be entered and exited in a direction that takes the user into or close to the moving traffic. If the curb height is considerable, the ramp must occupy much of the sidewalk corner, so that all traffic must move over it.

Providing a single curb ramp away from the corner is an even less satisfactory solution. People using it and wishing to cross in the other direction must enter the street against the red signal, into the moving traffic lane, before rounding the corner into the cross-

walk. And depending on the size of the ramp, the rest of the pedestrians must traverse the ramp across the slope.

A pair of curb ramps is better than these last two solutions, only because they permit those who wish to use them to enter straight into the crosswalk in the desired direction. But such a pair doubles the amount of uneven or crossramped surface to be crossed by everyone. If the ramps are located close together near the corner, they often leave at their intersection an area that is unusable for pedestrians. However, where the sidewalks and crosswalks are wide and the curb is low, then two curb ramps can be considered.

To circumvent the problems associated with cutting ramps into sidewalks, some cities have ramped

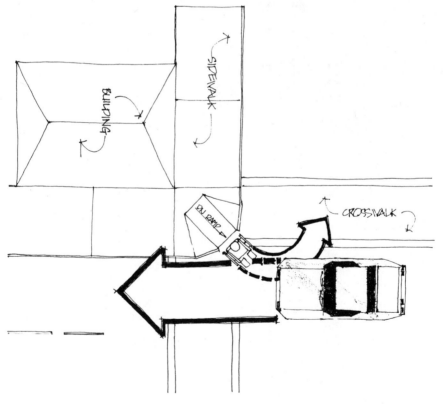

Figure 2–10
Corner curb ramp location.

out into the roadway. This is an inexpensive and simple solution, but it is impractical where snow plows and mechanical equipment may demolish the ramps. Care has to be taken to locate them where they will not interfere with vehicular traffic, particularly turning vehicles.

Bringing the sidewalk down to the level of the crosswalk can be achieved by several means, all of which must have special provisions to indicate to the blind whre the crosswalk starts. The whole sidewalk can be gently ramped down before the corner, so that the quadrant at the corner is at the crosswalk level. Of course, people on the sidewalk who wish to turn

the corner must go down a ramp and up another. Any shop entrances at the corner would need to be modified.

Where the sidewalk is wide, an alternative is to ramp the whole corner quadrant up from the edge of the street but to leave the remainder of the corner intact. A special problem with this and several of the previous alternatives is that many existing streets are graded to a corner drain, and in the event of heavy precipitation, the stream of water to be crossed may be substantially wider than that usually experienced at a curb (Figure 2-11).

Where the curb is very high so that any ramp will

Figure 2-11
Storm water drains are usually poorly located for pedestrians, and the gratings are a hazard for crutches, canes, wheels, and even heels.

have to be very long, a compromise is to reduce the curb height by raising the level of the pavement to an acceptable level.

This discussion on curb-to-street transition and other countermeasures has not, of course, covered all the problems nor all of the alternatives. But it indicates that for every problem and at every location, the costs and benefits of each alternative must be examined before selecting a solution. There are few universally applicable solutions.

THE ACCESSIBLE CITY

If the city is a large house, then walking through most of its rooms and passages is probably dangerous to our health. This is not altogether surprising; it has always been the case. But perhaps it should be surprising; after all, we know much more about safety and comfort than we did even fifty years ago.

If the city's pedestrian ways are uncomfortable, unsafe, inaccessible, or unavailable, then the fault is the city's; it is the city's domain to regulate, to erect, and to govern its streets. But the city represents a temporal continuum with its routes as the most stable and unchanging elements. Buildings pass through a cycle of birth, decay, and rebuilding, but streets change little except for infrequent repairs. And repairs are always just that: Streets are seldom rebuilt.

Cities respond to pressures in fairly predictable ways. Nothing is changed without a demand for change, and demand is generated as a response to patent crises. Most city building codes, health codes, and bylaws can be traced to nineteenth century responses to the threats of plague. Certainly the recent changes to the cities' movement routes have been responses to the growing number of vehicles (not to the growing number of pedestrian deaths and injuries; people are more compressible than vehicles). And even now the evidence of new interest in the pedestrian comes as a response to the general economic malaise of city centers. Perhaps city centers can be made attractive places for people again and

attract customers away from suburban shopping malls.

Political pressure for change without a patent crisis is more difficult to effect, and as we have seen, pedestrians do not represent a political power group. But the elderly and handicapped have, since the early sixties, begun to be a more effective lobby, and every state and the federal government now have architectural barriers legislation.

Much of the legislation is directed at making buildings accessible, but curiously, not the streets outside them. In some states the statutes are not only directed at buildings that are built with state or federal funds, but at *all* buildings for public use—but not the streets.

There is little question that the states are in a position to exert pressure on cities to embark on a program to make their streets accessible. But such a program is hampered by the fact that the states have no standards of accessibility as opposed to barrier-free building codes. There is no national standard for making cities accessible to the handicapped. Clearly such a standard is needed.

NOTES AND REFERENCES

This chapter describes research being conducted under Contract No. DOT-FH-11-8504, funded by the U.S. Department of Transportation, in the interest of information exchange. The U.S. government assumes no liability for its contents or use thereof. The contents of this chapter reflect the views of its authors, who are responsible for the accuracy of the data presented herein. The contents do not necessarily reflect the official views or policy of the Department of Transportation, Federal Highway Administration. This chapter does not constitute a standard, specification, or regulation.

1. "Accident Facts," National Safety Council, Chicago, 1974.
2. Ibid.
3. Ibid.
4. Jones, T. O., B. S. Repa, and J. L. Potgiesser, "A General Overview of Pedestrian Accidents and Protection Counter-

measures," *Proceedings, Third International Congress on Automotive Safety*, vol. 1, Washington, D.C., 1974.

5. *Travel Barriers: Transportation of the Handicapped*, PB 198327 (Cambridge, Mass: Abt Associates, Inc., 1969), distributed by National Technical Information Service, U.S. Dept. of Commerce, Springfield, Va.

6. Snyder, Monore B., and Richard L. Knoblauch, *Pedestrian Safety: The Identification of Precipitating Factors and Possible Countermeasures*, Vol. I (Washington, D.C.: U.S. Department of Transportation, 1971).

7. American National Standards Institute, *Making Buildings and Facilities Accessible to and Usable by the Physically Handicapped*, New York, 1961.

3

Barrier-Free Design: A Legislative Response

James S. Jeffers

James S. Jeffers who was appointed Executive Director of the Architectural and Transportation Barriers Compliance Board in March 1975 is the first person to hold this position. Prior to this appointment, he served as Special Assistant to the Administator of the Social and Rehabilitation Service, DHEW, where he had primary responsibility for implementation of the Rehabilitation Act of 1973. Before coming to Washington, D.C., in 1973, he served as Research Assistant to the Governor of Illinois and the Office of the State Comptroller. In these positions he was responsible for conceiving and drafting major legislative proposals regarding civil rights of handicapped people and providing for statewide architectural accessibility laws. Mr. Jeffers received his B. A. degree in public administration from Southern Illinois Unviersity, Carbondale, in 1969. He received the William S. Pollack Award as outstanding legislative intern for 1970–71. He was named "Rehabilitant of the Year" by the West Virginia Department of Rehabilitation in 1972. He received a Distinguished Service Award from the Illinois Congress of the Physically Handicapped in 1974.

BARRIER-FREE DESIGN: THE CONCEPT

Before embarking on a discussion of the process by which barrier-free design has surfaced as a legitimate subject of study, it is imperative that the concept of barrier-free design be explored and defined. For the purposes of this discussion, barrier-free design means the incorporation and utilization of design principles that result in the construction and creation of functional, safe, and convenient environments responsive to user needs.

Although barrier-free design is commonly associated with the environmental needs of disabled persons, it is a much more universal concept in its application. As a society, we have become victims of, and are controlled by, our environment. We have elected to adapt to inadequate and dysfunctional architectural design rather than to assert our needs and wants as basic components of functional design. Some of us have the ability to adapt more readily than others. For the physically disabled person, however, the ability to adapt to nonfunctional design is severely limited. For this reason, disabled individuals, for the purposes of survival and participation, are demanding barrier-free design that will benefit all by ensuring functional, safe, and convenient design of our manmade environment.

The three major components of barrier-free design are: functionality, safety, and convenience.

Functionality. The environments we create must be functional for the potential user. These environments must meet the functional activity needs and preferences of potential users and must be responsive to user capability. The component of functionality entails a concern for utility in arranging activities of similar or interdependent relationships in a functional manner. By so doing, the usability of the environment is increased, which in turn facilitates and eases the completion of activities.

Saftey. The environment and its component parts must be safe for potential users. At the very least, the environment and the products comprising that environment should not do bodily harm and damage to its users. It is evident that we as a society are becoming increasingly sensitive to, and aware of, the dangers of unsafe products and hazardous construction. This concern will continue to result in demands for safety in our environment.

Convenience. The convenience component is probably the most nebulous and most difficult element of barrier-free design to define. Convenience denotes the suitability and agreeability of the environment to needs and purposes. For example, accessible and usable transportation station facilities are not suitable and agreeable to the user if those facilities are not in close proximity to the respective transport vehicle. Convenience might be viewed as synonymous with "ease of access."

By incorporating these three elements of design, our manmade environment will not only be barrier-free, but will be functional and usable for all potential users.

This concept becomes increasingly important when viewed in the context that all potential users of our environment experience activity restricting limitations. Providing some indications of the number of individuals restricted by inadequate design may be useful. The U.S. Department of Health, Education and Welfare (DHEW) estimates that there are 41 million handicapped people in the United States. This number is approximately 20 percent of the population. The definition of handicapped persons used by DHEW does not include an estimated 30 percent of the population suffering activity-restricting injury. This figure of 30 percent represents those 62 million Americans who annually experience accidents and incapacities that prevent them from functioning in a "normal" manner.[1]

Lawrence D. Cohen and Phillip S. Stefanaik, two students in the Industrial Design Department at the University of Michigan, participated in the 1974 Armco Student Design Program, "Designing to Accommodate the Handicapped," which addressed the following question: "How many Americans are really normal?" It was indicated that in fact a very small number could be considered "normal." Cohen

and Stefanaik estimate that 50 percent of the population are "handicapped" in their day-to-day abilities to function.[2] Others contend, using criteria similar to Cohen's and Stefanaik's, that there are actually 160 million Americans who are not "normal"—that is, according to current design specification.[3]

Based upon the foregoing, barrier-free design is obviously a concept deserving of universal application, and we should view the historical progress of barrier-free design in this context.

THE LEGISLATIVE RESPONSE

Early Activity

In order to gain a proper perspective of the history and evolution of barrier-free design, we should note the genesis of activity in this area.

As a result of the massive numbers of disabled veterans returning from World War II and the Korean conflict and the increased life expectancies of persons incurring disabilities as a result of trauma, the necessity to focus attention and concern on the social and environmental needs of these persons began to gain momentum in the 1950s. Medical and rehabilitation services were expanded, and increased opportunities for vocational training for disabled persons began to surface.

As the disabled person began to acquire vocational and social skills necessary to develop full integration into the existing social structure, two facts became apparent: Neither the structure nor the environment were prepared for the challenge. Attitudes impaired social and personal acceptance, and structural barriers ensured the disabled person that integration would be impossible. In response to the obvious need for action to address these barriers, the National Easter Seal Society for Crippled Children and Adults formed a partnership with the President's Committee on Employment of the Handicapped to develop a strategy addressing architectural barriers and their removal. A research grant was awarded to the University of Illinois to develop standards designed to make public buildings accessible to the physically handicapped.[4]

As a result of this research activity, in 1961 the American Standards Association (now known as the American National Standards Institute) in cooperation with the National Easter Seal Society for Crippled Children and Adults, the University of Illinois, and the President's Committee on Employment of the Handicapped published standards entitled "Making Buildings and Facilities Accessible to and Usable by the Physically Handicapped." With the publication of these standards, a national educational program was undertaken to ensure adoption of the standards by state and local governments.

Due to the efforts of various public and private agencies, by 1965 thirty-four states had taken some type of action towards implementing the standards through legislation or adoption into building codes. Unfortunately, this activity had little success, due to its limited scope of coverage and a lack of effective sanctions to enforce compliance with the standards. Thus, while certain progress had been made, much remained to be accomplished to deal effectively with the removal of structural barriers.

National Commission on Architectural Barriers to the Rehabilitation of the Handicapped

The first major piece of legislation enacted at the federal level to further the barrier-free design movement was Public Law 89-333, the Vocational Rehabilitation Act Amendments of 1965, approved November 8, 1965. Section 15 of this Act established the National Commission on Architectural Barriers to the Rehabilitation of the Handicapped. The Commission was created as a result of the expressed desire of Congress to discover what had been achieved in relation to the elimination of architectural barriers. The duties of the Commission were to:

1. Determine how and to what extent architectural barriers impede access to or use of facilities in buildings of all types by the handicapped.

2. Determine what is being done, especially by public and other nonprofit agencies and groups having an interest in and a capacity to deal with the problem, to eliminate such barriers from existing buildings and to prevent their incorporation into buildings constructed in the future, and

3. Prepare plans and proposals for such further action as may be necessary to achieve the goal of ready access and full use of facilities in buildings of all types by the handicapped, including proposals for bringing together, in a cooperative effort, agencies, organizations and groups already working toward that goal, or whose cooperation is essential to effective and comprehensive action.

The Commission studied the issues for two years and in 1967 issued its report in a document entitled, "Design for All Americans."[5] The findings of the study were:

1. Architects were unaware of the problem. The National League of Cities conducted a study of 2,975 architects. Of the 709 who replied, only 251 had any awareness of the American National Standard Institute's accessibility specification (the ANSI 117.1 standards).

2. Manufacturers and suppliers of building materials were unaware of standards. Out of seven major national trade organizations, none had established any policies relative to meeting the standards and only three were familiar with them.

3. None of the four major building codes made any reference to architectural barriers.

4. A lack of public interest was the number one reason public officials gave for failure to develop public programs around this issue.

5. Voluntary action was deemed necessary but not sufficient. Even with an informal and concerned citizenry, change cannot be achieved by voluntary efforts. Legislative action must back it up.

5. Although lack of usable transportation by the aged and handicapped is the most serious problem, it has received almost no attention. There are no standard specifications that apply to accessible transportation.

7. ANSI standards do not cover residential housing or transportation. They do not spell out in just

what facilities and to what extent its specifications should be followed.

As a result of the findings, the Commission issued the following recommendations:

1. Enactment of federal legislation requiring that all new public buildings and facilities, which are intended for use by the public, must be designed to accommodate the elderly and the handicapped if any federal funds are used in their construction.
2. Issuance of an executive order to apply accessibility standards to new construction and to direct all federal agencies to plan and budget for feasible changes in their existing buildings and facilities.
3. Enactment or revision of state legislation to require that state and local buildings, constructed with public funds, meet accessibility standards and include strong enforcement provisions.
4. Revision of all building codes so that industries, shops, and other privately owned structures used by the public will be built for accessibility in the future and so that when existing buildings are renovated, feasible improvements in accessibility will be made.
5. Assignment of responsibility and resources to specific units of federal, state, and local governments, to administer the accessibility legislation, to conduct and/or support research and demonstrations, and to work with voluntary, professional, business, and industrial organizations to the end that all buildings and facilities will be readily accessible to elderly and handicapped people.
6. Expansion of publicly and privately supported educational information programs so that no longer, merely through thoughtlessness, will millions of citizens be unable to use buildings, parks, and other facilities.

These recommendations were substantially adopted in the legislation (H.R. 6589) introduced in the House of Representatives.

Architectural Barriers Act of 1968, Public Law 90–480

Currently, the basic statute providing for accessibility of federally funded and assisted buildings is Public Law 90–480. It requries the head of the General Services Administration, the Department of Housing and Urban Development, and the Department of Defense, in consultation with the Secretary of Health, Education and Welfare, to issue standards for federal buildings. The term *buildings* is defined to include those buildings and facilities constructed, or altered by, or on behalf of the United States; buildings leased after alterations in accordance with federal specifications; and buildings funded by grants or loans where the statute authorizing the grant or loan also authorizes the imposition of construction terms and conditions. The heads of the enumerated agencies are given the authority to waive the standards relating to accessibility and usability on a case-by-case basis only upon application by the head of another department or agency. GSA, HUD, and the Defense Department are also authorized to undertake surveys and investigations to ensure compliance.

Prior to enactment of this legislation, the administrator of GSA, had already adopted a limited accessibility program. Congress recognized that many other agencies, however, had no similar policy. The legislative branch felt a need to take action to adopt legislation that not only prevented construction of public buildings by and on behalf of the federal government that were inaccessible and believed that Congress should also set an example to encourage state governments and private industry to construct buildings over which they have jurisdiction, that would be accessible and usable by physically handicapped individuals.[6]

The Senate was most particularly concerned and most anxious to provide a legislative solution. The Senate chose to pass legislation even before the National Commission on Architectural Barriers had submitted its final report. Many of the executive agencies had advised the Senate to defer action on proposed S. 222 (the forerunner of P.L. 90–480) pending completion of the Commission's final report.[7]

The House of Representatives passed barrier-free design legislation, H.R. 6589, in the summer of 1968. After a conference to resolve relatively few differences, agreement was reached and bills were subsequently enacted by both chambers of the legislative branch. The legislation (P.L. 90–480) was signed into law on August 12, 1968, by President Lyndon B. Johnson.

Congress recognized from the time of enactment of Public Law 90–480 that approximately 22 million physically handicapped people, restricted in their ability to move from place to place, were a valuable asset and must be afforded every opportunity to enter the mainstream of American life. Congress indicated a need to legislate a mandatory legal requirement providing minimum accessibility to ensure the elimination of architectural barriers, since voluntary barrier-free design standards and policies, while helpful, had not assured the total accessibility and utility of the federal government to disabled individuals. The waiver provisions were to be narrowly invoked.[8]

In response to the statutory mandate of Public Law 90–480, the General Services Administration, and the Departments of Housing and Urban Development, and the Department of Defense each issued regulations and amended their construction manuals to include the American National Standard Institute specification for making buildings and facilities accessible to and usable by the physically handicapped. This standard is commonly referred to as ANSI A–117.1, originally issued in 1961 (subsequently revised in 1971). These standards were promulgated by the agencies after extended oral and written discussions with the Department of Health, Education and Welfare as was contemplated by Congress.

Washington Metropolitan Area Transit, Public Law 91–205

Public Law 90–480 was amended in March of 1970 to include buildings constructed under the authority of the National Capital Transportation Act of 1960, the National Capital Transportation Act of 1965, or Title 3 of the Washington Metropolitan Area Transportation Regulations Compact, so as to encompass within the ambit of the Architectural Barriers Act construction of subway stations, service stations, and other structures of the subway system being built in Washington, D.C. The legislation was needed because the Washington Metropolitan Area Transit Authority is a regional agency formed by compact and is not a federal agency. Thus, its buildings and structures were not otherwise subject to Public Law 90–480. It is significant to note that the legislative history clearly reflects that rolling stock—that is, the trains themselves—is not subject to or covered by Public Law 90–480.[9]

Urban Mass Transportation Act, Public Law 91–453

Section 16(a) of the Urban Mass Transportation Act provides:

It is hereby declared to be the national policy that elderly and handicapped persons have the same rights as other persons to utilize mass transportation facilities and services; that special efforts shall be made in the planning and design of mass transportation facilities and services so that the availability to elderly and handicapped persons of mass transportation which they can effectively utilize will be assured; and that all Federal programs offering assistance in the field of mass transportation (including the programs under this Act) should contain provisions implementing this policy.

This legislation was enacted in 1970 as an expression of the Congressional policy in this area.

Rehabilitation Act of 1973, Public Law 93–112

Public Law 93–112 established the Architectural and Transportation Barriers Compliance Board (A&TBCB). In establishing the board in 1973, Congress sought to ensure compliance with the Architectural Barriers Act of 1968. The legislative history is quite clear in that during the two years Congress took to create the board, the primary if not exclusive concern was the lack of an effective compliance program to ensure accessibility and usability of public buildings. The A&TBCB was designed to be the major force in assuring that handicapped people be given the opportunity to move freely in the society into which they must integrate themselves. All of the board's other functions, both in terms of investigating alternative approaches and increasing public awareness, must be viewed in their compliance-oriented context. Congress conceived the A&TBCB as a primary moving force to ensure the fullest implementation of a previously statutorily enunciated goal of a barrier-free federal environment.[10]

In 1972 Congress had twice passed legislation substantially similar to Public Law 93-112. Rehabilitation acts were vetoed by President Richard M. Nixon on two occasions for reasons largely unrelated to the Architectural and Transportation Barriers Compliance Board. The President disapproved of the bill as fiscally irresponsible. The veto message also indicated the President's disapproval of the diversion of various vocational rehabilitation program functions.[11]

The bills, S. 7 and S. 1875, and the reports, particularly Senate Reports 93-48 and 93-318, are the predecessors to Public Law 93-112 and Senate Report 93-391. It is sagacious to note that in the 1972 legislation, a National Commission on Transportation and Housing for Handicapped Individuals had been proposed to work in conjunction with the proposed Architectural and Transportation Barriers Compliance Board to define housing and transportation problems of the handicapped. In the revision of S. 7, after the first veto and the failure to override, Congress made several changes in the new bill, S. 1875, the most pertinent of which are that many of the functions previously prescribed to this National Commission on Transportation and Housing were given to the A&TBCB. The particular provisions may be found in section 502(c) relating to the extent of housing and transportation barriers as impeding the mobility of

handicapped individuals. The authority of A&TBCB to determine what measures are being taken to eliminate barriers on public transportation systems and to make housing available and accessible to handicapped people may be traced to the 1972 bill.[12]

The 1972 legislation had been predominantly composed of legislative authority currently found in section 502(b) related to compliance matters. Both the 1972 and 1973 Rehabilitation Acts authorized A&TBCB to hold public hearings as well as to invoke compliance procedures.[13]

1974 Amendments to the Rehabilitation Act, Public Law 93-516

Public Law 93-516, approved in December 1974, added the Department of Defense as a board member of A&TBCB and authorized the appointment of a consumer advisory panel, the majority of whose membership are to be handicapped people, to provide guidance, advice, and recommendations to the A&TBCB. The primacy of the board's compliance functions was underscored by providing that a compliance order of the A&TBCB could include the withholding or suspension of federal funds with respect to a noncomplying building. Congress also expressly authorized the employment of a board staff.[14]

Two additional changes of significance were made in the existing legislation. Congress revised the definition of a handicapped person to include a person who (a) has a physical or mental impairment that substantially limits one or more of such person's major life activities, (b) has a record of such impairment, or (c) is regarded as having such an impairment. Public Law 93-112 had defined handicapped people in terms of a disability constituting or resulting in a substantial handicap to employment. Public Law 93-516 also statutorily designated the Secretary of DHEW as the permanent chairman of the board. This measure is in keeping with what Congress believed to be the lead role of the Department of Health, Education and Welfare in matters relating to the A&TBCB.

A reading of the legislative report to Public Law 93-516 clearly shows that Congress expects A&TBCB to take an aggressive attitude in carrying out its functions as a quasi-independent agency. There is expressed language to that effect in reports from both the House and the Senate.[15]

THE REHABILITATION ACT OF 1973

Overview

The enactment of the Rehabilitation Act of 1973 must be viewed as one of the most important pieces of federal legislation affecting handicapped people. This Act extended and expanded the federal–state rehabilitation program begun in 1921 to provide rehabilitation and vocational training services to handicapped persons. During the half century the program has been in existence, the scope and degree of services had expanded to provide comprehensive rehabilitation services to handicapped persons.

The 1973 Act went further than any previous rehabilitation act in seeking to be responsive to the needs of handicapped individuals. A major emphasis was placed on first serving those people with severe disabilities. This legislative initiative was in response to criticism of the program by disabled people that persons with minor or marginal disabilities were receiving the majority of services of state rehabilitation programs. As a consequence of limited resources, people with severe disabilities requiring more time, effort, and money were being served on a much more restrictive basis.

Other provisions of the program included client-assistance projects to serve as legal advocates for clients receiving services from state vocational rehabilitation programs as well as provisions for the client to participate fully in the development of an individualized, written rehabilitation program. These provi-

sions addressed the consumer–due-process aspect of the service delivery system. Further, the 1973 Act required state rehabilitation agencies to involve disabled persons in the development of annual state rehabilitation plans submitted to the federal government as a condition for receipt of federal financial assistance. These and other major provisions in Titles I–III of the Rehabilitation Act of 1973 clearly focus on serving the needs and protecting the rights of disabled people.

In addition to these major changes in the federal–state rehabilitation program, the 1973 Act included a major title containing legislative provisions designed to preserve and protect the rights of disabled people and to expand the privileges extended to handicapped persons in order to ensure fair and equal treatment. Provisions in Title V congressionally recognize the enlarged scope of rehabilitation as a process and acknowledge the continual rehabilitation and developmental needs of disabled persons.

Title V—Rehabilitation Act of 1973—Major Provisions

Section 501: interagency committee on handicapped employees

Section 501 of the Rehabilitation Act of 1973 established the Interagency Committee on Handicapped Employees for the purpose of providing increased employment opportunities for the handicapped in the federal service. This committee, co-chaired by the secretary of DHEW and the chairman of the Civil Service Commission, is charged with designing the mechanisms necessary to facilitate the hiring, placement, and advancement of handicapped persons.

Agencies of the federal government are required under the Act to design and submit affirmative action program plans for the hiring, placement, and advancement of handicapped persons in their agencies to the

Civil Service Commission and Interagency Committee on Handicapped Employees. These affirmative action plans are to be monitored and evaluated with regard to performance levels and implementation.

To deal with the implementation of this provision, the Interagency Committee on Handicapped Employees has adopted a set of goals and objectives designed to address the comprehensive employment opportunities for handicapped persons. These goals and objectives include providing a focus for increased employment in federal service for handicapped persons by: (1) establishing a common and functional definition of "handicapped individual" for the purposes of federal employment; (2) establishing standards for evaluating and approving agency affirmative action program plans and the practices and achievements in effectively implementing those plans; (3) providing for a suitable and feasible information system for the collection of data regarding the employment of handicapped persons; and (4) initiating a review of existing federal employment practices and procedures and making recommendations deemed necessary or desirable to facilitate the employment of the handicapped. The goals also include assuring an equitable, suitable, and functional environment for the employment of the handicapped persons in federal service by: (1) consulting with the Architectural and Transportation Barriers Compliance Board to assure that all facilities that house federal employees comply with the architectural accessibility provisions contained in the Architectural Barriers Act of 1968 (P.L. 90–480) as amended; (2) identifying the transportation problems of handicapped persons, as those problems impair their employability; (3) promoting educational mechanisms necessary for overcoming attitudinal barriers that adversely affect the employment of handicapped persons; and (4) focusing attention on the development of the maximum potential of handicapped persons in employment, including, where appropriate, such consideration as job restructuring, use of assistance devices, employment of disabled veterans, and other aspects of job accommodations.

Section 502: architectural and transportation barriers compliance board

The Architectural and Transportation Barriers Compliance Board was established and authorized to enforce standards of accessibility prescribed in the Architectural Barriers Act. Congress believed that major efforts should be undertaken to provide handicapped persons with the opportunity to move freely and independently in the environment and society.

The Architectural and Transportation Barriers Compliance Board thus became the major governmental force to provide national leadership in eliminating environmental barriers that severely impede employment, education, and recreation of handicapped people.

An extensive review of the composition, functions, and activities of A&TBCB is provided in a later section of this chapter.

Section 503: employment under federal contracts

Section 503 of the 1973 Act provides that: "Any contract in excess of $2500 entered into by any Federal department or agency for the procurement of personal property and nonpersonal services (including construction) for the United States shall contain a provision requiring that, in employing persons to carry out such contract the party contracting with the United States shall take affirmative action to employ and advance in employment qualified handicapped individuals. . . ."

Section 504: nondiscrimination under federal grants

Section 504 provides for additional nondiscrimination provisions for qualified handicapped persons in participation and benefit of any program or activity receiving federal financial assistance.

Obviously, these provisions are designed to guarantee and promote equal employment opportunities of handicapped persons in the public and private sector. However, the success of these efforts will be substantially dependent upon the implementation and development of the programs of the Architectural and Transportation Barriers Compliance Board established in Section 502 of the Act. Access and use of the environment is a necessary condition to full and equal employment opportunities. Further, the subject of accessibility and usability of the environment is pervasive throughout all programs designed to further the independence of handicapped persons. Therefore, the mission of the Architectural and Transportation Barriers Compliance Board is to address this challenge by striving for a barrier-free environment.

NATURE AND FUNCTIONS OF THE ARCHITECTURAL AND TRANSPORTATION BARRIERS COMPLIANCE BOARD

The most recent major federal legislative enactment dealing with environmental barriers was the creation of the Architectural and Transportation Barriers Compliance Board in the Rehabilitation Act of 1973 (Public Law 93-112). In this Act, as in earlier rehabilitation acts, Congress expressed its intention to enlarge and expand the public programs for rehabilitation of disabled persons. To justify the expenditures authorized, however, it was deemed imperative that handicapped persons be enabled to move freely in the society into which they wished to integrate themselves. Earlier legislation to accomplish this end was not being carried out.

Congress recognized that compliance with the Architectural Barriers Act of 1968 had been very spotty. No initiatives were visible within the responsible federal agencies to meet the authorizing intent of the Act either in developing new and revised barrier-free construction standards or in establishing mechanisms to ensure compliance with the minimum standards already adopted. These conditions were attributed to the absence of any one central agency or force clearly responsible under statute or by administrative arrangement for ensuring the comprehensive and consistent development and enforcement of federal design standards. Congress, therefore, strongly believed that a new federal board was necessary to fulfill this function—and to achieve the goal of societal integration of the handicapped—by becoming a major national force for positive change in the elimination of all categories of barriers.

To carry out this charge, Congress fashioned the Architectural and Transportation Barriers Compliance Board as a collective instrument composed of the cabinet-level officials of those agencies responsible for nearly all federal programs affecting the construction and development of buildings and facilities. The Act established the A&TBCB as a quasi-independent body composed of the coequal Departments of Health, Education and Welfare; Transportation; Housing and Urban Development; Labor; Interior; General Services Administration; United States Postal Service; and Veterans Administration.

As implied by its title, A&TBCB was given the primary assignment of ensuring compliance with accessibility standards in all buildings and facilities covered by the provisions of Public Law 90-480. To carry out this function, it was charged with the authority to issue such orders, as deemed necessary, that affect any department, agency, or instrumentality of the United States. In carrying out its regulatory responsibilities, an order of compliance issued by the A&TBCB would stand as the final order for purposes of any judicial review.

The A&TBCB was also made responsible for initiating investigatory, evaluative, and developmental approaches into all categories of environmental barriers confronting the handicapped public. In this regard, Congress gave particular emphasis to those areas where new insight was needed most, thereby mandating A&TBCB investigation into the specific nature of architectural, transportation, and attitudinal barriers. Further legislative specification was made for A&TBCB attention to the barriers unique to such facility types as public buildings, monuments, parks and parklands, public transportation (including air, water, and surface transportation whether interstate, foreign, intrastate, or local), and residential and institutional housing.

In addition, this A&TBCB mechanism was selected to determine the activities being undertaken by other governmental units, public agencies, and nonprofit agencies with these same concerns and to prepare proposals for bringing together in a cooperative effort, agencies, organizations, and groups whose cooperation is essential to effective and comprehensive action.

Toward achieving its investigative mandate and role as a major national force in the elimination of barriers, the board was given authority to conduct investigations, to hold public and compliance-related hearings, and to prepare and submit to the President and Congress plans and proposals for such further legislative and administrative actions deemed necessary or desirable to secure a barrier-free environment.

In designing the establishing legislation, both congressional and administrative drafters recognized that the responsibility for implementing the A&TBCB's activities must be equally shared by its member agencies. Specific facility types and problem areas that were identified in the mandated research functions of A&TBCB were directly related to the particular program capabilities and mandated responsibilities of its member agencies (see Figure 3–1). The three standard-setting agencies cited in the Architectural Barrier Act of 1968, along with the Department of Health, Education and Welfare, were combined with five other construction-related agencies most affected by their implementing activities, especially those of the General Service Administration, which has the widest legislative scope of standard-setting activity.

Further, the drafters recognized that should a supervisory, lead agency be legislatively designated, the other agencies would perceive their role and responsibility on the A&TBCB as subservient, thereby, generating reactions of nonconcern and noncommitment. This situation would nullify the spirit of cooperation and joint reward that Congress intended for the A&TBCB and its member agencies. The under-

standing was that this A&TBCB combination of eight agencies, with the later addition of the Department of Defense, comprised nearly 95 percent of all construction-related activities of the federal government. The necessity of an independent body became more obvious with consideration of the A&TBCB compliance-related authorities as they would affect the massive construction related activities of its member agencies.

Also associated with this legislative approach was a rationale that recognized the unique research-, design-, and construction-related programs within each board member agency. Included within such program elements are those staff talents, experiences, expertise, and private organizational associations particular to the individual departments and agencies. Therefore, to fully activate the mission and role of A&TBCB, Congress instructed that each member department and agency "shall make available to the Board such technical, administrative, and other assistance as it may require to carry out its functions" and also authorized that the Board may supplement these resources by appointing such other "advisers, technical experts, and consultants, as it deems necessary."

Early Activities of the Architectural and Transportation Barriers Compliance Board

Section 502 of the Rehabilitation Act of September 26, 1973, evidenced serious congressional concern about environmental barriers and the need for an independent, high-level governmental force to deal with this problem. This same concern, however, was not translated into the necessary line-item appropriation of A&TBCB funds. Less than one-third of the authorized level of funds necessary to activate the mission of the A&TBCB was actually provided by congressional appropriation committees. Further, the Senate Labor and Public Welfare Committee's intent for an independent board was compromised when the appropriation was not earmarked as a board item, but was subsumed within the overall appropriation of

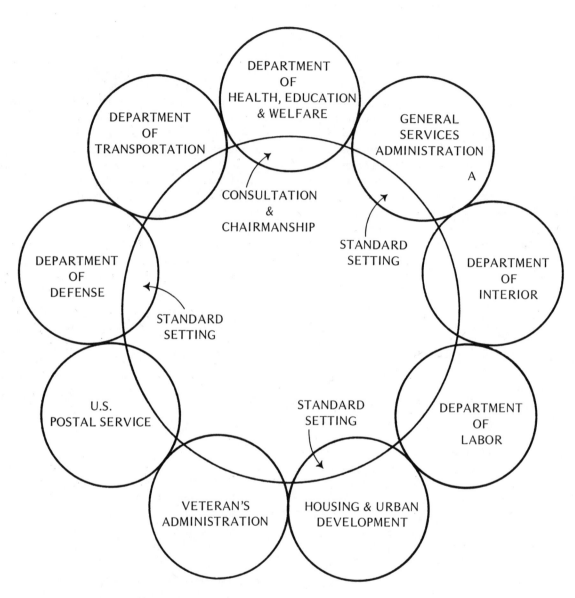

Figure 3–1
Composition and unique characteristics of A&TBCB member agencies.

the Social and Rehabilitation Service of the Department of Health, Education and Welfare.

Following the enactment of the Rehabilitation Act of 1973 and the creation of the A&TBCB, six months passed without substantial effort on the part of the eight member agencies to recognize its existence, let alone activate its functions. For this reason, and because of the likelihood that DHEW would be held accountable as a result of that agency's legislative and budgetary linkage to the board, DHEW's Secretary Caspar Weinberger convened the first A&TBCB meeting on March 26, 1974.

Discussions at the meeting clearly indicated the necessity for sharing information about each agency's activities directed toward the implementation of Public Law 90-480, thereby surfacing the fact that the four agencies cited under the Rehabilitation Act were not meeting their coordinating responsibilities. Members of the board agreed that its first activity should be the assemblage and review of each agency's report detailing compliance mechanisms and activities related to congressional mandates on building accessibility and usability by handicapped persons. Further, the need for an in-depth consideration of the mission of the A&TBCB was discussed at the first meeting, along with the determination of what resources in staffing, funds, and expertise were available to the board. The need for board chairmanship was noted. and it was determined that the Department of Health, Education and Welfare would retain temporary chairmanship, vested with the Assistant Secretary for Human Development, until the first report was made to Congress.

At subsequent meetings, presentations on the agencies' compliance mechanisms, to ensure the Public Law 90-480 related standards and standard-making activity, illuminated many overall problem areas. It became clear to the agency representatives on the Board that beyond the 1969 adoption and promulgation of certain minimum provisions for accessible building elements (American National Standards Institute Specifications for Making Buildings and Facilities Accessible To and Usable by the Physically Handicapped (A-117.1, 1961), there had been little activity.

The General Services Administration, responsible under the Rehabilitation Act for developing standards for all covered facility types except those of the Departments of Housing and Urban Development and Defense, was shown to be both negligent and unconcerned with the nonexistence of standards for parks, recreation, education, medical, industrial, and transportation facilities, to mention a few. Further, the GSA, having recognized through a 1971 agency-wide survey the scale of noncompliance with the minimum standards required, affirmed before the board its refusal to monitor the activities of other agencies and espoused a surveillance program based upon the self-policing efforts on the part of each agency.

The Department of Housing and Urban Development's presentation to the board told of their fullfillment of responsibilities under the Act by adoption of the GSA-promulgated minimum standards (ANSI A-117.1, 1961) for residential structures. This action was taken by HUD with approval by the Secretary of DHEW, despite the knowledge of both agencies that the standard was not intended for residential facilities, as is stated in its opening section. Even with this inappropriate minimum standard, however, HUD's implementing regulations redefined the scope of Public Law 90-480 by making the accessibility standard applicable to only 10 percent of those structures designed for occupancy by the elderly.

Similarly, the Department of Defense redefined the intended scope of the Act by making it applicable only to those structures "likely to be used by the physically handicapped." This agency's regulation even went so far as to make the major provisions of the minimum adopted standard (ANSI A-117.1, 1961) optional, through the use of such language as: "Unless otherwise required for a particular function, passenger elevators shall not be provided expressly for the physically handicapped."

As constituted and operating at that time, the A&TBCB was simply a high-level policy-making body, and the few clarifications and decisions it made regarding Public Law 90–480 were seldom implemented or recognized by the affected agencies. Therefore, a strong staff element was needed to present issues for resolution to the board and to assure the recognition of such resolutions by the member agencies.

Both the establishing legislation and the congressional appropriation, however, were silent on any permanent staffing authority, and despite the Executive Level IV agency representation on the board, no member felt willing to pledge full-time staff assistance.[16] Several A&TBCB members did, however, identify interested persons within their agencies to provide part-time staff. As a result, an interagency liaison staff committee structure began to meet to discuss the role of the board and to identify various project activities within their agencies that seemed to correspond to the A&TBCB mandate. The urgency of undertaking activities in support of the A&TBCB legislative mandate was heightened by the fact that an annual activity report, encompassing activities over fiscal year 1975, would be due to Congress by June 30, 1974.

As a result of the interagency liaison staff efforts, a number of projects, which were either in development or already underway, were identified for potential A&TBCB support during 1974. The projects that received A&TBCB funds were a Department of Transportation study of two approaches for providing special transportation or for improving existing transportation facilities for use by elderly and disabled persons; a HUD-sponsored project to develop information about how to make parks, recreation areas, parking lots, and outdoor spaces more usable by the handicapped; and a DHEW-sponsored project to develop the methodology and groundwork necessary for the evaluation of existing public and voluntary housing for disabled persons.

In addition, during fiscal year 1975, board liaison staff members attempted to develop a planning document that would identify the long-range goals, objectives, and activities to be undertaken by A&TBCB as well as a compliance mechanism to establish the

decentralized interagency procedures for monitoring and tracking construction activities. Although there was some information reported relative to what was developed by this group, a detailed planning document or compliance procedure was never fully prepared nor submitted to the board. The board, nonetheless, continued to operate without a plan or planning guidelines.

Rehabilitation Act Amendments of 1974, Public Law 93–516

The administrative difficulties hindering the full activation of A&TBCB functions reportedly stemmed from the ambiguities of staffing and granting authorities in the board's establishing legislation. In response, Congress again demonstrated its serious concern with environmental barriers by amending that legislation on December 7, 1974, and thus changing both the board structure and its operation. The congressional concern and rationale for passing the amendments were documented in both House and Senate legislative reports:

The Committee expects the Board to become a major force for positive change in the elimination of many categories of environmental barriers which now severely impede the mobility, the employment, and the recreation of handicapped people.

The Committee recognizes that a number of organizational and administrative difficulties have prevented the full development of Board activity. The Committee is concerned, however, that even with these difficulties the Board has not employed a single full-time executive director or professional staff member to begin its important functions.

The Committee understands that the Board has considered itself to be under severe limitations due to certain ambiguities it has found in section 502. Specifically, HEW, which has properly taken the lead in organizing the Board, has questioned whether there is authority for an enforcement or compliance mechanism in section 502, and has hestitated to issue grants or contracts to organizations outside the Federal Government to aid the Board in acquiring data and carrying out its functions.

The Committee substitute would resolve the problems

enumerated above by requiring the Board to employ an executive director and other necessary professional and clerical staff, by specifying a compliance mechanism, and by specifically authorizing grant and contract authority for the Board.

In this connection, the Committee reemphasizes that the Board was created as a quasi-independent agency with the power to hire personnel, notwithstanding individual department or agency limitations. The Committee expects the Board to take an independent, aggressive posture toward its functions, including application to the Office of Management and Budget and the Civil Service Commission for such professional and clerical positions and administrative law judges as it determines to be desirable and necessary to support its active role in the elimination of environmental barriers to handicapped individuals.[17]

Specifically, Public Law 93–516 amended the A&TBCB establishing legislation by (1) adding the Department of Defense as a board member by virtue of that agency's responsibilities under the Architectural Barriers Act; (2) specifying the Secretary of Health, Education and Welfare as permanent chairman of the Board; (3) enhancing the compliance powers of the board by authorizing that an order of compliance issued by the A&TBCB may include the withholding supervision of federal funds with respect to any building found not to be in compliance with accessibility standards; and (4) requiring the appointment of a Consumer Advisory Panel to provide advice, guidance, and recommendations to the board. The legislation requires that a majority of the members selected for this panel be handicapped persons "so that an increased awareness and sensitivity to the problems and needs of persons who are handicapped may be imparted to the Board."[18]

Organization of the Architectural and Transportation Barriers Compliance Board

With passage of the Rehabilitation Act Amendments of 1974, clear authorization was made for the appointment of a full-time staff to carry out the mandate of the A&TBCB. Recruitment of staff be-

gan in March 1975 and continued throughout the remainder of that year.

Today, the A&TBCB staff is headed by an executive director who reports to the chairman of the board, who in turn is responsible for providing supervision of activities through board policy direction. As depicted in Figure 3-2, there are three organizational units of the A&TBCB: (1) planning and research, (2) compliance, and (3) public information. The A&TBCB also has established an Office of General Counsel, which provides legal advice and counsel to the board members and staff in carrying out its activities. In the identified staffing areas in Figure 3-2, there are some instances of overlap. For example, in planning, plans for compliance are developed, or plans for publication information are coordinated. Note that the points where the unit lines meet the board agency circles are of no significance.

In addition, the A&TBCB Consumer Advisory Panel was created and appointed in December 1975. This panel is to provide guidance to the board and its staff so that consumer understanding and input concerning barrier-free activities can be added to the policy-making role of the board. The shaded area in Figure 3-2 between the board circle and staff circle represents this relationship.

If board planning is to be carried out (on the basis of the figurative graphic representation of the board functioning as a unit with staff) in association with member-agency liaison staff, we must ask what kind of target-group planning is necessary to carry out A&TBCB goals in a meaningful way. In Figure 3-3 the line marked "E" indicates that the first concern of the board is to ensure that within each agency of the board, there is compliance with the Architectural Barriers Act of 1968 (P.L. 90–480). The board must assist its own agencies to the fullest degree possible to achieve such compliance. Line "F" represents agents of member agencies, who through loans, grants, or contracts carry out those functions. These become the next important level of concentrated compliance emphasis. Line "G" represents constituent organiza-

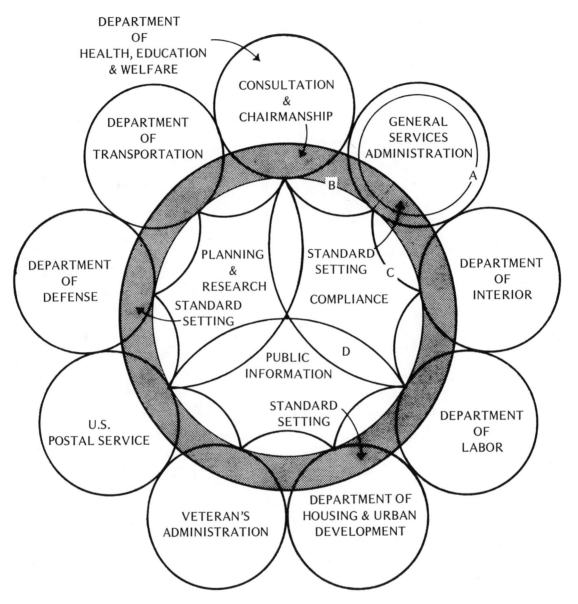

Figure 3–2
A&TBCB staff units and organizational relationships.

A-All other federal agencies
B-Administration, chairman, and executive director
C-General counsel
D-Areas of unit overlap

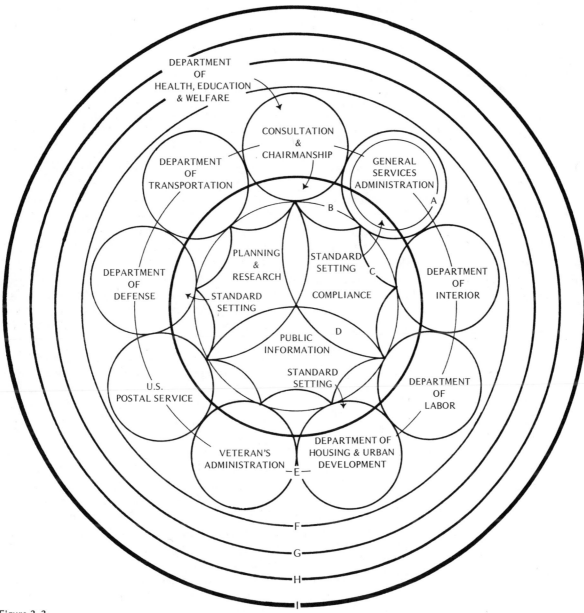

Figure 3–3
Target-group planning priorities.

E-Board member agencies   H-Disabled population
F-Contractor, grantees, and other agents   I-General public
G-Constituent organizations

tions, who would—through board efforts—be able to assist in developing and attaining full compliance with barrier-free legislation. The "H" line represents the entire disabled population, who are primary beneficiaries of the compliance program. The A&TBCB should address their concerns, solicit their assistance, and develop this resource on a priority basis. The outside ring, line "I," represents the emphasis that is placed on reaching and affecting the general public through activities and public information.

Mission of the Architectural and Transportation Barrier Compliance Board

It is within the aforementioned context of A&TBCB planning that a "Statement of Mission" and six basic planning goals and areas of activity concentration were developed and approved by the A&TBCB.

As defined, the Statement of Mission and goals are as follows:

Mission: The Architectural and Transportation Barriers Comance Board is established under section 502 of the Rehabilitation Act of 1973, as amended by P.L. 93-516. It is responsible at the highest level for setting policy and assuring the implementation of that policy to ensure compliance with standards pursuant to the Architectural Barriers Act of 1968, among and between member agencies and any other entity of the Federal Government or its agents by virtue of loans, grants, or contracts, in the construction and alteration of covered buildings. It is responsible for assuring both accessibility and usability of buildings, facilities, and transportation systems by handicapped individuals through the elimination and prevention of environmental and transportation barriers, through coordinated planning, regulation making, standards coordination, compliance related monitoring, investigations, hearings and technical assistance; research, study and training, public information systems, and advisory panel participation. It is responsible for reporting to the President and the Congress activities related to its legislated responsibilities.

Goals: (1) To assume a coordination role in the development and revision of prescribed standards, to ensure that such standards provide accessibility to and usability of all covered Federally assisted facilities. (2) To promulgate such regulations and guidelines as may be necessary to ensure compliance with barrier-free design standards prescribed in accordance with P.L. 90-480, as amended. (3) To exercise

a system of compliance, including such procedures of compliance as monitoring, investigation, hearings, litigations and technical assistance, as authorized by statutes and prescribed standards. (4) To exercise a system of research to investigate the existence of barriers in attitude and environment, the efforts made to eliminate such barriers, and to plan and propose alternative approaches. (5) To carry out a national program of public awareness to promote and facilitate the elimination and prevention of barriers. (6) To report to the President and Congress such information as required or necessary to detail the progress made in achieving the purposes of the legislation.[19]

Perhaps a better way to describe the mission and goals of A&TBCB, as well as its activities and accomplishments, is through its three fundamental roles in the creation of a barrier-free environment. As defined by the board, these roles are catalytic in causing an awareness of the needs and rights of handicapped persons and for creating and maintaining a broad variety of forums for exchange and interaction between consumer, public, and private agencies and organizations essential to the establishment of harmonious, productive, and consistent activity. With this same regard, the A&TBCB has a responsibility to be facilitative through its identification and supply of supportive policies, activities, and resources such as financial aid, technical assistance, coordination, consumer representation, legislation, and information—all of which are resources essential to accomplishment by the handicapped community and its supportive organizations. Lastly, and of equal importance, the board operates in a regulatory fashion in exercising its responsibilities to investigate and monitor, through a system of compliance, federal construction-related activities and to exercise when necessary its authorities to conduct hearings, issue orders, and suspend or withhold federal funds.

With respect to the A&TBCB catalytic activities, we have found the national public hearings process to be most productive not only in creating a greater awareness, but also, and perhaps most importantly, by reason of the permanent programmatic relationships that have resulted with both consumer and industrial organizations. To exemplify, many of the construction- and transportation-related organizations not previously exposed to the needs of handicapped persons are now working with the A&TBCB to identify supportive policies and activities best suited for such organizations and to develop and disseminate to their membership information necessary for affirmative actions.

Primary responsibility for A&TBCB's catalytic role is established within the Division of Public Information, which acts to continue and expand the hearings process and to develop and activate procedures and efforts necessary to supplement the hearings process by establishing and maintaining working relationships with federal, state, local, and other public and private organizations. The Division of Public Information has attempted to achieve these goals by operating an intense information-dissemination process to serve selected board audiences and by undertaking a general national awareness campaign through all media forms and vehicles.

The A&TBCB also has a very important obligation to be facilitative of supportive activities and policies in both the private and public sectors. While this role is achieved in part through the board's catalytic capacity to "spark" barrier-related attention and concern within the private and public domains, such awareness levels must be developed and translated into both support initiatives and accomplishments. In performing this role with the many consumer and representative organizations and federal and state governmental agencies, the board provides such technical activities as are needed for related policy and program development.

The A&TBCB completes its facilitating role through legislatively authorized investigation, evaluation, and development of solutions to architectural, transportation, and attitudinal barriers. It particularly deals with the barrier problems in public buildings and monuments, parks and parklands, transportation, and residential and institutional housing. In this respect, the board draws upon the expertise, resources, and constituent private organizations of the most responsible member agency. It either works directly with that agency's staff and financial resources in developing and disseminating information or undertakes

specific research or barrier-removal projects or requests the agency to perform the given task.

The facilitative role of the A&TBCB is carried out through its Division of Research and Planning, with the equal supportive efforts of the Divisions of Public Information and Compliance. These divisions undertake to bring together and involve all member agencies and outside organizations in the board's barrier-related activities. This goal is accomplished by developing and instituting, within the federal government, cross-cutting projects and by providing resources to support the board's goals and objectives. Further efforts include implementing research, study, and evaluative activities to support board staff efforts and influencing and targeting federal imformation-distribution activities to the most appropriate public and private agencies and organizations.

In a regulatory capacity, the A&TBCB is currently working toward the establishment of a consistent, comprehensive system of monitoring federally supported construction activities. The compliance mechanism is being designed to ensure that all construction receiving federal financial assistance provide for accessibility and usability by all disabled persons. Further, in this regard, the board is encouraging a federally coordinated approach in the development of research policies and standards related to environmental barriers and the establishment of the necessary federalwide incentive system to promote continuing agency input, modification, and expansion of barrier-free design standards.

The regulatory responsibilities of the A&TBCB are carried out by the Division of Compliance, which maintains technical design and construction assistance, barrier-related standards assessment, federal construction, monitoring, project certification of compliance, and complaint processing.

CONCLUSION

We have now reviewed the evolution of the legislative response to the need for barrier-free design. This process has been evolutionary in nature with a genesis of strong support and cooperation among various institutions and organizations, both public and private. Most particularly, we have witnessed the strong leadership role played by both the private sector and government in initiating the barrier-free design movement. The National Easter Seal Society and the President's Committee on Employment of the Handicapped deserve commendation for their pioneering efforts in this area.

The evolution of the barrier-free design movement has included a similar progression of legislative responses. To date, this legislative response has culminated with the enactment of the Rehabilitation Act of 1973 and the establishment of the Architectural and Transportation Barriers Compliance Board. However, it must be noted that law is organic and that each change in our economic, political, and social structure spawns the need for reappraisal of our legal base. In this context, then, we must continue to strive not only for additional legislative remedies that assure barrier-free environments but for the refinement of existing programs to ensure that they are truly effective and responsive.

Like many of the problems that face us at this time in our history, the access needs of disabled persons is one in which we must all participate. This involvement should not be difficult to achieve since the history of the movement has been one of participation and cooperation. However, there is need to ensure that the movement continues to be responsive to those persons most affected. Particularly, there must be a continual and concerted effort to seek the advice and counsel of disabled persons—that is, those people most affected by the barriers in our built environment. Without such involvement, the program risks the possibility of becoming incestuous and illegitimate.

As the A&TBCB pursues its goals and objectives, it becomes evident that full participation of the federal government and its cooperating agencies is essential for achieving the board's detailed mission. A full commitment must be made by the federal government to the elimination of existing architec-

tural barriers and, of equal importance, to the concepts of barrier-free design.

Another imperative is that the private sector become more involved and concerned with functional environmental design. The need exists to encourage the private sector to explore progressive design solutions to the various functional activities of our social existence. The success of the A&TBCB mission can be measured by its ability to effectively motivate institutions, professions, and organizations to create barrier-free environments.

Perhaps it is fitting to adjourn this discussion of a legislative response to barrier-free design by offering a quotation attributed to Richard Marsh Bennett, an American architect: "Architecture is a mirror, though not a passive one, reflecting the forces and ideas of a time."[20] As we gaze in that mirror, we hope the reflection is one that reveals that the forces and ideas of our time demand a responsive and functional environment for all persons.

NOTES AND REFERENCES

1. "The Handicapped Majority," *Industrial Design*, May 1974, p. 25.
2. Ibid.
3. Ibid.
4. Kliment, S. A., "Into the Mainstream" (Washington, D.C.: Rehabilitation Services Administration. U.S. Department of Health, Education and Welfare, 1975), pg. 4.
5. National Commission on Architectural Barriers to Rehabilitation of the Handicapped, *Design for All Americans* (Washington, D.C.: U.S. Government Printing Office, 1967).
6. Senate Report 90-538, House Report 90-1532, and House Report 90-1787.
7. Senate Report 90-538.
8. Ibid., House Report 90-1532, and House Report 90-1787.
9. Senate Report 91-658.
10. Senate Reports 93-381, 93-391, and 93-500; and House Report 244.
11. *Message of the President*, March 27, 1973.
12. Senate Reports 93-48 and 93-318.
13. Senate Reports 92-1135, 93-48, and 93-318; House Report 244; Senate Report 93-391; and Senate Report 93-500.

14. Senate Reports 93-1139 and 93-1297.
15. See Senate Reports 93-1139 and 93-1297.
16. Executive Level IV representation on the board is the lowest level that legislation allows—that is, assistant secretary or deputy administrator status.
17. Senate Reports 93-1139 and 93-1297.
18. Senate Report 93-1139.
19. The A&TBCB "Statement of Mission" was approved by the Board members at their November 11, 1975 meeting.
20. *The International Dictionary of Thoughts* (Chicago: J. G. Ferguson Publishing Co., 1969), p. 47.

Bibliography

Architectural and Transportation Barriers Compliance Board. *Freedom of Choice: Report to the President and Congress on Housing Needs of Handicapped Individuals*. Washington, D.C., 1975.

——. *First Report to the Congress of the United States*. Washington, D.C., 1974.

Dwight, James S., Jr. "Accessibility: Fact, Not Fiction." *The Social and Rehabilitation Record*, vol. 2, no. 2, 1975, pp. 16-18.

Farber, Alan J. "The Handicapped Plead for Entrance—Will Anyone Answer?" *Kentucky Law Journal*, vol. 64, no. 1, 1975-76, pp. 99-113.

Gailis, Ann, and Keith M. Susman. "Abroad in the Land: Legal Strategies to Effectuate the Rights of the Physically Disabled." *Georgetown Law Journal*, vol. 61, no. 6, 1973, pp. 1501-23.

Hammerman, Susan, and Barbara Duncan (eds.). *Barrier Free Design*. New York: Rehabilitation International, 1975.

Jacobs, Jane. *The Death and Life of Great American Cities*. New York, New York: Vintage Press, 1961.

Kirk, Larry B. "Design for All Americans." *HUD Challenge: Special Issue on the Handicapped*, vol. VI, no. 3, 1975, pp. 30-32.

Laski, Frank. "Civil Rights Victories for the Handicapped—Part I." *The Social and Rehabilitation Record*, vol. 1, no. 5, 1974, pp. 15-20.

——. "Civil Rights Victories for the Handicapped—Part II." *The Social and Rehabilitation Record*, vol. 1, no. 6, 1975, pp. 25-32.

McGaughey, Rita. "From Problem to Solution: The New Focus in Fighting Environment Barriers for the Handicapped." *Rehabilitation Literature*, vol. 37, no. 1, 1976, pp. 10-12.

Nau, Louis, and James S. Jeffers. "Rehabilitation Act Stresses Services to the Most Severely Handicapped." *The Social and Rehabilitation Record*, vol. 1, no. 6, 1974, pp. 9-12.

Obermann, C. Esco. *A History of Vocational Rehabilitation in America*. Minneapolis: The Brings Press, 1965.

President's Committee on Employment of the Handicapped. *A Survey of State Laws to Remove Barriers*. Washington, D.C., 1975.

——. *One in Eleven Handicapped Adults in America: A Survey Based on 1970 U.S. Census Data*. Washington, D.C., 1975.

Sommer, Robert. *Personal Space: The Behavioral Basis of Design*. Englewood Cliffs, N.J.: Prentice-Hall, 1969.

——. *Tight Spaces: Hard Architectural and How to Humanize it*. Englewood Cliffs, N.J.: Prentice-Hall, 1974.

Sykes, Robert. "Housing and Community Development for the Handicapped." *HUD Challenge: Special Issue on the Handicapped*, vol. VI, no. 3, 1975, pp. 6-7.

U. S. Congress, House of Representatives. *Bicentennial Planning in Washington, Hearings before the Subcommittees on Bicentennial Affairs, the Environment, and the International Community of the Committee on the District of Columbia*, 94th Cong., 1st Sess., June 3, 4, 5, and 13. Washington, D.C., 1975.

U.S. Congress, Senate. *A Barrier-Free Environment for the Elderly and the Handicapped, Hearings before the Special Committee on Aging*, 92nd Cong. 1st Sess., October 18-20. Washington, D.C., 1971.

U.S. General Accounting Office. *Further Action Needed to Make all Public Buildings Accessible to the Physically Handicapped*, Report to the Congress. Washington, D.C., 1975.

U.S. Department of Health, Education, and Welfare. *A Summary of Legislation relating to the Handicapped: 1963-1967*. Washington, D.C.: U.S. Government Printing Office, 1969.

——. *A Summary of Legislation relating to the Handicapped: 1968*. Washington, D.C.: U.S. Government Printing Office, 1968.

——. *A Summary of Legislation relating to the Handicapped: 1971*. Washington, D.C.: U.S. Government Printing Office, 1971.

——, Rehabilitation Services Administration. *Into the Mainstream: A Syllabus for a Barrier-Free Environment*, by Stephen A. Kliment. Washington, D.C.: U.S. Government Printing Office, 1973.

——, National Commission on Architectural Barriers to Rehabilitation of the Handicapped. *Design for All Americans*. Washington, D.C.: U.S. Government Printing Office, 1967.

U.S. Department of Housing and Urban Development, Office of Policy Development and Research. *Barrier Free Site Design*. Washington, D.C.: U.S. Government Printing Office, 1975

——. *HUD Challenge: Special Issue on the Handicapped*, vol. VI, no. 3, 1975.

Part II

Physical Barriers:
Towards a
Barrier-Free
Environment

4

The Fokus Housing System

Sven-Olof Brattgård

Sven-Olof Brattgård is a native of Goteborg, Sweden. He completed his medical education at the University of Goteborg. In 1952 he joined the faculty of that university as Professor of Histology and in 1970 became Professor in Handicap Research. Presently he is Head of the Department of Handicap Research at the University of Goteborg. During his distinguished career, Dr. Brattgård has written approximately one hundred and fifty papers in medicine, histology, neurochemistry, psychiatry, and social medicine. Since 1966 he has also written about two hundred papers dealing with the problems of the handicapped. Dr. Brattgård's community service record includes chairmanship of the State Board for Service to Disabled Students, the Fokus Society (an organization for housing, service, and work for the disabled), and Bracke Ostergard (rehabilitation center for children of West Sweden). He is also a member of the board of the Swedish Central Committee for Rehabilitation and serves on several expert committees of the Swedish Institute for the Handicapped.

INTRODUCTION

In spite of their circumstances, disabled persons like everyone else, long to have their own homes, to find work in satisfying occupations, and to enjoy normal leisure-time activities within a life of freedom and security. The Fokus Society supports these obvious goals and assists the severely disabled to achieve a satisfying life. Fokus is concerned with the problems of the severely disabled—that is, those who need not only specially adapted housing but also personal help in their daily living activities. *Fokus*—a way of life for living—has become a common term in many countries that refers to the solution of housing and living problems for the severely physically disabled.

The Fokus Society, started in 1964 in Sweden, supports the following basic rights of the disabled:

To live under the same conditions and with the same opportunities as the nonhandicapped,
To live in security with access to reliable personal service,
To live in a chosen geographical area,
To have a choice of suitable occupations,
To enjoy satisfying leisure-time activities.

While many people, once they have visited a tenant in a Fokus apartment and seen all the technical details, believe that they have grasped the main idea of Fokus, they are completely wrong. The Fokus Society is concerned with presenting a way of living. The very well-planned apartments are only a part of the system; another part is the service unit; and most important of all is the psychology underlying the idea that permeates the entire project. The psychological goal is to bring the disabled person into a situation where he or she has the freedom to make his or her own living choices and to take responsibility for choices.

THE IDEA OF FOKUS

What Fokus had in mind in developing the project was helping especially younger disabled—who are dependent upon technical aids and personal assistance —with housing, services, and guaranteed care, so that they could live in their own home under the same conditions as other people. They should not be reduced to isolation and idleness in nursing homes or to forced living at their parents' home.

Planning for the disabled, especially the severely disabled, starts with the goal of integration. From this point of view, building apartments for the severely disabled in the same block with those for nondisabled is necessary. All forms of segregation must be avoided. The necessity of day and night service means that the apartments for the disabled must be placed in the block so that they can easily be reached by the service personnel. Through the Fokus experience, we have found that the limit for the practical and economical dimensions of such a service unit is ten to fifteen apartments.

The apartments are in buildings in ordinary housing districts built near cultural and commercial centers. The buildings are situated in such a way that entering an apartment to visit the tenant is easy for the disabled and nondisabled. The location of the apartments makes taking part in activities in the city easy for the tenants. In the building, the apartments for the disabled are mixed with those for the nondisabled (Figure 4-1). All the Fokus apartments are designed from the very beginning for the severely disabled. In this way, the disabled (or as we prefer to say, the tenant with some disabilities) is physically integrated

Figure 4-1
One of the apartment buildings with integrated Fokus units.

and also has the possibility to be psychologically integrated. The degree of integration depends upon the tenant and his or her own desires.

In 1964, when the Fokus Society first presented its idea for such housing, many people were dubious. They believed that living outside of institutions was impossible for severely disabled people and that such a system would be very expensive for the community. Fokus first had to overcome these attitudes by showing that its plan was, for the majority of the disabled, the best way of living, that they liked it, and that it was less expensive than institutional care. After Fokus succeeded in doing so, the local authorities took over the total responsibility for the Fokus units in 1975 and are now planning to build more service units for the severely disabled. In this way, the Fokus principle has become an integrated part of the Swedish social welfare program for the disabled.

THE FOKUS SYSTEM IN PRACTICE

Unit Planning

The primary target group of the Fokus system consisted of younger persons suffering from severe locomotor disabilities. This group has to have technical equipment and personal assistance in order to cope with the activities of daily life, such as dressing and undressing, visits to the lavatory, cooking, shopping, and so forth.

In an investigation that covered the whole of Sweden (about 8 million inhabitants), Gunnar Inghe and Inga-Maj Juhlin found about 1,000 severely disabled persons between sixteen and forty years of age who were in need of apartments of the Fokus type while an additional group of about 1,000 were considered "borderline cases."[1] The investigation showed a preponderance of severely disabled in rural areas with fewer living in urban areas. This distribution is explained by the fact that handicapped youngsters cannot migrate as readily as others to the more attractive cities and towns. A higher proportion of the

severely disabled were compelled to stay with parents or relatives where they could be cared for or to live in nursing institutions. About 20 percent of the youngsters deemed capable of living in Fokus apartments were receiving institutional care. Many of those who were with their parents were living in old and inconvenient apartments.

This investigation was carried out under the auspices of the Fokus Society, and it provided a census of the severely disabled in Sweden that made planning activities comprehensively and assigning priority to the areas with the greatest need possible. On the basis of the funds that had been made available, starting units in thirteen different areas distributed over the whole country was deemed feasible. This effort would meet about one-third of the known need.

Guidelines for the design of dwellings and the microenvironment were developed for Fokus by a special team consisting of architects, rehabilitation experts, consulting engineers (heating, ventilation, sanitation, and electricity), and handicapped persons. The team sought to plan especially designed dwelling units that permitted maximum flexibility to accommodate individual needs. It was also called upon to plan the communal facilities that might be needed; for example, laundry, room for bathing and physiotherapy, hobby room, and so forth. This part of the project included the design of an emergency signal system that could be used by the handicapped tenants.

The team presented the first draft of a conceptual scheme in the spring of 1967. This proposal was then reworked into finalized form the following year. This manifesto, *Principles of the Fokus Housing Units for the Severely Disabled*, has formed the basis for planning the different Fokus units.[2] It is published in German and English versions.

Dwelling Design

A fundamental principle of Fokus planning is that every tenant shall have his or her own *apartment*. A single "all-purpose" room, even if equipped with kitchen facilities, cannot be accepted as a long-term solution to the handicapped person's housing problem. The recommendations drawn up by the Fokus planning team have been incorporated in the design of actual apartments.

Fokus has apartments for families as well as single persons. Figures 4-2, 4-3, and 4-4 illustrate three floor layouts of apartments in Mölndal near Goteborg. Generally speaking, floor layouts are the same for all apartments, even when specific allowance has to be made for structural technicalities. Some dwelling plans, especially those for one-person accommodation, provide for an "all-activities room" (Figure 4-2). The aim here is to have a dwelling that puts the tenant at the center of activity on every occasion, thereby enabling him to keep in touch with everything that happens around him, whether he is in bed,

sitting in the kitchen, on a sofa, or in an armchair. All interior fittings are detachable, which permits the tenant to shape his dwelling as he sees fit.

The floor area of the apartments is approximately the following:

one room and kitchen: 42–50 m^2 (Figure 4-2);
two rooms and kitchen: 64–76 m^2 (Figure 4-3);
three rooms and kitchen: 80–96 m^2 (Figure 4-4).

All the fittings are designed to offer tenants with some kind of disability the best possible opportunities. Most of the tenants are wheelchair users and thus function in a sitting position. Some others use crutches and have to work in a standing position. All fittings in the kitchen as well as in the bathroom are therefore flexible in height. An easily operated console-track system makes possible adapting the height

Figure 4-2
This Fokus apartment of one room and kitchen (48 square meters) in Mölndal is a one-person apartment that is planned as an all-activities room.

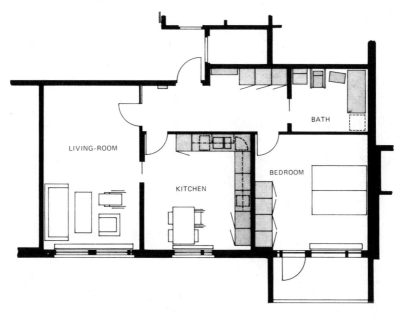

Figure 4-3
This Fokus apartment of two rooms and kitchen (76 square meters) in Mölndal can be flexibly furnished. Kitchen and bathroom equipment is adaptable to the tenant's needs; sliding doors take less space and are easy to maneuver for the wheelchair occupant.

of counters, cupboards, stoves, ovens, washbasins, and showers to the optimal height for each tenant.

The plan for the kitchen, as that for the whole apartment, is based upon a series of analyses and investigations from the research group at the Department of Handicap Research at the University of Goteborg.[3] The most suitable kitchen is the angle kitchen (Figure 4-5). The place for food preparation is between the sink and the stove. In this location, the tenant has the most effective working position. Movable units of drawers, preferably on wheels, offer the tenant the opportunity to decide where he wants to have his storage units and to move them when he wishes. With these movable fittings, he can always arrange work space where he prefers: at the stove, at the sink, or at the counter (Figure 4-6). The bathroom plan is based upon the series of investigations on

how disabled persons move and act.[4] Both the washbasin and the shower are placed on a console-track system that allows for individually adjusted heights. The wheelchair-bound person can therefore easily get his knees under the washbasin (Figure 4-7).

The apartments have a wide range of technical arrangements. The electrical switches are gathered into units and placed in handy positions on the wall, at the bedside, or on a movable table. If required, separate switchboards near the bed or on the wheelchair can be connected, sometimes with radio transmitters, so that the tenant is able to open the front door of the apartment, turn the lights on or off, or call for assistance from anywhere in the apartment. All apartments have a main entry telephone, an intercom for contact with the service staff, and an ordinary telephone.

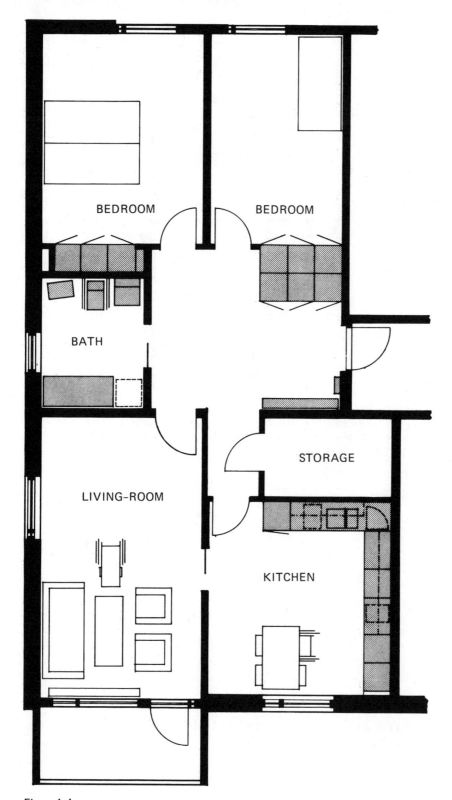

Figure 4–4
This Fokus apartment of three rooms and kitchen (96 square meters) in Mölndal is a multiperson apartment that offers greater opportunities for fellowship and family formation.

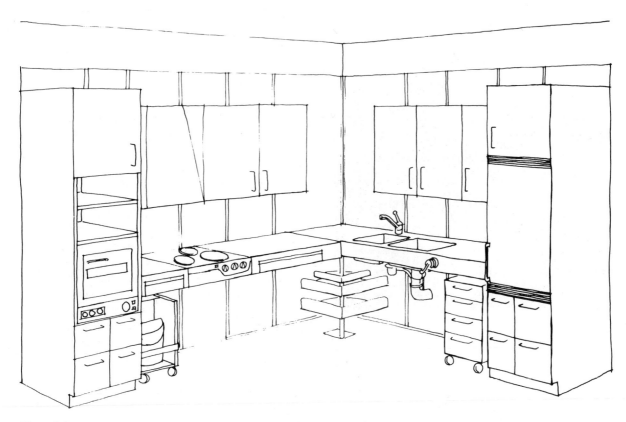

Figure 4-5
This angle kitchen in a single-occupant Fokus apartment has especially designed cabinets, appliances, and fittings.

The Communal Part of the House

Every building in which Fokus rents apartments contains special groups of rooms for different types of activities. These rooms are open to all tenants, disabled as well as nondisabled. There is a dining room and a kitchen for those tenants who prefer to have their main meal served there. There are rooms with facilities for daily physical activities and exercises, rooms equipped with all the essential accessories. There is a bathing unit with a sauna and a special bathtub for people with disabilities. There is also a special room for those tenants who wish to participate in some kind of hobby. The laundry is designed for the disabled. There is a room for television and for those who like to be together to play cards or to have discussions. Service personnel are provided with staff rooms as well as with an office or on-duty room.

All aspects of the building are designed to accommodate the disabled. Every kind of technical aid is utilized to offer tenants a life independent of personal assistance. The elevators and doors are equipped with automatic controls. Wherever feasible, parking stalls for cars are provided within the building. In other cases, garages equipped with electrical car heaters are provided. Planning is also underway to build garages for wheelchairs used outdoors.

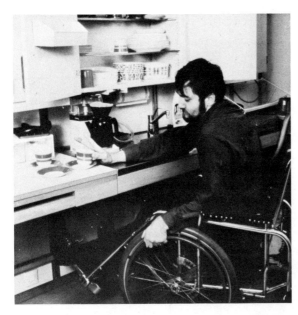

Figure 4–6
The counters and cabinets in the kitchen of Fokus apartments are designed to be used efficiently by a person in a wheelchair.

The Service System

Once a severely disabled person has been provided with a dwelling adapted to his handicap, the next important step is for them to enjoy well-functioning personal services. The handicapped tenants in a Fokus unit have that need met by the Fokus staff, over and above the services they may obtain from the public home help program.

Many handicapped persons, especially the severely disabled, need round-the-clock service for all functions that relate to life's daily activities. The most salient needs have to do with dressing and undressing, personal hygiene, getting food, and shopping. Moreover, the handicapped person who lives in his own dwelling needs help with cleaning, bed making, laundry, and so forth. Provided these tasks are not too heavy, many of them can be performed by the public home helpers or by another service organization. However, due to the severely handicapped person's need for twenty-four-hour service, as well as the size of assisting staff required, the Fokus system differs from that traditionally associated with home nursing. That is why we have chosen to call the Fokus system "full-care service."

The starting point for any assessment of the need for such service must be with what the handicapped person can do on his own and with the time it takes him to do it. Consideration must also be given to all technical arrangements that can reduce the need for service and make the handicapped person less dependent on others for help.

The Fokus service system for the handicapped differs slightly from one area to another. These differences reflect the philosophies prevailing among county councils and municipalities whose basic principle has been to allot to the handicapped person as many hours of help from a home helper as he would receive if he lived in a so-called interspersed invalid dwelling. The county councils and municipalities have generally allotted a maximum of four hours per day. For the severely handicapped person with whom Fokus is concerned, that is not enough. The vast majority must have access to personnel who can help them at different times of the day. To be able to meet that need, Fokus personnel must be employed to be on duty round-the-clock. This staffing pattern enables the handicapped person to receive help whenever he wishes, whether it is to go to the toilet, get undressed for bed, or have his sleeping position changed. These employees also assist home helpers whenever two people are needed to do heavy lifting or anything similar. Moreover, the home helpers program cannot easily find the manpower needed to work on weekends, which thus requires the especially employed personnel to assume this duty.

Several reasons prompted Fokus to adopt full-care service, which may be defined as a system of personal assistance and service during certain hours, with access to on-duty personnel in between. Most important of all, the tenants themselves have found this arrangement to be suitable. The handicapped person has someone familiar who takes direct care of his

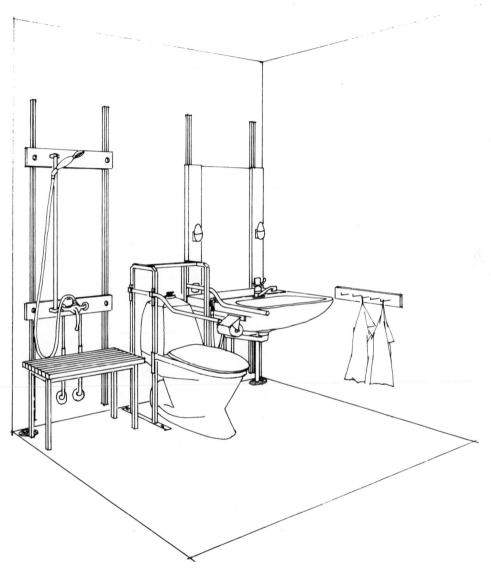

Figure 4–7
This bathroom in a typical Fokus apartment has especially designed, adjustable
toilet, washbasin, and shower.

dwelling and his service needs—that is, someone who knows his habits, where he keeps his clothes, and what he wants to eat. The plan thus makes initiating every new assistant in all the details unnecessary. Another reason is that a system based on personnel who come from the outside counteracts tendencies towards "institutional thinking" such as found in a hospital, or nursing home. A third reason is that the Fokus system requires the handicapped person to assume responsibility for himself. He knows how many service hours he can obtain and he must himself allocate them properly.

An important aspect of the full-care service is the attitude of the personnel. The staff must be open-minded and avoid all tendencies to treat the handicapped person as a patient. Showing respect for the handicapped person's right to independence and to management of his private affairs is also necessary.

Something to Do and Somewhere to Move

The rationale for Fokus is not only a matter of residence and service: It is also very important for the disabled to have something to do. All Fokus units are located in cities where relatively good job opportunities exist on the open market or in sheltered workshops. The apartments and workshops are never in the same building. The tenants must leave the house to get to their place of work.

Obtaining a suitable job takes time, and some tenants are unable to get jobs, or do not like the jobs that are offered. For those tenants, hobby facilities must be available. We prefer the tenants to establish contacts with hobby groups in the community, but if they like, opportunities exist for them to pursue hobbies in the Fokus unit.

A person cannot live exclusively for his or her job or for his or her hobbies. Contact with other people, cultural stimuli, and well-planned holidays are also important. Such concerns play an important part in the planning of Fokus units. Everything is done to help the tenant to obtain all the stimulus he or she

needs. Fokus units are located in cities where the opportunities for activities of various kinds are good. The city must have a special transportation system—taxis or buses—for the severely disabled. Tenants in one city can, when on holidays, exchange their apartments with tenants from other Fokus units. Everywhere the Fokus tenants go, they can enjoy the same service at the same cost.

The Fokus experiment has demonstrated an important factor in successful integration: Opportunities for the disabled person to go wherever he or she wishes. This opportunity requires an accessible transportation system. Only in this way can the handicapped person escape from his or her isolation. Despite all the improvements in public transportation, we must not forget that many disabled persons need access to special transportation. One method that has been tested in many urban districts in Sweden and proved valuable is *Fardtjanst*, a special transportation system for the disabled. In principle, the community provides assistance to the disabled not only during the trip itself, but also to and from the vehicle. Originally started as a private initiative, this system has now become a public enterprise.

THE TENANTS

To Be a Tenant in a Fokus Apartment

During the years when the Fokus Society was responsible for the apartments and the service, disabled persons who wanted apartments had to request them from the central Fokus board. Now that the local authorities have taken over the responsibility, prospective tenants must make their requests through local welfare offices.

The disabled tenant must rent an apartment on the same basis as other people—that is, with the same rights and the same obligations. When he has his lease, nobody can take the apartment away from him so long as he pays his rent. In Fokus units, no restrictions exist other than those common to all tenants in other apartments. What goes on inside the door is the tenant's business and no one else's.

The tenants in Fokus apartments have to pay their rent. According to the Swedish welfare system, they receive rent allowances from the local authorities if they are invalid pensioners without any extra income. If they have income in addition to their pensions, they have to pay 15–20 percent of that income for rent. The rest will be subsidized by the authorities.

The tenants have to buy and pay for their food. If tenants need help in shopping, they can get help from the Fokus service staff. In all units, tenants can have dinner served in the communal dining room. The medical care the tenants require is given to them, as well as everyone else, by the open medical service in the community or by the hospital. The Fokus Society does not take care of the medical treatment.

The Situation for the Tenants

Evaluating the new living conditions for the severely disabled tenants in Fokus apartments is very difficult. One way is to compare their situation today with their earlier conditions. In 1972, the Fokus Society published a report evaluating seven Fokus units that had been in service during more than one year. One year is a short time for evaluation, but the report gives some indication of the results.[5]

In 1972, all Fokus tenants had their own apartments—that is, their own homes. Before they moved to Fokus apartments, about 34 percent had lived in the neighborhood, while 66 percent had lived in other areas. Most of the handicapped, 48 percent, had formerly lived with their parents, while 24 percent had been at institutions, nursing homes, or chronic-care clinics. After moving into the Fokus units, the handicapped tenants became more active in work and studies. However, there was a time lag, which reflects the difficulties of their finding jobs during the short period that the program had been in operation. Nevertheless, 45 percent were in employment or edu-

cation one year after moving into the Fokus apartment. Before they came to Fokus, less than 10 percent were employed. The Fokus dwellings created opportunities for more handicapped persons to live together to form families with handicapped or nonhandicapped persons. Thirty-six percent of the tenants cohabited or were married after one to two years, in comparison to 8 percent earlier.

The handicapped tenants in Fokus apartments comprise a group of severely disabled who are utterly dependent on a full-care service that functions round-the-clock. The Fokus program has enabled them to live a more active and independent life under secure conditions. Moreover, the program has also permitted the handicapped persons a choice of living locations. They are no longer limited by provincial boundaries. They have the disposition of their dwellings on the same terms as others, and personal service is guaranteed to them. As a result, they are given new opportunities for employment, education, and leisure activities.

As a tenant of Fokus, the handicapped person derives special benefits. For some tenants, the Fokus apartment becomes a step in the rehabilitation process that leads to a more ordinary dwelling. Because of the Society's nationwide activity, a tenant can also move from one Fokus area to another and thus be closer to friends and relatives or to places with better job openings. During the vacation season, a Fokus tenant may switch apartments temporarily with a handicapped person in another area. Both then enjoy access to the home welfare service at the "holiday resort." A tenant may also provide guest accommodation over a weekend to another handicapped person, who likewise qualifies for service.

The Degree of Disability

The Fokus system is designed for those disabled who in one way or another are dependent on help from other people. They can require help several times a day or night or during only part of the day.

In Sweden, any disabled person who needs one or two hours help a day can usually obtain it. For them, moving into a Fokus apartment is not necessary. But many disabled need help every time they have to go to the toilet or when they want to get up or go to bed. Other people need help in preparing their food or in being fed. The Fokus system is designed for those persons.

In 1972, 77 percent of the Fokus tenants were wheelchair bound. Most of the others used crutches. More than half needed help with dressing and undressing, and one-third needed help with their daily hygiene. Nearly one in five needed help to change sleeping position during the night. Some tenants had such severe disabilities that they could only move around in their apartments by using electrical wheelchairs maneuverable with sucking and blowing. They could use neither their legs nor their arms nor their hands.

SOME ECONOMICAL ASPECTS

The Fokus Society was organized in 1964. In 1965, we obtained time during one day on radio and television to appeal for funds. That day gave us 11 million Sw. crowns ($2 million). With this money, Fokus rented 280 apartments in thirteen cities throughout Sweden. Each unit consists of 12–30 Fokus apartments mixed with those for nondisabled. The number of apartments in each unit is determined by the local conditions. Our experience indicates that the best size of a service unit is 12–16 apartments.

All blocks in which Fokus apartments are housed are mortgaged on government terms. This arrangement assures the tenants of a normal basic rent. To cover the extra costs that arise from adapting the apartment to handicapped occupancy, government subsidies are payable to up to 15,000 Sw. crowns ($2,727) per apartment. This amount usually suffices for a one-person dwelling, but it has proved to be too small for a larger apartment occupied by a severely handicapped tenant. Accordingly, certain extra costs of dwelling adaptation have had to be added into the

rental costs. The costs of renting communal facilities are distributed among the apartments according to an established formula.

The seven Fokus units that were evaluated in 1972 encompass a total of 141 apartments. Those 141 dwelling units were occupied by 174 persons, 151 of whom were handicapped. About half of the dwellings were one-room apartments of 43–48 square meters. The two-room apartments had an area of 55–79 m^2, the 25 three-roomers had 80–96 m^2. At all of the Fokus units, the apartments adjoined communal facilities such as lounges, hobby rooms, specially equipped laundries, bathrooms, training rooms, and on-duty and staff rooms. The annual price per square meter of floor area varies between 82 and 116 Sw. crowns. The lowest rent was found in units for which tenancy is subject to a down payment.

The costs of communal facilities, which amount to about 30 percent of the total, were added to the dwelling rent. To judge from this report, the rental cost per square meter of well-equipped and high-standard apartments for the handicapped did not appreciably exceed the costs of an ordinary dwelling in the general housing market. The cost for the day and night service varies from person to person. Some persons need a lot of service; others only a helping hand occasionally during the day. The average cost for the tenants in the seven evaluated Fokus units was $3,600 per year in 1971.

The total cost of housing and service in a Fokus apartment averages $5,000 per year for each handicapped person. This figure may be compared with the public cost of treating the chronically ill at clinics or homes for the elderly in similar locations. The costs per bed range from $9,300 to $13,000 at a chronic-care clinic and from $4,300 to $7,000 at a home for the elderly. Reservations must always be attached to comparisons of this kind, since different places vary widely in the quality of care and the residential environment they offer.

According to the Swedish welfare system, persons who need home help have to pay for this in accordance with their income. Those who have no income, above an invalid pension, receive service free of charge regardless of how much service they need. Thirty-five percent of the cost is paid by the government; the remainder by the municipality.

THE FOKUS SOCIETY AND THE COMMUNITY

The Fokus Society is a nonprofit organization. Its organization was comprised of three main groups: representatives of the community, the disabled themselves, and representatives of foundations and societies working with and for the disabled. The central board had the task of giving general directions for the work of the Society. In each city, where Fokus was established, the central board included representatives from the local community, from the tenants, and from the Fokus Society. Very close cooperation was thus maintained in local activities between Fokus and the community. At all stages, the tenants or their representatives had an opportunity to make their voices heard and to register their votes.

Before organizing in a city, Fokus held discussions with the local authorities about the location of the unit and the opportunities for the tenants to obtain jobs and education. A very important consideration in these discussions was the transportation system for the disabled in the city. As mentioned earlier, in all cities where Fokus was established, the community had a special transportation system whereby the disabled, by way of taxis or special buses, could obtain transportation to and from work, school, cinemas, theatres, or friends. The combination of a good day and night service at home and a good transportation service offered tenants with disabilities an opportunity to function like other people.

One important aspect in the cooperation with the community members was the contact between the disabled and the nondisabled tenants. Informing both groups about each other's situation is necessary, and they must in some way educate each other. Children and common neighborhood problems are focal points for achieving contact between the tenants.

The Fokus Society is to be regarded as a complement to the work of the community. The importance of the Fokus' work, apart from offering new possibilities to about three hundred severely disabled, is that it demonstrates to the community, to politicians, and to the general public, that even severely disabled can live a normal life if they can only obtain the technical and personal help that they require.

Today, when the Fokus housing and living system has been accepted and integrated into the normal social welfare system for severely disabled, the organization is different. Now the responsibility for the planning and running of the units belongs to the social welfare board in the city. The disabled have to make their influence upon the system through their organizations and politicians. The Fokus Society will continue, however, as a part of the central organization for the disabled and will follow the development of housing and service for severely disabled.

FOKUS—A WAY OF LIFE FOR LIVING

In the complicated community in which we live, there are many problems for all, but far more for those who are disabled. Three important things must be arranged: The disabled must have somewhere to live—their *homes;* something to do—their *jobs;* and someone who helps—their *service.* The way for the disabled person to be free and independent in spite of disability is to have the opportunity to influence his or her own situation. For many disabled, the way to that life can be very long and arduous, but it is the duty of the community to assist everyone to find his or her own particular mode of life. The Fokus Society has shown one way for the severely physically disabled.

NOTES AND REFERENCES

1. Inghe, G., and I-M. Juhlin, "Housing and Employment Difficulties for Severely Disabled Young People," Social-medicine Journal, Stockholm, 1968.
2. Fokus Society, *Principles of the Fokus Housing Units for the Severely Disabled* (Goteborg, Sweden: Fokus Society, 1968).

3. Brax, B., J. Paulsson, and L. Sperling, *The Standard Kitchen and the Physically Disabled, Vol. I: Kitchen Studies with Disabled Persons* (Goteborg: Department of Handicap Research, Goteborg University, 1973). Paulsson, J., *The Standard Kitchen and the Physically Disabled, Vol. 2: Planning Instructions and Examples of their Application* (Goteborg, Sweden: Department of Handicap Research, Goteborg University, 1973).

4. Andren, E., and B. Peterson, *Sanitary Rooms: Planning with Respect to the Needs of the Handicapped, Part I* (Goteborg, Sweden: Department of Handicap Research, Goteborg University, 1974). Andren, E., and B. Petersson, *Sanitary Rooms: Planning with Respect to the Needs of the Handicapped, Part 2.* (Goteborg, Sweden: Department of Handicap Research, Goteborg University, 1975).

5. Brattgård, S-O, F. Carlsson, K-E Hammerin, H. Nilsson and A. Sandin, *Housing and Service for the Handicapped in Sweden* (Goteborg, Sweden: Nordic Publishers, 1972).

5

Developing Standards for Accessibility

Edward Steinfeld

Edward Steinfeld is an Assistant Professor of Architecture at Syracuse University and a Faculty Associate at the All-University Gerontology Center. He previously was Research Architect at the National Bureau of Standards. His past research includes studies of preferences for age integration in housing, housing consumer information needs, and the development of self-instructional learning materials on barrier-free design. Currently, he is Project Director of the Department of HUD-sponsored project to revise and extend the ANSI Standard A-117.1, Specifications for Making Buildings and Facilities Accessible to and Usable by the Physically Handicapped. He is also Secretary of the ANSI 117 Standards Committee.

INTRODUCTION

This chapter will identify and discuss the major issues in the development of accessibility standards. Regulations abound for making outdoor and building environments accessible to and usable by people with disabilities. Every state in the United States, many municipalities, and many agencies of government at all levels issue such regulations. Most of them have been based in whole or in part on a model consensus standard, ANSI A-117.1, Specifications for Making Buildings and Facilities Accessible to and Usable by the Physically Handicapped. This "model" standard is a voluntary standard developed in 1961. Contemporary wisdom is that such a document reduces the proliferation of mandatory design criteria by serving as an authoritive source for the development of regulations. Such an eventuality, however, assumes that the model standard is truly authoritative and acceptable to all interest groups who are affected by the regulations. For several reasons ANSI A-117.1 was not satisfactory in its 1961 form to fulfill this mission. Thus, over the years, the regulations issued by many sources departed significantly from the basic ANSI model to the point where its validity became questionable and a proliferation of different criteria caused confusion. This situation has prompted a revision of the ANSI standard.

The process of revision must be responsive to the needs of all those affected by the standard. This includes not only citizens with disabilities, but also professionals who design the environment, administrative agencies who create and enforce regulations, and the building industry who must build the accessible environment.

In the development of a model standard of accessibility, certain pivotal issues must be raised and resolved. How this is accomplished will determine the success of the standard as an authoritative and generally acceptable document. Ultimately, the development of the revisions themselves, and their adoption by government agencies as regulations, will be based on political positions taken on these issues.

The discussion below is intended to help the reader develop awareness in regard to the political nature of standards and regulations and their social role as codified norms for a specific period of time.

A model standard or regulation must be a flexible document that can change as attitudes, opinions, and empirical knowledge changes. Too often, standards and regulations are viewed as inflexible "gospel." This attitude can be detrimental in achieving true social change. And that, after all, is what the quest for barrier-free design is all about.

TARGET POPULATION

ANSI A–117.1 was explicitly developed to provide accessibility for these kinds of people: (1) the non-ambulatory, (2) the semi-ambulatory, (3) those with severe loss of vision, (4) those with hearing impairments, (5) those with incoordination, and (6) the elderly. The actual criteria, however, implicitly omitted consideration of people who were very severely disabled and those with sensory disabilities. For example, the minimum toilet stall design requirements satisfy the needs of people who use wheelchairs only if they have full use of their upper body and limbs or some use of legs in addition to sufficient strength to lift and pivot themselves from a frontal position. Likewise, the few statements in the standard that make reference to features supportive to those with sensory disabilities are not sufficient for full and convenient use of facilities by people who are totally blind and those with partial sight. For example, no requirements are included to insure that blind people will know at which floor an elevator has stopped.

The reasons for these limitations were the state-of-the-art of research and rehabilitation medicine at the time, as well as the expediency of developing a standard that would be accepted on a nationwide basis. Today, with increased public consciousness of accessibility concerns and a larger number of severely disabled people who can live independently,

an extension of scope to a wider target population is timely.

By its very name, ANSI A–117.1 is addressed to the needs of disabled people. Thus, the standard identifies things that should be done to improve the quality of life for this group of people. This approach reinforces their "special" status in society. Certainly, all people may benefit from an environment that is more convenient to use. Linked to this notion is the idea that those who are disabled are a finite group of people, which is not the case. Inevitably, most people will experience disability, but those who are disabled in youth will become more disabled in old age. Yet the goal of the standard is still to obtain accessibility for those to whom it has been denied. If they are not explicitly identified, opponents may question the need for a standard to promote accessibility of buildings for all people, most of whom can obviously use them easily already.

People with the same disability may have different abilities. For example, a person who uses a wheelchair may be well trained in the use of the chair or have absolutely no training at all. Training, multiple disabilities, or advanced age can all result in different ability levels. Given any disability, which ability level should we use as the basis for generating criteria? Current statistics on disability focus on conditions of impairment rather than functional ability. Thus, deciding on the extent of "environmental disability" that should be considered in design is a basic policy question. For example, elderly people are likely to have multiple disabilities and have little rehabilitation needs. On the other hand, a blind person with no mobility training is unlikely to live or travel independently. We may be expecting too much for environmental design to make up for lack of such a minimal level of ability except in an institutional setting.

Thus, consideration of the target population for accessibility standards raises these issues:

1. Which disabilities should be considered?
2. Should a standard or regulation address the gen-

eral concept of accessibility and usability for the entire population or focus on disabled people?

3. What levels of environmental competence should be assumed for people with each disability?

SCOPE OF APPLICATION

ANSI A-117.1 focused explicitly on providing basic principles for accessibility and usability of publicly used buildings in general. As it was adopted into regulations, however, its use has for the most part been limited to publicly used buildings built in whole or part with public funds. This approach was certainly the most feasible politically, given that accessibility had never been mandated before. However, access to such facilities as stores and restaurants is necessary for normal, independent living. Should privately owned but publicly used buildings also be included? Implementing regulations based on a standard that deals explicitly with private buildings would be more difficult than one that doesn't.

As the civil rights movement for racial minorities moved from concern with public accommodations to concern with housing, so has the movement for barrier-free design. Making housing accessible is a major goal of the revisions to the ANSI standard. The basic issues here are: (1) Should accessibility be built in from the start, or should units be made adaptable, so that modifications that are needed can be made with minimum cost and effort and (2) should only some units be made accessible, or should they all be accessible? A model building standard can have design criteria for built-in accessibility, adaptability, or both. Specifying how much housing should be built in these ways may be more appropriately determined by regulations of local and state levels of government where needs, resources and the characteristics of housing markets and site conditions can be more specifically assessed.

There is, however, a relationship between local decisions and a model standard. It the standards include only criteria for built-in accessibility, local and state decisions would likely be to build only a limited and specific number of such units. These would have to be reserved for people with disabilities; thus, developers (both public and private) would resist such an approach, and few units would likely be built. On the other hand, adaptable units would be better received; but since the intention of criteria for such units would be to apply them to as much of the housing stock as possible, criteria for adaptability may fall short of the provisions necessary for housing those with very severe disabilities. The provision of adaptable housing alone may not help to prevent institutionalization. In the case of apartment layouts and circulation, for example, with adaptability, floor plan relationships could not be specified in a standard, doorways would have to be the minimum width required for accessibility, and kitchens and bathrooms would have only limited flexibility. The very severely disabled may not find such minimal conditions satisfactory enough to make living independently feasible.

Similar issues arise when considering other building types. Should only publicly used buildings and housing be given consideration or should place of employment also be considered? The issues here are that many employment settings are typically inaccessible to people with certain disabilities. Boiler rooms in subbasements or second-story offices in supermarkets, for example, are usually inaccessible to the person who uses a wheelchair. Hiring disabled people involves the need for special equipment in many cases. Often the disabled can be hired simply by rewriting a job description or moving an office from one floor to another. Full accessibility of a building is neither a prerequisite nor the full solution to equal opportunity in employment. However, basic access to personnel offices is necessary in order to find a job. Adaptability of work settings, given the eventual hiring of a person, must be possible if employment opportunities are to be fulfilled in the sense of upwardly mobile careers. Full access to places of employment may be appropriate as a concern of regulations, but not necessarily standards. Yet, without discussion of such places in a standard, in all likelihood local regulations would not be extended to include them.

Thinking ahead for the next five to ten years, makes it apparent that accessibility to *new* buildings alone is not sufficient to normalize life for people with disabilities. The goal is real accessibility to the community as a whole. Buildings last a very long time; thus, a very real part of achieving full accessibility in the community is changing that part of the built environment that already exists and is not accessible. This effort could be infeasible if renovations must meet the same criteria as new construction. For example, structural and topographical conditions may preclude making every entrance or floor to old building accessible although these features are desirable in new construction. Obviously, some allowances must be made for renovation work, including historic preservation. Without specific attention to renovation and rehabilitation, application of a standard to old buildings may often be infeasible.

In summary, the major issues concerning the scope of accessibility standards or regulations are:

1. Should privately owned buildings be explictly considered?
2. Should the amount of accessible housing units be part of a standard or regulation?
3. Should criteria be included for dwelling units adapted for the severely disabled or only minimally adaptable or both?
4. Should places of employment be considered and in what terms?
5. Should construction for purposes of renovation and historic preservation be given exceptions to the criteria for new construction?

USABILITY OF STANDARDS AND REGULATIONS

A different set of issues regarding development of standards and regulations for accessibility arises from

the use of the document itself. Again, by referring to the original ANSI standard, we can see that the criteria were stated in minimal terms. Unfortunately, applications of these criteria have usually been minimal as well—that is, the minimum features required for accessibility become the maximum provided.

A related issue is the form of some of the criteria. Ideally, standards and regulations should specify objectives rather than the means of achieving them; yet this "performance approach" can be a two-edged sword. If standards and regulations are overly prescriptive of solutions, they become unwieldy and inflexible for use in design. For example, specifying only one acceptable bathroom layout would be too prescriptive. On the other hand, specifying performance objectives that do not give adequate measures of success can often leave too much leeway for poor solutions or be too vague to be of much use for the designer. For example, a standard or regulation might require only that an elevator be "usable by blind people", but this requirement does not indicate when such a state is achieved. Many of the differences between actual regulations in force today and the existing ANSI A–117.1 voluntary standard are that the former are much more prescriptive in certain areas because of vagueness in the ANSI version. The best form of standards and regulations usually lies somewhere between these two extremes.

Standards for accessibility are only one of the many sets of standards that are used in the building industry. Adopted as regulations, they have not only been issued by government agencies but also incorporated by the four model building codes (National, BOCA, Southern, Uniform). These model codes are, in turn, adopted by local municipalities and states. The model codes are organized into sections dealing with general provisions and specific provisions for building types. The existing ANSI standard, as discussed above, does not make distinctions among building types. The building industry is not monolithic, but is actually a group of industries focusing on specific types of construction. The most notable subindustry is housing. Each area of the industry has its own specific problems. A standard that is organized by building types is more compatible not only with the model codes, but also with the various elements of the building industry.

Other standards used by the industry are trade specific, such as those of the elevator or metal railing and stair manufacturers. Some are actually ANSI standards, such as ANSI A-17.1, the safety code for elevators, dumbwaiters, escalators and moving walks. If a new ANSI standard for accessibility is not compatible with these other voluntary standards, confusion will result. The same can be said about compatibility with other mandatory regulations, such as those of the Occupation Safety and Health Act (OSHA). The major issues regarding usability of standards for accessibility are:

1. Should they include only minimal provisions?
2. How performance oriented should they be?
3. Should they be made compatible with building codes and other voluntary standards?

THE ROLE OF RESEARCH

At the time that ANSI A-117.1 was written, little empirical research on accessibility existed. As a result, many of the criteria used in 1961 are not applicable to the target population of today. Over the years this lack of applicability, which became apparent as reports from the field were obtained, resulted in lack of confidence in ANSI A-117.1, and many modifications were made through local, state and federal regulations. Research has been completed and/or is now underway to improve the state of knowledge.

Contemporary research focuses on accessibility for disabled elderly people and those with low stamina, multiple disabilities, and little or no formal rehabilitation. Stairs have received attention as well as mobility in the external environment. (See Chapters 2, 6, and 7.) Sidewalks and intersections are being investigated. Also, research on the mobility of blind people has been initiated. Studies have been done and are now underway on the use of kitchens by people with severe disabilities. The costs of accessibility are also being studied. The influx of well-documented empirical research will continue to improve the data base for design and standards.

The use of this data base, however, is not necessarily guaranteed. If those who write standards and regulations are not aware of empirical research, or if they choose to ignore it, the data base will not be incorporated. We should emphasize that in this area of knowledge there is a great tendency to ignore research since professionals and disabled individuals often have strong opinions that might be contradicted by research results. However, empirical research can provide more generalizable data that are open to public scrutiny and replication, unlike anecdotal, undocumented, and limited observations or speculations. Today the validity of technical criteria can be improved significantly by consideration of available empirical findings. Thus, a significant issue in the development of accessibility standards is the attention given to current research.

IMPLICATIONS OF POLICY DECISIONS

The issues discussed above are fundamentally policy issues. If, in the process of developing the model standard and later while converting it to mandatory regulations, they are not resolved adequately, the standards may have serious flaws in use. The most critical flaw would be restrictions on accessibility for people with disabilities. What good are accessibility standards if they don't measurably improve accessibility? Another serious flaw would be major cost implications. In the years ahead, economics will play an even greater role in policy making than in previous years. For example, we can argue that spending money on accessibility in housing rather than appearance is an attitudinal issue and that the time has come to change values toward accessibility. However, not everyone agrees with this position. Housing must be priced within the means of the consumer. If the cost of accessibility detracts from marketability through cost cuts in other areas, we can be sure that some very powerful people—including consumers—will object to the accessibility require-ments. Another flaw would be "red tape." If the new standards and regulations are difficult to use as an evaluation tool or they are unreasonable to satisfy, delays in obtaining approval or in construction can result. Given the profusion of such problems as this one with which the industry is already plagued, in all likelihood another difficult regulation will not be greeted calmly.

CONCLUSION

Professionals tend to be heavily involved in the development of standards for accesssiblity. The issues described here cannot and should not be resolved by this one interest group alone. They are issues of political significance that require input from many interest groups. That is why ANSI committees that approve standards must include broad representation. This consideration also applies to local, state and federal efforts to enact regulations. Of course, bring-ing people together in a group does not imply that they will function in the best interests of developing a standard or regulations. Group-dynamic factors of power and influence are involved: Consumers may be viewed by professionals in the group as uninformed guests, while they in fact may accept this role and defer opinions to professionals since the technical considerations of standards are often beyond their cognizance. But who is a better judge of the issues related to target populations or scope of application than the consumers themselves?

From another perspective, the building industry is often cast in the role of adversary of accessibility standards. Often, this group is not represented by industry spokesmen, but rather indirectly by archi-tects. Architects may understand the industry but few share industry attitudes. Industry spokesmen, in the form of homebuilders, trade association repre-sentatives, or property managers are best equipped

to address cost and certain scope of application con-cerns. The building industry should not be viewed as an adversary, but as a source of valuable input that will minimize problems of acceptance and usability.

Research in human factors and costs can be a valuable means toward resolving many of the pivotal issues. However, research results will be received differently by different interest groups. Professionals may be unwilling to accept new results that contra-dict their established beliefs. Consumers also may not accept findings that are different than their personal experiences; yet their lack of technical expertise may modify such a position. Industry may not accept findings that create problems for their business, but they will be ready to support findings that help it at a moment's notice. Research results can only be use-ful if attitudes toward research are positive and objective.

In the end, the development of an authoritative and acceptable standard for accessibility is based on who is involved in the process, how they work to-gether, and what their attitudes are, as well as the quality of information they have to use. All of these factors affect how the pivotal issues are resolved.

Clearly, these issues are interrelated. Cost impli-cations cannot be determined until valid research results can be obtained on what is required. Human factors and research results, together with cost studies, will in part be useful for identifying the target population, but decisions on the approach to housing may also affect the parameters of the popu-lation. It is also evident that one cannot resolve the issues one-by-one as if checking off items on a shop-ping list. They form a complex system. All the issues must be reviewed periodically as a document takes shape and then repeatedly, as it is used over the years. Perhaps the most important lesson to be gained from the first experience with the ANSI A–117.1 standard is that such a document must not become fixed for more than five years. It should evolve as conditions require and allow.

BIBLIOGRAPHY

American National Standards Institute. *Making Buildings and Facilities Accessible to and Usable by the Physically Handicapped*. New York, 1961, reaffirmed in 1971.

Brattgård, Sven-Olaf et al. "Maneuver Space for Indoor Wheelchairs." Goteborg, Sweden: Department of Handicap Research, University of Goteborg, 1974. Mimeo.

Howie, P. M. *A Pilot Study of Disabled Housewives in their Kitchens*. London: Disabled Living Foundation, 1968.

Leonard, J. A. "Studies in Blind Mobility." *Applied Ergonomics*, March 1972, pp. 37–46.

McCullough, Helen E., and Mary B. Farnham. *Kitchens for Women in Wheelchairs*, Circular 841. Urbana, Ill.: College of Agriculture Extension Service, 1961.

Steinfeld, E. H., M. Bishop, R. Faste, S. Schroeder, R. Buchanan, P. Cardell, J. Duncan, C. Fisher, H. Sommers, and P. Wirth. "Access: The State of the Art." Syracuse, N.Y.: Syracuse University, School of Architecture, 1975. Mimeo.

Steinfeld, E. H., S. Schroeder, R. Faste, M. Bishop, J. Aiello, S. Ambrose, and R. Buchanan. "Human Factors Research on Building Standards for Accessibility to Disabled People." Proceedings of the Seventh Annual Conference of the Environmental Design Research Association. Vancouver: Environmental Design Research Association, 1976.

Walter, Felix. *Four Architectural Movement Studies for the Wheelchair and Ambulant Disabled*. London: Disabled Living Foundation, 1971.

Wright, James W. *Performance Concepts in Buildings*, Special Publication 361, edited by Bruce E. Foster. Washington, D.C.: National Burea of Standards, 1972.

6

Access to the Environment

Alan G. Winslow

Alan G. Winslow is Professor of Landscape Architecture and Chairman of the Landscape Architecture Program at Virginia Polytechnic Institute and State University. He received his A.B. degree from Dartmouth College and B.S. and M.S. degrees in landscape architecture from the University of California at Berkeley. He has taught at the University of Illinois and Syracuse University. He has been a practicing landscape architect and urban and regional planner for twenty-five years and has had extensive experience in all regions of the United States. Most recently, he has been Research Associate on the A.S.L.A.F.–HUD project on Barrier Free Site Design. He is now a professional consultant to the HANDEPED Project at Georgia Tech and the ANSI Standards Project at Syracuse University and a full member of the American Institute of Planners and the American Society of Landscape Architects.

INTRODUCTION

Traditionally, urban and regional planning has been concerned primarily with the distribution of land uses, public facilities, and transportation networks to form functional, physical interrelationships that provide for the convenient exchange of goods and services to the entire population. Only recently has the emphasis changed to concern for more effective human development and social planning services that include such elements as mental and physical health, drug and alcohol abuse, day-care services, employment training, housing for the elderly, integrated social services, and other socioeconomic issues. In 1976, the emphasis in urban planning grants shifted back to land use and housing.

During this evolution of the planning process, provision of local barrier elimination programs for the elderly and the physically handicapped have not fully entered the mainstream of program development. The recent Older Americans Act and the Community Services Administration have generated some funds for programs, which include the handicapped, that are related primarily to transportation facilities. However, broader programs need to be established and funded whereby the elderly and disabled, as taxpaying citizens, may enjoy barrier-free access to expanded public services and facilities and may lead normal, independent, and self-fulfilling lives. Independent living for the disabled should entail a combined program of human adaptation and task simplification as a goal.

The goal of equal access to the urban environment is a social, economic, and physical problem. It can be compared equally with those social, economic, and physical problems that are generated in slum and blighted areas for which planning was once heavily funded through Model Cities legislation.

Although more than 10 percent of the population of the United States may have restricted mobility due to age or various physical handicaps, these people should be granted the opportunity to lead as active and fulfilling a community life as the rest of society.

The majority of people in the United States are aware of the problem of environmental barriers, although they are not particularly concerned about correcting these problems, according to results of a survey by the National League of Cities in 1967.[1] This survey found in general, that women, the young, and the highly educated are more aware and concerned than the general populace. Once people become fully informed, however, they tend to consider the issue of environmental barriers a fairly serious problem, and the majority would approve the use of tax money for elimination of architectural barriers to the handicapped.

DEMAND

In community planning, we might wish to do a study of demographic characteristics of the permanently disabled in order to determine the priority for designing facilities that would provide full access for elderly and handicapped persons. Although this type of study, in addition to state legislation, would perhaps increase the likelihood of establishing official policies, the wide varieties of recordkeeping make collection of specific information on number, type, degree and age of handicapped persons and where they reside very difficult. The U.S. Bureau of the Census, Social Security Administration, National Center for Health Statistics, Veterans Administration, and other agencies may provide some general information, but nothing short of a house-to-house planning information system would give us the desired results. If we were to use the estimated figure of "one out of ten people have limited mobility due to a temporary or permanent physical handicap,"[2] the target group is appreciable and one that should command concern by local administrators. There are plans to get more information in the 1980 Census of Population. (For a more thorough analysis of this demand, see Chapter 2.)

States that have adopted handicapped sections in their building codes, like Minnesota and North Carolina, usually refer to "appropriate number of specific items necessary to accommodate individuals with specific disabilities, who would use a particular building or facility."[3] Although this number may vary depending upon building function and regional location, the rule of thumb could be established at one person in seven to possibly one person in ten of the population who would find the specific provision useful.

The principle of physics, which is also used in the art of judo, that "least action" leads to the maximum results should be recognized as a basic principle of urban planning and design. Some surveys on the use of ramps versus the use of steps for changing levels in exterior environments have shown that although the major number of people will use the easier route, alternative circulation routes should be established wherever possible in order that physical competence (through more extensive exercise) may be maintained by all (Figure 6-1).

Frequently, surveys of business and civic leaders indicate that they don't feel there is a need for barrier-free design, because there aren't that many handicapped people in the community.[4] In reality,

Figure 6-1
This is a good example of a combined ramp and step design for an entry to a building: It provides an alternative for people with different abilities; the handrail on the ramp, however, should follow the slope of the ramp. (Northern Virginia Community College, Annandale, Virginia)

the elderly and many people with mobility-related disabilities simply don't make as many shopping trips or utilize community facilities due to architectural or transportation barriers. The personal activity that might take place with barrier-free design changes to dependence on friends or relatives for shopping and personal business. Likewise, many elderly and disabled share a low socioeconomic position, because of lack of employment opportunities, that curbs activity and choice of residential location. Thus, the number of elderly and disabled we may observe on the street may be very few in contrast to the actual number who reside in the community.

Fully understanding the perceptual psychological responses of the physically and mentally handicapped to the man-built environment is difficult for the "average" person. As an example to illustrate these factors, let us take an environmental extreme in which few of us would feel competent. Suppose that, either for pleasure or challenge, we attempted to climb a peak like Mount Everest. Think about the many route conditions with which we would be concerned. Think of the psychological reactions.

Starting out on this trip at lower elevations would be easy going and pleasurable in anticipation of our conquest of the summit. As time progressed and the going became more treacherous, however, we would develop more concern for potential hazards to life and limb, and we would have to consider many questions:

1. What happens if I get fatigued halfway up the mountain where there is no place to rest and a possibility of being stranded?
2. What if it gets dark during the ascent so that sight of the path becomes obscured? During daylight, will reflections from strong sunlight inhibit the safety of my traverse and cause me to misguage my position?
3. Will snow or rain make my footing slippery and lead to an accident? Will the wind be so strong that I may be thrown off balance and lose stability with nothing to hold onto?
4. Because of the restricted path, will there be

less-than-adequate space for maneuverability that may lead to a fall?
5. Will the condition of the rocks or other material be too smooth and cause slipping or will it present too much roughness that may lead to tripping or stumbling?
6. What happens when I need drinking water and toilet facilities? Will there be provisions at intermittant locations to satisfy these needs?
7. How will I know the best route for ease and safety in climbing? There certainly won't be signs or other means of orientation, and I may have to travel at night without sufficient lighting and physical clues for determining location.
8. How will I recognize unprotected and/or undesignated hazards like a suddenly perceived chasm into which I could fall?
9. Will some of the climbing steps be so high that I may be thrown off balance if I don't have something to hold onto? How will I proceed if I lose the support system of others in the party?
10. Even if I can make it without excessive fatigue will there be some place to rest so that I will have enough energy to return safely to the bottom of the mountain?

Looking back at this list of questions, we may wonder whether so many considerations could be made about an urban environment. Although the elderly and handicapped will probably never climb Mount Everest most of them do ask similar questions before they undertake any journey in the urban environment by progressively considering the typical barriers that they will face. The "average" person may ask no questions whatsoever except: "Should I take an umbrella" or "Should I wear a warm coat?" This author has had experience climbing major mountain peaks, skiing, hiking, and performing other demonstrations of physical competence until stricken with a cyst on the spinal cord that caused cessation of this type of activity. Now I observe the urban environment in similar ways while utilizing braces for better mobility. There are many places I would like to go in the urban environment, but many are so restrictive that my potential activity becomes unwillingly limited.

FUNCTIONAL BARRIERS

Once this perspective has been adopted with respect to the perception of and psychological responses to the environment by the elderly and physically handicapped, we can then form a classification of physical functional mobility barriers found in the urban environment, whether the trip is for employment, shopping, social, cultural, recreational, or personal business. When we perceive our built environment, we must bear in mind that all forms of transportation, site elements, public spaces, and buildings are interconnected in a continuum of access and that the improvement of only one of these interdependent components does not insure accessibility.

The intent of this chapter is to develop an awareness of the physical difficulties encountered by various types of handicapped people in the exterior environment and to suggest ways in which this environment can be made more adaptable and usable by all people. All designers and planners should be aware of these constraints and the acceptable modifications that can be employed, as well as possible means of implementation through the planning process. Typical interrelated problem areas that may pose access barriers to the handicapped are classified and discussed in the following sections of this chapter.

Transportation Mode Change

There are many places in the urban environment where transportation mode changes occur, most of which involve changes from pedestrian access to a vehicle or vice versa. At each of these points, the transfer should not be confusing, dangerous, or cause delay. Pedestrian and bicycle traffic should be separated from each other, and both should be separated from vehicular traffic. The principle types of trans-portation mode changes of concern to the planner-designer occur in the following locations.

Drop-off zones

Most elderly and handicapped people use the automobile, van, or taxicab as their basic form of transportation because they usually find ingress and egress to be reasonably convenient. The act of slowly gaining access to a motor vehicle can be difficult in fast moving traffic. Thus, zones should be provided at major housing, employment, and public activity areas for the purpose of picking up or dropping off passengers who may be pregnant, laden with packages, have children in strollers, or are physically disabled. Drop-off zones provide an environmental setting that suggests each person has a reasonable period of time available for gaining access to the vehicle.

On city streets that allow parallel parking, these drop-off areas can be simply designated in a 45'-0" yellow zone sufficient for two cars. However, on streets that do not allow parking at rush hours, a paved inset should be set back from the edge of the traffic way to allow several cars to pull out of the major circulation route for this purpose. This form of drop-off–pick-up zone could also be used by police and emergency vehicles during rush hour so that traffic is not impeded.

Where there are curbs in these areas, several curb ramps should be provided. Lighting should clearly designate these areas, and they should possess direct access to major barrier-free building entrances. Walkways should be set in back of this zone to avoid confused pedestrian traffic and to provide room for seating facilities for use during long waiting periods.

Parking lots

In using parking lots, the independent or assisted disabled person usually faces several questions: Will I be able to park close enough to gain safe and convenient access to a major building's walkway system? Will I be able to fully open my car door so that I can get out comfortably or not get out at all because only conventional 8'-6" or 9'-0" parking spaces have been provided? Will I have to walk or wheel behind cars that are backing up to gain access to a walkway system?

All major parking areas, whether for employment, commerce, services, or public activities should contain designated spaces that are at least 12'-0" wide for perpendicular or diagonal parking. These spaces should be located within reasonable proximity to major entrances of the principle activity the parking lot supports. People should be able to get out of their car onto a smooth, hard, level surface suitable for walking or wheeling. Where curbs are present, curb ramps should be provided to lead conveniently to unimpeded, smooth-surface access to major walkways or building entrances (Figure 6–2).

If these wider spaces are provided, we would not be concerned about the handicapped parking illegally to obtain access. Many disabled people now park in distant overflow areas to insure the ability to open their car doors. Imagine your plight as a wheel-

Figure 6–2
This is a properly designed parking area and building entry for the physically handicapped person: The parking space is near the facility entrance; it is of sufficient width; it is designated with the international symbol of access; and there is a curb ramp with handrails. (Rustler Restaurant, Charlottesville, Virginia)

chair-bound person when you park in an outer area, with sufficient space to unload, and then return to find your car hemmed in on either side by newly parked cars, which usually don't park in the middle of the parking space.

When wider, convenient spaces are designated for use by persons with physical disabilities, the spaces themselves should be properly identified and, in large parking lots, there should be signs at the entrances to note the location of specialized parking spaces. Many retail outlets already provide for these wider spaces and designate them with the international symbol of access. A maximum of one percent of the total parking spaces designed to accommodate the handicapped, plus the given number of disabled persons known to frequently use the facility, is recommended.[5] In lots with less than one hundred spaces, this percentage should be greater.

Bus stops and other waiting areas

Transfer on and off buses and trams is a frequent activity of the elderly and many handicapped in large cities. These waiting areas should present a sense of protection from passing pedestrian activity and comfort during long periods of waiting. Thus, screened spaces with overhead shelter that provide seating and places to accommodate packages would be welcome street furniture for all residents. The loading area itself should be simple enough for all to use, and it should have textural warning strips in the pavement to aid in identification for the blind. Access to the bus or tramway itself is being solved in some areas by means of hydraulic steps and lifts in the doorway to assist boarding and unboarding in an operational time of four seconds or less each way.

Pedestrian Circulation Routes and Changes in Level

Ease of access between transportation facilities and buildings or recreation areas is probably one of the most fundamental considerations in site planning to accommodate the handicapped and all citizens in an unencumbered manner. Pedestrian circulation routes include walks, paths, plazas, courtyards, bridges, underpasses and changes in level by means of steps or ramps. Any change in level should be planned to provide a minimum amount of expenditure of energy, sufficient room for comfortable pedestrian passage, and safe usage of facilities by ambulatory and nonambulatory persons alike. All site planning and design should endeavor to find a natural way of accommodating access that is sympathetic with the existing forms of the landscape. If we do not endeavor to do so, unnatural, man-built environments will cause less enjoyment in our daily activity and may even make everyone feel psychologically ill at ease. When more natural transitions from one area to another are utilized, we then have more energy and desire to use these pedestrian routes instead of relying on vehicular transportation.

Most of us generally move through the city as pedestrians without consciously thinking about the type of pavement material, the quality of its maintenance, the length of a steep walk, locations of places to rest, the true height and number of steps, or the need for handrails. However, concerns such as these occupy a significant part of the conscious thinking of the disabled. While many mobility safety precautions, such as handrails on stairs, are included inside buildings, these precautions may not be adequately provided in the exterior environment for the safety and general welfare of the public. Thus, it should be the designer's role to direct his attention to those constructed details of progressive pedestrian movement that will create more use of urban facilities in a safer manner.

Each building and its corresponding site should be planned and designed as an integral unit from the very beginning of the design process. The location of each structure can be adjusted vertically and horizontally to assure ease of potential accessibility and still conform to zoning setback restrictions where these are applicable. Often, the architect and the landscape architect collaborate on the initial site planning and design process, thus exploring alternatives that will unify the building and site components in the most harmonious manner possible. Such initial planning is better than waiting until building plans have become too firm to permit easy adaption of site circulation elements. These basic studies will include methods of grading and shaping the land to provide, wherever necessary, alternative routes of access, such as a combined ramp and steps to accommodate a major change in vertical elevation.

All pedestrian circulation systems should be constructed of suitable surface materials (Figure 6-3). Anyone with a mobility handicap, including the blind, will find soft surfaces like crushed rock, lawn, soil, cement, and bare earth difficult to negotiate. These soft surfaces are useful only for light traffic, and they present high maintenance costs in spite of low installation costs. Likewise, while variable surfaces provide faster movement, they may present some hazards. Such irregular surfaces as cobblestones, coarsely exposed aggregate concrete, flagstone, bricks laid in a sand base, wood decking, and wood discs in sand often cause bumpy rides for wheelchairs, stumbling for people who can't lift their toes high, and

Figure 6-3
Paving brick set in a mortar base provides a good walking surface for all pedestrians. Openings in the drainage grate are small enough not to create a hazard. The drainage way is subtle enough not to cause stumbling and next to it is a texture strip of stone that can serve as a guideway for the blind. (Main Street Mall, Charlottesville, Virginia)

trapping of crutch tips, cane tips, heels, and narrow wheels. Most of these surfaces have moderate maintenance requirements and average-to-high costs of installation. Hard, smooth, continuous surfaces like asphalt, concrete, closely spaced brick, and tile set in a concrete base are probably the most desirable materials for walking and wheeling. They are also the best for snow and ice removal processes. They have a relatively high cost of installation, but are the most durable and easily maintained.[6]

Most circulation spaces and routes should utilize these hard surface materials in their construction. Variable surface materials can be utilized in smaller areas, such as walkway edgings or caution strips for the blind (where path routes change or there is a hazard), and in areas that are not intended for intensive circulation, to provide color and textural interest.

Plazas, courtyards, and other large paved areas

In large paved areas, the major circulation routes within the space should be over continuous hard surfaces. Minimum lateral pitch for drainage is usually about .5 to 1 percent and maximum pitch would be 2 percent (2 feet per 100 feet). Because these spaces are relatively level, few people encounter mobility problems, except for the blind. The blind may experience many more difficulties in these spaces than they do on walkways because of the absence of clues like reflection of sounds from building walls and the linear quality of most walkways. In large paved areas, the blind can benefit from textural changes in the paving so that they can sense changes in circulation movement. For the partially blind, simple changes in the reflectiveness of pavement materials may provide sufficient guidance.

In large paved areas, everyone enjoys places to rest, water features, plantings, and other amenities, and these features should be provided for aesthetic interest and comfort. There may be need for directional signs for the blind and others, but care should be taken not to put any three dimensional objects in the middle of principal circulation routes where they may become an impediment to effective circulation or a hazard to the unsighted.

Protection from inclement weather or the hot sun is also an important consideration in the design of large paved spaces. Many elderly and disabled people cannot move quickly through open spaces, and they would benefit from the provision of some shelters with seating in case of thunderstorms or excessive heat. Likewise, walls or screens would serve as protection from extremely strong winds that can limit mobility security.

In addition to the street furniture already mentioned, consideration should be given to the provision of adequate lighting of large paved areas. Areas with the most circulation, resting locations, and changes in level should have the strongest light value to achieve a feeling of security and protection against crime. Thus the location, height, and types of lights used are fundamental considerations in furthering public use and enjoyment.

Walks and paths

Walks used by the public should be designed to enable a wide variety of people to ambulate or wheel in a safe, unencumbered manner from place to place. For these purposes, walks should not be so narrow that people cannot pass each other comfortably. The average person occupies 2'-0" of space and if that person is pushing a stroller, has a cane, or is in a wheelchair, he will occupy 2'-6" of space. If the person is carrying packages or suitcases he will occupy 3'-0": if he is on crutches, possibly a 3'-6" space. Thus, a minimum walk width would be 4'-0" for ease of functioning of passing pedestrians, and 5'-0" will allow two wheelchairs to pass each other. If we are to allow for all possibilities, such as a person on crutches and a parent with a small child, then 5'-6" or 6'-0" is preferable for moderate two-way traffic. This dimension allows everyone to proceed at their own desired speeds.

As in large paved areas, the surfaces should be of a hard, relatively smooth, and continuous common surface material, which is not slippery when wet, and they should be free of drainage gratings. Expansion or contraction joints should be as narrow as possible so that heels, narrow wheels, crutch tips, or cane tips can't get lodged in them.

Walks must have some slope, which is usually between .5 to 1 percent laterally, for the purpose of surface draining. Linear or longitudinal walk gradients should not exceed 5 percent (5 feet in 100 feet) and should maintain a maximum average of 3 percent slope for ease of movement (Figure 6-4). While walk routes with sustained grades of 4 to 5 percent can be utilized by people in wheelchairs, or with braces, these slopes should have intermittant 4'-0" to 5'-0" level areas for resting at about sixty-foot maximum intervals. When walks exceed 5 percent gradient, they are considered ramps and require curbs and handrails. The only condition on a walkway that would require protection, like 3" to 4" curbs and a guardrail, would be where a sharp drop in terrain occurs next to the walkway.

Figure 6-4
Here a change in level is accomplished with both steps and a sloping walk to allow both handicapped and nonhandicapped to circulate freely. The walk has the correct gradient and an exposed aggregate concrete surface to prevent slipping. (Northern Virginia Community College, Annandale, Virginia)

In order to better understand these walk gradient requirements, let us examine the standards for interstate highways as an analogy. The maximum grade for interstate highway design is 3 percent and the desirable grade is 1.5 percent in a normal situation. The absolute maximum grade for these highways is 4 to 5 percent, in which case on long grades extra lanes for slower moving vehicles, like trucks, must be provided.[7] Trucks lose speed climbing along 4 to 5 percent grades in the same way as some pedestrians and people in wheelchairs lose speed and strength over long stretches of steeper walkways. Also, in the same way that trucks may lose their brakes going down steeper highways, handicapped people may not be able to control their movements when going down steep sidewalks.

Even on major city streets, maximum grades for short distances are usually set at 6 percent to prevent slipping on ice and to provide better visibility at street intersections. This gradient can be compared to the classification of a ramp that would need some protection and movement assists for ascent and descent.

Rest areas, at the same level as the walk, are useful to all pedestrians and particularly to the elderly and handicapped as they move through the city. Benches should be offset from the principle walkway so that they don't impede circulation. Most business districts and shopping centers could benefit from the provision of more places for people to comfortably rest.

All walkways should be lighted well enough so that the pavement edges can be easily discerned at night. The greater the pedestrian movement and potential hazard, the more the need for adequate lighting for personal safety. Overhead walkway lights should be 10 feet to 15 feet high with below eye level lights (less then 3'-6") at hazardous locations such as changes in level.

Curb ramps should be planned at principal intersections with streets and building entrances in order to facilitate movement by those with physical handicaps. These short ramps should be a maximum proportional gradient of 1 in 6 with a nonslip surface.

Curb ramps should not present a sudden challenge to the normal pathway of the blind and should be preceded by caution strips 3 to 5 feet prior to the crossing. These caution strips, of a contrasting paving material, should also occur at the intersection of walkways to aid orientation. Gratings, manholes, and similar impediments should not be located in walks (Figure 6–5).

Ramps

Significant necessary changes in level are usually best accommodated by ramps with surfaces constructed of nonslip materials. As stated earlier, once a walk exceeds 5 percent, it is considered a ramp and requires 3″ to 4″ curbs and 32″ to 36″ high handrails. Normally, ramps will range in slope between 5 and 8.33 percent (1 in 20 to 1 in 12) maximum for wheelchair operation. All maximum gradient ramps should have level 4′–6″ (minimum length) rest areas every 30 feet, but level rest areas may be further apart for lesser slopes. The best gradient for the elderly and people who wear braces is a maximum of 7 percent for ease and comfort in directing the feet straight ahead up an incline. For some, the foot-lifting

Figure 6–5
These concrete curb ramps have been installed at many intersections in downtown Seattle, Washington. They have a nonslip surface and are located to one side of the walkway, at the corner.

capacity of the tibialis anterior muscle augmented by the peroneaus longus and brevis muscles, which are usually the first muscles to lose strength and the last to return to normal as a result of a disfunction in the nervous sytem, requires that braces be worn to aid ambulation and to avoid tripping because of a "dropped foot." People in a cast and on crutches because of injuries to the lower leg and foot face similar difficulties in swinging their leg straight ahead because they have no vertical flexibility in their foot. Normally, braces lift the toes 4 to 10 degrees, but 10 degrees can usually only be maintained by a rigid, inflexible brace. Thus, a gradient of 4 degrees or its equivalent of 7 percent should accommodate most everyone in a reasonable manner.

Ramps should be wide enough to allow use by ambulatory and nonambulatory people, as well as service deliveries, at the same time. Therefore, most ramps should be a minimum of 4′–4″ and preferably 6′–0″ clear width to allow for two-way traffic of varying types. If only sufficient space can be provided for a one-way ramp, it should be a minimum of 2′–8″ clear width and preferably 3′–0″ wide. Where ramps must turn, space of 5′–0″ minimum must be provided for turning wheelchairs and for aiding circulation flows. Handrails must be available on both sides of a double-loaded ramp with a double railing, one at 30″ to 32″ actual height for use of children and those in wheelchairs, and the other at 36″ to 38″ for ambulatory adults. There should be an extension of 18″ at the top and bottom of the ramp and designed in such a way that they will not be a hazard (Figure 6–6).

The bottom of each ramp should have 6′–0″ of clear level space so that a "running" start, or slowing down if descending, may be accomplished. Where the top of a ramp is near a doorway that swings outwards, there should be a level platform that exceeds the swing of the door by 4′–0″ for maneuverability. This platform should also extend 1′–0″ beyond each side of the doorway for safety purposes. The blind could also benefit from caution strips in the pavement placed 3′ to 5′ prior to the top and bottom of

Figure 6-6
This ramp has continuous handrails on both sides, a brick nonslip surface, and a level area at the bottom for starting up and slowing down. (Charlottesville, Virginia, Parking Garage)

the ramp. Average illumination that insures safe use in darkness should be provided. Ramps exposed to inclement weather should either be protected by a canopy or be provided with automatic snow and ice melting equipment in cold climates.[8]

Steps

Outdoor stairs are normally referred to as steps. Because our spatial perception of exterior environments is quite different from our perception of interior environments, the standards for step design must be different. There has been a long-standing rule in the practice of landscape architecture that no exterior step should be more then 6" in riser height with a tread of at least 12" in width. Many architects and the A-117.1, 1961 standards of the American National Standards Institute recommend 7" maximum riser height for both interior stairs and exterior steps. The American Society of Landscape Architects Foundation suggested that the maximum riser height be 6 1/2" with a minimum tread of 11", but they recommend 5 3/4" as the preferred riser height.[9] Most landscape architects follow the formula

of "two times riser height plus tread width equals 26."[10] To demonstrate this formula, let us look at the following examples:

6 1/2" R = 13" T
6"   R = 14" T
5 1/2" R = 15" T
5"   R = 16" T
4 1/2" R = 17" T
4"   R = 18" T

A further look at recommendations shows that Goldsmith in England recommends a 6 1/4" maximum riser height,[11] the New York State University Construction Fund specifies a 5 3/4" maximum riser height,[12] and in Sweden 4 3/4" to 5 1/2" for riser height is recommended.[13] The number of conflicts in the recommendations is probably a result of insufficient testing procedures, but these varied recommendations can be resolved in the following way. As with ramps, we should not plan and design on the basis of maximum or minimum allowable figures, but on the basis of comfort. Somewhere between a 5 1/2" or 6" maximum riser height, and 4" minimum riser height, would seem to be the most comfortable for children, handicapped adults, and the elderly as well as the general public. By no means should it exceed 6 1/4" (Goldsmith) or 6 1/2" (ASLAF), unless 6" or less is impossible to achieve. The tread width should then correspond to the formula that has been given. By following this formula, each tread will be deep enough to allow any person to place their entire foot on the step, rather than just the ball of the foot, for greater security. Usually there is more space for changes in level in the exterior environment, and we should plan accordingly for people who cannot lift their legs high because of limited muscle strength in the thigh.

Many people, who have limited strength, tend to raise their foot with the toe pressed against the riser to keep their balance. Therefore, the riser design must not permit the possibility of catching the toe under a projecting nosing. Thus, many shadow lines, while interesting from an aesthetic viewpoint, can be uncomfortable and may even present a hazard to some people. The riser should provide only a slight outward projection with a 3/4" to 1" rounded or chamfered nonslip nosing that permits pulling one's toe over the lip without catching it. All treads and risers in a series should be uniform.

On a long flight of steps, 4'-0" landings, and continuous handrails, should be provided for every 4'-0" change in elevation. If the total grade change does not exceed 6'-0", then intermediate landings are unnecessary. Steps should never be used when only two or three risers are needed. They then can be a hazard. Just as for interior stairs, landings are important as rest areas, for those who have activity as well as mobility impairments.

The width of exterior stairways should conform to the projected amount of pedestrian traffic they will need to carry. Minimum width for two-way traffic should be no less than 5'-0". Where no people are likely to pass one another, this could be reduced to a 3'-0" clear width. Regardless of the width of the steps, wall-secured handrails, 36" high, should be provided on both sides to aid those with balance and foot-lifting problems as well as to enhance security for all people when the steps have rain, ice, or snow on their surfaces. Where the stairway is very wide to accommodate large numbers of people, intermediate handrails should be installed at appropriate intervals between the outer edges.

For the partially sighted who may have difficulty distinguishing treads on ascent or descent, using a color on the nosing of a step that contrasts with that of the treads is helpful. The blind and partially sighted will need textural caution strips that precede by at least 3'-0" to 5'-0" both the top and bottom of the steps. The general public, as well as the partially sighted, will benefit from an adequate, average-maintained light level cast down toward the risers to insure safe use at night. All stairways should drain surface water by establishing a pitch of 1/8" per foot on each tread in order to insure the maintenance of a nonslip surface.

In summary, walks under 5 percent gradient are the easiest and least expensive method of access for all people. These walks should be hard surfaces that are smooth and free of barriers that could prove restrictive to the elderly and handicapped. Where significant changes in grade require steps for direct and immediate access, then at least one major entrance should be served by a ramp as an alternative means of access. These alternative means of access are important so that people will have a choice that is appropriate to their physical abilities. In terms of space requirements, a 6' change in level will require a 7 percent ramp, which is almost seven times the linear dimension of a vertical stairway utilizing 6" risers. If the street slopes or there are level changes in the building, the ramped surface can lead in from the high side and the steps from the lower side to provide immediate access for most people from either direction. Although ramps require greater horizontal area, they are much less expensive to build than steps, if laid on graded surfaces. Building steps of concrete or brick is more expensive because of the amount of material used and the required form work.

Comfort and Convenience Facilities

Places to rest with usable facilities are important to the enjoyment of all and particularly essential to those who lack stamina and become easily fatigued. Too few cities provide enough of these facilities for the average person and many people become upset over the long distances they must travel to avail themselves of useful conveniences. Outdoor comfort and convenience facilities would include seating and benches or seat walls, kiosks or announcement boards, rest rooms, drinking fountains, trash receptacles, and telephones. Most of these can be classified as street furniture that will be used and enjoyed by people out for a day on the town or even for a few hours.

Benches

The easiest and least expensive amenity to install are benches, but their actual design for the best usefulness is often neglected. In considering the selection of a bench, we should note that the average person will occupy two linear feet. For comfort, the bench should have a slightly sloping back that is about 32" high and arm rests with an approximate height of 2'-1". The seat itself should be between 14" and 17" high but not over 19" or 20". The reason for this minimum seat height is that many elderly and handicapped people cannot stand up from a seat height that is too low because their knees are overly bent and too much of a strain is put on their thighs. When the seat is too high, they cannot rest comfortably. Likewise, arm rests and back rests are important as leverage points for the arms to assist the lowering and lifting action of the legs. The accommodation of back supports and arm rests also make the bench more comfortable for the average person to use (Figure 6-7).

Seating in large paved areas should be offset 24" from walkways and near the tops and bottoms of steps and ramps in parks and waiting areas, or wherever else deemed appropriate, provided that it does not create an obstruction to the pathway. Paved space, of about 36", next to benches would allow people in wheelchairs to converse with others who are seated. All benches should be made of materials that do not retain heat or cold and are not rough or likely to splinter.

Figure 6-7
This sturdy wood bench for two people has a sloping back and arm rests for leverage when sitting down and standing up. (Lee Park, Charlottesville, Virginia)

Seat walls

Seat walls are another means of providing spots for resting. Raised planting areas are attractive and also provide the opportunity for seating; if they are between 18" and 21" high they can comfortably accommodate those who are physically limited. Walls that are lower than this height can become a hazard, particularly for the blind. Seat walls should be at least 12" wide. If the walls are only 8" wide and no higher than 18", wooden members that are 12" wide can be attached to the top for seating (the overhang makes standing up easier since the heels are under the center of gravity). Low retaining walls between 2'-0" and 2'-6" are useful for leaning against in a half-sitting manner and for wheelchair users to rest packages. Higher walls are not useful for sitting, but where one can grasp the top, they may be useful for keeping balance. Sometimes, handrails are helpful alongside these high walls.

Trash receptacles

Trash receptacles are relatively simple pieces of street furniture that are an asset to shopping districts and parks if they are attractively designed. Any trash receptacle should be about 3'-0" high and securely stationed so that, if people lean against it for support, it won't move or tip over. The openings should be large enough to receive the estimated trash sizes, and if spring-loaded doors are used, they should be easy to push with one hand by those with upper extremity handicaps. Foot-operated controls and remote buttons or levers should not be used because of difficulties some people have in comfortably operating these devices.

Kiosks

Kiosks and other forms of displaying announcements of public, charitable, and commercial events are very useful devices that add interest to the urban scene when they are well designed. These display techniques, which are used extensively in Europe, are very helpful to the visitor, especially when orientation information is provided. In addition, such information centers could provide information to assist the disabled in learning about barrier-free access routes. The blind could be provided with the same information in braille.

Public restrooms

Public restrooms that were once provided in many urban areas have disappeared because of vandalism, crime, and the difficulties of providing attendants or proper maintenance. These serious problems have caused many public conveniences to be discontinued, but there is need for safe and easily accessible restroom facilities for use by the physically disabled who cannot travel quickly or as far as the able-bodied when the need arises. Many people with physical disfunctioning may have problems of incontinence and need ready accessibility to restrooms. While many shops and other establishments in the business community provide rest rooms that are open to the public, many keep them only for employees.

Public restrooms that are provided in public buildings and recreation facilities should be readily accessible to those in wheelchairs and provide at least one wider stall with an outward swinging door. Importantly, these facilities should be adjacent to principal walks, should have no encumberances like steps to impede fast and smooth access, and should have good illumination for the sake of safety at night.

Drinking fountains

Drinking fountains are particularly important to paraplegics and quadriplegics who need frequent water intake due to dehydration, but many exterior fountains are too high for people in wheelchairs to use. Thus, free-standing fountains should have two units: one nozzle at 36" to 39" for ambulatory adults and one at 32" to 33" for children and those confined to wheelchairs. All drinking fountains should be on hard surface areas that are accessible to people in wheelchairs. Stepping blocks that may be provided for children should be kept clear of the access area for totally ambulant or wheelchair-dependent people. The controls should be lever operated, rather than knob controlled, for ease of operation by upper-extremity handicapped people or those with arthritis.

Telephones

Outdoor telephones installed in a group should have at least one telephone that is no higher than 4'-0" to the coin slots, so that it can be operated easily by those in wheelchairs and even by children in an emergency. A paved space that is 30" wide should be provided in front of each of these special installations. Such telephones can also be provided with instructions in braille, volume controls on headsets for people with hearing problems, and push-button dials for easier use for people with extremity disabilities. Lighting directly above the telephone as well as a fold-down seat are helpful additions for increased usability.

Protection from the Effects of the Weather

Although everyone enjoys some protection from the hot summer sun, rain, and intense winter winds, most people with activity or mobility handicaps are affected much more by changes and extremes of daily weather conditions. People who suffer from activity impairments cannot move about rapidly in the direct hot summer sun because they may exhaust themselves. People with mobility impairments and even temporary impairments cannot run in the event of thunderstorms and can thus become drenched within a short distance. Those with mobility impairments that affect balance may also be blown over in strong gusts of wind and then find standing up again very difficult. Excessive coldness will also limit the normal activity of many people who have poor blood circulation. Thus, the more seasonal weather protection we provide, the more usable the exterior environment will be for all urban citizens.

Man-built structures for climatic control include free-standing or attached shelters for protection from rain and snow, canopies for overhead protection from hot sun, and free-standing walls and fences for protection from strong cold winter winds. These structures are very useful at transportation mode changes (bus, taxi, and automobile waiting areas), building entrances, in parks and plazas, and at various pedestrian gathering nodes in the business district. Any shelter should have vertical protection on the windward side for comfort during long waiting periods.

In addition to structures, many trees and shrubs can provide climatic control as well as functional control of erosion, dust, pollution, and air quality in urban areas. Deciduous trees along major circulation routes and in places of congregation are a welcome relief to the hot summer sun and reflective pavement surfaces. Deciduous trees also provide shelter from rainstorms during six months of the year. Protection from rain during the balance of the year can best be provided by shelters in most climatic zones of the United States. Many coniferous trees and tall evergreen shrubs will provide some reduction in wind velocity, and these should be used in northwest parts of the site for protection against cold winter winds. When evergreen material is used in this section of the site, it will not impede the melting of ice from paved surfaces.

Earth mounds can often be formed on sites by utilizing excavation material. These mounds, in combination with evergreen shrubs, can reduce noise and wind to some degree. The selection of plants for public urban spaces should be done in consultation with a landscape architect since many trees and shrubs may create hazards or nuisances, particularly to the physically disabled if they are not properly selected and placed.[14]

Communication

Many handicapped people have difficulty in interpreting their location and orienting themselves within the environment. A person in a wheelchair is less than four feet high, and he cannot see well while in a crowd; a person who is blind needs signs with raised or indented letters, because less than 10 percent of the blind read braille; a person who is partially sighted needs contrasting colors and clues, like contrasting textures, alongside walkways and audible signals for dangerous areas; a person who is deaf or hard of hearing needs visual signals; and the physically handicapped, in general, benefit from knowledge of the most comfortable and accessible routes to follow as well as information on rest areas, public toilets, special car parking, accessible entrances, and directions to major building complexes. Much of this information will also be beneficial to visitors and the general public.

The main purpose of signs should be to provide a clear designation of places, warnings, and routing information. In order to make signs more useful to everyone, they should be designed so as to be easily seen from eye level, readable by moving the fingers over the surface of the letters, and well-lighted for night time identification. Larger, higher signs will have to be used in certain locations, but supplementary signs at lower elevations are useful for most pedestrians. These signs can combine graphic symbols with lettering so that everyone can easily understand the message.

General rules for sign design include proper location to avoid sign clutter by grouping directional signs into unified systems, combining lighting fixtures with signs to reduce unnecessary posts, and placing signs at natural gathering places that are out of the way of major circulation routes for safety. While overhanging signs are useful in the business district, they should clear the walkway by at least 7'-6".

Outdoor lighting, when it is well done, increases the activity in the city at night by providing aesthetic enjoyment, clarity of orientation, and safety from crime and accident. Many urban areas need to reevaluate the usefulness of their outdoor lighting systems by considering the type and location of light fixtures and not just the number. Many new lighting sources, like "cut-off" lights, have improved light distribution without glare to surroundings. These new sources deserve careful consideration for new areas as well as for renovation. Good general reference for lighting considerations has been given in the publication "Barrier Free Site Design."[15]

Building Access

Although access has been mentioned in the section on ramps, a few more comments are important when considering building entrances. Any entrance threshold should be flush with the floor and never exceed 3/4" maximum for wheelchair access. The clear opening of the door should be 32" minimum and (36" preferable) 7' 0" high. In heavy traffic areas the best doors for speed in activation are automatic sliding doors. Where doors must be pulled open, they should be controlled by lever action, instead of knobs, for use by people who have difficulty in grasping.

Door pressure, for self-closing doors, should be kept below 8 pounds for operation by the elderly, people in wheelchairs, and those who have difficulty with balance.[16] Where there are a series of swinging doors, a space of about 6'-6" should be provided between each to prevent people from getting trapped.[17] Raised or etched letters, about 4'-6" above the floor at doorways, and caution strips, 3' on the sides and 6' in front of the door, help the blind to identify the premises.

All of these guides make doors easier to open for people with packages, those wheeling strollers, and

the general public, as well as those with temporary or permanent mobility impairments. As stated earlier, at least one main entrance to any public-use facility should be accessible to all handicapped persons, and low signs should direct those people to such entrances from the major circulation route. Handicapped people like to avoid the stigma of having accessibility only through the service entrance.

Gates to gardens and courtyards should also be considered in a similar way as entrances to buildings—that is, by providing 32" clear opening, lever-type opening mechanisms, and between 5 and 8 pounds maximum pulling pressure on self-closing mechanisms. Paved level space of almost 4' should also be extended from the end of the gate swing when open.[18]

POLICY PREPARATION AND IMPLEMENTATION PROCEDURES

Policies to eliminate architectural barriers to the handicapped are established by many different means. Laws at the state level have been enacted in a variety of ways: Many states have adopted the American National Standards Institute standards (ANSI Standard A–117.1, 1961) as part of the law, and others have established their own standards. Some states apply the law to just new buildings constructed in full or in part through the use of public funds, whereas others extend the coverage to include publicly used but privately owned buildings. This latter situation is more desirable. In addition, the laws of almost half the states apply to buildings undergoing substantial remodeling, rehabilitation, or renovation, and a few also apply to temporary and emergency construction. Only a few states, such as Minnesota and North Carolina, have adopted the ANSI standards and additions to these standards into their state building codes. This procedure holds the most promise, provided that local building inspection is carried out, the code is clearly understood, and violation of the code carries a penalty.

Although all states have enacted legislation, the

great majority of the nation's cities have not under-taken programs to eliminate architectural barriers. The results of a survey by the National League of Cities in 1967 indicated that only 34 percent (95) of the responding local units (278) had made an effort to eliminate barriers. More than half of these (56) based their barrier elimination programs on some form of official municipal action, but only half of these (26) had taken legal action, either by the adop-tion of an ordinance or by amending their local build-ing code. Of these, only 33 percent (9) had incorporated the ANSI specifications into their ordinances. Most communities used state legislation as a basis for local programs and reported relatively high effectiveness, although most of these programs were directed only at new local public buildings. Cities that lacked effectiveness attributed this to the fact that the program was permissive and lacked penalty clauses to insure compliance. Overall, city officials ranked "elimination in the design state," "state law," "amendment of state and local building codes," and "local ordinance" in descending order of preference as means for achieving the goal of making public buildings accessible to the physically disabled.[19]

Since this study in 1967, many more communities have probably formulated policies to eliminate archi-tectural barriers to the physically handicapped. The means for doing so should be through consultation with building architects and landscape architects, through amendments to state and local building codes or ordinances, and through changes in the four na-tional building codes. Local informal action or execu-tive order of the mayor or governor have not been found to be very effective. In any case, there must be some substantial policy commitment at the local level that includes mandatory regulations for the public good and enforcement procedures. These should apply to publicly used but privately owned facilities as well as public facilities. Once this commitment is realized, an architectural barriers committee could be established to help the cause of the program. This action may allow for a better review process of cur-rent projects rather than leave these decisions solely to the building inspector.

Once a policy and its attendant requirements have become an official document, implementation can proceed through several future governmental actions that affect the use of the land. The zoning ordinance is one implementation tool that almost all local plan-ning agencies utilize. Zoning, as a governmental re-striction on the use of private property, must promote public health, safety, morals, or general welfare, and the physical needs of the elderly and handicapped should be included as part of this requirement for constitutional enforcement. Within these standards and restrictions on the use of land, the creation of barrier-free environments could appropriately become a required part of all future development. This re-quirement would probably best be upheld as part of a section in the ordinance on requirements for site plan review.

The site plan review process is a relatively new amendment to most zoning ordinances, but it has gained public acceptance as a logical planning tool whereby public and private interests for health, safety, and the general welfare can be maintained. Most site plan review sections of the zoning ordinance stipulate provisions for insuring the proper setbacks, drainage and run-off controls, driveway and curb-cut locations, the planting of buffer screens for bordering districts, and even the preservation of significant trees and other landscape features (i.e., grading practices). Within these considerations, provisions for adequate walks, changes in level, and entrances to buildings could be included in order to prevent development errors that could be costly to change at some future time.

Besides zoning ordinances, subdivision regulations could incorporate a few provisions for controlling the development of new, low-density residential areas. The existing regulations typically control the width and organization of streets, the facilities for drainage and lighting, the size and shape of lots, the provisions for open space, locations and size of sewer and water systems, and the grading, surfacing and curbing of streets. Within this list, we might attempt to include adequate pedestrian lighting on walkways to insure no dark spots, barrier-free access to open-space systems and parks, curb ramps at major pedestrian street crossings, lighted internal walkways with rest areas that are not a part of the street rights-of-way, and changes in the texture of street surfacing to warn motorists of major pedestrian crossings or school zones. In addition, there may be success in developing a standard for wider lots in proportion to the increased steepness of slope in order to permit easier access by the elderly and handicapped on traversing inclines.

A fourth form of implementation may take the form of enforcement of local and state building codes that protect the health, safety, morals, and general welfare of the public. Planners are sometimes involved in stipulating the minimum standards for the design of buildings as a part of the municipal police power. Likewise, in urban renewal programs that involve the conservation of the existing quality of developed property, rehabilitation of properties that are in poor condition, and/or the complete redevelopment of dilapidated structures, planners involved in the administration of the program may establish conditions to be met for barrier-free design.

Finally, consideration of the need for improving the problems imposed by architectural barriers in public facilities should become part of every capital improvements program. Capital programming, as a form of financial planning for public facilities, is becoming a successful tool for implementing the comprehensive plan. The survey by the National League of Cities has shown that a substantial majority of the public approve the use of tax money to remove barriers in public buildings.[20] Recent legislation has even made capital improvements programming mandatory[21] and related it to the regular operating budget, so that the projected physical and social priorities can be successfully scheduled for implementation. In determining the nature and cost of the proposed projects, criteria and estimates should include provisions to insure adequate accessibility by the elderly and handicapped. Perhaps even remodeling of existing forms of access in public spaces and buildings could be included in the capital improvements program.

Costs of barrier-free design are frequently assumed to be prohibitive, despite the fact that this form of construction would provide greatly increased benefits for the general public as well as to those with actual handicaps. Surveys that have been conducted by architects conclusively show that, for new construction, additional money to meet these requirements will be substantially less than 1 percent of the total cost of construction and even as low as 1/10 of 1 percent.[22]

One of the problems present in accepting the comparatively low cost of barrier-free design involves the traditional thinking of the architect and builder. Although architects are making headway in incorporating the principles of barrier-free design into their design methodology, most builders have not been sufficiently exposed to these techniques and continue to utilize traditional construction methods. An example of this occured in the construction of the Watergate complex in Washington, D.C., which consisted of gracefully curving wall forms. The supervising architect was plagued by contractors who said it couldn't be built, but ultimately, it was! Thus, the whole question is one of general acceptance of barrier-free design as an inherent and natural component of man-built environments for all.

Although studies have been made on the cost-benefit to new buildings and sites, little research has been applied to remodelling and renovation of existing buildings to allow access by handicapped groups. However, this research will soon be completed as a result of action taken to improve access to federal buildings by the Architectural and Transportation Barriers Compliance Board. Some cost examples for remodeling the site conditions of typical buildings were included in a study conducted by the Department of Urban Studies in 1967,[23] which would now bear the added cost of inflation. The important facts lie in the proper consideration of suitable materials and construction methods. A great deal can usually be done by regrading sites in order to save construction materials that are needed for the formation of such site elements as ramps.

As a reward for initiating remodeling to provide barrier-free access, communities might utilize an incentive system. Thus, removal of architectural barriers in privately owned buildings used by the public could be a condition for granting a tax incentive. In North Carolina, building owners who perform such a service have been granted unlimited tax deductions for barrier-free renovations.[24]

In conclusion, access to the environment depends upon public acceptance and understanding of the needs of the physically handicapped in using an interconnected continuum of site facilities. Changes in the practice of environmental design can best be demonstrated by professional architects, landscape architects, and planners by such means as expanding the scope of site design considerations, becoming familiar with and utilizing the laws and codes effectively, and continually searching for suitable means of implementation in private or public practice.

NOTES AND REFERENCES

All photographs in this chapter were taken by Michael J. Bednar.

1. Department of Urban Studies, National League of Cities, *State and Local Efforts to Eliminate Architectural Barriers to the Handicapped* (Washington, D.C.: U.S. Department of Health, Education and Welfare, 1967).
2. Task Force of the American Institute of Architects, "National Policy for a Barrier Free Environment" (Washington, D.C.: The President's Committee on Employment of the Handicapped and the National Easter Seal Society for Cripppled Children and Adults, 1974).
3. Mace, R. L., in B. Lalett (ed.), *An Illustrated Handbook of the Handicapped Section of the North Carolina State Building Code* (Raleigh: North Carolina Building Code Council and North Carolina Department of Insurance, 1974).
4. Department of Urban Studies, National League of Cities, *State and Local Efforts to Eliminate Architectural Barriers to the Handicapped*.
5. Kirk, L., *Accent on Access* (McLean, Va.: American Society of Landscape Architects Foundation, 1975).
6. American Society of Landscape Architects Foundation, *Barrier Free Site Design* (Washington, D.C.: U.S. Department of Housing and Urban Development, 1975).
7. American Association of State Highway Officials, "A Policy on Geometric Design of Rural Highways" (Washington, D.C.: American Association of State Highway Officials, 1965).
8. New York State University Construction Fund, "Making Colleges and Universities Accessible to Handicapped Students" (Washington, D.C.: President's Committee on Employment of the Handicapped, 1965).
9. American Society of Landscape Architects Foundation, *Barrier Free Site Design*.
10. Church, Thomas, *Gardens are for People* (New York: Reinhold, 1955).
11. Goldsmith, Selwyn, *Designing for the Disabled* (London: Royal Institute of British Architects, 1963).
12. New York State University Construction Fund, "Making Colleges and Universities Accessible to Handicapped Students."
13. National Swedish Building Research, *Accessible Towns-Workable Homes. Planning with Consideration for the Handicapped*, Stockholm, Sweden, 1972.
14. American Society of Landscape Architects Foundation, *Barrier Free Site Design*.
15. Ibid.
16. Kirk, *Accent on Access*.
17. New York State University Construction Fund, "Making Colleges and Universities Accessible to Handicapped Students."
18. American Society of Landscape Architects Foundation, *Barrier Free Site Design*.
19. Department of Urban Studies, National League of Cities, *State and Local Efforts to Eliminate Architectural Barriers to the Handicapped*.
20. Ibid., p. 109.
21. Legislative Task Force, Virginia Chapter, American Institute of Planners, "Planning Enabling Legislation Task Force Report," Richmond, 1976.
22. American Society of Landscape Architects Foundation, *Barrier Free Site Design*.
23. Department of Urban Studies, National League of Cities, *State and Local Efforts to Eliminate Architectural Barriers to the Handicapped*.
24. National Easter Seal Society for Crippled Children and Adults, News Service, Chicago, 1972.

7

Moline, Illinois: Planning a Barrier-Free Environment for the Elderly and Handicapped

Gunduz Dagdelen Ast

Gunduz Dagdelen Ast, born in Istanbul, came to the United States in 1958. She received her Bachelor of Architecture degree from the University of Illinois in 1962, and her Master of Urban Design and Architecture degree from Washington University, St. Louis, in 1963. After three years of practice with Harry Weese and Associates, in 1969 she opened her own architectural firm in Chicago, in partnership with Bruno Ast. The firm of Ast–Dagdelen specialized in variously scaled housing projects and residential renovations and has conducted research in the following areas: "A Documentary Research to Assess the Responsiveness of Turkish Vernacular Architecture to Climatology," "Chicago's Vernacular Houses," and "Establishing New Design Tools through Behavioral Science Methods and User Participation." She is a member of the Turkish Chamber of Architects (branch of UIA) and The Chicago Women in Architecture.

INTRODUCTION

Environment consists of all the conditions and circumstances that surround and influence the development and existence of a person.[1] From birth to death man is continually interacting with environmental forces—both natural and manmade. Natural environmental forces provide benefits (sunlight, warmth) and create problems (storms, cold), but they affect us all equally; they discriminate against no one. Manmade environmental forces, however, are different.

Manmade environmental forces, shaped by modern technology, do not affect us all equally. While the achievements of modern technology in communications, transportation, and architectural design have changed the environment that surrounds us in ways that often seem to benefit us all, interaction with the manmade environment, with its components and modifications, soon convinces many people that the manmade environment does discriminate. It discriminates against the elderly, the infirm, the handicapped, and the less-than-physically-perfect. It is, in fact, designed for the ideal person—that person of perfect physical health, dimensions, and mobility and that mythical ideal of the human species fostered by consumer product advertising and fashion journals. This ideal human is frozen in time, never to grow old, to be ill, to be blind, or to be deaf.

This case study is addressed to the fact that due to a general acceptance of a mythical human ideal, the modern, manmade environment is often designed in a way that deprives many persons of freedom of movement and access to public facilities. Specifically, the elderly and the handicapped are frequently forced to confront difficult and unnecessary architectural barriers when performing the most routine of daily tasks; they are denied access to public buildings by these barriers and are even faced with dangers seldom encountered by the able-bodied. The achievements of modern technology, such as those that enable us to land a man on the moon or travel one hundred miles an hour in a car, can kill or cripple a less than perfect man as he negotiates the earthly environment. Actions such as crossing a street, boarding a bus, or going through a revolving door can be hazardous for the fit, but especially so for the elderly and handicapped. In the United States, for example, 45 percent of all traffic fatalities are pedestrians, and a breakdown of this statistic reveals that these victims are almost always in certain subpopulations: the elderly, the very young, the handicapped, and those impaired by infirmity or alcohol.[2]

In a society that is presumably concerned with equal opportunity for all of its citizens, many of the needs of the elderly and the handicapped are virtually ignored. They themselves are often seen as a burden to that ideal self promulgated by current attitudes and the increasing sophistication of our society. The contention of this case study is that the needs of the elderly and the handicapped can no longer be ignored. People involved in the design of the modern, manmade environment must take responsibility for designing that environment for the benefit of all users. Advances in communications, transportation, and architectural design must be incorporated into the environment so that freedom of movement and access to public facilities are ensured for the elderly and the handicapped as well as for the young and the able-bodied. The specific objectives of this case study are as follows.

1. *To identify architectural barriers that inhibit public movement and reduce access to public-use facilities in the urban environment.* Access to and use of public facilities is both a humanistic and a legal right. Legislation has been passed at the federal and state levels requiring that public-use buildings, both old and new, financed with federal or state funds be accessible to and usable by the handicapped as well as the physically fit.[3]

2. *To design support elements for public movement systems (crosswalks, curbs, public vehicles, and so forth) that will facilitate movement through the macroenvironment and provide adequate access to public-use facilities for the handicapped as well as the able-bodied user.* The macroenvironment consists,

among other things, of natural elements, such as climatic conditions (wind, rain); of combinations of natural and manmade elements, such as movement and noise (traffic); and of specifically manmade elements, such as buildings and their exterior parts (stairs, doors), streets, curbs, lampposts, and so forth. Although public-use buildings are now often designed with the handicapped user in mind, ways for the user to get to such facilities are frequently overlooked as design issues—that is, facilitation of movement for the handicapped person from his place of residence to those physical facilities that have been made useable to him has been largely ignored. There is a need for movement support elements that remove barriers and increase accessibility for the handicapped user.

3. *To coordinate support elements for public movement systems and to thus create an integrated system that will provide easier movement and public facility access for all user groups.* Facilitating macroenvironment accessibility does not lie solely in the use of especially designed vehicles, special doors in existing transportation modes, rear building entry doors, and freight elevators, as is frequently the current practice. Not only is the use of such solutions too often sporadic and uncoordinated, but these solutions tend to segregate and restrict the freedom of movement of the elderly or handicapped users, thereby encumbering them and making them dependent on the assistance of able-bodied people. The effect is to inhibit rather than encourage efforts to make public-use buildings accessible and usable by all user populations.

4. *To develop design solutions with the handicapped user, and not just for the handicapped user.* The contentions of this study is that experiments conducted by architects that simulate the experiences of the handicapped do not result in reliable findings. Experiments, such as having an able-bodied person perform daily tasks in a wheelchair, leave the designer only at the threshold of fully understanding the complexity of the problems faced by a person with restricted mobility.

5. *To develop a model that will promote action*

and awareness programs. This study is primarily a process model for producing a barrier-free environment in the central business district of a medium-sized midwestern town. The process model developed can also be used by other towns of similar size and geographic conditions. The design model resulting from the process model is in its preliminary stage and thus requires further design development, testing, and financing for implementation. It was developed for the site in Moline, Illinois, based upon local data. The design model would need to be adjusted to local conditions, needs, and circumstances in its application to other sites in other towns.

Hopefully, the study will act as a catalyst and raise further questions about design for all users. The results are by no means ultimate or final, but they can provide a basis for future action programs and further public awareness.

RESEARCH METHODS AND PROGRAM DEVELOPMENT FOR THE CASE STUDY

The thrust of this case study was directed toward the development of an empirical model illustrating programmatic criteria for environmental barrier modification in the central business district of a medium-sized city. Environmental barriers for this study were defined as those elements in the urbanscape that deter access to the "downtown" and make the "downtown" unnegotiable to a part of its resident user population, specifically the elderly and the handicapped users. The empirical model was evolved from the study objectives supported by the research findings. The findings of the study and the implementation of the proposed solutions should not only increase accessibility and mobility for the elderly and the handicapped users, but the resulting improvements and amenities should also revitalize town centers by attracting a large segment of the total user population.

The research methods and program development consisted of three phases:

Phase I: Site selection criteria;
Phase II: Reconnaissance of the study site, including site analysis, user group identification, and mapping of the study site area;
Phase III: Data and information gathering, including survey questionnaires and open-ended interviews.

The researchers decided that establishing communication links with local agencies and decision control groups associated with the target area, in the early planning stages of the study, would allow them to focus on the programmatic issues of the study in later phases. For this reason, and for purposes of obtaining direct and accurate data, the following sources in the Moline governmental and business hierarchy were contacted: the mayor and the planning commission of Moline, the Moline Housing Authority, the Downtown Development Corporation, the Chamber of Commerce, and one of the major local industries.

Phase I: Site Selection Criteria

Moline, Illinois, was selected for the case study. The criteria used for this selection were as follows.

Population

According to the 1970 U.S. census, the population of Moline was 46,237. Comparisons of the 1960 and 1970 census indicate an 8.3 percent population increase, thereby reflecting a stable growth rate (a factor deemed relevant to the thesis of the study).[4] In evaluating the population makeup of Moline, the researchers found that 14.3 percent belong to the sixty-two years or over age group. This fact allows an assumption of a population group beginning to experience at least partial failure of its motor and sensory abilities.[5] Furthermore, based on national statistics extrapolated to the Moline population, an additional 10 percent of the total population belonging to younger age groups can also be classified as handicapped. Adding the two figures together makes apparent that a substantial portion of the city's population, 24.3 percent, has mobility limitations. This factor alone justifies research on environmental modification related to public facility accessibility and use by the physically disabled and the aged.

Redevelopment programs

A major redevelopment program to revitalize the central business district (CBD), which has been seriously affected by peripheral shopping center developments, is currently underway. The Downtown Redevelopment Corporation, formed by prominent business enterprises, has initiated a program of land acquisition to carry out the proposed CBD development. This program, coupled with the planning proposals for a barrier-free environment, increases the possiblity for implementation of the case study proposals.

Phase II: Reconnaissance of the Study Site

The user group

The researchers determined that a stable user group was required for the proposed data-gathering phase of the project. The selection criteria for the user group further required that the subjects be familiar with the Moline central business district and be dependent on its services and amenities on a daily basis. Handicapped subjects were sought, but few seriously handicapped people were found in the immediate downtown area because of the physical access barriers that this study is attempting to eliminate. (One paraplegic interviewee stated that the inaccessibility of the environment makes handicapped users "hermits" in the urban setting.) Because of this situation and

because they met the selection criteria, the residents of the nearby Hillside Heights Housing Project (for the elderly) were asked to participate in the research project as the user group.

The location of the Hillside Heights Housing Project is in good juxtaposition to the study area. The complex is relatively new (built in 1971) and was financed with a federal housing subsidy specifically for the elderly and handicapped of moderate income. The location is three and a half blocks from 5th Avenue, the primary downtown shopping street. This fact is significant because three and a half blocks is the maximum desirable walking distance for the elderly.[6]

A second significant factor for the study was the housing authority requirement that tenants admitted to the housing project be able to look after themselves. This housing authoirty requirement assured the researchers that this group of people would be mobile, alert, and self-reliant, regardless of their handicaps.

Mapping the study site

Home range. The "home range"[7] is the area falling into the user's capability radius and includes the path most often frequented by him. Visual observation generated the hypothesis that the "home range" of the Hillside Heights residents extended to 5th Avenue and that the most frequently used path was along 17th Street. This street is used not only because it provides the shortest route to 5th Avenue, but also because a number of service facilities are located on it. These service facilities include the library, the YWCA, the post office, and some retail shops that break the routine and monotony of this path for elderly users. A cognitive navigation map was requested during the survey phase to test the accuracy of this hypothesis (Figure 7–1). Cognitive maps are mental images of the physical environment that people form as aids to comprehending and functioning in their everyday environments. They are internalized perceptions that provide a basis for orientation and activity for the person by linking current perceptions of the environment with past perceptions of that environment.[8]

The study corridor. Accepting the "home range" concept and the identified barrier conditions on the path from Hillside Heights to the downtown led to the evolution of the concept of a *mobility corridor* The "study corridor" was chosen as the area for demonstrating the proposed innovations and modifications of the existing setting that were designed to provide a barrier-free environment and to facilitate independent mobility.

The limits of the study. Within the limits of the study were the urban transportation systems, natural area conditions, and manmade structures affecting the macroenvironment. Manmade structures make up much of the urban fabric, but the macroenvironment is also subject to the influence of natural and climatic forces, as well as to physical conditions created by man and his governmental organizations. The combination of these forces yields specific results that, at times, conflict with the basic needs of individual people and are too powerful for man to deal with.

This study proposes to identify physical constraints to individual mobility within the macroenvironment and to recommend possible solutions to eliminate these constraints. The portions of buildings that are considered in this study are the outsides of buildings and their projections or extensions, such as canopies, doors, and steps, that contribute to the character of the exterior environment and link the outside to the inside. Architectural problems encountered by the disabled that pertain to the interior of buildings (i.e., the microenvironment) are deliberately excluded from this study. The difference in the set of conditions and the range of scale between the macro- and microenvironments requires two separate studies.

Target area for design models. The barriers within the macroenvironment and the design solutions needed to eliminate these barriers are of a complex nature. A "target area" was selected to provide a focus for specific design solutions. The selected target area was the intersection of 17th Street and 5th Avenue where all city networks, infrastructures, vehicular and pedestrian movements, and city services meet.

Phase III: Data and Information Gathering

Survey questionnaire

An Urban Activity Questionnaire and a Satisfaction with the Urban Environment Scale were developed for the elderly and administered to the residents of Hillside Heights.[9] The questionnaire was designed to gather information on the interaction of age, disability, and architectural barriers as they affect the lifestyle and satisfaction level of the aged. The 85 of Hillside Heights' 127 residents who were interviewed represent a 67 percent sample of the total group of residents. The questionnaire consisted of three parts:

1. General information about the subjects interviewed, including their backgrounds, their characteristics, their activities, and their handicaps;
2. Information about the neighborhood as viewed by the subjects, including the way they relate to it and the way they negotiate it (a cognitive navigation test between the residence and downtown was given);
3. Evaluation of the physical environment in terms of a qualitative and quantitative satisfaction test.

Open-ended interviews

A limited number of open-ended interviews were also carried out with the residents of Hillside Heights. The purpose of these interviews was to gain insight into the circumstances and problems relating to age, mobility, and architectural barriers, that were not revealed by the questionnaires. These interviews were recorded on video tape.

SUMMARY OF SURVEY AND INTERVIEW FINDINGS

Survey Findings

Demographic characteristics

The residents of Hillside Heights are predominantly over the age of sixty-five; the median age for this group is between seventy and seventy-four. The population is 84 percent female, which is a typical characteristic of this age group in the United States.

On the average, a majority of this population group had been out of the labor market for more than nine years or had not worked in their lives. Sixty-eight percent of the group had been living in Moline, in Hillside Heights, for four years; they were the first residents to move in after the completion of Hillside Heights. No specific data was gathered on the geographic place of origin and various places of residence of the group. However, the informal interviews revealed that a large segment of the group had spent a majority of their lives in the midwest, mostly in the quad-cities area.

Health characteristics of the group interviewed show that 59 percent suffer from at least one physical ailment and the rest suffer from multiple ailments. Note that all of the identified ailments (see Table 7-1) impair mobility at some level. However, everyone in the group has the qualifications necessary to reside in Hillside Heights, which means that none are bedridden and all are able to look after themselves.

Analysis of data on mobility, transportation modes, and activities of the elderly

Data on mobility clearly show the continued ability of most of the residents to get out and around beyond their place of residence. The two modes of

TABLE 7-1
Present Ailments of Hillside Heights Residents

Ailments	Percent of Residents
Heart Trouble	31
Respiratory Problems	25
High blood pressure	28
Hardening of arteries	28
Crippled limbs	22
Poor sight	35
Poor hearing	21
Rheumatism	46
Nervousness	35
Tiredness	60
Other	44

individual mobility most curtailed are climbing steps and driving (see Table 7-2). This information suggests that the scope of individual mobility might very well be enlarged, or at least maintained, by increasing and improving the presently available public transportation system.

The mode of transportation used by the elderly to actually get around outside of their residences and to get to places beyond walking distance is affected by the means of transportation available to them. More than half of the residents (68 percent) are forced to rely primarily upon the assistance of relatives and friends (see Table 7-3). Qualitative data gathered from interviews with the residents, however, indicate that this dependence upon the good will and schedules of others for transportation can be oppressive,

TABLE 7-2
Mode of Mobility of Hillside Heights Residents

Activity	Percent of Residents with Activity Curtailed
Walking	20
Climbing steps	32
Driving a car	25
Taking public transportation	19

TABLE 7–3
Mode of Transportation Used by Hillside Heights Residents

Mode of Transportaton Frequently Used	Percent of Residents
Private auto	25
Taxi	22
Public transportation	46
Driven by friends or relatives	68

TABLE 7–4
Leisure-Time Activity of Hillside Heights Residents

Activity	Percent of Residents Engaging in Activity
Taking walks	73
Attending church	61
Taking auto rides	58
Attending club meetings	37
Community and social activities	33
Library	21
Movies	16
Cultural activities	16

humiliating, and destructive to a person's sense of freedom, as well as severely limiting to his or her range of mobility.

The second most frequently used mode of transportation is public transportation. The qualitative data from the interviews indicate that for most of the residents, public transportation is the preferred mode of transportation. There are, however, a number of very serious drawbacks related to the usefulness of public transportation. First of all, available bus routes do not adequately serve the housing facility. Residents must walk a number of blocks to the nearest bus stop. For many of them, this fact puts public transportation effectively beyond their reach. Secondly, many residents are unable to negotiate high steps to board buses. Again, this serves to make public transportation effectively unavailable to them. Finally, the residents indicate that bus schedules are not aligned with their needs. There is no bus service on Sundays or after 6:00 p.m., which are precisely the times when residents might wish to visit friends and relatives.

Data obtained on modes of transportation indicate relatively little use of taxis and private autos. Taxis are expensive and are used only when no other means of transportation is available. Maintaining private automobiles is also expensive and impossible in some circumstances where driving abilities are curtailed.

Given these constraints upon mobility, the leisure-time activities that the residents of Hillside Heights presently engage in outside of the housing facility provide an important commentary on the lifestyle of this age group. By far the most predominant activity

is taking walks, alone or in pairs (see Table 7–4). This activity is indicative of three things: (1) the mobility potential of the residents, (2) their desire to do something with their time, and (3) the basic solitude of their existence. The second activity most often engaged in, church attendance for the sake of social interaction, reinforces this observation. Taking auto rides for pleasure, on the other hand, usually depends on the willingness of another driver, and thus the frequency of this activity is limited. Activities in which the aged residents interact with other people are much less frequent. There is a significant decline in the extent to which the residents of Hillside Heights participate in community and social activities and club meetings. This fact is most likely due to an inability to attend (e.g., due to the absence of means of transportation) rather than to a lack of desire. Other, even less-frequent, activities such as visiting the library and attending cultural activities basically depend on personal preferences that vary with each individual person. Note, however, that within range of the residents' walking ability are no social activities that might bring the residents into social and interactive relationships with others. To seek such situations requires traveling outside the "home range" and immediate neighborhood. Thus, the quality of life for the residents is impaired by their limited mobility and by the limited social offerings of their immediate neighborhood.

Residents' perception of the immediate neighborhood

Residents were asked a number of questions about their perception of the neighborhood environment and its architectural features. A summary of their responses describes the extent to which residents view their environment positively or problematically.

The residents tend to find the sidewalks in the area problematic: 44 percent feel that they are not sufficiently well illuminated, and 81 percent view them as neither well maintained nor safe. Fifty-five percent of the residents feel that there are not sufficient traffic lights in the area to allow them to cross streets without going too far out of their way. Moreover, 52 percent of the residents feel that the red-light traffic signal does not give them enough time to cross the street; 55 percent of the residents complained about the volume of traffic in the streets; but only 21 percent complained about the noise level on the street.

With respect to a question about their ability to get on and off buses, responses from only forty-five interviewees are available. This represents 77 percent of those who use this mode of transportation. Most (91 percent) of these residents feel that they have little difficulty in boarding and getting off buses. However, the qualitative sections of the interviews produced responses that indicated that many residents do not use public transportation precisely because they find getting on and off buses too difficult.

Of forty-three residents who responded to questions regarding bus signs, 81 percent stated that they have no problem reading signs on buses and knowing which bus is arriving. However, 91 percent of these respondents indicated that they have serious problems stemming from the absence of adequate bus-stop signs on the street and from not knowing where each bus stops or what is the operation time schedule. All of the residents responding to these questions indicated a real need for sheltered bus stops.

Fifty-three percent of the respondents are not satisfied with rain drainage and snow removal in the streets and intersections. Most feel the streets are not well drained. Many (78 percent) feel the streets are

well lit, and 83 percent feel the intersections are sufficiently well lit. A similar 83 percent consider the intersections well marked. However, in the qualitative section of the interviews most residents feel that the intersection markings, although visible to pedestrains, are ignored by drivers most of the time and are not effective in stopping motorists.

There is considerably less satisfaction with "street furniture." Sixty-eight percent of the residents feel there are not sufficient public telephones available on the streets in the area. Even more (84 percent) think that there are not sufficient public alarm systems (police and fire call boxes) in the neighborhood, and 91 percent complained about the lack of public benches and the poor quality of those few available.

Effects on mobility of age, disability, and architectural barriers

A series of questions was asked to determine the residents' extent of activities and satisfactions, as patterned by age, disability, and architectural barriers. These findings are discussed in relation to the effects of age and in particular to the extent to which age and age-related disabilities limit activities. The data analyses for this section of the report are primarily in terms of two statistical tests: Chi-square, which indicates the probable level of statistical significance of the relationship between variables; and Gamma, which is a measure of the strength of association between variables (see Table 7–5).

Note that limitations to an activity resulting from age can be distinguished from those resulting from disability. The analysis of correlation between age and the number of disabilities affecting the residents revealed a very low .10 Gamma. This analysis does not provide information about any relationship that might exist between age and specific disabilities and activities, but it does indicate that age is not necessarily related to an accumulation of disabilities and associated limitations to activity.

A number of strong, significant relationships

TABLE 7-5
Significant Relationships between Age, Disability, and Activities

	Significance Level (P) of Chi Square[a]	Strength of Relationship Gamma	Direction of Activities
Age related to:			
walking	.04	.31	curtailment
driving	.01	.59	curtailment
taking taxis	.02	.58	increase
Heart trouble related to:			
climbing steps	.001	.69	curtailment
reading	.01	.58	curtailment
passive activities[b]	.02	.80	increase
Respiratory problems related to:			
walking	.03	.56	curtailment
climbing steps	.003	.67	curtailment
taking public transportation	.02	.60	curtailment
taking walks for leisure	.02	.57	increase
Crippled limbs related to:			
climbing steps	.0007	.76	curtailment
taking public transportation	.04	.57	curtailment
Poor sight related to:			
walking	.01	.59	curtailment
climbing steps	.003	.63	curtailment
driving	.01	.69	curtailment
taking public transportation	.03	.55	curtailment
reading	.0001	.88	curtailment
getting rides from relatives	.04	.54	increase
community activities	.05	.53	increase
Tiredness related to:			
walking	.004	.79	curtailment
climbing steps	.0009	.73	curtailment
driving	.04	.60	curtailment
Loss of hearing related to:			
driving	.009	.87	curtailment
taking walks for leisure	.04	.55	increase
Nervousness related to:			
reading	.02	.55	curtailment
taking walks for leisure	.006	.63	increase

[a]Significance level (P) becomes stronger as the number decreases.
[b]Passive activities are window shopping, watching people, watching traffic, sitting outdoors, and going to picnics.

were obtained between specific architectural features that create barriers for the aged and particular disabilities. The data gathered on the mobility of residents, particularly on their access to the library and the city hall, document the presence of severe architectural barriers to those who have difficulties in negotiating stairs. Steps to climb are significantly problematic for aged residents suffering from heart trouble (P = .001, γ = .69), hardening of the arteries P = .001, γ = .86), crippled limbs (P = .0007, γ = .76), and poor vision (P = .003, γ = .63).

A relationship was also found between the problem of crossing the street and heart trouble. This problem was due to the shortness of crossing time provided by the timing of the signals (P = .005 γ = .66).

Nonsignificant but strongly suggestive relationships between specific disabilities and architectural barriers were also obtained. For those residents suffering from heart disease, suggestively strong Gamma's (associations) were obtained with respect to difficulty in climbing stairs, walking on sidewalks, crossing streets, using public transportation, and the lack of street furniture. Among residents suffering from respiratory disease, there is an indication of a strong relationship between this disability and problems related to climbing stairs, using sidewalks, using public transportation, crossing streets, and the lack of street furniture. Similar problems are encountered by Hillside Heights residents suffering from high blood pressure, hardening of the arteries, crippled limbs, poor vision, rheumatism, and general tiredness.

The data relating disabilities to problems generated by architectural barriers does not, however, adequately reflect the true nature of the situation. First of all, in many instances the residents have become so well adapted to living with and compensating for their disabilities that they fail to perceive architectural barriers as problematic. A second factor tending to distort the data is the residents' personal pride and their unwillingness to admit that their disabilities limit their activities. Thus, while the interviewers personally observed limitation of activities due to architectural

barriers, the data from the interviews often do not adequately reflect that reality.

Another reason why the data do not fully show the relationships between specific disabilities and environmental barriers is that problematic situations among the aged tend to affect all of them and are not specific to any one segment of the age group. What represents a barrier to elderly people suffering from heart disease is also likely to cause activity curtailment for those suffering from other ailments as well.

Thus, although the collected data reveal only a limited number of relationships between specific ailments and activity curtailment that are statistically significant, a large portion of the sample group are, in fact, limited in their activities. For those aged persons suffering from an accumulation of disabilities, the range of activities is even further curtailed. The data indicate that as the number of disabilities increases within the resident sample, the percentage of residents whose ability to walk is curtailed also increases (P = .005, γ = .64). In this sample, the relationship is most dramatic among persons with four or more ailments. A very similar finding exists in regard to the relationship between the number of disabilities and the ability to climb steps (P = .0005, γ = .68) and to use public transportation (P = .005, γ = .44).

Cognitive Navigation from Residence to Downtown

The Hillside Heights residents who were interviewed were asked to map verbally the path they most commonly selected when going downtown. They were asked to describe, step by step within the limits of their recollection, the physical features they remembered, the events that happened, and the buildings, landmarks, and special places they noticed along this path (Figure 7-1). Sixty-three percent of those interviewed prefer to walk along 17th Street; 20 percent choose 16th Street, and 17 percent do not have a preference between 17th Street and 16th Street.

For those who select 17th Street at all times, the

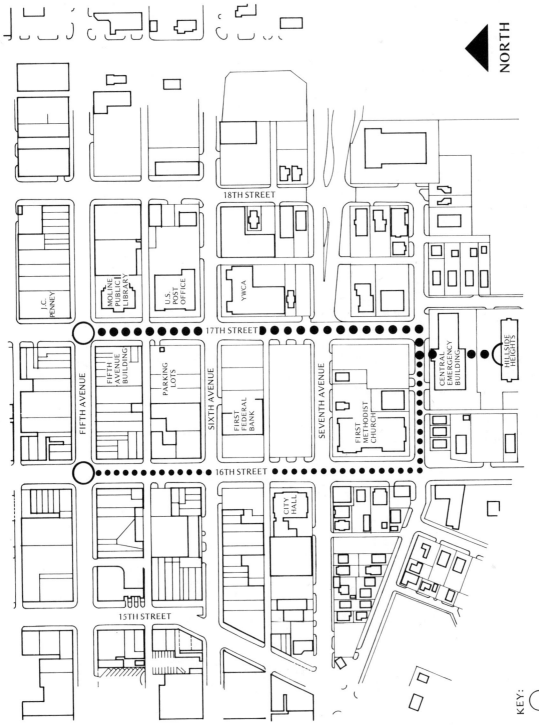

18TH STREET

MOLINE PUBLIC LIBRARY

U.S. POST OFFICE

YWCA

17TH STREET

FIFTH AVENUE

FIFTH AVENUE BUILDING

PARKING LOTS

SIXTH AVENUE

FIRST FEDERAL BANK

SEVENTH AVENUE

FIRST METHODIST CHURCH

CENTRAL EMERGENCY BUILDING

HILLSIDE HEIGHTS

J.C. PENNEY

16TH STREET

CITY HALL

15TH STREET

NORTH

KEY:

⭕ Point of departure and destination

⚫ Path selected by 63%

• Path selected by 20%

Figure 7-1
Cognitive Navigation from Hillside Heights Residence to Downtown Moline.

walk is usually uneventful except at one point: the intersection of 7th Avenue and 17th Street where the pedestrian often encounters great difficulties. Seventh Avenue to the east of this intersection merges with Interstate Highway 74. At rush hours, the accelerated heavy traffic emerging from 1–74 makes the intersection dangerous. Due to the on-going construction of a new 1–74 in the same vicinity and the widening of the adjoining streets to compensate for the traffic volume, the traffic lights and signals have been temporarily removed from the intersection. This situation leaves the pedestrian totally vulnerable while crossing the street. At this point the preferred side for crossing is the west side of 17th Street. This preference could be due to the fact that the street is narrower on the west side than on the east side and requires less time to cross. However, once 7th Avenue is crossed, most of the elderly switch to the east side of 17th Street. There are two significant reasons for this choice. The west side of 17th Street is lined with parking lots almost up to 5th Avenue, but the east side is lined with such significant buildings as the YWCA, the post office, and the library, which thus create a more pleasant sidewalk. In addition, cars emerging at frequent intervals from the parking lots on the west side are obstructive to pedestrians who are thus required to be constantly on guard.

Two other significant places along the preferred path are recollected because of the dependency of the elderly on two particular facilities. The first is the elevator of the emergency building that connects the entrance level of Hillside Heights to the street level on 17th Street. Hillside Heights is situated at the edge of a bluff, and the elevation between the building's ground floor and 17th Street varies a great deal. The entrance of the Hillside Heights building and the roof of the emergency center have a common elevation point. The elevator eliminates descending or climbing a steep hill, and, therefore, serves as a significant element of access affecting the daily lives of the elderly. Without this simple device the world outside would stretch only to the threshold of their residence for most of these people.

The second place is the only point within the "home range" that provides a social gathering place. The YWCA on 17th Street is the most popular eating place for the elderly, in spite of the fourteen steps that must be climbed at the entrance of the building.

Summary of Open-Ended Interviews

The results of the open-ended interviews indicate a number of barriers that do not fall into the category of physical barriers, but nevertheless, strongly affect and add to the physical barriers confronted by the elderly in their daily environment. These barriers affect the elderly in particular, but in some cases they also affect the handicapped in general. The economic, social, and psychological barriers, the attitudinal barriers presented from the outside, and the motivational barriers all relate to the environment. In some cases, they are direct products of experience in the urban environment, and in others they are universal problems of humanity related to the quality of the environment.

In general, the people interviewed seemed to have very strong feelings about themselves and about their environment. These feelings can be placed into two categories: their fears and their desires.

The fears of the elderly include their fears

Of not being accepted in the same circle anymore because of age;

Of being lonely and being left without any friends;

Of having to depend on someone or having to ask someone a favor, such as being driven someplace;

Of falling, especially in winter;

Of unknown conditions outside the home range;

Of overspending;

Of getting mugged or having a purse snatched;

Of being a burden to others;

Of embarrassment in awkward circumstances created by physical barriers;

Of not being able to take care of oneself;

Of losing one's lease and having to go to a nursing home;

Of being taken advantage of;
Of losing the respect of others;

The desires of the elderly include their desires

To be able to drive and take care of oneself now
and in the future;
To have adequate delivery services that do not
charge too much;
To have a park nearby;
To be needed by others;
To have cultural programs, symphonies, and concerts, "big name" bands, and musical shows nearby and to have someplace to go;
To have a variety of restaurants to choose from
when going out to eat;
To have a better and more flexible bus system;
To have more department stores so that there
would be a larger selection of merchandise to
choose from.

PROPOSED COORDINATIVE DESIGN MODELS

Proposed design models were developed to satisfy
the needs identified by an analysis of data and information gathered from the subjects of the case study.
The design models were also developed with reference
to the following resources:

1. Available standards and specifications for the
handicapped;
2. Design proposals already developed for other
cities and urban environments;
3. Products available in the world market.

In addition, design criteria were evolved to make sure
the users' general needs of comfort, required services,
legibility of the physical environment, and safety-security were met.

Problem areas uncovered by the case study that
are remediable through design basically fall into four
groups, and design models were developed to satisfy
these following specific needs:

1. Transitional elements to bridge the scale and
speed gap between pedestrian and vehicular

movements—need to improve legibility of the
environment and protect the user;
2. Sidewalk improvements—need to maximize
comfort and protection of the pedestrian;
3. Improvement of existing transportation systems
and support systems—need for required service
provisions;
4. Access to public buildings—need to provide
comfort as well as accessibility.

Provisions for meeting these needs consist of the
redesign—either partial or complete modification or
structural reorganization—of the following presently
existing components, structures, and systems to
eliminate the obstacles they present to mobility:

1. Street furniture;
2. Traffic signal system;
3. Street lighting;
4. Sidewalks and crosswalks;
5. Mass transportation system;
6. Shelters and seating;
7. Doors and steps in public-use buildings.

The design models to meet the criteria established
and to satisfy the needs identified were developed in
the following stages: New design proposals were
schematically developed for each of the listed problematic components, structures, and systems with the
aid of a photographic inventory of existing conditions
and the listed reference material. The need for design
coordination among these separate parts and for
refinement of the physical dimensions of the proposals led to the construction of a three-dimensional
model. For this model, the actual site, a corner of
the 17th Street and 5th Avenue intersection was
selected. The scale selected for this model is 3/8" =
1', which allows a maximum amount of detail to be
demonstrated on the model.

Evaluation of each part of the model led to the
discovery that some elements could be combined into
one structure, thus eliminating clutter on the streets.
The model also helped in the study of the effect of
solutions, such as action graphics and curb-cuts, on
the total environment.

Design Solutions to Satisfy Identified Needs

*Transitional elements between vehicular
& pedestrian movements*

The scale and speed gap between vehicular and pedestrian movements creates a problem that is most apparent at intersections where they overlap. Streets in general are too wide in proportion to sidewalks. An average street for four-lane traffic is four times as wide as a sidewalk, and it creates a barrier between the two sides of the street for the pedestrian. Measures to help alleviate this problem are described below.

Curb-cut ramping. Curb-cut ramping is essential at intersections. The width of traditional curb rampings is designed to allow use by one person at a time. This design is inconvenient and creates a bottleneck in crowded situations. The recommended plan is that the entire corner be ramped to everyone's advantage and for the convenience of those who have to cross two streets at one time. The ramp can be extended beyond the sidewalk and projected into the street, thus shortening the street crossing distance for the pedestrian (see Figure 7-2). Narrowing the street at this point could also provide a physical barrier to traffic on the street and to force the traffic to slow down.

Crosswalk markings. The standard method of marking pedestrian crosswalks is not strong enough

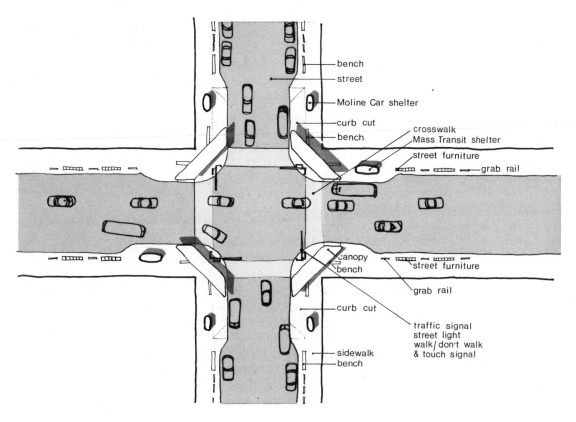

Figure 7-2
Plan of a typical intersection modification.

to provide a visual barrier for the motorist. Brightly colored stripes or patterns (Figure 7-3) serve the purpose better, both as a visual message to the motorist and as a definition of territory for the pedestrian. A well-selected color scheme or pattern can also be an asset to the environment in that it provides a warm and pleasant variation to the black-top of the street pavement.[10]

Intersections: canopies and covers. Most traffic accidents involving pedestrians occur while the pedestrian is crossing the street.[11] One way to prevent or reduce these accidents is to overcue the motorist at those intersections where increased haz-

ards to the pedestrian exist. This study recommends using sidewalk canopies at the corners of intersections (see Figure 7-3). Canopies can function as visual cues to the motorist and can provide weather protection for the pedestrian as well. The fascia of these canopies can be brightly colored or lighted at night to reinforce the message of the traffic signals. Street names can be mounted on the fascia and incorporated into the structure to provide better orientation for motorist and pedestrian.

The height and size of visual information is critical for the motorist. In the case of sidewalk canopies, the height must be carefully selected so as not to

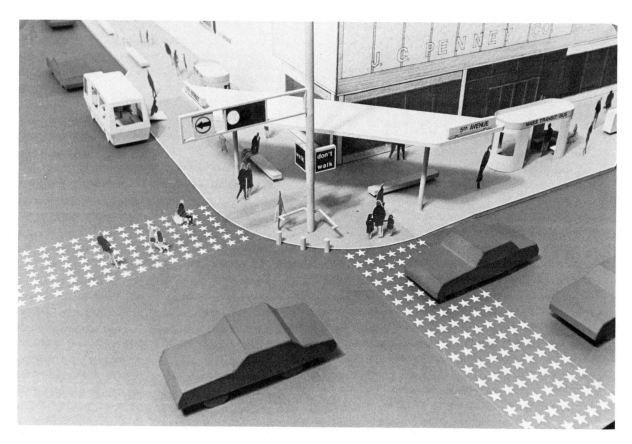

Figure 7-3
Model of proposed street intersection design.

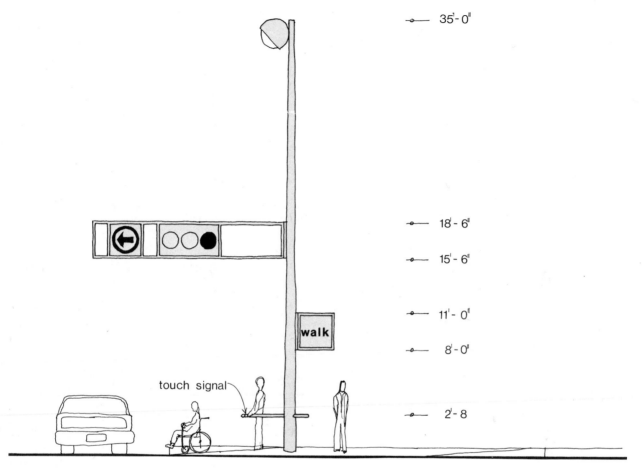

35'- 0"

18'- 6"

15'- 6"

11'- 0"

8'- 0"

walk

touch signal

2'- 8"

Figure 7-4
Coordinated street light, traffic signal, and traffic sign pole.

create confusion with the traffic signal system. The canopy height selected for this case study takes surrounding architectural features into consideration. The eleven-foot height coincides with the second floor line of the existing buildings at this intersection.

Coordinated street light, traffic signal, and traffic sign pole. Centralizing at one place all information relating to pedestrian and vehicular traffic simplifies the visual task of the driver and the pedestrian (Figure 7-4). The street lighting fixture, when incorporated into the same component, further defines the street intersection at night. This plan also eliminates clutter

at the corner of sidewalks, enables simplified operation and maintenance, and is thus an economic advantage to the city.[12]

Other desirable elements of a coordinated traffic pole include horizontal traffic light signals, which are far more legible than those arranged vertically. Horizontal signals, placed in the direct axis of the on-coming pedestrian and vehicular traffic flow would also eliminate "the error of the perpendicular green" that occurs when signal lights for all four streets of an intersection are clustered in the center of the intersection. The pedestrian wanting to cross the street on the green light responds to the light perpendicular to his version. In spite of his intentions to obey the light, he crosses the street on a red light and possibly causes an accident. This visual confusion is especially common among the elderly.[13]

To aid the visually handicapped, a touch signal device on the traffic pole that is proposed would be electronically activated to vibrate when the "Don't Walk" signal is on. This device is attached to the main pole and also serves as a railing.

Sidewalk organization

Sidewalks in general present many problems to the pedestrian. Some of these problems arise from

weather conditions. Others are due to a lack of adequate comfort and safety devices. With physical improvement, sidewalks can actually become places for people to stop, to rest, to congregate, to play chess, to enjoy window shopping. Recommended sidewalk design improvements are discussed below.

Street furniture clustering. The randomly scattered street furniture elements found along sidewalks should be rearranged in linear groups and situated at regular intervals (Figure 7-5). This arrangement allows for a free flow of pedestrian movement. It also creates a buffer between the street and sidewalk to prevent jaywalking. The clusters are easily found because of the consistency of their location on all sidewalks: In case of emergency, a person would know ahead of time where to locate a public tele-

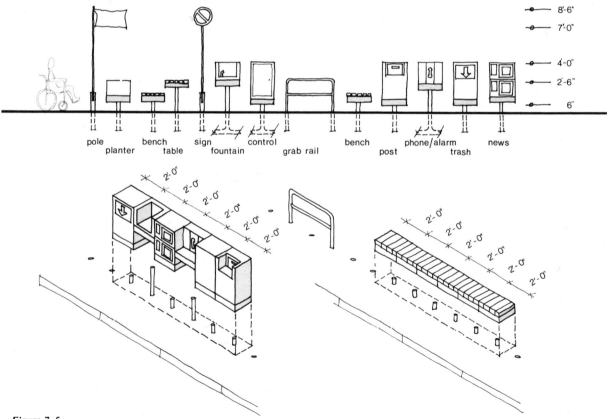

Figure 7-5
Street furniture clustering system.

phone or an emergency alarm. Awareness of these conveniences increases the pedestrian's sense of security.

Another advantage of such furniture clusters is that the standardized four-foot height of the cluster arrangement shields the cars on the street from view without interrupting the visual openness of the street. Special markers can be placed along crowded sidewalks to cue the location of street furniture. Such markers could consist of banners on poles mounted on either side of the cluster. The banner would be seven feet high from the sidewalk for clear visibility.

The system of grouping street furniture is flexible enough to incorporate several elements. Those illustrated in the study proposal are a mail box, trash can, water fountain, telephone, police and fire alarms, traffic control boxes, newspaper vending machines, benches, and a railing. This system has the economic advantage of using some of the conventional street furniture already in use, such as mail boxes, and traffic signal control boxes, which can be adapted to the system.

Canopies and covers on sidewalks and at intersections. A covered pedestrian area on the corners of sidewalks at intersections can provide protection from weather conditions (Figure 7–6). Installations of push-putton, automatically controlled space heaters can provide comfort in extremely cold weather for those who have to wait for signal lights to change before crossing a street. Heat radiation from this device would melt snow and ice on the adjacent ramped surface of the sidewalk. Lighting fixtures installed in the canopy structure would illuminate the sidewalk surfaces at night. Regular placement of these covered structures at every intersection would provide an oasis for those pedestrians who experience difficulties in walking great distances.

Action graphics on blank walls adjacent to sidewalks. One way to liven up the sidewalk environment and to break the monotony of some of the empty sidewalls of buildings is through the use of action graphics. Action graphics can also serve more functional purposes, such as giving specific information about the city. However, action graphics that are too bright and overpowering in color and design not only can distract a person's attention from vital signals and information but can create visual confusion.

The action graphic developed for this study is a map of the "study corridor" illustrated at two different scales (see Figure 7–7). The large-scale map is addressed to the motorist; the small-scale map, the total height of which is only seven feet, provides information for the pedestrian. This map could provide tactile or printed information for the blind by use of an optocon.[14]

Sheltered seating. Sheltered seating areas are es-

Figure 7–6
Model of proposed street corner design.

Figure 7–7
Proposed action graphics.

pecially needed at bus stops. Waiting for a bus in bad weather can be uncomfortable as well as hazardous for those who are physically weak. Shelters can also provide refuge for anyone on the street in the event of one of the abrupt weather changes that often occur in the Midwest.

The different components of the suggested system can be assembled in many ways to provide various types of shelters.[15] They can provide a spacious pavillion in the park or a compact shelter to fit the edge of the sidewalk at a bus stop (Figure 7-8). For the comfort of the handicapped user, certain features should be added to these shelters. A vertical grab bar can be installed to provide a safety gripping device for people of various heights. The inside of the unit should be well lighted at night. A push-button heating device can provide additional comfort. Units that are exclusively used as bus shelters should also include route information on the outside surface of the shelter.

Existing transportation systems and related support systems

Transportation systems are important services that seriously affect the mobility potential of the

Figure 7-8
Proposed sheltered seating.

elderly and the handicapped. Barrier problems related to transportation vehicles are of a highly technical and mechanical nature. Therefore, developing complete and effective solutions for these problems falls beyond the scope of this project. However, some suggestive and informative solutions relating to available equipment are presented below and a number of support systems to increase the efficiency of the present transportation system are proposed.

Mass transportation buses. Loading and discharging passengers, especially handicapped passengers, presents serious problems in the use of buses. Solutions to eliminate these problems have been developed by various bus manufacturing companies. A prototype that is currently being tested is "Transbus," a 40-foot, 45-passenger vehicle. In comparison to conventional buses, it is quieter, faster, easier to board, and less bumpy. It provides for entry by a person in a wheelchair. American General Corporation, GMC Truck and Coach Division, and Rohr Industries have been building and testing prototypes for this bus under a contract supported by an Urban Mass Transportation Administration grant. These buses should become available for public service in 1978 after consumer testing.[16]

Other possible solutions are presented by Twin Coach Highway Products, Inc., which manufactures the mass transit buses currently operating in Moline. The company produces two features designed to increase accessibility that can be installed in their buses at an additional cost. These are (1) a hydraulic wheelchair lift that can be mounted on the rear door of buses and (2) an extendable step, or a flexible first step, that can be lowered to convenient height for elderly and handicapped users. At the time of this study, none of the mass transit buses in use in Moline were equipped with these features.

The opening and closing time of doors can also present a problem for bus users. Automatic doors shut too quickly, and manually operated doors require a great deal of strength to operate. This study recommends that all mass transit vehicle doors be automatically operated. However, if necessary,

Figure 7-9
Entrance to a streetcar in Zürich with push-button devices that allow for manual control of automatic doors.

manually extending the opening time should be possible with a push-button device; for example, a red button mounted on the side of the bus near the door at a height reachable by everyone and visually emphasized by an emblem (see Figure 7-9).

Two major problems related to the interior design of buses are the bottlenecks created at entrances because of the current fare-collection system and the narrow aisles. These problems result in pushing, crowding, and delay. The fare-collection system occupies the driver and prevents him from assisting people who need special help.

To help alleviate the first of these problems, fare collection should occur outside the bus at the sidewalk, either prior to boarding the bus or at the end of the trip. Mechanical fare-collection devices adapted for this purpose are already being used successfully in several European cities. This system allows freedom in boarding buses from both front and rear doors.

Provision for an empty space inside the bus, near either one of the doors, would compensate for the narrow aisles. This space should be wide enough for a wheelchair or a perambulator and still allow free movement of people. A couple of foldable seats provided in this space, and reserved for handicapped persons, would guarantee seating at all times. These

seats could be equipped with grab bars for additional safety and comfort.

Improvement of signs that provide information about bus routes and schedules can encourage the use of mass transportation. Route numbers and schedule information can be mounted on panels at either side as well as in front of buses. The lettering on these panels should be large enough to be read from the sidewalk. For quick identification, the panel can also include a color code of the route. Route and schedule information should also be located at a convenient location on the bus shelter. In this study, a push-button audio device is also suggested to assist the visually handicapped.

Moline car as a support system to mass transit. Because of their size and operational expense, mass transit buses can only operate within fixed routes along important streets and avenues. As a result, pedestrians must often walk great distances in order to have access to main bus routes. The limited range of service routes could be extended by introducing a transportation support system consisting of small, flexible, limited-speed vehicles. These vehicles could operate along flexible routes; they could shrink or extend their field of coverage according to passenger demand, provided that they maintain links with the main line of the mass transportation network at regular intervals.

Because of their size and slow speed, the small vehicles would be able to operate along sidewalks or special lanes such as bicycle routes. There are several vehicles of this type available that can be adapted to this system with minor adjustments. The most familiar example would be the golf cart. The criteria for selecting the vehicle illustrated as "Moline Car" in this study were based upon inherent design considerations for the handicapped passengers.[17] In addition to presently existing features, this car should also be equipped with a hydraulic wheelchair lift to make up the level difference between the sidewalk and the step of the bus (Figure 7-10).

Delivery service cart. Delivery service, an amenity badly needed by the physically weak and the handi-

Figure 7-10
"Moline Car" mass transit vehicle with delivery service cart.

capped, is gradually becoming extinct in urban areas. The system proposed here could revitalize this service without too great an economic burden on the enterprises that have to support it. A light-weight delivery cart, jointly maintained by shops and stores, could be attached to the "Moline Car" at certain times of the day, preferably excluding rush hours, for distribution of deliveries (see Figure 7-10). Several enterprises as well as public services could use the same system: postal delivery, portable library service, and even garbage pick up service could utilize this system.

The cart itself can have a special compartment for small packages and hand-carried parcels. Passengers could check packages in at a bus stop, for instance, and reclaim them at their point of destination from a special kiosk in a manner similar to that used for airline baggage. Freedom from carrying packages can stimulate extended walking or leisure enjoyment of the downtown area on a nice day. The proposed kiosk can be assembled from the same prefabricated components recommended for the bus shelters.

Access to public buildings

Two basic architectural elements, stairways and doors, are usually the cause of inaccessibility of build-

ings. Exterior stairways are a common stylistic feature of certain buildings. The problem of doors, on the other hand, exists in all buildings, regardless of their age and type of construction. Improvements in door and stairway design are presented below.

Stairways. Stairways are the transitional elements between the public and the private domain. The use of stairways in monuments can be found in architectural history dating from the Egyptian pyramids, Asiatic ziggurats, and Grecian temples. However, the use of stairways in these monuments generally was not as a means of entrance; on the contrary, the monolithic quality of the buildings symbolized the unapproachableness of the deities housed in them, and the stairways were used to reinforce this concept. In the ancient Greek temples, for example, the general public worshipped in the forecourt, and only a priviliged few were allowed to enter the sacred precinct of the temple, which was very distinctly marked by the transitional stairway.

Adaptation of the exterior stair as a design feature in twentieth-century buildings has been most commonly used as a means of achieving an historic architectural relationship. Many of the public buildings in the "study corridor" serve as examples of this design concept, as shown by the adaptation of the neoclassic style to their exterior design. These buildings are the public library, the YWCA, the post office and the city hall. All date from the early part of this century, and all have the following common characteristics: The main entrance is reached by a number of generously wide stairs that are set back from the property line; at the top of the stairs and immediately in front of the entrance door is a wide landing; and usually the door opening is about ten to twelve feet wide. At his juncture of stairs, landing, and building entrance the use of mechanical devices to facilitate barrier-free access is recommended. The proposed wheelchair lift selected for this study requires minimal space and is operated by an electric hydraulic mechanism.[18] By utilizing the space in front of the building (the result of the building setback requirement), the lift mechanism can be installed at the side of the stairs without destroying the building's character and without requiring major renovation (see Figure 7-11). Note that the public buildings considered for modification in this study have historic significance and that the changes proposed will not destroy their historic characteristics and features.

Doors. This study recommends that all entrance ways be equipped with automatic doors for maximum safety and comfort. Entrance ways that are subject to heavy traffic flow should be equipped with air-doors.[19] The initial cost of air-doors is high; however, the air-door attracts more people into a building and is economically feasible in heavy traffic areas, such as retail stores, department stores, and supermarkets.

For public buildings with less, but steady traffic, automatic sliding or swinging doors are recommended. The choice of the type of door depends on the space available for operation and installation. The wide stair landings at the entrances of public buildings in the "study corridor" suggests that there is adequate space for automatic doors. In those cases where the landing width does not allow for the installation of doors that swing out, without hitting people, this study recommends that stair platforms be widened by taking advantage of the building setbacks previously mentioned. The study also suggests that existing stairs be reconstructed at the edge of the property line and the landing can then be extended without significantly changing the overall character of the building.

CONCLUSION

This study reveals that some street elements in downtown Moline, Illinois, such as sidewalks, signals, and crosswalks, are inadequate and present problems to people with limited mobility. At times, these problems even create dangerous circumstances and discourage the elderly and the handicapped from utilizing public streets and public facilities. These conditions of the public environment are not unique to Moline; they exist in many towns and urban centers, regardless of their size.

The design models proposed in this study have

been developed from survey and research findings and are responsive to the needs of the identified user group in downtown Moline. This user group consists of elderly residents of the downtown area. As survey findings revealed, they have a wide variety and degree of disabilities as well as combinations of disabilities. Regardless of their physical disabilities, however, they are motivated and active within their limits, and they constantly seek stimulating opportunities to be involved. Design solutions that answer the needs of this particular group can certainly satisfy the requirements of other groups, such as the handicapped, with minor design revisions. The study models demonstrate programmatically how street conditions can be improved, and how the public environment can be made safer and more attractive to the handicapped and the elderly as well as to the able-bodied. These programmatic design models can be developed into prototypes and implemented in Moline, as well as in other cities.

The process of implementing proposed design solutions should take place in several stages and will require the attention and participation of several groups, such as administrative agencies, political bodies, industries, and commercial enterprises.

The first stage of implementation would be to establish a citywide policy to remove all identified physical barriers and to make all public property and public services accessible to and usable by the handicapped. To translate such a policy into action would require the support of such political bodies as the mayor's office and the city council. The proposed design models, on the other hand, also need to be evaluated by the public and supported by the elderly and handicapped citizens. For this evaluation process, a physical model, similar to the one developed and illustrated in this study, could be utilized. This model could be publicly displayed, and public support could be measured by administering a simple survey. Once public support is won, the program could move into design refinement, physical development, and the involvement of manufacturers for prototypes. Some of the components recommended in this study, such as the bus shelter, are already available on the market. Others, such as the coordinated light and signal pole,

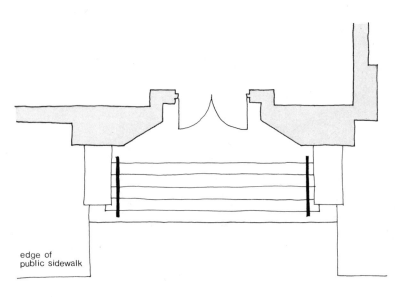

edge of
public sidewalk

EXISTING ENTRANCE

relocating steps next to public
sidewalk provides space for
lift and automatic door
activator mat

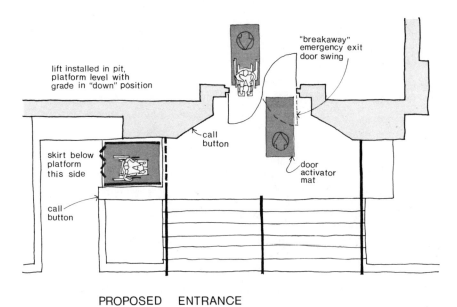

lift installed in pit,
platform level with
grade in "down" position

"breakaway"
emergency exit
door swing

call
button

skirt below
platform
this side

call
button

door
activator
mat

PROPOSED ENTRANCE

Figure 7-11
128   Typical building entrance modification

Figure 7-12
Hydraulic lift manufactured by Trepel U.K. Ltd, New Road,
Sheepness, Kent, England.

need custom-manufactured accessories. This phase should also incorporate field testing of full-scale models or mock-ups by different categories of elderly and handicapped users. The purpose of testing would be to correct anthropometric errors and to eliminate conflicts between the needs of different types of users. For instance, eliminating curb-cuts at all edges of sidewalks, although ideal for a wheelchair user, would be disastrous for the blind user.

Implementation of the recommended design solutions, in some cases, would require coordination between different agencies. In this study, special attention was given to minimizing the need for inter-agency coordination. The street furniture clusterings, for instance, although unified in appearance, allow each component to be installed, operated, and maintained independently. A system that does require coordinated operations, however, might be more economical to the city in the long run, because of its shared maintenance.

Cost estimates of the proposed design models are not included in the scope of this study. However, one can easily determine that the initial cost of the elements proposed in this study would run higher than standardized, widely distributed, conventional street furniture. To reduce cost, every effort should be made to recycle the existing street furniture in as many circumstances as possible. The existing traffic signal lights, for instance, could be revised by reorganizing them horizontally and reinstalling them on a new support frame. New fixtures could replace old fixtures that are ready to be renewed, over a period of time, as part of the regular maintenance program.

The overall cost of this project should be weighed against the benefits of the proposed policy to be adopted by the city. This policy should set forth the criteria to be used in creating a barrier-free public environment and should place importance on making the downtown area accessible to everyone. An action program supported by such a policy can create a physically functional public environment and attract more people to the downtown area. More people mean more life and more activities, which thereby betters the economic potential and benefits both the public and the private sectors.

NOTES AND REFERENCES

The study reported in this chapter was made possible by grants from the National Endowment for the Arts, The Rehabilitation Institute of Chicago, and the University of Illinois, Chicago Campus, College of Architecture and Art. The project's organizational pattern and staff includes the following: *Project Directors*, Henry Betts, Vice President and Medical Director, The Rehabilitation Institute of Chicago; and Bertram Berenson, Dean, College of Design, Architecture and Art, University of Cincinnati; *Project Coordinators*, Gunduz Dagdelen Ast, Architect and Urban Designer, Ast Dagdelen Architects, Chicago, Illinois; *Survey Application and Evaluation*, Yildiz Y. Fidel, Research Psychologist; *Film Documentation and Photography*, Hans Schaal, Professor, University of Illinois, Chicago Campus; Robert Kuntsmann, Photographer, and Balthasar Burkhard, Photographer; *Illustrations and Graphics*, Stephen R. Knutson, Architect.

The section in this chapter describing the summary of survey and interview items is based on "A Summary Report on Urban Activity Questionnaire and Satisfaction Scale for the Elderly," prepared by Yildiz Y. Fidel for this case study, June 1975.

1. *Webster's New World Dictionary*, Second College Edition (New York: The World Publishing Company, 1970), p. 468.
2. Planek, Thomas W., William A. Mann, and Earl L. Weiner, *Aging and Highway Safety—The Elderly in a Mobile Society* (Chapel Hill: The University of North Carolina Highway Safety Research Center, 1973), pp. 54-55.
3. Vash, Carolyn L., "Discrimination by Design: Mobility Barriers," paper presented at Environmental Design Research Association Conference, University of California, Los Angeles, January 1972.
4. "Analysis of Development Potentials, Moline Central Business District—Moline, Illinois," prepared for First Moline Neighborhood Redevelopment Corporation by Larry Smith and Company, Inc., Moline, Ill., 1973, p. Y-2; Loralee Mengel, "Transportation Needs of the Elderly and the Handicapped Citizens of the Quad-Cities: A Report on the Analysis of the 'Senior Citizens Survey' and the 'Transportation Survey for the Mobility Limited'," prepared for the Bi-State Metropolitan Planning Commission, 1974, Chapter 1.
5. Pastalan, Leon A., "The Simulation of Age Related Sensory Losses. A New Approach to the Study of Environmental Barriers," typewritten report, Institute of Gerontology, The University of Michigan, Ann Arbor, 1973.
6. Mengel, "The Transportation Needs of the Elderly," Chapter 5.
7. Gelwick, Louis E., "The Older Person's Relation with the Environment: The Influence of Transportation," E. J. Cantille, J. L. Schmelzer et al. (eds.), *Transportation and Aging, Selected Issues* (Washington, D.C.: U.S. Government Printing Office, 1970).
8. Eribes, R. A., and V. A. Regnier, "Neighborhood Service Delivery: A Cognitive Mapping Approach." paper presented to the American Society of Planning Officials Annual Meeting, Los Angeles 1973.
9. Several survey methods and questionnaires applicable to our study were carefully studied. Out of the available material, three samples were selected to be used as models in developing an Urban Activity Questionnaire for the Elderly. These reference samples are: (1) Martineau, Thomas R., "The Urban Activity Model," paper presented at the Environmental Design Research Association Conference, University of California, Los Angeles, January 1972; (2) Hunter, W. W., and H. Maurice, *Older People Tell Their Story* (Ann Arbor: The Institute for Human Adjustment, Division of Gerontology, University of Michigan, 1953); and (3) Gellman, William, "Changing Career Patterns for the Vocationally Disadvantaged in a Polytechnic Multicultural Model Cities Area," final report, Jewish Vocational Service of Chicago, June 15, 1970–May 13, 1973.
10. The star-patterned crosswalk selected for this study is from a *Report to U.S. Commission of Fine Arts on the Environmental Design of Streets in Washington, D.C.*, prepared by Cambridge Seven Associates, Inc., Cambridge, Mass. and New York, 1966.
11. Planek, T. W., W. A. Mann, and E. L. Weiner, *Aging and Highway Safety—The Elderly in a Mobile Society* (Chapel Hill: The University of North Carolina Highway Safety Research Center, 1973), pp. 54-55.
12. Reference sources for the design and critical dimensions of this component are: *City Sign and Lights: A Policy Study*, prepared for the Boston Redevelopment Authority and the U.S. Department of Housing and Urban Development by Stephen Carr, Asley/Myer/Smith Inc., Architects and Planners, Boston, 1973, and *Operation Street scape: A Demonstration Furnishing the City Street*, conducted for the Department of Urban Development, City of Cincinnati, by Harold Lewis Malt Associates, Inc., Environmental Designers and Planners, Washington, D.C., and Miami, 1973.
13. Planek, Mann, and Weiner. *Aging and Highway Safety—The Elderly in a Mobile Society*, p. 58.

14. An optocon is a portable, battery-powered device, the size of a tape recorder, that enables the blind to read any printed material without the use of braille. A miniature camera moves along a line of print and the optical image is converted to a tactile form that a blind person can read with his fingers. In spite of its currently high market value ($2,985.00 per unit), its wide range of applicability represents a major breakthrough for the blind.

15. The type of shelter selected for this study is designed by Richard Dattner and manufactured by 2001 Inc., New York. Richard Dattner is also the designer of a number of playgrounds for handicapped children, and the author of the book *Design for Play* (Cambridge, Mass.: MIT Press, 1969).

16. Vrchota, Janet, "Take a Bus," *Design and Environment*, no. 21, Spring 1975, pp. 20–23.

17. The reference used for "Moline Car" in this study is the Steyr City Bus manufactured by Steyr-Daimler-Puch AG in Vienna, Austria.

18. The proposed wheelchair lift selected for this study is manufactured by Trepel (U.K.) Ltd. in Great Britain.

19. The automatic door and air-door utilized in this study was selected from Stanley Doors, manufactured by JED Products Company, Elk Grove Village, Ill.

Part III

Social Barriers: Theoretical Perspectives

8

The Normalization Principle, and Some Major Implications to Architectural-Environmental Design

Wolf Wolfensberger

Wolf Wolfensberger was born in Mannheim, Germany, in 1934, and came to the United States at age sixteen. He majored in philosophy at Siena College in Memphis, Tennessee, received a master's degree in clinical psychology at St. Louis University, and earned his doctorate in psychology at George Peabody College for Teachers where he specialized in mental retardation and minored in special education. He was a researcher for seven years at the University of Nebraska, and later a visiting scholar to the National Institute on Mental Retardation in Toronto, Canada. Currently, he is Professor in the Division of Special Education and Rehabilitation at Syracuse University and Director of the Training Institute for Human Service Planning, Leadership, and Change Agentry.

Wolfensberger's involvement with handicapped and devalued groups has been very diverse. He has worked in public institutions for the disordered; held administrative, research, and training positions in institutions for the mentally retarded; been a researcher and planner in mental retardation; and served as a consultant in services for the blind. His current interests and involvements have extended to the problems of transient men and the elderly and have resulted in the founding of a citizen action group entitled ADVOCATE! (Advocates Dedicated to Vigorous Ongoing Change of Attitudes Towards the Elderly!). His publications in the form of books, monographs, articles, and reviews are too numerous to mention here. Among his most well known books are Changing Patterns in Residential Services for the Mentally Retarded, *which he edited with R. Kugel in 1969 for the President's Committee on Mental Retardation, and* The Principle of Normalization in Human Services, *published by the National Institute on Mental Retardation in 1972.*

INTRODUCTION

This chapter deals with those interior and exterior aspects of a human service facility that have social or physical implications to a citizen's skill development, personal growth, self-image, public image, or social integration. It will *not* (or only tangentially) deal with physical design features that constitute access or utilization obstacles to physically handicapped persons because that issue is covered in other chapters.

The theoretical base for this chapter consists of an orientation to the research and theory concerned with the processes by which people value or devalue other people. As explained later, the principle of normalization is merely a systematic formulation of how to maximize the likelihood that people who have been socially defined as deviant (devalued) become socially valued or revalued. We propose that the process of systematic valuation (i.e., normalizing) is practically impossible to accomplish unless we deeply understand how devaluation (i.e., deviancy making) comes about in the first place.

THE SOCIAL DEFINITION OF DEVIANCY

A number of definitions of deviancy exist. Differentiating among these is of utmost importance. The definition on which all of my work, including this chapter, is based has four components that must all be present: A person can be said to be deviant if (a) some characteristic or attribute is (b) judged different by others who (c) consider this characteristic or attribute (or a combination thereof) of importance and who (d) value this differentness negatively. An overt and negatively valued characteristic that is associated with a deviancy is called a *stigma;* for example, the hearing aid of a person who hears poorly, the facial features of an ethnic minority member, and so forth. Table 8–1 shows one possible way of classifying the sources of people's deviancies or stigmata.

We must keep clearly in mind that deviancy is socially "made"; it is not a characteristic of a person but rather of an observer's (or society's) social values. An observed quality only becomes a deviancy when it is viewed as negatively value charged. The same quality that may be negatively valued in one culture may be positively valued in another. Obesity in women is a good example because it is positively valued in some middle eastern cultures, but negatively valued in our own culture.

Handicapped persons are generally perceived as at least somewhat deviant. We need only to consider the history of attitudes toward and the management of the mentally retarded and disordered; the visually, auditory, physically, or speech handicapped; and people who are aged or epileptic. In addition, people whose differentness may not necessarily constitute a disability may be perceived as deviant; for instance, people who are unusually tall; the cosmetically disfigured; members of ethnic, racial, or nonconformist minorities; people who have offended against the law;

TABLE 8–1
Sources of a Person's Deviancy and Stigmata

Deviancy	Stigma
1. Physical Characteristics	
A. Primarily Inherent:	
Physical features	Height
Congenital handicaps	Albinism
Age	Old age
B. Primarily Acquired:	
Physical features	Odd or offensive grooming
Secondary handicaps	Amputation
2. Behavior	
A. Overt:	
Acts	Crime, addictions
Attire	Outdated fashions
Social associations	Counterculture membership
Physical associations	Residence, possessions
B. Covert:	
Beliefs	Atheism, sectarianism
Ideas	Delusions
3. Descent, Nationality, Attribution	Caste

and even those who stand out because of special talents, high intelligence, or virtue.

When a person is perceived as deviant, he is cast into a role that carries with it powerful expectancies. Strangely enough, these expectancies not only take hold of the mind of the perceiver, but of the perceived person as well. The well-established facts that people's behavior tends to be profoundly affected by the role expectations placed upon them and that generally people will play the roles they have been assigned, permit those who define social roles to make self-fulfilling prophecies by predicting that someone cast into a certain role will emit behavior consistent with that role. Unfortunately, role-appropriate behavior will then often be interpreted to be a person's "natural" mode of acting, rather than a relatively plastic mode elicited by environmental events and circumstances. There is profound truth in Shakespeare's statement in *As You Like It:*

All the world's a stage,
And all the men and women merely players.
They have their exits and their entrances;
And one man in his time plays many parts.

[2.7.139–42]

MAJOR SOCIOHISTORICAL ROLE PERCEPTIONS OF DEVIANT PEOPLE AND THEIR ARCHITECTURAL-ENVIRONMENTAL IMPLICATIONS

When we review history and literature, we see that regardless of time or place certain roles are particularly apt to be thrust upon deviant persons. The way in which these roles transcend time, distance, and culture is remarkable. Most of these sociohistorical role perceptions reflect fairly clear-cut prejudices that have little relationship to reality. However, as with many prejudices, the lack of objective verification is not a crucial element in the shaping of a social judgment or social policy. The major roles to be reviewed below include those of the deviant person as subhuman, a menace and object of dread, a diseased organism, an object of ridicule, an object of pity, an object of charity, an eternal child, and a holy innocent. Most of these roles have distinct architectural as well as larger socioenvironmental implications. In fact, the perception that decisionmakers have of a particular group of people will determine (or at least deeply influence) almost all aspects of the decisions they will make in regard to that group, from the largest systemic decisions all the way to the most minute aspects of individual personal interaction with a member of that group. Elsewhere I have attempted to demonstrate how some of the above role perceptions have shaped the entire history of the management of the retarded in United States society since about 1850, including the evolution of the prevailing institution system.[1]

Naturally, the design of human service buildings is merely one expression of how the potential client-users are perceived. Most human services are rendered inside of buildings, and these buildings often affect the way these services are or can be rendered, how these services are perceived by the public, how the public perceives the recipients of these services, and how the recipients perceive themselves. Thus, the design, location, and history of a building interact most intimately with the nature, quality, and direction of any service that may be associated with it.

Within a facility, role performance of client-users is influenced not only by the interpersonal stimuli to which these clients might be exposed on the part of the personnel, the public, and each other, but also by the opportunities and demands of the physical environment. For instance, the environment can very clearly express the expectation that a client-user will act out violently, is not supposed to assume any responsibility for his actions, and so forth. By the same token, the physical environment may impose a demand for controlled and highly socialized behavior that is clearly communicated to the prospective client-user. Thus, the building can usually tell us whether it is appropriate for the mission as stated by a human interpreter.

The Deviant Person as a Subhuman Organism

Historians and sociologists have long recognized that deviant subgroups within a culture may be perceived as not being fully human. To this day, for example, large segments of our population deny full human status to members of certain minority groups. Even ordinary army recruits may be said to need "being broken" or tamed, like wild beasts or horses. But the retarded, severely handicapped, emotionally disordered, and elderly are particularly apt to be unconsciously perceived or even consciously labelled as subhuman, as animal-like, even as "vegetables" or "vegetative." The literature of retardation is richly endowed with allusions to the alleged subhuman nature of retarded people and with labels that suggest subhuman status.

Deutsch has pointed out that the mentally disordered are often apt to be stripped of their human attributes, together with their rights and privileges as human beings.[2] Logically, if we dehumanize a person who once had reason but lost it, then dehumanizing a person who never possessed much reason in the first place, such as a retarded person, is even easier. For instance, a comment in the *Atlantic Monthly* called for "... sacrifice of mentally defective humans, or human vegetables..." to provide organ transplants and "... increase the intellectual betterment of mankind...."[3]

Mowrer has proposed that operant conditioning is so effective with autistic children because it is also effective with animals, and the autistic person "is least removed from the 'animal level.'"[4] In a footnote, he refers to the good results of these procedures with retarded children. Dehumanization of the retarded is so accepted, even in this day and even by workers in the field, that we can witness a public statement by a superintendent of a state institution who referred to some of his retarded residents as "... so-called human beings ... [who are] ... below what we might call an animal level of functioning...."[5]

Some of the implications of the subhuman role perception are: attribution of animal-like qualities or even skills; belittling of the learning capacity; abrogation of a sense of aesthetics; need for extraordinary control, restriction, or supervision; denial of citizenship rights and privileges (which may partially explain why residents in public institutions have been treated since about 1900 in a fashion that today is being ruled illegal or unconstitutional); and abrogation of human emotions, sensibilities, shame, and even sensation and perception.

In regard to the last point, the idea that the mentally afflicted lack sensory acuity—that is, that they are insensitive to heat and cold—was popular into the mid-1800s.[6] This myth resulted in their often being denied heat in their cold institution cells during the winter, and may well have contributed to the image of the mentally disordered or retarded as insensate vegetables. Indeed, even new buildings designed specifically for the disordered at that time did not provide for heating of the residents' cells nor were their windows glazed.[7] Parallels to this interpretation of a devalued group as being insensate nonhumans can be found even in contemporary society. As recently as 1972, the South African government was planning to build high-rise housing for nonwhite laborers, in which these laborers would be "kept" segregated by sex, four persons to a room, without any heating.[8]

Obviously, the atmosphere and design of a building can very clearly express an expectancy that the client-user will behave in a subhuman fashion, no matter how vociferously the staff may deny adherence to dehumanizing attitudes. Such expectancies are implicit in any of virtually hundreds of dehumanizing practices encountered in institutions and enumerated by Vail.[9] Some of the more common expectancies will be listed and briefly elucidated here.

The perception of the deviant person as an animal usually implies an expectation that he or she behaves in a primitive, uncontrolled fashion. Thus, the environment may be designed to be "abuse-resistant," which implies measures such as:

Walls, floors, and so forth made of material that is indestructible;

Unbreakable, shatterproof, or wire-enmeshed glass in windows and partitions;

Installation of the sturdiest, most heavy-duty furniture and equipment;

Screw-heads that can only be fastened but not unfastened;

Minimization of moving parts;

High ceilings and/or light fixtures that are recessed or especially shielded or laminated to minimize damage from thrown objects;

Extensive soundproofing to muffle the (animal?) sounds that client-users are expected to emit (such soundproofing may even be installed in areas designed for clients quite capable of considerable adaptive behavior);

Lack of any soundproofing (which makes the environment unbearably loud for most people);

Television sets protected with wire screens, recessed into protective housings, and/or placed above reach.

Presumed subhuman persons are usually perceived as being potentially assaultive, destructive, and lacking in self-direction and constructive purpose. This attitude necessitates restricting their movements—both to control them more easily and to protect either the humans from the subhumans or one subhuman from another—and characteristically leads to a number of measures:

Locked areas and living units;

Locked areas within locked areas (in the case of children or the physically handicapped, door knobs may be set high and above reach or complicated release mechanisms may be installed, thereby permitting staff to perceive the facility as "open" even though it is de facto locked);

Doors made from heavy material and bedroom doors that can be locked only from the outside and often open outward rather than inward as in most homes or offices;

Barred windows (more sophisticated but equally effective are reinforced window screens—or so-called security screening—that are incredibly strong but not readily as identified by an observer as being extraordinary) and windows so small or subdivided that a person cannot slip through them;

Fences or walls surrounding entire buildings or even an entire facility complex;

Segregation of the sexes (such segregation may assume absurd proportions and more clearly reveal the underlying ideology) when practiced with infants and children or with the aged;

Outdoor activity areas enclosed by either high walls or high, strong fences or by both.

Often, the outdoor areas are quite small (and therefore easier to control) and are not sufficiently large (or equipped) for adequate exercise. Such small areas again permit the staff to engage in conscience-salving self-deception. I once inquired of a nurse whether the seminaked retarded children in her locked living unit were ever dressed and taken outdoors. She assured me that the children were dressed and taken for outdoor walks every day. The woman was not hypocritical; she was only rephrasing reality so that she could live with it. The reality was that these moderately to severely retarded ambulatory children did not leave the building confines for months, perhaps years, at a time. "Dressing" meant putting on more clothes than merely underpants and diapers, and "going for a walk outdoors" meant being turned loose in large groups with minimal supervision in a small outdoor enclave enclosed by high brick walls on two sides and high wire fences on the other two sides.

A typical programmatic, rather than architectural, expression of the subhuman view surrounds the "feeding" of clients. To this day, food and drink may be served in unbreakable tins reminiscent of prison riot films of the 1930s. Knives or forks may be prohibited, which in turn, necessitates the serving of special foods, such as finger foods or soft homogenized pap that can be spooned. The latter situation is particularly apt to be encountered in institutions for the retarded. (In nursing homes, this situation may be due to a child-like perception of the residents).

Since the perceived subhumans are not believed to be capable of making meaningful choices, they are permitted minimal control over their environment. This attitude typically implies the following measures:

Light switches in client areas such as "day rooms," sleeping quarters, toilets, and so forth that are made inaccessible by placing them in such staff-controlled areas as nursing stations or locked cabinets, or by keying (i.e., a key is required to turn a light on or off);

Thermostat controls for water temperature in lavatories, showers, and so forth and removable and portable handles that permit the water flow to be controlled only by caretakers;

Temperature, humidity, and air movement controls that are locked or keyed and radiators that are locked, recessed, or screened;

Rules that forbid residents to carry matches or lighters.

In residences, perception of the deviant person as an animal implies an emphasis on the efficient "keeping" of clients rather than their interaction with caretaker personnel. Consequently, the environment is designed for efficient supervision. For example, caretakers work behind isolating (protective?) partitions that keep out residents and perhaps even their sounds, but permit extensive or complete visual monitoring. (Today, this supervisory measure might even include closed-circuit television.) A stated rationale here may be that the isolation makes for greater efficiency in certain necessary caretaker tasks such as visual supervision, recordkeeping, and administration of medications. Residents sleep in large dormitories with no, or only low, partitions that would restrict vision between the beds. Lights may burn even at night to facilitate supervision. If bedrooms exist, they may lack doors.

A number of other factors minimize chances for interaction with caretaker personnel. For example, supervisory staff may be isolated in a separate building. Living units on a campus may be widely dispersed and removed so that ready interaction between staff and residents is difficult to achieve. In one such widely dispersed residential complex, low staff interaction with residents was partially due to the facts that walking was both time-consuming and often not feasible due to bad weather and driving was inconvenient because of lack of parking space near the residential units.

Even staff meetings and in-service training activities can become an unconscious legitimization of noninteraction with residents. Another example is the emphasis put on the use of drugs (chemical straight jackets?), rather than human interaction, to control and shape behavior. Lastly, the placement of residential centers far from population centers and towns

can, in some cases, be a correlate of a "keeping" or "controlling" desire.

Subhumans are perceived to "live like animals"—that is, to soil themselves and their habitat. This view results in design of an environment that can be cleaned easily, frequently, efficiently, and on a massive scale. These measures include:

Walls and floors made of a material that is virtually impossible to deface (i.e., scratch, soil, stain, and so forth) and that can be hosed down as in a zoo (there may be drains in the floors of living areas);

Beds or bed stalls designed to be picked up and immersed in cleaning solutions in their entirety by means of cranes;

Bathing facilities designed for efficient cleaning of large numbers of clients by small numbers of caretakers (there may be slabs, hoses, and mass showers, rather than installations conducive to self-conducted cleansing or the learning thereof).

Typically, subhumans are not expected to learn or to develop appreciably, or their growth potential is considered so small as to be irrelevant since it will never lead to complete "humanization." In other words, the state of subhumanity is perceived as being essentially permanent or at least to last as long as the person resides in the building. In consequence, the environment may be designed to maintain a client's level of functioning at best, but not necessarily to provide opportunities for further growth and development.

If animals have no rights, it follows that deviant persons perceived to lack humanness are also perceived to lack certain rights. Among these are the rights to privacy, property, communication, and individuality.

The right to privacy. Bedrooms often lack doors—not to mention that in some cases the bedrooms themselves may be lacking. Where doors exist, they almost always have window panes or so-called Judas-windows (complete with wire-enmeshed glass or peepholes). Private visiting space may be nonexistent.

Toilets and showers may lack partitions, curtains, or doors. There may be physical continuity between space for living, elimination, and bathing. I have seen modern, intensive-treatment buildings for the disordered in which the showers were openly (and visibly) accessible from the day room, and I have visited new institutional buildings for the retarded that had huge "picture windows" between the day room and the toilet.

The right to property. Residents may have few or no possessions. Often they have little or no space to store possessions, or they lack ready access to and control over such space. Residents may be denied the privilege of locking up their possessions, carrying the key, and using it without restrictions. They may be denied personalized clothing, and residents of the same size (sometimes of various sizes) may share the same supply of clothes. All of these points have implications for architectural design, especially regarding space allocations and selection of built-in furniture. Residents may not be entitled to receive payment for their work or to carry actual currency even if they do own money: "Poverty in a mental hospital is no less dehumanizing than in a slum. . . ."[10]

The right to communicate freely. There may be censorship of in-coming and out-going mail, although some forms of censorship may not be perceived as constituting censorship. Telephone usage may be severely restricted. Visiting is often restricted for several weeks after admission.

The right to individuality. As described so well by Vail,[11] clients are regimented and managed in groups, even where individual management might be feasible. For example, residents are mass-showered even where individual showering is feasible; residents may even be mass-toileted, which accounts for the fact that some living units for the retarded have many more toilet seats than would be needed for, say, an equivalent-sized college dormitory.

Many of the above features, plus additional ones, may be derived from or reinforced by the belief that subhuman clients should be kept under close and convenient surveillance. This view can also be found as part of the "menace–dread" and "disease" (medical) models described below and can result in "panoptic" designs,[12] where the staff can view vast parts of the environments from a single location. Such designs have accounted for institutions that are built like wheels (with the staff at the hub) and for the open-faced, multi-tiered cell rows in prisons.

The assumption that deviant people lack aesthetic sensibilities is a subtle but important corollary of the subhuman view. This corollary results in the creation of unattractive environments because the funds spent on beauty are seen as wasted. The drab, monotonous design and the furnishings of many human management residences (sometimes in contrast to staff living quarters) are usually a testimony to this view. Rarely do we see furniture that is both comfortable and attractive of line and color in institutions for the disordered and retarded, and even yet more rarely do we find culturally typical (at least middle-class) zoning of living space so that the furniture reflects the mood and function of different living areas in an attractive fashion. The degree to which a deviant client can appreciate beauty is really only one of two important issues involved here. The second important issue is that observers' (e.g., the public's or employees') attitudes are shaped by the context in which deviant people are presented to them. For example, to deprive a deviant person's environment of beauty is likely to predispose an observer to view him as subhuman.

Caretakers sometimes claim that drabness is due to lack of funds, but this argument is often untrue because much beauty can be provided at little or no cost. In my own institutional work, I recall trying to mount attractive pictures on walls of several retarded children's living units that had a severely deprived atmosphere. There was no support for this project from the institutional power echelons; nursing and housekeeping services objected to the "defacing" of the walls; and the pictures that actually got put up were pulled down (by personnel) within days. Quite possibly, the human managers' compulsion to preserve drab environments is motivated by their malignant need to maintain a difference between themselves and those they perceive to be so different they are no longer human.

A 1964 set of specifications written by the staff of an institution contained the following instructions to an architect regarding the design of a new residence building for adults and young adults:

All interior wall surfaces shall be of a smooth material, and without wall projections other than those specifically stated. All thermostats should be protected with a guard to avoid tampering. Window areas shall be kept consistent with patient needs. Excessive window areas are not desirable. Consideration should be given to using shatterproof glass in patient areas. Door louvers in patient areas should be made of a steel material to withstand patient abuse. Mechanical and electrical equipment and controls throughout the building shall either be tamperproof or located outside the patient areas. Maximum water temperatures for bath and lavatories must be automatically controlled to eliminate the possibility of scalding. Switches in large patient areas shall be located on the outside of the rooms. A cubicle measuring 24″ x 12″ x 12″ should be provided for each patient.

While such instructions are not conclusive evidence that the instructors (staff) held a "subhuman" view of the prospective residents, such instructions certainly appear to be consistent with such a view. Today, people of the type for whom this environment was designed live in small home-like community hostels (group homes). These generally provide a lower middle-class atmosphere and not one that is too much different from the homes of most readers of these lines.

The Deviant Person as a Menace and Object of Dread

Unknown events or objects, if alien enough, tend to arouse negative feelings in both human and beast. Mankind's history is filled not only with incidents of persecution of fellow humans of different features, skin pigmentation, size, shape, language, custom,

dress, and so forth, but with evidence that people have been very apt to see evil in deviance. Therefore, it is not surprising that one role perception prominent in history is that of the deviant person as a menace—that is, a person is perceived as being a menace individually, because of alleged propensities toward various crimes against persons and property, or as a social menace because of alleged contribution to social disorganization and genetic decline. This role perception has been a very prominent one during the so-called genetic scare or alarmist period (c. 1890–1925) when most of society's problems were attributed to inherited defects.

A building environment based upon the menace perception has much in common with the subhuman model. Certain features—such as segregation from the community as well as segregation of the sexes—are likely to be accentuated. Since the menace model may ascribe a certain willfulness and evil intent to deviant people (in marked contrast to the disease (medical) model), an element of vindictiveness and persecution may enter into their management, and some of the protective features inherent even in the subhuman model may be omitted.

The Deviant Person as a Diseased Organism

A historically prominent role perception is that of the deviant person as being sick—that is as an incumbent of what sociologists refer to as the "sick role." Much of what has been said and written about the medical model generally implies the perception of a deviant person as a "sick" "patient" who, after "diagnosis," is "prescribed" "treatment" or "therapy" for his "disease" in a "clinic" or "hospital" by "doctors" who have primary administrative and human management responsibility and who are assisted by a hierarchy of "paramedical" personnel and "therapists"—all of which hopefully leads to a "cure" rather then "chronicity." Conditions that have been widely subsumed under such a model include homosexuality, mental disorder, mental retardation, stuttering, alcoholism, drug addictions, aging, and even reading problems and sex education.

When a deviant person is thus seen as sick, then education, work, and recreation can come to be interpreted as educational, industrial, and recreational therapy; those who "administer" such therapy (perhaps in "doses" rather than lessons, and so forth) may be called therapists; finally, a pessimistic preoccupation with the issue of curability versus incurability often exists because of the perceived "chronicity" of a condition.

Perceived as sick, the deviant person may be seen as entitled to the privileges and subjected to the demands generally characteristic of the sick role that have been proposed by Parsons[13] and Parsons and Fox[14] and partially verified empirically by Gordon.[15] The privileges include exemption from normal social responsibilities and recognition that the condition is not the person's fault; the demands are that the person must want to get well or at least better and must seek suitable and appropriate remedy for his or her condition.

Note that the "disease" model can be expressed in two variants: One of these embodies the best tradition of medical service to fellow humans, and the other one is concerned with health but not with human values. The latter model can be likened to veterinary medicine and is particularly apt to be encountered in residential institutions.

When clients are viewed as diseased organisms, their service facilities are structured on the (medical) hospital or clinic model and tend to have similar characteristics. For example, the facility is administered by a medical hierarchy: The chief administrative officer (e.g., the superintendent) is a physician, a hierarchy of other physicians is under him, and a hierarchy of nurses is under them. Preoccupation with medical power and prerogatives tends to result in a tightly controlled perpendicular administrative structure rather than a flexible subunitized one.

The facility is identified or even labelled, at least in part, as a clinic or hospital. Thus, a public institution for the disordered is often called a hospital (e.g.,

"state hospital"), and a common name for public institutions for the retarded has been "hospital and school." The living units are referred to as nursing units or wards, and the residents are referred to as patients, while their conditions are identified as "diseases" that require "diagnoses" and "prognoses." Resident care is referred to as nursing care, and case records are referred to as charts.

Hospital routines prevail. For example, residential admission procedures may require days or weeks of "observation" and residence in an "infirmary" or similar unit prior to "diagnosis" and to assignment to regular living quarters. Daily routines may resemble hospital routines in regard to rising, body inspections, sick call, charting, and so forth. Indeed, the daily schedule may revolve around medication schedules. Dispensing of medication, in turn, may become the model for intake of all nourishment and for other "treatments" as well.

Such other treatments, even if "administered" in the form of education, may be referred to as "dosages." Usually there is at least moderate emphasis upon convenience of "nursing care." Physicians, whether qualified or not, make decisions about nonmedical matters; for example, clients' rights and privileges, visits, work assignments, discipline, schooling or training, and participation in various programs. Even if these decisions are made by nonmedical personnel because of temporary or permanent lack of physician manpower, this situation is often perceived as delegation of medical authority, and as such is interpreted as undesirable and transient.

Departments with the greatest affinity to medicine are given priority in program development. For example, dentistry, orthopedics, and physical therapy may receive stronger support than behavior shaping, education, and so forth. Physical and medical techniques are more likely to be used in managing the behavior of clients than other techniques. Thus, disturbed clients are more likely to be physically restricted or settled with drugs than to be counselled or trained; persons with seizures may be placed on anticonvulsant medication with little thought given to environmental manipulation of seizure-precipitating events or to educating the person to develop preventive behavior habits.

Concern with professional symbols and status differentiation, often encountered in a hospital atmosphere, may be expressed by features such as presence of hierarchical staff lounges, showers, and private toilets. There may be separate vending machines (and areas) for staff and "patients." Staff and client-users may eat in separate areas, which thus requires separate dining and sometimes even cooking facilities. Caretaker personnel may wear uniforms. Even professional and semiprofessional personnel may wear uniforms, coats of different colors, badges, name plates with academic degrees listed, and similar insignia of their role and rank.

Architecturally, a prominent place is given to the space (locus) from which human management is "dispensed." Often a "nursing station" is given a central and perhaps large space. This space, which is often so designed as to afford maximal surveillance of the client area with minimal engagement therewith, reflects the assumption that "nursing manpower" is very limited and that "nursing personnel" must perform many functions (e.g., charting) that require seclusion from the "patient." This seclusion may be perceived necessary either because of the confidentiality of the activity to be performed or because of the tranquil setting it requires. Status concerns may also have a bearing on the design (spaciousness, sumptuousness, or exclusivity) of the human management locus, while the space where drugs are stored may take on the importance of a shrine.

Nonmedical personnel may emulate the medical role—that is, social workers and psychologists may wear white coats or jackets, and prestigious professionals may be referred to as "doctor" even if they do not possess a doctorate degree.

The human management programs are referred to as "treatments" or "therapy." For example, recreation and work assignments may become recreational and industrial therapy, and even ordinary schooling may become educational therapy.

There exists an excessive abhorrence of any chance or likelihood of injury to the client. On the one hand, this concern is exemplified by lack of stairs and steps, sharp objects and corners, conventional electrical outlets, and access to conventional hot water faucets. On the other hand, it is exemplified by the presence of special features such as ramps, screening of radiators, and screened stairways.

A disease conceptualization of deviancy tends to result in a management dilemma. On the one hand, such a conceptualization often results in pursuit of treatment that is hoped to result in cure; on the other hand, unless a "cure" is seen as likely, the management atmosphere is often permeated with hopelessness and treatment nihilism. In other words, the disease conceptualization tends to be correlated with inappropriate extremes of management attitudes, and it seems to be one reason why the quality of service for people with conditions that have been defined as "chronic" is often very poor in those residential facilities that operate on a medical model.

The Deviant Person as an Object of Ridicule

The role perception of the deviant person as an object of ridicule is similar to one defined by Vail as "man as trivium"[16]—that is, as unimportant or not to be taken seriously. Thus, for many years, the Negro was virtually always depicted by the mass media, particularly the movies, in the role of a servant, a comic figure (the eye-rolling superstitious porter), or at best a light entertainer. Similarly, the retarded have frequently been cast into the movie roles of village idiots, and in folk humor they are almost without exception depicted as objects of ridicule. A relatively recent manifestation of this role perception is the so-called moron joke rage of a few years ago, and a classical scene of the retarded person as an object of ridicule was contained in the award-winning film *Charly*, based on Keyes' book *Flowers for Algernon*.[17]

In medieval society, the retarded and deformed achieved some distinction as court fools or court jesters who would dress in garish costumes and engage in comic and silly antics for the merriment of the high-born. Thus, Horsfield relates that "the court of Philip IV of Spain, 1621–65, was crowded with a horde of zanies, jugglers, tumblers, clowns, buffoons, jesters, an incomparable assortment of dwarfs, in fact almost every sort of person that might be included in fooldom. . . . These individuals, most of whom were probably mentally deficient folk, many with marked physical defects, were gathered from the highways and byways of the kingdom and brought to the palace, primarily for the amusement of royalty."[18]

The role of the object of ridicule generally does not have architectural implications today. But there have been exceptions throughout history. Montezuma, the last of the Aztec kings, kept an extensive zoo in Mexico City that made considerable impression upon the Spanish chroniclers who accompanied the conquistador Cortes. It is noteworthy that in the same building in which the beasts were kept and displayed, he also "kept" men and women who were crippled, deformed, dwarfed, hunch-backed, and albinos. At times (apparently especially at meal time), some of these persons played the role of jesters by amusing Montezuma and his court who might feed them leftovers from the table.[19]

Similarly, at the Royal Bethlehem Hospital in London, popularly known as "Bedlam," the curious public in the 1700s would pay their coins to be able to stare and laugh at the writhing and screaming of the chained inmates.[20]

Up to so late a date as 1770, this famous hospital was still regarded as the raree show of the city, superior even, in the attractions it offered the pleasure-seeker, to a bull baiting or a dog fight. No more diverting entertainment could be devised by the average citizen for guests visiting him from the country than to take them, for a hearty laugh, to Bedlam, to see the madmen cursing, raving, and fighting. There was to be had on show St. Paul or Julius Caesar chained to the wall, or Semiramis or Joan of Arch ironed to the floor, while the general throng, left more at liberty, were guarded by brutal keepers, ready on the slightest provocation to knock them senseless with heavy clubs. The annual fees derived from this public entertainment amounted to several hundred pounds. No one seems to have felt any pity for the poor wretches. The abyss which opened up between them and ordinary humanity was too deep and wide for any sympathetic imagination to span. A madhouse was a menagerie, nothing more; and it was as legitimate to look through the bars at one class of wild beasts as at another.[21]

The famous 1735 painting by Hogarth, *The Rake's Progress,* shows snickering ladies "enjoying" the antics of Bedlam's popes, kings, mad scientists, and other unfortunate inmates.

Today, one of the most common environmental expressions of afflicted persons as objects of ridicule is found in the totally unconscious (a) use of labels based on ridiculous names of animals, fruits, vegetables, or other objects (e.g., the lemons, the giraffes, the jay birds, the turtles); (b) the juxtaposition of service buildings near zoos, burlesque shows, and similar entertainment spots; and (c) the incredibly common decoration of environments (especially for disordered and retarded people and for legal offenders) with hobo, clown, and circus motifs. In one recent tour of services with associates of mine, we found such motifs in half of the twelve services toured—without any awareness by the personnel that these motifs constituted a systematic pattern of interpretation encountered so widely across human services.

The Deviant Person as an Object of Pity

Frequently, a deviant person is viewed as one who is handicapped because of a misfortune for which he or she bears no responsibility and who therefore should receive special attention, services, and so forth. The deviant person may even be seen as "suffering" from a condition, even though such an interpretation may be highly subjective and even inaccurate. While efforts may be made to relieve this alleged suffering, the person may also be seen as possibly unaware of the condition causing the deviance. Much as in the sick role perception, pitied persons are likely to be held blameless for their condition and perhaps unaccountable for their behavior. They are very apt to be viewed with a "there but for the grace of God go I" attitude.

This "pity image" will tend to be expressed in a paternalistic environment that shelters the client against injury and risk by having few environmental dangers such as stairs, sharp edges, hot water, hot heaters, and electric outlets, as discussed previously. While the pity model has some features in common with the disease and subhuman models, there are important differentiating features. The benevolent version of the pity model strives to bestow "happiness" upon the person, often by emphasizing recreational programs, religious nurture, and activity for its own sake. This emphasis, in turn, is likely to result in allocation of generous space and facilities for music, arts, crafts, parties, picnics, and worship (e.g., a chapel on the grounds or in the building).

The Deviant Person as a Burden of Charity

The pity perception is usually benevolent up to a point, at least temporarily, and it is accompanied by compassion and acceptance, although it may be devoid of respect for the deviant person. However, a variant of the pity perception is one that is upheld more by a sense of duty than compassion. Persons possessing a strongly moralistic conscience, but not much genuine humanism, are particularly apt to perceive deviant persons as objects of sour charity. This attitude can be likened to the one widely held in the Victorian age toward orphans and epitomized by the Victorian response to Oliver Twist's request for "more." While the affected person was usually (but not necessarily) viewed as innocent, his parents often were not. Thus, the advent of a handicapped child was sometimes interpreted as a punishment for parental sins, and occasionally the handicap was even attributed to a sin committed by the handicapped person himself prior to the presumed onset of his impaired condition.

For instance, colonial New Englanders often looked upon handicaps as the consequences of a stern providence meting out judgment for wickedness.

According to Suraci, such a view is quite common today in the Puerto Rican subculture in New York City.[22] Where such a view prevails, the family members of a malformed or impaired person are likely to feel shame, and outsiders are more apt to be contemptuous rather than sympathetic toward them and the handicapped person. Any charity extended with such views can be expected to be cold, and the person receiving such aid might be labelled rather aptly as a "burden of charity." Thus, the sour humanist may look upon a deviant recipient of services as a "kept" object of charity, and while such charity clients may be seen as entitled to basic assistance and sustenance, they are not seen as entitled to anything interpretable as luxuries, frills, or extras.

As Coll has pointed out, the Puritan Ethic had a strong influence in the formulation of the "less eligibility" doctrine in the history of welfare services and charitable agencies.[23] The doctrine states that no matter what the need of a person supported by public funds may be, assistance to him must be below the level of the lowest prevailing wage.

A service based on the charity model will be austere and will lack privacy, individuality, and opportunities to have personal possessions. Clients are expected to be grateful and to work as much as possible for their "keep." An example of a Victorian "burden of charity" view is found in the following quotation taken from the Massachusetts report at the 1890 National Conference on Charities and Correction.

As to the State schools, it recognizes the value only of such teaching, mental or manual, as shall develop the boy or girl and tend toward an honest and respectable life outside the institution. It disapproves of extravagant or luxurious appointments in institutions, as foreign to the spirit of true charity. The inevitable weakening of character by life in institutions, the arrest of development, must be prevented, if possible, by some hardships and privations, such as these boys and girls would be sure to encounter in their own homes or those to which they would be sent.[24]

Again much of the physical environment implied by this model will be similar to that of the subhuman model; however, there are certain differentiating architectural and program implications. In a residence built on the charity model, there will be less emphasis upon segregation from the rest of society. There will be a grim and unimaginative emphasis upon eventual self-sufficiency, and while there will be little stress upon environmental enrichment as a means of fostering development, education and training in traditional occupational skills may be strongly valued, especially training that can be accomplished in a brief period of time.

The Deviant Person as an Eternal Child

A very strong role perception of some deviant people is that of persons who are, and perhaps always will be, much younger than their age. For instance, the book *The Child Who Never Grew*[25] by Pearl Buck and a Canadian film entitled *Eternal Children* render such a depiction of the retarded person. An article by Fendell entitled "Israel's Eternal Children"[26] is another example.

While the mentally retarded are the most common candidates for the child role, other groups are also at risk. These include people who are seen as being "simple minded," such as some mentally disordered persons. Also, elderly people may especially be said to be "in their second childhood." They may once more be referred to as "boys" and "girls" and may be addressed in high-pitched melodic voices—the same as some people adopt when they want to speak affectionately to children.

One implication of the child role to environmental design is that those who hold this role perception generally do not place strong or even reasonable developmental and adaptational demands upon the persons so perceived. Instead of expecting persons to adapt to the environment, those who see them as children would adapt the environment to them. Also, adults are frequently placed into environments more suitable for children, and in fact adults may be housed *with* or closely adjacent to children and sub-

jected to the same general management. A very common phenomenon is the decoration of the environment with children's pictures and themes—even in nursing homes for the aged.

The Deviant Person as a Holy Innocent

In a number of cultures and eras, deviant people (particularly the mentally afflicted) have been accorded a religious role interpretation as the special children of God, as saints, or as holy or eternal innocents. Those incompetent to perform everyday tasks might be perceived as having religious thoughts on their minds or as being endowed with saintly powers. Another belief may be that such persons have been sent by God for some special purpose. Perceived in a religious light, the afflicted are usually seen as incapable of consciously or voluntarily committing evil, and consequently they may be considered to be living saints. Religious role perceptions of some kind were reportedly prevalent among the Eskimos, North American Indians, and Arabs, as well as in Russia, Central Asia, and medieval Europe. Since this role is elaborated elsewhere,[27] suffice it here to say that this perception tends to express itself in the physical environment in two major ways.

One of these expressions is retention of the afflicted person as a valuable member in his natural surroundings, home, and community. A contemporary example is the Hutterite communities in the United States and Canada that have been studied by Eaton and Weil.[28] In these communities, not one mentally handicapped person has been institutionalized on a long-term basis; instead, they are accepted, perhaps sheltered, and integrated into the community life.

Secondly, while the holy innocent perception has generally inhibited the development of residential placement, it has not prevented it altogether. What residential placement has been achieved in this view tends to be of a very special kind. It might involve placement of persons in a child-like role in godly homes, as menial workers in religious communities such as monasteries, or as workers in nursing homes or hospitals run by religious orders. One variant of this historical practice still exists in the Belgian town of Geel where, since the Middle Ages, thousands of the mentally handicapped have been boarded in an atmosphere of sheltered benevolence in ordinary homes, and they have the liberty of the city. The presence of a religious shrine to St. Dymphna—long (but no longer officially) believed to be the patron saint of the mentally afflicted—gave rise to this practice.

Where the afflicted person is placed in an environment especially oriented toward a holy innocent perception, expectations are usually modest, and offensive behavior is relatively forgivingly accepted. The environment may be relentlessly interpretive of religious themes (chapels, statuary, pictures, symbols, decorations, religious quotations, and so forth). However, a holy innocent environment is *not* to be interpreted as identical to a religious one. A religious approach can be fused to virtually any of the role perceptions discussed above and below, and such a fusion can be particularly powerful when it involves the developmental-normalizing model.

The Deviant Person as a Human Being, Citizen, and Developing Organism

Since some of the above role perceptions are valid for only some of the people, and usually for only some of the time, the most common basis of environmental design should be normalization—that is, a perception of the client-users as (a) human beings, (b) citizens possessing legal-constitutional identity and rights, and (c) organisms that are capable of adapting as long as they live—indeed, as a sign that they are alive. To my knowledge, anyone who will not be dead in a matter of days is capable of emitting at least some kinds of adaptation responses. Because of the enormity of the normalization concept, the developmental model and rationale is discussed separately in the remainder of this chapter.

THE PRINCIPLE OF NORMALIZATION

Elsewhere readers will find much more systematic statements of the Normalization principle;[29] here we will define the principle as "the utilization of culturally valued means in order to establish and/or maintain personal behaviors, experiences, and characteristics that are culturally normative or valued." The normalizing features of the physical-architectural environment discussed here are drawn especially from the third edition of *Program Analysis of Service Systems.*[30] PASS 3 is a normalization-based evaluation instrument devised to assess a wide variety of human services in a quantitative fashion.

The normalization principle calls for the use, as much as possible, of human service methods that are culturally understood *and* valued, so that these techniques, processes, and hardware do not stigmatize the client more than is necessary. Furthermore, the normalization principle implies that persons be enabled to take full advantage of their culture, to have access to the same privileges and amenities as other citizens, to play valued roles, and to lead valued lives. In regard to severely handicapped persons especially, it calls for the aggressive use of the highest technical competence, equipment, and processes. In regard to service facilities, it implies value- and competency-enhancing structures, appearances, locations, designs, and appurtenances. A summary overview of the action implications of the normalization principle is provided in Table 8–2.

A normalization perception usually reveals that even the best-intentioned service environment for devalued people reflects at least some of the larger cultural devaluations—often in a deeply unconscious fashion. How many people are aware of the statistically unexpectedly common location of service facilities (especially for the mentally handicapped) on elevations (hills, mountains, and more recently, the top floors of high-rise medical facilities)? How many know that this commonly found phenomenon is derived (a) from medieval etiological concepts that saw insanity as the successor of

TABLE 8-2

A schema of the Expression of the Normalization Principle
on Three Levels of Two Dimensions of Action

Levels of Action	Dimensions of Action	
	Interaction	*Interpretation*
1. Person	Eliciting, shaping, and maintaining socially valued skills and habits in persons by means of direct physical and social interaction with them	Presenting, managing, addressing, labelling, and interpreting individual persons in a manner emphasizing their similarities to rather than differences from others
2. Primary and intermediate social systems	Eliciting, shaping, and maintaining socially valued skills and habits in persons by working indirectly through their primary and intermediate social systems, such as family, classroom, school, work setting, service agency, and neighborhood	Shaping, presenting, and interpreting intermediate social systems surrounding a person, or consisting of target persons, so that these systems as well as the persons in them are perceived in a valued fashion
3. Societal systems	Eliciting, shaping, and maintaining socially valued behavior in persons by appropriate shaping of large societal social systems, and structures such as entire school systems, laws, and government	Shaping cultural values, attitudes, and stereotypes so as to elicit maximal feasible cultural differences.

leprosy and (b) from ancient (miasmic) theories that mental disorders are transmitted by vapors, mists, winds, and low-lying swamp-like conditions?[31] How many are aware that a disproportionate number of service facility names imply location on an elevation (Hilltop, Elmcrest, Highpoint, and so on and so forth) *even where no such elevation exists in fact?* How many people are aware of the very strong tendency to juxtapose (co-locate) different services to devalued people and of the equally relentless physical juxtaposition of such services to devalued sites (cemeteries, garbage dumps, railroad tracks) and symbols

(dead-end and one-way streets, deviancy-suggestive facility names or agency logos, and so forth)?

The normalization principle is not simple, as some people suppose; it has a vast number of subtle and unexpected corollaries, many of which are (almost universally) violated in current services. These include avoidance of congregating more devalued people together than the surrounding social systems can absorb; the separation of domiciliary (residential) from other life functions; avoidance of funding from deviancy-imaged sources; selection of staff that possess a positive societal image; and conscious and systematic uses of images, symbols, and language that have positive (though often also unconscious) long-term impact on social stereotypes and attitudes. This latter corollary also includes a tough orientation to the personal appearance of handicapped people and the appearance of the settings they are found in—in terms of age-appropriate and otherwise culture-appropriate norms. In order to have large-scale and long-term impact upon public attitude improvement, these appearances need to be not merely minimally stigmatizing, but should even be on the positive ("conservative") side of social valuation.

Both the exterior as well as interior environment of a facility strongly affects behavior by setting physical limits, by imposing environmental demands that influence a person's growth and development, and by expressing underlying assumptions about the utilizers' characteristics and abilities. These assumptions are translated into powerful role perceptions and role expectations that will substantially determine how utilizers are treated by others and, ultimately, the way they actually act and see themselves.

Although all aspects of the environment operate strategically in all of the above ways, some elements are likely to affect a person's development and growth more immediately. For the purposes of this discussion, we have labelled these aspects "concrete and programmatic functions" of the environment. Other aspects that are more likely to influence the way in which a person is perceived by others, we have called "symbolic or interpretational functions." As a framework for this chapter we have rather arbitrarily chosen the format shown in Figure 8–1 as an analytical tool.

The reader should keep in mind throughout the discussion that follows that the "concrete–programmatic" and the "symbolic–interpretational" functions of the environment are *conceptually* distinguishable, even though in practice they often overlap. Similarly, the environmental aspects within the four cells are

| | | Functions of the Facility Environment for Clients | |
		Concrete and Programmatic	Symbolic and Interpretational
Dimensions of the Facility Environment	External	Location and Program Related Design Elements: —Location and access —Size	Social Role and Image-Affecting Features: —Building perception —Program facility and location names —Age-appropriate facilities, design, and decor
	Internal	Program-related Internal Designs: —Comfort —Internal design —Overprotective features —Intensity equipment and technology —Innovativeness	Social Role and Image-Affecting Appointments and Design Features: —Culture-appropriate internal appointments —Environmental beauty —Individualization —Influences on interactions and status equality

Figure 8–1
Normalization-related dimensions and aspects of the facility environment.

conceptually separable and distinct, although empirically they tend to be positively and moderately intercorrelated.[32]

Finally, from a purely clinical perspective, the *internal* environment is the one that is more critical to a person's learning success. The internal design and physical features of a building have much to do with both the shaping of skills and habits as well as the development of normative independence. In contrast, the *external* environment is especially influential and important in terms of the interpretations and images communicated by the facility to the public at large.

We should note in regard to residential settings specifically, that on a temporary basis people may live in large hotels, dormitories, and so forth, on a long-term basis the overwhelming majority live in apartments and family homes. Thus, as a common cultural medium, facilities might follow two general rules as guides to the client congregation issue: (1) Services to handicapped persons should not be much larger than analogous services to citizens in general—that is, special schools, classes, and vocational and residential settings should conform to the general size patterns typically found in a given region; and (2) people who are devalued by a majority of the culture should not be congregated in larger numbers than the surrounding social systems can absorb.

INTERNAL VS. EXTERNAL ENVIRONMENTAL FEATURES

The External Environment

Concrete–programmatic aspects

The major issues here are (1) the effects of facility location and accessibility and (2) the effects of facility size.

Location and access. The location of a service facility can greatly affect the type of "world" and people with whom clients will have contact. This aspect of physically integrating the client via facility location is important in our urban-oriented culture. The historical pattern of locating services to mentally handicapped persons in rural and remote sites is part of a real (largely unconscious) system of segregation that has pervaded the service scene.[33] Location can also have multiplicative effects—such as the creation of disjointed service areas, the difficulty of attracting qualified personnel, and transportation and accessibility difficulties—that are often naively overlooked by planners.

The abyss created by physical distance from population concentrations decreases the ability of clients to reach the service setting for day programs, and in residential programs, it can contribute to a sense of isolation from friends, relatives, and familiar surroundings. Even with speedy and convenient transportation systems, the ability to attend socially integrative public services and events is seriously hampered.

Additionally, service facilities located in a "geographic vacuum" constrict the availability of resources through which people are socially integrated. Recreational services in certain locations are sparse or nonexistent. The range and availability of factories, stores, restaurants, libraries, or churches can seriously affect the development of social interaction skills.

Size. The physical size of a facility has both programmatic and symbolic functions that create important consequences. Large facility size is highly correlated with large congregations, either of persons with the same deviancy condition or with different deviancies (persons with physical handicaps juxtaposed with mentally retarded persons; youth with drug problems served in the same setting as illiterate adults; and so forth). In addition to differing program needs, age-related needs often vary greatly in such facilities, and thus the needs of certain groups can "get lost" due to the predominance of staff concern with one particular age group. Thus, in mental health settings, the needs of children have been typically subordinated to the needs of adults, while the opposite can be said for mental retardation settings.

As client numbers and facility size increase, there is a strong tendency to become inward-oriented in meeting client needs, and the dynamics toward deindividualizing treatment becomes almost irresistible.[34] This inward-centered tendency of settings is often compounded when large client numbers occur at locations of poor resource availability. Thus, the clients' needs to participate in societal functions are denied for administrative-management expediency. Particularly in residential settings, small size almost forces dependence on generic services and thus allows clients to experience greater variety.

Another extremely important consideration of building size that has programmatic implications is the ability of the surrounding social system to absorb a deviant group into its resources. Thus, a sheltered workshop serving 120, or even fewer, handicapped clients may completely inundate the restaurants located in that neighborhood during lunch hours. Also, large facilities (i.e., large client congregations) typically create obstacles to social integration by increasing citizen resistance. Thus, the neighborhood that might accept six mentally handicapped persons living in a nearby group residence may strongly object to ten, twelve, or twenty residents in the same facility or within close proximity. Thus, client congregation can become a *functional* obstacle because it first was an *image obstacle*.

Symbolic–interpretational aspects

Both the exterior "building perception" of a facility, including its name, and the interior design and appointments can speak a powerful interpretational language about the people who use the facility.

Exterior building perception. As we pass by buildings and architectural forms commonly found in our culture, we can often predict or envision the type of activity that would be "expected" to take place in such a facility; we can even map a mental picture of

what we could expect to encounter in such buildings, including the people and their appearances. For example, as we pass by a bank, bar, factory, or school, certain preformed notions of the processes we commonly and typically expect in such settings come to mind.

In human services to handicapped persons, we have often violated common cultural norms, thereby creating unnecessary "differentness" and accentuating the often temporary or remediable conditions of clients—even when the internal environment is perfectly suitable and appropriate to client needs. Service planners, constructors, and designers need to be conscious of this frequently overlooked external aspect of a facility and be concerned with three key issues: (a) the appropriateness of the external appearance of a building relative to its function; (b) the appropriateness of the building relative to its neighborhood; and (c) the relationship of building size to neighborhood "image."

The relationship between function and the building (which we have called "function congruity image") can be succinctly stated as follows: Does the building look like what it is supposed to be (i.e., what goes on inside)? If the setting serves as a school, its external features should look like a school. "Special schools" located in church facilities, office buildings, former bars, or in hospitals often violate this criterion and serve either to draw unusual attention to their clients or to project odd images upon them. Iron bars, grates, and other forbidding appendages should be purged from most facilities. Community residential facilities should be perceived as typical homes in neighborhoods and communities. Whatever the level of functioning of clients, workshops for them should be located in buildings that are perceived as work-related facilities. Of utmost importance is a need to orient clients, staff, and public to the normatively expected separation of one's place of work, residence, recreation, congregational worship, and so forth.

The relationship between building and neighborhood (which we have called "building–neighborhood harmony") may be framed as follows: Does the building fit harmoniously in its neighborhood? We often find settings that serve for training or rehabilitation in grossly atypical and incongruous locations, thus increasing the image of "specialized," different, and usually outright "deviancy programming." For example, sheltered workshops are often positioned in residential rather than commercially or industrially zoned areas. Other examples of neighborhood–building and/or neighborhood–program incongruity (which we have called "program–neighborhood harmony") include the guidance and counseling clinic located above the factory warehouse; the dilapidated group home in the upper-middle-class neighborhood; the "halfway house" located on the grounds of the large mental hospital; the newly constructed mental health clinic located next to the garbage dump. These incongruities signal the facility and its clients as grossly different.

An important fact to recognize is that facility size —quite apart from the number of clients congregated there—can be an image obstacle. A nursing home designed for one hundred people can be an integrative obstacle even if only eight clients live in it.

In addition, there is a need for service managers to beautify the exterior of a setting through up-keep of the grounds, furnishings, and seasonal decorations, so as to be consistent with the slightly idealized community norm. This issue of harmony with neighborhood norms is particularly important in residential settings, where neighborhood hostility can be devastating.

Program, facility, and location names. Facility names, titles, and labels are particularly powerful image carriers. They can often be traced to outmoded and erroneous theories, beliefs, and practices, some of which date as far back as the Middle Ages and even beyond.[35] The following small sample of facility names illustrates the unconsciousness with which facility names proclaim loud deviancy messages:

Apartness Image:
  Outwood
  Wildwood
  Rolling Acres

  Echo Hills
  The Retreat
  Charity Refuge
  Fairyland Forest Day Care Center
  Camelot
Dependence Image:
  Carefree Lodge
  Good Samaritan Village
  Rest Haven
  Camp Lend-A-Hand
  HELP School
Hopelessness Image:
  SOS Workshop
  St. Jude Deliverance Center
  Sunset Lodge
  Last Chance House
  Homeward Bound
  Park Lawn Personal Care Home
Presence of Deviancy and Other Imagery:
  Sumerset Low-Level Workshop
  Alberta Rehabilitation Council for the Disabled Group Home Pilot Project for Physically Handicapped Young Adults
  Maiden Lane Residential Home for Wayward Girls
  Salvation Army Workshop
  Redemption Acres Farm
Deviancy Sound-Alike Associations:
  Looney Day Care Center (for the retarded)
  Battey State Hospital
  Madden (Mental Health) Zone Center
  Bahr Treatment Center (for alcoholism)
  Keeling Personal Care Home (for the aged)
  D. H. Bury Nursing Home
  Toomey-Abbot Towers (for elderly and severely physically handicapped)

The list of (often unconscious) deviancy–image-transmitting service names is endless. This author has a collection of thousands of them from all areas of service to devalued people.

Age-appropriate facilities, design and decor. Another important issue is the age expectancy people "read" from the environment. In most instances, the question is whether the environment—both interior and exterior—suggests that its utilizers are younger than they are—that is, more childish, if they are actually adults. The co-location of a sheltered workshop and child development center in the same setting is a common finding that usually conveys age devaluation. Other child-associated elements (playgrounds, decorations, equipment, and so forth) in adult- or elderly-oriented settings can create or strengthen the perception of clients as less adult or less capable than they actually are. Similarly, in work training centers, signs, decorations, and work products (toy soldiers, craft work) may lower already low expectancies for adult production. Also, some such symbols or products draw attention to the "mental" aspect of the condition. One example is weaving, which is much more commonly found in "mental" and institutional settings than it is in normative societal settings.

Facilities for persons perceived or "diagnosed" as devalued should consciously encourage and promote structures, imagery, and symbolism that surround clients with value, growth expectations, and the firm belief that their condition or disorder will improve. Age-reducing environmental design and decor typically reflect paternalism, condescension, and low expectations.

The Internal Environment

Concrete-programmatic aspects

Features of the internal environment that are to be discussed in this section are: (1) comfort, (2) internal design, (3) overprotective features, and (4) program intensity—equipment and technology.

Comfort. An obvious way in which the internal environment affects client development (and even image) is in its attention to normative comfort requirements. Physical safety and comfort are normative prerequisites for many typical behaviors. Depending on the facility type and the amount of time spent there, the client's experience in terms of temperature, humidity, noise, odors, lighting, furniture, carpeting, food, and clothing will strongly affect personal achievement and adjustment. Adequate space, and separation of spaces for different functions, are also comfort requirements. These are especially important in residences where a client is likely to spend a great deal of time each day.

The comfort issue also illustrates quite clearly the distinction between, but also the correlation between, "concrete-programmatic" and "symbolic–interpretive" elements. Lack of attention to physical comfort reinforces an old and damaging perception of the mentally handicapped person as being impaired in sensory acuity and therefore indifferent to physical discomfort. On the other hand, a similar environmental issue—the presence or absence of aesthetically pleasing decor—has only modest functional implications since its major impact is interpretive.

Other internal design aspects. To the extent that the internal design of the facility is culturally normative and consistent with its function, clients will have the opportunity to learn to enjoy the freedoms, and to respect the limitations, of typical environments—and therefore of reality.

The importance of culturally typical internal design is frequently ignored for financial or political reasons, or it is simply overlooked through lack of awareness of the issues. Numerous instances can be found of factories and warehouses becoming schools, clinics, and even residences; schools becoming factories; and churches and hospitals being converted into schools, residences, and workshops. The exterior aspects of such "function incongruity" typically create interpretive problems (as seen in a previous section). Internally, the effects can be both interpretational *and* functional. A section of a hospital, church, or school that has been converted into a workshop is less likely to have loading areas, convenient storage space, or other features of typical industrial design. Lunch, rest breaks, and recreational activities may have to be conducted on the work floor, rather than in separate, designated areas, thus confusing the work–recreation distinction. Churches or hospitals converted into secondary schools are not likely to have student hall lockers, dismissal bells, and so forth. In each case, clients have reduced opportunities to learn the skills, habits, and attitudes that are commonly experienced by normative citizens.

As mentioned before, in many residential facilities, culturally typical internal design has been sacrificed in order to facilitate supervision of clients. Such an environment may be characterized by large living, dining, sleeping, and bathroom areas that afford little, if any, privacy and/or tend to create a noisy or otherwise offensive environment.

Building materials and construction features may also be culturally inappropriate. In many facilities, the environment is designed to be abuse resistant and/or able to be cleaned easily, frequently, efficiently, and on a mass scale. Walls and floors are made of indestructible materials that are impossible to deface and easy to clean—even by hosing. Drains may be installed in the floors to facilitate this process. Unbreakable, shatterproof, or wire-enmeshed glass is used in windows and partitions. Ceilings are high, and light fixtures are recessed or specially shielded. In such an environment, when there is little need or demand for controlled, responsible, behavior, it is unlikely that positive individual growth will occur—or will even be expected by the staff.

Overprotective features. An overprotective feature might be defined as (1) one that reduces physical hazards below a level that might exist under comparable cultural circumstances in the community and does so without compelling rationale; and (2) a reduction of risk even beyond what is needed on the basis of a realistic consideration of the impairments of the clients. Since the risk-taking aspects of ordinary life are necessary for normative human adaptation, a person should be permitted to confront the maximum amount of *normative* risk with which he or she can cope with reasonable probability of success.

The implications of this idea are numerous and sometimes subtle. As much as possible, clients should be able to interact with their environment. Rather than be restricted by the physical facility, potentially objectionable behavior should be modified by social interactions with staff. In spite of the importance of client awareness of the external environment (i.e., daily, monthly, and yearly rhythms), facilities have been built without windows or with windows that are small, inoperable, out of reach, and barred or screened.

Within the limits of prudence and cultural norms, clients should be exposed to the normative risk of injury. Generally, clients cannot be taught to act safely in an environment without stairs and steps, sharp objects and corners, conventional electric outlets, exposed radiators, playgrounds, pools and baths, tools and machinery, and so forth. Thus, a commendable effort to reduce barriers to physically handicapped people may unintentionally also diminish the challenge to other clients to grow and adapt. This dilemma can be resolved or reduced by building in redundancies (ramps *and* stairs, more than one type of faucet, and so forth).

Equipment and technology for service intensity. An environment that is designed to promote development of functioning (and sometimes even for its maintenance) is likely to include a wide variety of media adaptation. Equipment and technology ranges from simple objects of daily life with which ordinary citizens are expected to cope (e.g., window blinds and shades, can openers, vending machines) to sophisticated and recent innovations. In looking for evidence of the intensity of environmental equipment, we should keep two points in mind: (1) Availability of equipment does not necessarily insure effective use (for example, prosthetic devices may be displayed or stored in a locked cabinet, distributed in inappropriate areas, or available but not actively employed); and (2) the presence of special equipment and technologies does not automatically reflect appropriateness. Ingenious modification of equipment and systematization of operations may open up many tasks to severely impaired persons. For more capable persons, however, such modifications may unnecessarily limit further growth and development.

Symbolic–interpretational aspects

The following sections are devoted to discussion of four aspects of the *internal* architectural environment that have a primarily *interpretational*, symbolic, or "image-transfer" (and secondarily programmatic) importance: (1) culture-appropriate internal appointments, (2) environmental beauty, (3) environmental aspects of individualization, and (4) environmental influences on interpersonal interaction. These involve or even become symbol systems through which client social identities are created, sustained, and transmitted. A later section will present some empirical findings from a recent study of the adequacy of human service environments on the internal–external and concrete–interpretational dimensions sketched in this chapter. The four image-related aspects of the internal environment discussed in this section are conceptually distinquishable, even though in practice, they tend to be significantly correlated.

Culture-appropriate internal appointments. The essential issue is whether, within the intended function of the service, the appointments (furnishings, decorations, and general interior decor) of a facility are culturally appropriate in addition to being age appropriate. Harmony of "fit" between the internal appointments of the facility and its function enhances the role image and status of clients; incongruity detracts from both. For example, the vocational center furnished as a typical industrial mini-environment (e.g., time clock punch-in and work stations) and painted in normative coloration and design will portray the handicapped person as a worker or trainee. The small group home for adults amply furnished with chairs, sofas, floor lamps, carpeting, plants, and framed pictures will convey a sense of warmth and respect, as well as a set of expectations for responsible behavior by the residents whose home it is. The same setting communicates a very different mood and message if it features a uniform and somber color scheme, industrial blinds rather than curtains in the bedrooms, worn-out and/or heavy-duty furnishings, and "Exit" signs above the front and rear doors.

Incongruence between internal appointments and facility function are common in many residential, vocational, educational, and developmental settings. However, they occur most frequently and most blatantly in residential (and particularly institutional) settings. Without exception, such violations appear to derive from (and to maintain) one or more of the stereotyped deviant role perceptions commonly imposed upon the handicapped person: the person as a menace; as subhuman; as an object of pity, charity, or ridicule; as a child; as a sick organism, and so forth. Even well-intentioned clinical measures may project devastating interpretations. For example, unlike in a normative residence, the hallways and passages of a nursing home or institution may be labelled "Streets," "Avenues," "Squares," and so forth, perhaps even in a pity or child-imaging fashion (e.g., Rainbow Street, Moon Square, Water Avenue).

The acid test of the appropriateness of a service facility's internal decor and appointments (and of the adequacy of most other environmental features) is a simple, powerful, and yet typically violated one: Would *most* valued members of society (or even a significant minority) gladly use the facility for long periods of time for the purpose for which it was intended? If the service is of a long-term residential nature, we can ask: Would the architect, human service worker, or member of the public be pleased to live in the housing imposed upon the handicapped person?

In the long run, only through the adoption of developmentally oriented role perceptions and normalizing service ideologies, with concomitant reform of building and fire codes and regulations, will present environmental deficiencies be overcome.

Environmental beauty. Attention to aesthetics often portrays man as a sensitive and even spiritual being, and thus environmental beauty is a powerful expression of how program managers perceive clients and interpret them to the public. The fact that contemporary service facilities appear to be almost normatively unattractive and drab subtly but clearly points to the continuing influence of the historically pervasive role perceptions of the deviant person as subhuman or object of charity. Funds spent on beauty are seen as clinically irrelevant and wasted. Given the immense financial resources poured into the construction (now above $200,000 per client in some institutional settings) and upkeep of service facilities, the argument that a lack of beautification stems from a lack of funds must be challenged. Visually pleasing lighting and decor, furnishings of tasteful lines and color, and culturally normative zoning of living spaces are matters of ideological, more than monetary, commitment. Much beautification can be achieved at little or no cost.

Individualization. Individualization is here defined as (1) differentiation of a person from other persons and (2) self-expressivity in one's uniqueness.[36] The normalizing influence of the architectural environment on individualization (and on individualizing perceptions of clients) can be enhanced by providing individual life spaces and privacy (e.g., private or semiprivate bedrooms), by encouraging clients to decorate their rooms or work settings in a personal way, and by promoting the possibility of clients' purchasing or bringing their own furnishings to suit their individual needs and taste. Particularly in residential settings, lack of sensitivity to client individuality is manifested in the use of built-in furniture, in dormitory-like sleeping quarters, in doorless toilets and bathrooms, in prohibitions against attaching personal memorabilia or pictures to one's life spaces. (The formulations of privacy into solitude, intimacy, anonymity, and reserve as expressed in the work of Westin[37] and by various writers in the text by Proshansky, Ittleson and Rivlin[38] are especially recommended.) In counseling or interviewing offices, deindividualization may be manifested by partitions that do not extend up to the ceiling or that fail to contain sound.

Influences on interactions and status equality. Subtly, architectural environment both influences and symbolizes the process of status equality (or conversely, status differentiation) between staff and clients. Physical features such as the following have both an interpretational and an interactional distancing significance: separate staff lounges for meals, coffee, smoking, rest, and so forth; separate toilets for clients and staff; conveniences such as air conditioning for staff, but not for clients; special parking conveniences for staff; and so forth. This issue and some of its implications are so critical, especially in residential settings, as to be examined separately under the next heading.

A fundamental issue for residential facilities: life sharing

A large proportion of those who live in special service settings are deeply wounded people who have been frequently and prolongedly rejected, often abandoned by their families, and sometimes even abandoned professionally. Prisoners, street people, many elderly, and so forth are among this group. Often, there exists a wide culture and class gap between them and their professional staff—as is common in the mental health field. Finally, the helping relationship often has an aura (whether justified or not is irrelevant) of being "unreal." At the very time that broken people need to feel they are worthwhile and that there is something lovable and acceptable in them, they may get placed into an environment that is segregated (perhaps even isolated) and into juxtaposition with *other residents who are rejected and devalued.* Just about the only people who will work with them are those who come in on short shifts for a few hours a week (typically, 40 hours out of 168) and who are paid to do so.

Ultimately, professional and technical skills are totally inadequate in serving other human beings; that these skills be coupled with humanism, charity, or good intentions is not even sufficient. Beyond these, viewing the people served as peers and being prepared to adopt service forms and lifestyles that result in significant life sharing with them is absolutely essential. The superficially weak members of society may in fact be no weaker and no different from anybody else. We all have profound weaknesses and immoralities, and it is only proper that human services not be conceptualized and structured as a one-way street in which the handicapped are always the recipients. The fact is that the apparently nonhandicapped may receive just as much service as the other way around.

The "boughten" relationship can perhaps be just as genuine as the one freely given. But somewhere along the line, the wounded person must have the "world building"[39] and world testing to prove the reality of the relationship. He must have someone who accepts him and sees something worthwhile in him and loves him without the doubt that the help is being given because the helper is paid to do so or because doing so is his or her profession. No, the helper must be seen as caring and giving because there is something in the devalued person that brings forth acceptance or at least a genuine perception of great value. The person must be made to feel: "By golly, it's within me; I'm worthwhile."

World testing is largely mediated by generous life sharing. One major method with deep design implications is to break down the difference between staff and client. One way to do this is by their sharing space and activities: meals, toilets, recreation and fun, shopping, worshipping, joy, and domiciliation—that is, by living together. Living together does not merely mean that some people like the superintendent live on the same grounds as the clients, but live *together with* wounded people, in one's own home or building or in theirs.

Breaking down the barrier between staff and client—server and served—also implies that staff give up status symbols such as uniforms, badges, special parking privileges, private toilets, different forms of address, and so forth. Obviously, all of the above have extensive design implications. For instance, life sharing is very unlikely to occur if environments are so located and internally designed and appointed so as to repel ordinary people who might be willing to engage in life sharing or so as to make them unhappy, disordered, uncomfortable, depressed, and so forth if they were to reside there.

Finally, life sharing can be facilitated by lionizing (rather than consciously or unconsciously depreciating and trivializing, or status degrading and subverting) the clinical involvement of unpaid volunteers. Most people will claim that volunteers are great, but in reality, they are often assigned trivial activities. Their contributions are devalued, poked fun at, often discouraged, and all sorts of systemic obstacles are put in their way. And yet, in settings in which we deal with psychically wounded people, the volunteer could be the single most important medium of carrying in the culture and of carrying on constructive relationships, and they could be more important than the most highly trained professional whose relationship is perceived as "bought." The trivialization of volunteers is, of course, often unconscious because cultural norms superficially demand lip service to volunteerism.

At one time, the idea of handicapped and nonhandicapped individuals fully sharing their lives and residing together in a communal, rather than we-staff/they-clients atmosphere, would have struck many people as unreal, utopian, or at least rare. Today, such settings are becoming increasingly more common, especially in community residences for retarded people. The Camphill movement has a tradition of voluntary (largely unpaid) and even life-long life sharing. The newer l'Arche movement has the same tradition. In twelve short years since 1964, it has mushroomed into worldwide prominence, with establishments in numerous countries and almost all continents, united by a common ideology, bonds of deep love, and a sense of community.[40]

Voluntary, and especially unpaid, life sharing proves to devalued people that they are worthwhile and that not just other "crazy" people who are not right in the head can live with somebody who is crazy himself. Yet, that is what we are saying by the very nature of our residential service. For instance, the psychiatric residential model is based almost entirely on the assumption that when a person has something wrong in his psyche that requires residential service, then he must live with someone else who also has something wrong and anyone who does not have something wrong would or could possibly live with him. What a terrible thing to say about a wounded person.

We pervert and we medicalize the human condition. We artificialize and medicalize human suffering, and then we professionalize both it and the most basic, culturally normative states and activities. In fact, we sometimes become liars; and, sometimes, when we offer a substandard, prison-like, ugly, regimented, dehumanized, nonprivate, and humiliating living environment and call it "milieu therapy," we even become criminals. This fact has been brought out in lawsuits such as the recent *Donaldson* case.[41]

Where do we build residential treatment environments? We build them in such a fashion and in such places that our prophecies come true: Nobody in his right mind would choose to live there. Would *you* go there and say: Okay, I'm going to set up house for six months, a year, five years, for life? You would not—and you could not—because many of the environments are unlivable. I have been in modern, expensive treatment environments for children that were absolutely unlivable for *any* human being, and I am not talking about those facilities that were dictated by politics, but those dictated by professionals when they had the authority and funds. Such places demonstrate how far our devaluation goes, and how terribly unconscious it is.

The "Conservatism Corollary" of the Normalization Principle

Some readers may have noted that several of the practices we have mentioned as sources of deviancy making may be encountered in the lives of ordinary citizens without our imaging them as devalued. This idea brings us to one of the most subtle and least-accepted corollaries of the normalization principle: Valued people can afford exposure to processes and juxtapositions that do not devalue them, or that may even enhance them, while the same processes or juxtapositions may denormalize an already deviant person or one who is at risk. For example, the mayor's home may be enhanced by being adjacent to the park-like peace of a cemetery, but a nursing home so located would merely reinforce the image of its elderly residents as already dead or dying. Boy Scouts can collect garbage and be lionized for it; retarded people or prisoners will merely be further imaged as being trash, worthless, and discardable. In most high-rises, the top floor is the most valued one; but in almost all veterans' hospitals, and many general hospitals, the top floor (being most segregated) contains the psychiatric unit. There is nothing wrong with selling brooms and brushes—unless a blind person does, since this activity has been traditionally and stereotypically forced upon and associated with blind people.

Consequently, the "conservatism corollary" of the normalization principle states that if a person or group is *already* devalued, or at risk, processes and juxtapositions should not merely be statistically normative ones, but should even go further by being supranormative in the sense of actually adding extra value projection to the person or group. For example, a classroom for handicapped children might be located in the most desirable space of a school; the staff working with devalued people should be even more valued and "glamorous" than equivalent staff serving the general public; the interior of a residence for devalued people should be even a bit more attractive and clean than average homes; a sheltered workshop might be in a valued building in an industrial park instead of a condemned building in a slum.

THE DIFFICULT ISSUE OF THE MASSIVE UNCONSCIOUSNESS OF SOCIETAL DEVALUATION

The General Issue of Unconscious Symbolic Expression of Devaluation

Devaluation of a human being is so contrary to the other ideals and values that a perceiver may hold as to prohibit the conscious recognition and labelling of the devaluation. Therefore, it is important to be aware that while many persons hold devaluing perceptions, they cannot admit these perceptions to their own awareness, because the implied interpretation of a human being would clash with other, concurrently held perceptions and values. Thus, we commonly encounter persons who devalue or even dehumanize a certain group without being conscious of the meaning of their overt behavior and the reality of their attitudes. Only by understanding this process of repression of an unacceptable impulse can we also understand certain valuing behavior, or why most people are remarkably unaware that their behaviors and attitudes are devaluing of at least some group of people and may be perceived to be so by others.

Vail has probed this problem with considerable sophistication.[42] For instance, how can we explain why people who, by all ordinary criteria, can be described as model citizens suddenly become cold-blooded killers of millions. This phenomenon can only be understood if we understand the reality and process of the dehumanization of devalued persons. The explanation is that if an organism is perceived as being not fully human, then it does not matter whether this organism is destroyed, dislocated, disowned, or otherwise used at the convenience of those perceived to be human. Animals are thus used all the time.

The remarkable fact is that persons who are relatively moral in every other sphere of their lives are capable of imposing nonhuman role perceptions upon certain groups and are then very readily capable of treating such groups no better than animals. Only this reality can explain how otherwise moral and loving people can be unfeeling and dehumanizing human managers in certain spheres of their functioning. For example, it explains a phenomenon such as why the senior personnel of an institution with about seventy-five years of collective experience in work with retarded children design a new building for severely handicapped children that has toilets that are too large and too high to be usable by such children and has soap dishes and towel racks attached so high on the wall as to be unreachable by the children. Had the designers been charged with planning a building for human children, they would have anticipated such problems, but because they perceived nonhuman entities, the designers were unable to muster the empathy necessary to anticipate this problem even with generations of experience behind them.

Only by fully understanding the dynamics and the accompanying unconsciousness of dehumanization will we be able to fully perceive and relate to the symbolic ways in which dehumanization often manifests itself. For example, there are many documented instances in which a parent has destroyed his handicapped child. The motives, which have been varied, include disappointment, frustration, hostility, pity, and so forth. However, sometimes but not often, a middle-class parent not only merely destroys his own child, but also commits the highly symbolic act of discarding the child literally in the garbage, as happened recently in a large North American city.

As Buddenhagen points out, there may be similar symbolism in the fact that severe, aversive punishment is particularly apt to be used with the retarded, and perhaps for reasons that are not quite conscious.[43] With less impaired persons, we are much more apt to use rewards. While some ingenuity might be required to devise an appropriate reward system for the profoundly retarded, such ingenuity is probably quite within the scope of ability and grasp of most experimenters. Thus, their sometimes too ready recourse to severe stimulation, when dealing with the profoundly retarded, may well derive from an unconscious perception of these people as nonhuman.

Similarly, the use of the electric cattle prod to administer aversive stimuli in the shaping of the behavior of the profoundly retarded may carry with it profound symbolic meaning. Assume for the moment that the administration of electric shock is more humane than permitting the person to engage in extreme self-destructive behavior, as some of the profoundly retarded and disturbed may do. We can still ask why such stimuli are not administered in a fashion that strips the symbolism of animal-handling and particularly of "dumb cattle" from the methodology that is chosen.

In the physical environment, devaluation may be

expressed symbolically in innumerable ways, some of which have already been mentioned. Especially common are: (1) juxtaposing various devalued groups to each other, thereby implying that they have something in common (e.g., prisoners and retarded or disordered people); (2) juxtaposing older people with children, which conveys the image that the older group is child-like (e.g., co-location of a sheltered workshop and a children's day care center, both for the mentally retarded); (3) placing services for devalued people in such devalued image–laden locations, as cemeteries, garbage dumps, former execution sites, isolation places, islands, and so forth, (4) juxtaposing risky symbolisms to service facilities (e.g., "dead-end" signs, "no hunting" signs, functionless fences and walls, and so forth).

In order to illustrate the relentless inconsciousness of the implicit message in service location, we cite evidence that took over two years to collect (we had to break down our own blindness) that involves only one type of service in only one city: services to the elderly in Syracuse, New York. We found that three such services were located in/on cemeteries, ten were adjacent or nearly so to cemeteries, at least one had a death-suggestive name (i.e., "Toomey") and was located in and next to a cemetery, seven were adjacent or nearly so to funeral homes, one was close to the county coroner's office, one was housed in a former funeral parlor, three were adjacent to garbage dumps, one was located on not just one but two dead-end streets, and one was managed by an embalmer.

Obviously, something very explicit and definitive about elderly people in Syracuse is loudly shouted at the public, but we are not aware of one single member of the professional gerontology power structure in the city admitting it, nor is it being admitted by the largest voluntary association of elderly citizens in the area. The most immediate denial we encounter is that these facts are not facts; the second line of defense is that the locations are "unintended" and coincidental and therefore carry no meaning or message. Similar unconsciousness of the devaluation of groups of people, which every person harbors to some degree, is universal—and practically has to be by definition.

Some Other Largely Unconscious Meanings of Buildings

Facility designers and other service planners are apt to be victims of certain other "unconsciousisms"—namely, the incredible power of communication contained in a building regarding its real purpose, and its intended beneficiaries.

The language of buildings

To begin with, we must recognize that buildings have many symbolic purposes and meanings as well as many purposes other than, or in addition to, those that are overtly stated or even privately admitted. Often, a building has a much louder and more honest voice than the people who may talk to us about it and its purpose.

Samuel Gridley Howe was probably the most remarkable and foresighted figure in the American history of special education. In 1866, he gave the dedication address at the cornerstone-laying ceremony of a new institution for the blind in Batavia, New York. By that time, he had been instrumental in founding the early U.S. institutions for both the blind and retarded, had been superintendent of the first such public institution for the retarded (in Massachusetts), and had already perceived and accurately defined most of the shortcomings under which residential institutions were to labor for the next one hundred years. To capture fully the eloquence of Howe's statement on the language of architecture, several excerpted passages from his 1866 dedication address follow:

Language is of vast extent, and speech is only one of its powers. By speech and by print, men of our generation hold intercourse with each other. There are, moreover, some sorts of language by which the generations of men hold intercourse with other generations, and by which they converse across centuries and cycles of time. Among the various forms of language between generations, and between the ages, monuments hold a high place.

As men and women unwittingly, and sometimes unwillingly,

reveal their character and even their secret motives of action, by the sort of language which they use, so the generations unwittingly reveal the prevailing ideas of the men who lived in them, by the works which they leave behind them. Consider the Pyramids of Egypt, and read the speech which they utter. . . . What say the ten million cubic feet of solid masonry, enclosing two or three small chambers, whose entrances are so narrow that the enclosed sarcophagus must have been placed therein before the walls were built; and those entrances afterwards closed up by huge blocks of stone, too heavy to be moved by any common force? What does all this tell? What is the language of that generation, spoken by the tongues of the pyramids to this generation?

It is, that the monarchs were absolute, selfish, cruel and short-sighted. That they built these vast monuments to preserve their fame from oblivion, and their bodies from disturbance. . . . The monuments tell us, moreover, that the people must have been ignorant, oppressed, and like "dumb, driven cattle."

They tell us, that great multitudes of men and women were driven in from towns and villages, to toil and moil, and lift stones and carry sand for weeks and months; and when some had died and all were exhausted, then that fresh gangs were driven in to take their places.

And so of smaller monuments, whether the triumphal arch, where the chained captive walks sadly behind the sculptured conquerors; or the storied column, with its winding procession of battles, assaults and sieges, leading up to the proud victor standing self-glorified on the top. And so of those which tell a better story—the aqueducts, the fountains, the bridges, the canals, the docks and the like.

If we study the monuments which a generation built, and the kind of men in whose honor they raised statues, we may learn much of the character of the people themselves.

You are assembled to lay the foundations of a monument which will speak to future generations; and although what you grave upon the cornerstone, and what you put within it, should never be seen, the monument itself will talk to future generations; and what will it tell them?

It will disclose that the physical condition of the human race in this country was imperfect and unfavorable and that there were born to this generation, and expected to be born in the next, . . . children, numerous enough to form a persistent class. That children of this class were not only loved and cherished by their parents and kindred, but also cared for by the public. That there was no Mount Taygetus* here, on which to expose them, with other infirm folk, to perish

*The mountain upon which the Spartans abandoned infirm or unwanted infants.

or be devoured, but asylums into which they were gathered and nurtured.

It will prove that the social and political union which here leagued three million people into one powerful State, was formed and maintained not only for defense against enemies, for common commerical interest, for great enterprises, for social prosperity and enjoyment, nor yet for mental culture and high civilization of the many, but also for the protection and care of the weak and infirm. That the State of New York, which could dig out a navigable river clear across her broad land, which had just armed and sent forth three hundred thousand sturdy soldiers to serve the common country and the cause of humanity, that this great State, while holding on in her high career of material prosperity, and providing schools for all the children, took thought also, that not even the . . . little ones should be neglected.

In such language will be the building, those foundation-stones you this day lay, speak to many generations in coming time.

But, while thus noting with pleasure and even excusable pride, the humane impulses which prompt and which will carry forward the work, pardon me if I utter a word of warning.

Good intentions, and kind impulses, do not necessarily lead to wise and truly humane measure.

Nowhere is wisdom more necessary than in the guidance of charitable impulses. Meaning well is only half our duty; thinking right is the other and equally important half.[44]

A later superintendent from Massachusetts offered and equally relevant insight:

This history of the development of the human race has been most enduringly written in its architecture. A study of the architecture of a people reveals their dominant thoughts and ideals. The caves of the cave-dweller suggest man's early struggle for existence against wild beasts; the tents of the ancient shepherds the nomadic traits of these people in their moving from place to place in search of food for their flocks. The religious fervor of the middle ages is unmistakably recorded in the cathedral monuments of Europe. The creative and commercial ideals of nations are accurately recorded in their factories, warehouses, docks, highways, and office buildings, and their warlike instincts are well gauged by their forts, armories, battleships, tanks and aeroplanes; their educational interests by their schools and higher seats of learning; their interest in the sick and handicapped are clearly recorded in their hospitals and eleemosynary institutions.[45]

The hidden purposes of buildings

Human service buildings, like other buildings, can also project images of many purposes and meanings. Certain of these meanings are of particular relevance to our discussion. At least three such relevant meanings can be readily recognized in human management facilities: the building (1) as a monument, (2) as a public relations medium, and (3) as a medium of service. Each will be discussed briefly.

The building as a monument. Buildings are often erected, consciously or unconsciously, as monuments. In human management facilities, this characteristic is especially likely to be true of administration and medical treatment units. The monument may be to a political person, such as a governor, minister, prime minister, and so forth; a famous man; a foundation donor or donor dynasty; or an administrator or professional who may want to achieve identity or "immortality" through the monument building. Common examples of the latter are the aged superintendent or administrator who wants to make one last, only, or major contribution before retiring or dying.

While such aspirations often result in genuine benefits to mankind, they can also pervert the consciously verbalized or officially defined purpose of the building. For example, in order to fulfill its function as a monument, the building may be erected in a locality not consistent with normalizing and optimal program development; available funds may have been so plentiful as to result in a building that is either larger than optimal or overequipped; limitations of funds may result in a building so small as to require wasteful duplications and adjustment later; the ambitions of the initiator may require a free-standing building where an additional wing or floor on existing buildings would have been preferable; or the concepts that the initiator imposes upon the building plans may force future human services into undesirable and hard-to-remedy patterns.

Examples of the latter are donations of facilities such as swimming halls, medical buildings, churches,

or institutions. The existence of such facilities often create later difficulties for establishing patterns of increased and integrated use of the community for recreation, medical services, and church attendance. Similarly, an expensive new service building, designed to serve large numbers of residents, can become a great obstacle to reduction of a facility to a smaller size consistent with normalizing dispersal.

Kirkbride has aptly summarized another aspect of the building of service facilities as monuments: "Let us remember that our purpose is not to build costly monuments, at the expense of the taxpayer, to architects, legislators and governors or indeed to ourselves . . . ."[46]

The building as a public relations medium. A building, or an entire facility, can become a medium of public relations. While such a medium may produce desirable and beneficial results in the long run, the public relations function may also be irrelevant and even detrimental to the welfare of client-users. A number of examples follow.

A building may function as an advertisement for the architect, as in the many instances of widely acclaimed buildings that have serious functional shortcomings. Innovations in design may become means of aggrandizement or advancement to staff or administrators, and the real benefits of novel designs may be blown up beyond all proportion. Other widely hailed design innovations may later be recognized as unworkable solutions. For example, one institution for the retarded in the late 1950s erected a new showcase nursery in which the infants' cribs had solid, visually attractive, and expensive marble sides with wire mesh fronts. Among other things, these materials could obviously lead to injuries, especially for children with seizures. Soon after construction, the cribs had to be rebuilt at great expense. The new style was hailed as another dynamic innovation rather than as rectification of a predictable blunder.

The building as a medium of service. A building may truly be intended primarily as a medium of human service; however, this intent by itself does not ensure that the actual service rendered will be appropriate in type and quality. Many human service buildings fail to offer either.

The focus of convenience of a building

Importantly, we should recognize that a building can tell us much about the question that concerns whose convenience it was designed to serve. Social norms demand that when a human service building of some sort is constructed, we must pretend and proclaim that the building is designed for the convenience of the prospective client-users. In reality, the building may be designed to serve the convenience of the builder or architect. If buildings are erected with public funds, the convenience of the community can easily become a primary consideration. If the prospective client-users belong to a deviant subgroup that requires special management, then the building may be designed for the convenience of the "manager" rather than the "managed" client-user.

The convenience of the architect. Some buildings are designed for the convenience of the architectural agent. Such buildings may have required the least imagination, planning, and work from the architect or engineer and thus perhaps result in the largest profit to him. Many ill-designed, ill-constructed buildings and building complexes bespeak an utter disregard for the prospective client-user. This convenience characteristic is especially true of residential buildings. However, the building as a monument to the architect, though perhaps well-designed for external beauty and effect, may also fall into the "convenience of the architect" category if client-user welfare is neglected.

The convenience of the community. The location of a large proportion of institutions has been determined by economic considerations. Institutions were often placed in areas where jobs were needed, and site selection became a very political matter. In many instances, institutions were located through the "accident" of land donations by job-hungry communities. Locations of this nature are not only ill-

advised as far as the client-users are concerned, but often also inconvenient to their families. Furthermore, they result in professional and scientific isolation of the staff. To locate any human service agency with the needs of the server rather than the served in mind is analogous to requiring people to eat in order to provide employment to cooks.

The convenience of the staff. Many buildings, when entered, leave little doubt that staff convenience was paramount in the designer's mind. Characteristic elements may include the following:

"Segregated" staff lounges to which the caretakers withdraw for meals, coffee, rest, and so forth;
Air conditioning for staff, but not for client-users;
Caretaker stations that provide maximal visual control over client-user areas while minimizing staff involvement (the glass-enclosed nursing station is a classical example);
Location of services such as classrooms, beauty shops, barber shops, and therapy areas inside of residential buildings to save staff the effort of dressing residents and escorting them to other buildings or arranging for them to leave the grounds.

The convenience of the client-user. Designing a human service building with only the convenience of the intended client-users in mind is not always possible. Staff are also human, and cost is a justifiable element of importance. However, when all is said and done, surely the client-user should be considered the most important consumer of the building; otherwise, providing a human service facility is like eating to support cooks. The building should reflect an attitude of client-centeredness.

THE MEASUREMENT OF THE QUALITY OF SERVICE SETTINGS

The measurement of the quality of human service has been a persistent and perplexing problem. Lately, a flood of literature on the topic has appeared, and while some people seem to reject the notion that service quality can be quantitatively and objectively assessed, a number of such assessment schemas have been devised. To my knowledge, all of these are specific to specific types of services (workshops, nursing homes, institutions, and so forth). However, one such schema is designed for universalistic application to any type of human service: the Program Analysis of Service Systems (PASS).[47]

PASS is designed for the objective quantification of the quality of a wide range of human service programs, agencies, and even entire service systems. Examples of services that might be evaluated include child development and (special) education programs, treatment and training centers, special camps, sheltered workshops, clinics, residential homes and institutions, rehabilitation facilities, psychiatric settings, nursing homes, homes for the aged, hospitals, reformatories, and corrective facilities. Such services may be addressed to a wide range of human problem areas and deviancies: physical and sensory disability, mental disorder and retardation, social incapacity, poverty, delinquency, addiction and habituation to alcohol, or drugs.

In assessing a particular human service program or agency, a team of qualified "raters" familiarizes itself thoroughly with all aspects of the service by drawing upon a combination of written descriptions of the projects, site visits, and interviews with clients, key administrators, and direct service staff. By applying well-defined guidelines and criteria, the raters evaluate the project on fifty ratings consisting of three to six levels each. These ratings are statements about various aspects of service quality (e.g., speed and convenience of client access to the service, building–neighborhood harmony, physical comfort of the service setting, intensity of relevant programming, individualization, and so forth. The lowest level of each rating implies poor or even unacceptable service performance, and the highest one implies near-ideal but attainable performance. Each level carries a weight (score), with the highest level of a rating carrying the maximum weight for that rating. While the rating statements are brief,

each rating is accompanied by a lengthy narrative that not only explains the rationale but provides guidelines on the scoring as well as examples that illustrate typical performance at different levels of the particular rating.

The weights received by a service on all ratings are successively summated into a total score for that service. The maximum attainable score is +1000, or in other words, each point is a "millage" of the possible total. The scores of the members of a rating team are consolidated, and the total score represents the quality of the proposed or actual project. This score reflects a number of agency characteristics and/or practices that bear upon service quality. Major categories are: adherence to the principle of normalization (73 percent of the total); presence of other ideology-based service and administrative practices (13 percent); and administrative efficiency (14 percent). The score reflects both the product (outcome) and the process of a service.

Among the fifty ratings, some are completely concerned with aspects unrelated to the physical environment (e.g., the way clients are labelled and addressed); others are totally concerned with the physical environment; and some fall in-between in implying part physical and part social expression. The ten ratings that can be assessed entirely in relation to the building alone can be combined into a facility score, even though the other forty ratings cannot be interpreted as a program score because of the many areas of overlap.

PASS raters are persons with prior human service sophistication and with extensive training in the principle of normalization and the PASS technique. In order to use PASS validly, they must have studied certain materials, participated in a total-immersion workshop and practicum lasting at least five days, and conducted a number of assessments under the guidance of experienced raters. Raters, however, need not necessarily be professionals. Intelligent, well-prepared consumers of human services and citizens with volunteer service or other relevant experiences can also become raters. They can thereby achieve greater effectiveness in their indispensable but too-often-neglected roles as change agents and as monitors of agency service quality.

Since PASS can be applied not only to existing services but also to plans and proposals, it is a most useful tool in the planning stage. It has been used in order to optimize service locations or to determine whether a proposed service should be funded.

Initially, PASS was designed to serve simultaneously and equally as a tool for training personnel in the principle of normalization, as well as for assessment. Experience has shown that PASS does serve this training function extremely well and that participation in a PASS training workshop often brings about radical changes and updating in service ideology and conceptualization—even among senior service workers.

PASS is issued in two volumes and with a set of checklists and scoring forms. The first volume, the *Handbook*, explains the system and enunciates its rationale and structure. The second volume, the *Field Manual*, is for the use of raters on assignment and contains detailed instructions for the assessment of services. The present version of the system is the third edition; additional editions derived from recent applications of the materials are likely.

A recent analysis[48] of 151 service program evaluations made with the earlier (second) version of PASS[49] provides some indication of the "environmental quality" achieved on the current service scene. The analysis (see Table 8-3) suggests two major conclusions:

1. There is a considerable range in the adequacy

TABLE 8-3

Performance of 151 Human Service Programs on Environment-Related Aspects of Program Quality, as Measured by PASS (Second Edition)

Concrete–Programmatic Dimension		Interpretational Dimension		
PASS 2 Rating	*Score (%)*	*PASS 2 Rating*	*Score (%)*	
1. External Dimension:				
Proximity to societal resources	61	Program & facility labels	34	
Access to the facility	60	Building perception	38	
Physical context (including socially integrative resources)	30	Age-appropriate facilities, environmental design, & appointments	56	
Size/dispersal of clients	34		—	
	Mean = 46		Mean = 43	Mean = 45
2. Internal Dimension:				
Physical overprotection	77	Environmental beauty	18	
Intensity of relevant programming	−2	Individualization	43	
Physical comfort	55	Interactions	61	
	Mean = 42		Mean = 41	Mean = 41
				Grand Mean
	Mean = 44		Mean = 42	= 43%

Note: Score is the mean achieved on each PASS 2 rating, expressed as a percent of the maximum attainable score. Negative scores are possible on PASS, if the service dimension is considered unacceptable by the PASS raters. This factor accounts for the one negative score (−2 percent) shown in this table.

of environment-related aspects of service quality. Lack of "Physical overprotection" (77.3 percent of the maximum achievable score) appears to be the most satisfactory feature of service environments, at least in this sample. The least satisfactory feature is "Intensity of relevant programming" (near-zero percent), although this rating is a measure of more than the environmental aspects of intense, relevant programming.

2. Overall environmental quality is only about forty-three percent of the maximum possible, which thus indicates that service facilities can and should be greatly improved. Also, the mean quality within each cell hovers only slightly above the forty percent level of performance.

CONCLUSION

Ideology must be recognized as the single most important determinant of human service environments. Values, ideologies, and role perceptions, not money or technical architectural considerations, are the ultimate source of most of the environmental features, just as they are the sources of most clinical and administrative processes. The ideologies that we adopt must therefore be developmental, normalizing, and status enhancing, rather than growth inhibiting, segregative, and stigmatizing. Careful orientation and attention to the real meaning of the terms *environment* and *rehabilitation* are needed. Environment must be viewed in its *totality* as a complex set of factors that shapes human behavior and includes both interior and exterior aspects as well as functional *and* symbolic dimensions.

Planners should cautiously and consciously examine the long-term public attitude implications of locating, constructing, furnishing, and naming facilities that will be used as the point of service delivery for devalued persons. Facilities should be designed more in accordance with service type (e.g., residential, vocational and educational), rather than primarily in terms of the perceived functioning level of utilizers. Names of facilities, programs, or locations need to be chosen not only so as to avoid the creation of differentness

of clients, but so as to maximize positively valued images. Names should be chosen to be analogous to the use of similar facilities in our culture (e.g., people's houses *do not* normatively have names). Much consideration must be given to the labels placed upon facilities in light of the very serious nature of the effects of labels upon devalued individuals.[50] Generally, persons of different ages should be grouped together only in ways that have valued cultural analogues, and the location of facilities should be relevant to clearly stated client and agency goals (e.g., to integrate persons as much as possible). Careful consideration needs to be given not only to access to the building but also to access *from* the building to relevant societal and integrative resources.

The utilization of existing and/or new structures needs to be planned for maximum adaptation (should the particular service no longer be necessary) and for future usage. Central to the creation of small, decentralized, and specialized community residential services is the question of what to do with our current institutional structures. Firstly, we must consider some facilities as totally and hopelessly unusable because of their age and/or remote location. Rather than pouring monies into such facilities for renovation or redevelopment, we should utilize these funds to create small, adaptive, and feasible service systems.

Secondly, some objectionable residential facilities of newer vintage that have adaptive features and locations might be converted into other rental and leased-income uses such as child development centers, classroom space, governmental offices, youth recreation facilities, modular shopping centers (e.g., shoe, grocery, or clothing stores), commercial laundries, 4-H centers, church or civic group meeting places, dormitory space (in college or university locales), or offices for law firms, insurance companies, or fundraising organizations. Such schemes have already been tried and found to be successful; for example, Eleanor Roosevelt Developmental Services in Schenectady, N.Y.[51]

There is a dire need to examine state and local requirements, ordinances, codes (e.g., zoning, health), certification standards, and evaluation standards to determine their viability and suitability. In some instances, laws and ordinances constitute serious roadblocks to the development of community residential service systems and may subtly deny the citizenship rights of handicapped persons. The reader may have noticed that fire and construction codes, health and other regulations, various types of laws and funding provisions, have not been discussed as factors in deviancy making or as obstacles in deviancy unmaking. Such obstacles are real, but human service planners must first know what the relevant concepts are if they are to discern the appropriateness and validity of these obstacles and how inappropriate ones may be circumvented. Human service concepts must precede law, funding, and so forth, or compromises and trade-offs will never be recognized as such, and inappropriate obstacles will not be combatted.

Projects should be initiated to raise the level of awareness that *perpetuation of devaluation is more destructive than poor service quality* and that such perpetuation is taking place in large degree by unconscious juxtaposition of devalued people with negative images. Rehabilitation must be seen as a process that restores to rank, and privilege, and image, as well as to function. One of the many means to this end is more extensive consumer representation on bodies that have responsibility for funding services for devalued persons. This action might be viewed as a minimal measure to counter perhaps well-intentioned but often growth-inhibiting and image-impairing professional influence.

NOTES AND REFERENCES

The author acknowledges the assistance of Bernard Graney, Robert Flynn, and Terri Johnson (all present or former students) in conceptualizing and writing the middle part of this chapter.

Information on the PASS training workshops described in this chapter can be obtained from the Training Institute for Human Service Planning, Leadership and Change Agentry, Syracuse University, 805 South Crouse Avenue, Syracuse, New York 13210. Telephone: 315-423-4264.

1. Wolfensberger, W., *The Origin and Nature of Our Institutional Models* (Syracuse, N.Y.: Human Policy Press, 1975).
2. Deutsch, A., *The Mentally Ill in America: A History of Their Care and Treatment from Colonial Times*, 2nd ed. (New York: Columbia University Press, 1949).
3. *Atlantic Monthly*, October 1967, p. 49.
4. Mowrer, O. H., "Learning Theory and Behavior Therapy," in B. B. Wolman (ed.), *Handbook of Clinical Psychology* (New York: McGraw-Hill, 1965), p. 49.
5. *Frontiers of Hospital Psychiatry*, vol. 5, no. 1, 1968, pp. 5-6.
6. Deutsch, *The Mentally Ill in America*, and Thompson, J. D., and G. Goldin, *The Hospital: A Social and Architectural History* (New Haven, Conn.: Yale University Press, 1975).
7. Tiffany, F., *Life of Dorothea Lynde Dix* (Cambridge, Mass.: Riverside Press, 1891).
8. *Time*, May 15, 1972.
9. Vail, D. J., *Dehumanization and the Institutional Career* (Springfield, Ill.: Charles C. Thomas, 1967).
10. Bartlett, F. L., "Present-Day Requirements for State Hospitals Joining the Community," *New England Journal of Medicine*, vol. 276, 1967, p. 92.
11. Vail, *Dehumanization and the Institutional Career*.
12. Thompson and Goldin, *The Hospital*.
13. Parsons, T., *The Social System* (Glencoe, Ill.: Free Press, 1951).
14. Parsons, T., and R. Fox, "Illness, Therapy, and the Modern Urban American Family," in E. G. Jaco (ed.), *Patients, Physicians and Illness* (Glencoe, Ill.: Free Press, 1958).
15. Gordon, G. A., *Roles, Theory and Illness: A Sociological Perspective* (New Haven, Conn.: College and University Press, 1966).
16. Vail, *Dehumanization and the Institutional Career*.
17. Keyes, D., *Flowers for Algernon* (New York: Harcourt Brace & World, 1966).
18. Horsfield, E., "Mental Defectives at the Court of Philip IV of Spain as Portrayed by the Great Court Painter Velasquez," *American Journal of Medical Deficiency*, vol. 45, 1940, p. 152.
19. de Fuentes, P., *The Conquistadors: First-Person Accounts of the Conquest of Mexico* (New York: Orion Press, 1963) p. 40; and Diaz del Castillo, B., *The Discovery and Conquest of Mexico: 1517-1521* (New York: Farrar, Straus and Cudahy, 1956) p. 210.
20. Thompson and Goldin, *The Hospital*.
21. Tiffany, *Life of Dorethea Lynde Dix*.
22. Suraci, A. B., "Reactions of Puerto Rican and Non Puerto Rican Parents to their Mentally Retarded Boys," unpublished doctoral dissertation, New York University, 1966 (University Microfilms No. 67-4930, Ann Arbor, Mich.).

23. Coll, B. D. *Perspectives in Public Welfare: A History* (Washington, D.C.: U.S. Department of Health, Education and Welfare 1969).

24. "Reports from States," *Proceedings of the National Conference of Charities and Correction*, 1890, p. 329.

25. Buck, P. S., *The Child Who Never Grew* (New York: John Day, 1950).

26. Fendell, N., "Israel's Eternal Children," *Journal for Special Educators of the Mentally Retarded*, vol. 4, no. 1, 1969, pp. 19–22.

27. Wolfensberger, W., *The Principle of Normalization in Human Services* (Toronto: National Institute on Mental Retardation, 1972), chapters 2 and 6.

28. Eaton, J. W., and R. J. Weil, *Culture and Mental Disorders: A Comparative Study of the Hutterites and Other Populations* (Glencoe, Ill.: Free Press, 1955).

29. Wolfensberger, *The Principle of Normalization in Human Services*, and Wolfensberger, W., and L. Glenn, *Program Analysis of Service Systems: A Method for the Quantitative Evaluation of Human Services* (2 vols.), 3rd ed. (Toronto: National Institute on Mental Retardation, 1975).

30. Wofensberger and Glenn, ibid., vol. 2.

31. Foucault, M., *Madness and Civilization: A History of Insanity in the Age of Reason* (New York: Vintage Press, 1973).

32. Flynn, R. J., *Assessing Human Service Quality with PASS 2: An Empirical Analysis of 102 Service Program Evaluations*, Monograph No. 5 (Toronto: National Institute on Mental Retardation, 1975).

33. Deutsch, M., *The Mentally Ill in America: A History of Their Care and Treatment from Colonial Times*, Rev. ed. (New York: Columbia University Press, 1967).

34. Goffman, E., *Asylums* (Garden City, N.Y., Anchor, 1961).

35. Foucault, *Madness and Civilization*.

36. Wolfensberger and Glenn, *Program Analysis of Service Systems*, vol. 2.

37. Westin, A., *Privacy and Freedom* (New York: Atheneum, 1967).

38. Proshansky, H., W. Ittleson, and L. Rivlin (eds.), *Environment Psychology: Man and His Physical Setting* (New York: Holt, Rinehart and Winston, 1970).

39. Miller, D. H., "Worlds that Fail," in S. E. Wallace (ed.), *Total Institutions* (Chicago: Aldine-Atherton, Trans-Action Books, 1971).

40. Wolfensberger, W. (ed.), *A Selective Overview of the Work of Jean Vanier and the Movement of L'Arche*, Monograph No. 1 (Toronto: National Institute on Mental Retardation, 1973); and Wolfensberger, W., "Review of *Enough Room for Joy*," *Canadian Welfare*, vol. 50, 1974, pp. 14–17.

41. *J. B. O'Connor* v. *Kenneth Donaldson*, June 26, 1975 (422 U.S. 563; or 95 Sct 2486).

42. Vail, *Dehumanization and the Institutional Career*.

43. Buddenhagen, R. G., "Until Electric Shocks are Legal," *Mental Retardation*, vol. 9 no. 6, 1971, pp. 48–50.

44. Howe, S. G., *Ceremonies on Laying the Corner-Stone of the New York State Institution for the Blind, at Batavia, Genesee Co. New York* (Batavia, N.Y.: Henry Todd, 1866), pp. 13–16.

45. Wallace, G. L., "Plan and Construction of an Institution for Feebleminded," *Journal of Psycho-Asthenics*, vol. 29, 1924, p. 256.

46. Kirkbride, F. B., "Types of Buildings for State Institutions for the Feeble-Minded," *Proceedings of the National Conference of Charities and Correction*, 1916, p. 256.

47. Wolfensberger and Glenn, *Program Analysis of Service Systems*, vols. 1 and 2.

48. Flynn, R. J., *Measuring Normalization, Integration, and Administrative Effectiveness with PASS: Some Sobering Findings on Agency Service Quality*, unpublished manuscript, Syracuse University, Syracuse, N.Y., 1976.

49. Wolfensberger, W., and L. Glenn, *Program Analysis of Service Systems: A Method for the Quantitative Evaluation of Human Services*, (2 vol.), 2nd ed. (Toronto: National Institute on Mental Retardation, 1973).

50. Mercer, J., *Labeling the Mentally Retarded: Clinical and Social System Perspectives on Mental Retardation* (Los Angeles: University of California Press, 1973); and Hobbs, N. (ed.), *Issues in the Classification of Children* (2 vols.), (San Francisco: Jossey-Bass, 1975).

51. La Fave, H. G., R. Woodhouse, and F. Grunberg, *A New Generation of Programming for Children with Developmental Disorders and the Retarded of All Ages*, unpublished manuscript, Eleanor Roosevelt Developmental Services, Schenectady, N.Y., 1974, cited in N. Hobbs, *The Futures of Children: Categories, Labels and Their Consequences*, (San Francisco: Jossey-Bass, 1974).

9

Environmental Stimulation and Design

Maxine Wolfe

Maxine Wolfe is Associate Professor in the Environmental Psychology Program and a member of the Center for Environment and Behavior Studies at the City University of New York Graduate School. She received her B.A. degree in psychology from Brooklyn College and her Ph.D. in social psychology from the City University of New York. Her recent research and consulting has been in the area of design and evaluation of children's environments and on the nature of privacy. Recent papers include "Privacy and Institutionalization" and "Private Places: The Concept of Privacy in Childhood and Adolescence," both of which were presented at the Environmental Design Research Association Conference in Vancouver, B.C. She has also published "Room Size, Group Size and Density: Behavior Patterns in a Children's Psychiatric Facility," in Environment and Behavior, *vol. 7, no. 2, 1975.*

INTRODUCTION

Over the past decade there has been a strong movement towards removing the stigma that has for too long been associated with mental and/or physical disability. Historically, mentally and physically disabled people were placed in "special" environments (homes for the aged, state training schools, psychiatric hospitals) that largely served the purpose of isolating these persons from the rest of society. While the stated purpose was to "treat" them and then to return them to a "normal lifestyle," most of the residents remained in institutions for all of their lives or were returned, shortly after discharge, because they "could not make it on the outside."

Many persons have begun to point out what should have been obvious a long time ago: We *all* have disabilities of one kind or another. Furthermore, we have also begun to realize that in many ways the environments we *all* live in do not help us to overcome these disabilities and may in fact support or create disabilities. Some of us disabled people end up living in "special environments" for either part of our day or all of our lives. It may be that we need (or someone thinks we need) more care, different kinds of care, or extended care. It may simply be that we have no one else to care for us. Yet, when we speak about *designing for the disabled*, we are usually speaking about *designing for differences*. We design these special environments—that is, *institutions*—so that they primarily "take care of" what we consider to be the unusual aspects of these people. Therefore, I want to stress in this chapter that in designing for the developmentally disabled we also *design for those parts of people or those parts of people's daily lives that are not disabled.*

We must also understand that the environments we design, both socially and physically, can help to create disabilities. People who live in our institutions, have a right to lead a life as close as possible to the normal way of living. Many of us know of this idea as the "goal of normalization." It is not new but it needs to be restated. These people certainly have a right, as we all do, not to have the environment create new disabilities. They also have a right to special treatment. In the balance between normalization and special treatment, our institutions give more of a message of special treatment (sometimes positive; very often negative) and certainly can be seen to create some disabilities—that is, institutionalized behavior. I will get back to this point later when I discuss various aspects of institutional design. Now, however, I want to clarify a second concept that needs some definition: the issue of environmental stimulation.

A usual problem with the concept of environmental stimulation is the implication that stimulation comes from the environment and that people passively receive it via the sense organs and then respond to it. This view of environmental stimulation is far too simplistic. Stimulation does not simply come from an environment "out there." People, who are part of the environment and stimuli themselves, are in that environment with certain goals, needs, expectations, abilities, styles of living, and so forth. The way in which any particular aspect of the physical environment relates to behavior, cognition, or emotions must be viewed in terms of these goals, needs, expectations, and so forth. For example, we can define *noise* as sound above a given decibel level—a certain loudness or harsh quality. This definition is a "stimulation" definition of noise. We can, however, also define *noise* as "unwanted sound." This later definition reflects the view I bring to the notion of environmental stimulation. While clearly there are sound levels that are damaging to the human ear, this aspect is only one basis for thinking about noise. Under certain circumstances, many sounds at a low decibel level will be perceived as noise; under other circumstances, sounds of a high level are not perceived as noise. That someone says, "Yes, it was noisy in there," doesn't mean that the sound interfered with what people were doing. In fact, the noise may have supported what they were doing. What would a football game be without the roar of the crowd? Thus, environmental stimulation should be viewed in the context of its meaning components, and, its meaning components

can be different for the different people living in that environment. Noise, for the staff member, may be defined as "the sounds that children make." For the children, it may be "all those announcements over the loudspeaker." In the same sense, environmental stimulation does not occur on a particular day or only in a particular place or at a particular time; nor is color separate from size or noise or from what people are doing. People do not live particular parts of days in particular places separated from other spaces, places, noises, colors and people—that is, the question of those aspects of the environment with which the individual person interacts or transacts and their meaning for the person can only be dealt with if we consider such aspects as they interact with one another over time.

With the goal of normalization in mind and with the idea that any concept of environmental stimulation must take into account the goals, needs, and expectations of people in order to understand the meaning they give to certain environmental stimuli and their behavior over time, let me discuss some research findings that will highlight the need for considering these views in order to apply our knowledge to designing for the developmentally disabled.

The research focused on children in a (physically) large psychiatric facility. While we could question whether the findings are relevant to other groups of disabled children and/or to issues of designing small group homes and other types of community residences, my belief is that the results are relevant to these different circumstances. First of all, the studies focus on issues that are common to all environments: the occupancy process, the match of program and environment, privacy, bedroom size, and so forth. Secondly, there are specific ways in which these issues are commonly dealt with in many "special-care" environments. For example, institutional settings (whether for physically, mentally, or emotionally disabled persons) rarely provide for privacy needs because residents are believed to require more surveillance than people in ordinary environments. Finally, while small group homes and community group homes are the new design and program thrust, many older large institutions are still in use and new ones are still being built. More importantly, while large physical size may be thought of as a key descriptor of institutional environments, I submit that almost any environment can quickly become "an institution" on the basis of physical attributes (interior and exterior), site location, and programming unless we become aware of the subtle and not-so-subtle ways in which institutions are created. Therefore, I think we can learn a good deal from the research in this psychiatric facility that can aid us in future design and programming for a variety of special-care environments.

RESEARCH FINDINGS AND IMPLICATIONS FOR DESIGN

Factors Affecting the Evolution of Use Over Time

A major issue in institutional design is size. In the past, institutions have been designed for hundreds, or even thousands of people. Present treatment ideas focus on facilities for small groups of people (i.e., community group homes) or the breaking up of larger facilities internally into smaller groupings (cottages). This movement in design for the disabled is paralleled by similar movements for persons who do not reside in institutions; for example, the trend towards creating mini-schools within larger schools. Research has indicated that settings with small numbers of people provide a wider range of activities, greater sense of importance for each person, and an increased sense of self-identity.[1] But size can be, and is, thought of as more than the number of people in a given space. It can also refer to the actual total square footage, the number of square feet available per person, the arrangement, the location, and the distance between spaces. It can even refer to the meaning various combinations of space and number have in terms of everyday experiences, needs, goals, and so forth.

Over the past five years, we have been studying the relationship between the physical design of a children's residential psychiatric facility, the therapeutic philosophy, the administrative policy, and the patterns of use and behavior that evolved over time.[2] Several aspects of our studies relate to the issue of size. The 80,885-square-foot building was designed as a total institutional facility for 192 children ranging in age from five to sixteen (see Figure 9–1). The two-story building has a rectangular plan being organized around a central open court. The four functional areas of the building (living, community, school, and administration) radiate from the rectangular corridor plan that connects them all. The architect's distribution of private, semipublic, and public spaces was predicated on the assumption that there would be 192 children and sufficient staff to supervise them. With the building fully occupied, patients and staff would be spread throughout the building, and there would be few areas into which a child would go where staff would not be present.

This aspect of the design would act to provide a subtle sense of supervision—that is, a covert form of observing the children without having to follow them around. This intention was quite consistent with the director's therapeutic philosophy of an unstructured program, on-the-spot therapy, and a de-emphasis on control (no locked doors, no seclusion rooms, and so forth). However, the hospital opened with only four full-care and twelve day-care patients and a staff of about fifty. Even fourteen months after opening, there were only twenty-two full-care and thirty day-care children. The small number of children and staff, which under other physical circumstances might be considered an ideal size of group, under these circumstances resulted in large, unoccupied, unpopulated sectors of the facility. The long corridors, separate functional areas, and lots of unlocked doors leading to lots of inside rooms and outdoor spaces meant that children could and did easily slip away from supervision.

The *potential* loss of control is significant because it is here that we must deal with the meaning of the

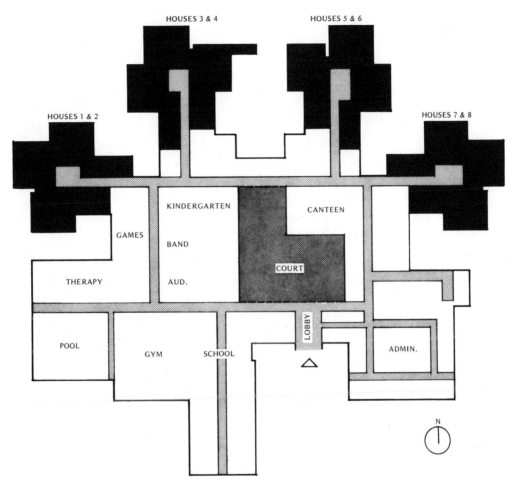

Figure 9-1
Original floor plan of children's hospital.

situation and the actions we take to deal with it—that is, how the children, the "institution," and staff roles are perceived and actions taken based on these perceptions. The staff, in such institutions, is responsible for the children. The idea that the children *could* do certain things, impulsively or without understanding the consequences, operates to create more tension than would be the case for those who do not require special care. Although a variety of different ways of dealing with the problem may have been offered at

this point in the facility's history, an important fact to recognize is that the solution selected was administrative rather than architectural. Over time, all doors were locked, all activities structured, and ultimately, almost every moment of the child's time was programmed. This decison acted to contain the children physically but also influenced their freedom of choice of activities within areas. Certain spaces became "appropriate" for certain behaviors. A child who "acted out" or did not participate during a programmed activity was sent to the living areas (houses). The houses (see Figure 9–2), which had been designed to provide for private, small-group, and large-group activities, became places for detention and withdrawal. As a result, even when all of the children were in the house, the space became known as or had meaning as a space for withdrawal, and very little social behavior took place there. Both the community and house areas were affected by this characterization of spaces. In fact, the general milieu of the hospital became more subdued. The physical location of the one occupied living area, far from the community areas in the building, reinforced its role as a place for total withdrawal. But soon, detention in the house became even more specific. An office was turned into a "quiet" or "seclusion" room (no furniture, mattress on the floor, peephole drilled in the door) and subsequently we have seen a single-bed room in each apartment (for eight children) turned into a quiet room and there are quiet rooms in each activity area.

Now, there are sixty to seventy children in three living areas, many day programs using other spaces, and the facility has been almost totally inhabited. However, the patterns of space use that developed at a particular point in time have repercussions, long after the disappearance of the conditions (large space, few people) that created them. Few people remember the initial therapeutic philosophy. In fact, I heard staff members who had been there since the hospital's opening tell some visitors "how much foresight they had to include quiet rooms in each house." Our analysis has suggested that these changes in philosophy were the results of attempts by the administration to meet realities, many of which were unexpected, but not unusual, in terms of an occupancy process. All grew out of the best intentions, by the most dedicated of staffs. However, often the consequences were diametrically opposed to the working philosophy that opened the building. I raise this part of our case history to point out that (1) the number of people in a space can not be thought of as separate from the size of that space and the location of areas within the space, and (2) that the size of space and

size of groups within that space and other spatial issues can create problems that are interpreted and gain significance in terms of the meaning properties of the environment. The solutions to these problems can have long-term consequences for therapeutic philosophy and for total milieu even when the original conditions creating the problems have disappeared.

Room Size, Group Size, and Density

Another aspect of our work relates to size of institutions, both in terms of numbers of people and size of spaces. In most residential treatment settings for the emotionally disturbed, one goal of therapeutic treatment is to foster socially interactive behaviors among the children and between the children and staff. Often, programming emphasizes group activities as a major means of supporting this behavior among the children. Yet, one of the clearest findings in behavioral research, both inside and outside of institutions, is that increasing the number of people in a space decreases the amount of social interaction.[3] In our own research, we looked at the relationship between group size, room size and density in the children's psychiatric facility.[4] The analysis was based on observational data collected over a period of two and one-half years and focused on the use of bedrooms. Various combinations of room size (total number of square feet) and group size (number of children assigned) occurred naturally and yielded densities ranging from 29.01 square feet per person to 220.99 square feet per person. What did these data show? First, in support of work done in adult institutions,[5] we found that no matter how many children were assigned to a bedroom, on the average, only one child would be in there at any one time and, on an individual basis, each child would use the room less as the number assigned increased. Thus, assigning more children to a space did not mean that children would use it as a group space. Also, we found that in examining the relationship between group size or density and bedroom use, our analysis would have to focus on *potential* group size and *potential* density.

Figure 9–2
Floor plan of house units.

This approach is significant in terms of the notion of environmental stimulation, which I discussed earlier, because the potential characteristics of spaces and places are psychological components of all naturally occurring, stable environments. Our behavior in and ideas about spaces are not just based on what is occurring this moment, but they are based on our past experience in those environments and our expectations about what will or may occur. In fact, we found that the amount of use of rooms and the things children did in their rooms were related to potential group size and to actual room size but that they were not related to potential density.

Potential density, the number of square feet per person if all people were present, is used in almost all architectural space planning, whether for housing or hospitals. Yet, we found that potential density was not related to bedroom use patterns. Our data, collected in an environment that might be considered special—a children's psychiatric facility with "disturbed children"—support the main point of recent literature on the behavioral effects of density: Behavior is influenced more by the manner in which given levels of density are achieved than by the level of density itself. A minimum number of square feet per person is a necessary but not a sufficient basis for decision making. Size of space and number of people are significant, not as parts of a mathematical density factor, but as they interact to create certain psychological density conditions. Size and number take on meaning as related to issues of privacy, territoriality, control, and the emotional relationships possible between people sharing spaces.

We had, in this study, the ability to look at fairly equal potential densities created by the proportionate increase of size of room and number of children assigned. While the one-child, one-bed room, the two-child, two-bed room, and the four-child, four-bed room had nearly equal potential densities, our data showed that the amount of use of these rooms and the behavior patterns in them were very different. In terms of the psychological aspects of space and number, the one-child, one-bed room, which was used most often, is clearly the most "private" environment.

The total space is, by definition, one child's territory (with unambiguous defense rights) and there is no need for considering use or coordinating use in relation to another child. We found that children in a two-child, two-bed room used their room least with the four-child, four-bed room falling in between. These latter two rooms differ from the one-child, one-bed room in that they are not "private" for any child assigned and will clearly require territorial defense and/or coordination of activity. Why then should the two-child, two-bed room be used less often than a four-child, four-bed room when in fact the amount of square footage per child is approximately the same?

A variety of research has indicated that two person groups have unique properties—that is, they show the lowest amount of overt disagreement, but have high rates of tension.[6] Bettelheim has made the same point about two children sharing a bedroom at the Orthogenic School.[7] The emotional dependence of each child on the other made the use of the room by either one uncomfortable. Thus, one reason for the higher use of the four-child, four-bed room may be that two person groups have unique properties that support avoidance. However, potential group size is not enough to explain the findings since two children in a four-bed room each used their room more than two children in a two-bed room. Here the total amount of space available and its relation to emotional dependence would seem to be critical. When interpersonal demands (or emotional dependence) are high (a two-child group) additional space can serve to lessen those demands while less space can serve to heighten them. In a larger space, each child can enter the room without physically confronting the other; their activities can be spatially more separate and dependence can be lessened.

In comparing the amount of use and type of behavior of sole occupants assigned to bedrooms originally intended for one, two, or four children (increasing space), we found that there was decreasing use of the bedroom as size of space increased. When the child did use the room with the largest amount of space, he or she used it for social and isolated active behaviors as well as isolated passive behaviors. A sole occupant assigned to a space, especially a child (with or without emotional difficulties), may experience a large amount of space as frightening. One way the child seems to deal with this is to use the space less often. When the child uses the space, he or she seems to pattern his or her behavior to make time in the space less frightening; for example, by inviting others in to play or talk or engaging in active rather than passive behaviors. Thus, when one child is sole occupant of a bedroom, a smaller room probably provides more physical and hence psychological security. We could argue that the lower use and greater dispersion of activities we found for one-child in the larger room is positive in terms of the therapeutic goal of an institution (i.e., more social interaction, less withdrawal) and that we should in the future design very large one-bed rooms. I am glad this approach is economically unfeasible because the interpretation and applicability of this finding in such a manner would be disastrous. In this instance we have to look at the notion of environmental stimulation within the context of the total day of the child and the total institution. We cannot look only at a particular point in time or consider such behaviors as withdrawal or social interaction as inherently positive or negative.

In our study of children's use of bedrooms, as well as in a similar study for adults,[8] isolated passive or withdrawal behaviors (sleeping, sitting alone, lying awake) predominated in *all* bedrooms as it probably does in bedrooms in normal living environments. However, in the adult studies, which considered only group size, patients in private rooms engaged in the widest range of activities while in the children's hospital this was only true for the very large private room. In the adult hospital studies, the diversity of activities in the private room was interpreted as reflecting the freedom of choice quality of privacy. In the children's hospital did the diversity of activities in the large private room also reflect the freedom of choice of privacy? The answer is no.

In this institution, programmed activities involving many children took up almost all of the day. If we consider aloneness and interaction as balanced needs, the children's institution provides many forced and/or potentially interactive settings and few, if any, alone settings. In this hospital, as in others, the child's exhibiting withdrawal behaviors in situations defined by the program as "social" was considered inappropriate. The bedrooms, when they could be used, became the only place considered appropriate for these withdrawal behaviors by the adults in authority. The private room, as compared to a shared space, offered the possibility of engaging in these behaviors without interruption, and because the larger private space had other qualities that acted to diversify behavior and lower its use, the smaller private room offered the greatest possibility to engage in passive behaviors. Thus, freedom of choice as a quality of environments does not necessarily have to be reflected by the use of one space for a wide variety of behaviors, but may be reflected by the use of certain spaces for specific behaviors that are not possible elsewhere.

The findings and implications of this work lead me to two other areas of research that I think are relevant to this discussion. The first deals with privacy; the second with age differences in designing for the developmentally disabled.

Privacy: Physical and Social Aspects

As mentioned above, *privacy* is one of the psychological aspects of space and number. Recent conceptual approaches to privacy state that in addition to individual differences, concepts and patterns of privacy are seen to reflect and/or be reflected by the sociophysical context in which people live.[9] In given social systems (an institution, for example), achieving privacy, freedom of privacy, invasion of privacy, the consequences of invasion, and so forth are all elements in the rights and privileges that define the role relationships between people. However, privacy as behavior and experience is also rooted in spaces and places. By design, activity, and meaning, physical spaces achieve their privacy character. The person learns to accept, identify and, indeed, act private in certain places and spaces over others. Thus, socio-physical contexts have a number of aspects that can facilitate or inhibit, create or eliminate, certain forms and patterns of privacy. Members of given groups, therefore, are likely to attach different meanings to privacy and to have different patterns of privacy behavior as a result of both the social organization of the group and the physical environment it inhabits.

Our behavioral data, presented before, indicated that a "private" room gave a child the opportunity to engage in behaviors considered "inappropriate" elsewhere because it required no coordination of activity, fostered no problems of emotional dependence, and had the least amount of visual distraction and stimulation. We have also examined the concepts of privacy of children in this setting by the use of an interview. We compared the concepts of privacy for the hospitalized children with a nonhospitalized sample matched by age, sex, ethnic background and socioeconomic status (from a larger sample of 1,000 children interviewed in another study).[10] We found that concepts of privacy for these groups differed, and instead of being attributable to pathology versus nonpathology, thus reflected differences in the contrasting sociophysical contexts in which these children lived.[11] In response to the question "What does privacy mean to you?" significantly, almost one-third of the nonhospitalized children said, "no one bothering me," while none of the hospitalized children gave this response. Furthermore, compared to the hospital sample, three to five times as many nonhospitalized children gave definitions of "being alone in a room or place," "being away from people," and "quiet." On the other hand, nearly one-quarter of the children in the hospital mentioned "privacy for undressing," while none of the outside children did. One-fifth of the nonhospital sample responded with some idea that privacy involves "choice" (doing what you want to, being alone when you want to), while none of the hospitalized children gave responses of this kind. In discussing "private places," hospitalized children never mentioned outdoor settings, while one-fifth of the nonhospitalized sample gave this response. In response to a variety of questions about the meanings

of private places, things, things to do, and so forth, the use of "no one knows about it" as a defining characteristic was rarely, if ever, mentioned by the hospitalized children and yet was very often mentioned by the nonhospital sample.

The clearest picture that emerges from this comparison, and from our analysis of data from the larger study of nonhospitalized children, is that concepts of privacy strongly reflect the environmental experiences children have been or are being exposed to. In the total institutional setting, some forms of privacy are so out of the person's control (i.e., controlling information about yourself, no one bothering you, choice) that they are not even connected to the idea of privacy. For other aspects of life under these circumstances, privacy becomes increasingly salient (undressing, using the bathroom, taking a shower) probably in contrast to what is possible and, indeed, acceptable outside the hospital environment. We have to ask what consequences the choices and options we provide for the outlet of privacy needs within the hospital and other special care settings may have for our therapeutic goals, as well as for the children's behavior, when they are inside the hospital or outside of the hospital environment, either temporarily or permanently. For example, most adolescents, whether inside or outside of institutions, are dealing with questions of sexuality. However, adolescents who are in our institutions are frequently seen as having special difficulty in this area—that is, for example, being overly demonstrative at inappropriate times and in inappropriate places or having problems with homosexuality (from a staff point of view). The one area of privacy most universally accepted in our daily lives is privacy for undressing, toileting, showering, as well as for intimate relationships that often have some sexual component. The lack of privacy for such behaviors could exacerbate or support exactly the behavior the staff may see unacceptable or unhealthy and can create conflicts for children when they leave the institution.

There are other ways in which our definition of privacy in relation to spaces may have negative consequences. In this institution, a number of the children saw the seclusion room as the only private place. In fact, in other interviews with the children, several said that they often became disruptive in order to be sent to the quiet room where they could be alone and unbothered. When asked "How do other people on your unit let you know when they want to be private?" one of the responses the hospitalized children give is that they hear children ask if they can go to the quiet room.

Some aspects of privacy may be impossible to provide within the context of a "total" institution (lack of surveillance, control of information), but others can be provided (some places where the child cannot be bothered, some choice for aloneness, privacy for dressing) and, indeed, may be necessary and important developmental needs. Certainly, we want to be aware that we may be teaching these children that "aloneness" is a negative need or something only necessary for dealing with negative emotional states or received as a reward for "inappropriate" behavior. If we provide "private" rooms, we want to make sure that what this means to an incoming child (i.e., no one bothering me; a place to be alone, and so forth) is what it means to the staff. If we do not clarify its meaning to both children and staff, we set the stage for conflict and tension.

Finally, I should add that privacy is not only a need expressed by the children, but by the staff as well. While the children are on "full view" all of the time, so are the staff. In our interviews with staff, the need for a place to retreat, recoup, to think, and to be alone with a child or with another staff member was frequently mentioned. While, clearly, the staff members do not spend their total days in the hospital, the kind of intense involvement we expect from them seems to require some places of retreat during the day.

Age Differences in the Use of Space

Our work on privacy with children outside of the hospital focused on age-related differences in the concept of privacy. Unfortunately, the sample at the hos-

pital was too small for such an analysis. However, the whole idea of age differences and their implications for design should not be overlooked. There is a tendency, which I talked about earlier, when considering the design of special-care settings, to focus on pathology as the major component dictating design decisions. On the other hand, in the design of facilities for "ordinary" persons, the age of occupants is frequently a major consideration. A question we looked at was whether there were age-related differences in the use of space in the children's hospital, despite the "idiosyncratic" effects of disturbed behavior and the conformity resulting from long-term institutionalization.[12]

We compared the use of physically identical living areas by two groups: one, ages eight to twelve; the other, ages thirteen to sixteen. While the general types of activities in the living areas as a whole did not differ for the two age groups, there were differences in the sizes of groups involved in activities, the dispersion of activities across rooms, and the extent to which different rooms were the focus of different types of activities. The younger children seemed to use unstructured spaces more spontaneously and more diversely. Their activities seemed to be more a reflection of an immediate reaction than a deliberate review of the total range of environmental possibilities. When there was a strong external definition, it acted as an immediate influence on choice of activity. The older children seemed to be more able to match what they wanted to do with the total range of spaces available and to select a space on the basis of this match. They could apparently set up some unspoken shared normative uses for physically identical spaces and adhered to this pattern. These observations parallel others we have made in open school settings.[13]

Our findings indicated, at the very least, that designers and administrators of facilities to be used by different ages should consider the need of younger children for clear definitions of spaces. Frequently, the "inappropriate" use of certain spaces is attributed to the child's pathology, aggressiveness, negativity, and the like, when in fact, lack of clear definition of the space may be the issue. If planners, teachers, group leaders, or administrators desire to have spaces used in specific ways, younger children may require explicit environmental cues. When specific behavior is the goal, the design components must communicate the message at the child's level of understanding.

CONCLUSIONS

I have chosen to address a few specific issues that are considered relevant to an understanding of environmental stimulation in designing a special-care environment. There has not been time to consider many areas of concern. I have focused on psychiatric facilities because I have done most of my work there and I know this area better than others. But, as discussed earlier, I believe many of the issues to be relevant to a variety of "special-care" environments. I hope to have emphasized the complexity of the issues in this area and the need to avoid the temptation of simple solutions. Yet, I also want to emphasize that there are ways to deal with these issues both architecturally and administratively.

In any specific setting, special environmental attributes must be considered in terms of the people who live and work there, therapeutic goals and attitudes, the overall design of the setting, the availability of spaces for a variety of activities, and types of interaction. Furthermore, within any setting there must be an on-going awareness and evaluation of the design and use of space in relation to the behavior of individuals and the therapeutic goals of that setting. Problems are often *not* related to pathology. They may be related to patterns and rules for space use or to design itself and certainly may well be a function of the interaction of people in places. Environments communicate messages about what may and may not occur in them and about who the people are who live in them. The messages are not the same for all persons using them. Environments are not static; they can and do change over time—both physically and socially. Unless we are aware of the messages being communicated, of the changes that are occurring, and

their relationship to the behavior that occurs we cannot use the physical environment as part of a therapeutic program. In fact we can end up with a therapeutic policy created by default and with a physical/social environment that can support the very problems it was designed to help alleviate.

NOTES AND REFERENCES

1. Bechtel, R., "The Undermanned Environment: A Universal Theory?" in: R. Bechtel (ed), *EDRA 5: Undermanning Theory* (Washington, D.C.: Environmental Design Research Association, 1974).
2. Rivlin, L. G., and M. Wolfe, "The Early History of a Psychiatric Hospital for Children: Expectations and Reality," *Environment and Behavior*, vol. 4, pp. 33-72; and Wolfe, M., and L. G. Rivlin, "Evolution of Space Utilization Patterns in a Children's Psychiatric Hospital" in W. Mitchell (ed.), *Environmental Design: Research and Practice*, Proceedings of EDRA III Conference, University of California, Los Angeles, 1972.
3. Ittelson, W. H., H. M. Proshansky, and L. G. Rivlin, "Bedroom Size and Social Interaction," *Environment and Behavior* vol. 2, pp. 255-70; Wolfe, M., "Room Size, Group Size, and Density: Behavior Patterns in a Children's Psychiatric Facility," *Environment and Behavior*, vol. 7, pp. 199-224; Hutt, C., and M. J. Vaizey, "Differential Effects of Group Density on Social Behavior," *Nature* vol. 209, pp. 1371-72; Loo, Chalsa M., "The Effects of Spatial Density on the Social Behavior of Children," *Journal of Applied Social Psychology*, vol. 2, pp. 372-81; and McGrew, P. L., "Social and Spatial Density Effects on Behavior of Pre-School Children," *Journal of Child Psychology and Psychiatry*, vol. 2, pp. 197-205.
4. Wolfe, "Room Size, Group Size, and Density."
5. Ittelson et al., "Bedroom Size and Social Interaction."
6. Thomas, E. J., and C. F. Fink, "Effects of Group Size," *Psychological Bulletin*, vol. 60, pp. 371-84; and Bales, R. F., and E. F. Borgatta, "Size of Group as a Factor in Interaction Profile," in A. D. Hare, E. F. Borgatta, and R. F. Bales (eds.), *Small Groups* (New York: Knopf, 1955), pp. 396-413.
7. Bettelheim, B., *A Home for the Heart* (New York: Knopf, 1974).
8. Ittelson et al., "Bedroom Size and Social Interaction."
9. Altman, I., "Privacy: A Conceptual Analysis," in S. Margules (ed.), *EDRA 5: Privacy* (Washington, D.C.: Environmental Design Research Association, 1974); and

Laufer, R., H. M. Proshansky, and M. Wolfe, "Some Analytic Dimensions of Privacy," in R. Kuler, (ed.), *Architectural Psychology* (Stroudsburg, Pa.: Dowden, Hutchinson & Ross, 1974).

10. Wolfe, M., and R. S. Laufer, "The Concept of Privacy in Childhood and Adolescence," in S. Margules (ed.), *ERDA 5: Privacy* (Washington, D.C.: Environmental Design Research Association, 1974).

11. Wolfe, M., and M. Golan, "Privacy and Institutionaliza-tion," paper presented at Environmental Design Research Association Meeting, Vancouver, May 1976.

12. Rivlin, L. G., M. Wolfe, and M. Beyda, "Age-Related Differences in the Use of Space," in W. Preiser (ed.), *Environmental Design Research* (Stroudsburg, Pa.: Dowden, Hutchinson & Ross, 1973).

13. Rivlin, L. G., M. Rothenberg, and F. Wheeler, Personal communication, Environmental Psychology Program, City University Graduate School, New York City.

10

Normalization as a Social-Physical System

R. Christopher Knight, Craig M. Zimring,
and Margaret J. Kent

Christopher Knight is an advanced doctoral student of social psychology at the University of Massachusetts, Amherst. He holds a B. A. degree from Occidental College and an M. A. degree from San Diego State University, both of which are in psychology. His primary research interest is in the application of multidisciplinary social science to the planning and evaluation of social ecologies.

Craig Zimring is an advanced doctoral student in environmental psychology at the University of Massachusetts at Amherst. He hold a B. A. degree from the University of Michigan and an M. S. degree from the University of Massachusetts. His primary research interest is in the application of behavioral information to design and development of environmental design evaluation techniques.

Margaret Kent is a designer with a B. F. A. degree in design from the Tyler School of Art at Temple University and an M. S. degree in design from the University of Massachusetts at Amherst. She had worked for four years as a professional designer for several organizations before attending graduate school.

Together, these three authors have been Co-Directors of the Effects of the Living Environment on the Mentally Retarded Project sponsored by the Social and Rehabilitation Service, DHEW.

INTRODUCTION

The past few years has witnessed a confluence of interest by designers and behavioral scientists in the emerging field of environmental behavior, a discipline that focuses much of its attention on the built environment. Our own explorations of this field have recently centered around the "Effects of the Living Environment on the Mentally Retarded" (E.L.E.M.R.) Project, which we are undertaking in collaboration with Arnold Friedmann and Harold Raush. E.L.E.M.R. is a multidisciplinary, longitudinal study that is examining the effects of providing semiprivate spaces and other renovations for developmentally disabled adults in a large state school.

The E.L.E.M.R. Project originated when we were approached by a top administrator from the John Q. Adams (J.Q.A.) State School,[1] a training facility for the developmentally disabled. JQA was in the process of undertaking a major renovation program. Although the staff was convinced that an improved physical environment could have a positive effect on residents, the administration had found little data to guide them in their design and planning decisions. The renovation program seemed to be an excellent opportunity for research to help provide this guidance for the future.

The E.L.E.M.R. Project has been developed with two purposes: (1) to evaluate the impact of the designed environment on its users at JQA, and (2) to generate exploratory data on the basic issues of the environment–behavior relationship. We are concerned that both specific and general design decisions be made with the most complete information available about the impacts of those decisions on users. Moreover, by studying the residents within the context of the state school system, we hope to begin to understand some basic issues concerning the complex interactions of people and built environments.

In this chapter, we discuss the "E.L.E.M.R. Model," the emerging conceptual framework of the E.L.E.M.R. Project.

As of this writing, the renovations at J.Q.A. are yet to be completed, and most of the postrenovation data are not yet collected. We therefore base the present comments on our experiences and our preliminary observations. Although our model is primarily concerned with large institutions, we are addressing basic questions that have relevance for a variety of settings: How does the built environment affect behavior? What are the processes and paths of influence? What is the role of built environments in planning social ecologies to meet the needs of users.

Although the answers to these questions and to more specific design-oriented questions are as yet ambiguous, some clarity is beginning to emerge. In order to enhance this clarity, we must go beyond a narrow focus on environmental *determinants* of behavior: That architectural design be treated as only one of the many interrelated components of the social–physical system in which the developmentally disabled are living is necessary. In presenting our approach, we will first briefly describe normalization and environmental research. We will then discuss both "systems"- and "person"-level perspectives on the J.Q.A. State School and present our model and our empirical approach. Finally, we will discuss some implications of this model for those concerned with environments for the developmentally disabled.

NORMALIZATION AND ENVIRONMENTAL BEHAVIOR RESEARCH

Planning and design for the developmentally disabled has been dramatically altered in recent years by the general acceptance of the "normalization concept." Because this topic is treated at some length by Wolfensberger and other authors elsewhere in this volume, we shall discuss it only briefly as a way of setting the stage for our later deliberation. Nirje has described the normalization concept as, "making available to the mentally retarded patterns and conditions of everyday life which are as close as possible to the norms and patterns of the mainstream of society."[2] In our view, this normalization concept has been justified principally in two ways: on ethical-civil rights grounds, and as a behavioral hypothesis.[3]

The "ethical position," which has been primarily emphasized, calls for an end to the societal practice of labelling these citizens as "deviant"—a practice that has led to their isolation behind the walls of bleak, overcrowded, and dehumanized asylums. The belief is that the developmentally disabled deserve the same rights and privileges as other citizens to pursue normal, rich, and meaningful lives.

The "behavioral hypothesis" suggests that much of the bizarre behavior associated with the mentally retarded in large institutions (and perhaps their developmental deficit itself) actually stems from the institutional environment rather than from organic problems. The argument is that when moved to the community and given a supportive social and physical climate, the developmentally disabled will act in a more normal manner. Stated very simply, not only do the developmentally disabled deserve to live in normal home-like environments, but these are the only circumstances in which they may develop their potential to achieve important personal and social skills; normal environments influence or cause normal behavior.

Before continuing, we should note that *normalization, normal environments,* and *normal behavior* are all terms that may be criticized for their vagueness and implicit value content. They may imply typical, average, positive, or ideal. Moreover, the meanings of these terms are highly dependent on personal values, social class, and culture. In this sense the terms present some vexing conceptual problems unless they are carefully defined. Throughout this chapter, *normal behavior* will refer to behaviors that are positively valued, adaptive, and socially acceptable in the wider culture (e.g., high personal and social competence, independence). *Normalization* of built environments is taken to suggest positive and healthy settings that facilitate adaptive behaviors within this same value context. Moreover, "normalized" environments fall on a continuum of adaptiveness. In moving away from institutional settings, the "home-like" environments (which are seen as the goals of normalization) fall somewhere toward the more positive and healthy end of this continuum. However, the ends of the continuum are undefined. We may be fairly sure that these home-like environments are not *optimally* healthy or adaptive, just as the homes of many non-institutionalized people are not optimally healthy.[4]

Although we personally support both the "ethical position" and the "behavioral hypothesis" arguments, the behavioral hypothesis has some special aspects that should be stressed. By accepting this position, some advocates have endorsed assumptions that have yet to be proven and that can produce an overly simplistic view of what we *do* know about environmental influences on behavior. The hypothesis implies that the environment, and especially the designed environment, has a clear, direct, and understood influence on people. Moreover, it suggests that a normal environment rather than a compensatory one is the best way to produce normal behavior. This hypothesis is a reasonable one, but its validity is an empirical question to be answered in part by careful observation of people in normalized environments. The exploration of this question forms the crux of the E.L.E.M.R. Project, and we will discuss it in some depth later. Also, the behavioral hypothesis is in danger of leading us to believe in a sort of "architectural determinism" in which we may assume that by planning and designing houses and buildings we can plan the behavior and moods of the users of these buildings. As will be seen, this belief is overly simplistic in most situations.

The growing field of "environmental behavior"[5] has begun to explore the relationship between the designed environment and its users. Although the findings are both complex and as yet somewhat contradictory, we can state with some assurance that several conclusions are relevant to our approach.

These will be discussed more fully in the section on the "person" level later in the text. Briefly, these conclusions are:

1. People have needs for information and stimulation that can be met or frustrated by the environment. They also seem to prefer a moderately challenging, and interesting environment[6] and one in which they can control both physical stimulation (e.g., noise and color) and social stimulation.[7]
2. People seem to prefer a personally defined level of social interaction and therefore must be able to both encourage and discourage it.[8] Social interaction can be affected by interaction-fostering or interaction-discouraging furniture arrangement,[9] and by the provision of a "hierarchy of spaces" which includes a transition of control and usage from public to semipublic to private.[10]
3. The effect of the environment on behavior is complex, with physical aspects such as color, space, and noise interacting with social variables such as emotional needs and personal traits to influence behavior in a variety of ways.

Most environmental behavior studies have used easily accessible and observable groups such as college students, psychiatric or geriatric patients, or armed forces personnel. While even this literature is limited, systematic study of built environments for the developmentally disabled is almost nonexistent. Various anecdotal accounts suggest that normalizing environments for the developmentally disabled produces remarkable effects. However, there are very few intensive and systematic investigations with this population. Conclusions, including many of ours in this chapter, are often generalized to the disabled from research involving other groups. Although such generalizations may often be justified, we must exercise caution in interpreting such findings. We will propose a framework that may help to tie some of these findings together and may help to organize the badly needed work with the disabled.

As we began to formulate an approach for studying the normalization of built environments for the mentally retarded, certain key concepts emerged. First, normalization can be most reasonably viewed as a social–physical system that includes a number of interrelated factors. The influences on residents' behavior come both from people (e.g., direct-care staff, professional staff, and administrators) and from the physical environment (e.g., number of people per bedroom and furniture arrangement). Second, these various influences are highly interdependent. The effects of built environments may not be investigated without consideration of the interactive influences of the staff. Finally, the direct system of influences is itself sensitive to outside influences. We must keep in mind that the community of residents and staff in a building is affected by such outside influences as state budgeting decisions, shifting treatment models, and even national economic conditions that may bring changes in the type of persons seeking staff positions. Although our stated concern is with interior design and its role in personal development, we believe these aspects may only be understood within the context of the wider community system.

A SYSTEMS APPROACH

In the preceding sections we have begun to lay the groundwork for our conceptual approach. The E.L.E.M.R. Project is an attempt to examine the behavioral hypotheses implicit in the normalization principle. Although these are very complex issues, we believe they may be rendered more comprehensible if conceptualized at two levels of analysis.

1. At a systems level, the J.Q.A. physical and social environment is viewed as a set of constituent parts. We may map out each influence or combination of influences as they influence the J.Q.A. residents, and this general framework may then be used to guide more specific investigation.
2. On a more detailed "person" level, we focus on

the residents and direct-care staff by examining more specifically the relationships between the designed environment, the residents, and the direct-care staff.

The Systems Level

Although fully exploring the systems approach is beyond the scope of this chapter, understanding at least some of the more general characteristics of this perspective is necessary. A *system* has traditionally been defined as a group of interdependent elements that form a larger entity. *Systems analysis* focuses on the elements and their interrelationships and serves as a convenient way to study both the individual elements and workings of the larger system.

Recently, individual persons have been seen as components of social systems, although the scale of the systems has varied. In some cases, the multiple influences that act on a person's life have been viewed in this system perspective, and on a grander scale entire societies have been seen as constituting a system. Clearly then, a system may itself be only one component of a larger system. An important quality of all systems, however, is that they are somehow discrete. The elements that compose the system must have something in common with each other that they do not share with elements outside the system.

The components of a system are generally interrelated in complex ways, with each component singly and jointly affecting every other component. And, some components may intervene between others. For example, in the J.Q.A. system, the direct-care staff both affect residents and are affected by them. These groups are both affected by the physical environment and in turn alter that environment; yet the effect of the environment on residents is partially mediated by staff. The staff decide which doors, if any, are to be locked, which range of behaviors is to be tolerated in each space and who the users of those spaces are to be.

The extreme interrelatedness of many social systems means that they react to change in complex ways. The introduction of a developmentally disabled person into a community setting often changes both the person and the setting. Also, the physical setting is only one among many influences affecting behavior. Much of behavior is determined by relations with other people and with the larger community. These social relations may either intensify or largely negate the effect of living in a normal setting.

The great impact of the larger community, and of the norms of society, illustrates the *openness* of most social systems. Most social systems with which we are concerned, especially those that include interaction with the community, are directly affected by the outside world. The J.Q.A. system has recently felt the impact of several external influences. A federal court has awarded substantial funds for remodeling. Medicaid standards have dictated shifted staffing patterns, the economic recession has changed the type of job applicants, and the recession has slowed the creation of community placements.

The J.Q.A. system is an open social–physical sys-

tem that encompasses both the various groups of people within the state school as well as the physical environment. We examine the system in terms of the *residents*, and focus on the influences that affect them. The system itself consists of the state, school administration, professional staff, parents association, volunteers, direct-care staff, architectural environment, and the residents (see Figure 10-1). There are many outside influences on the system, such as the values and perceptions of the society as they dictate treatment models, funding, images of residents and staff, availability of community settings, and federal and state regulatory policies. The residents, for whom the system was created, are highly dependent on other groups in the system. Limited functional abilities, stereotypes of the retarded, and a custodial treatment model" have served to maintain this dependency.

Figure 10-1 provides a simplified overview of the system. The boxes represent the prime actors, and the arrows represent our conception of the paths of influence as they relate to residents. The thickness of

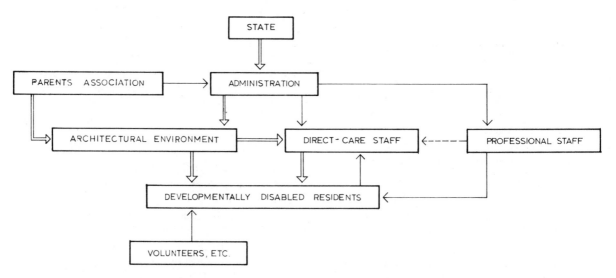

Figure 10-1
Principal paths of influence in the living milieu of residents at J. Q. A. State School
(thickness of arrows represents approximate strength of influence).

the arrows represents the approximate strength of each influence. For example, the direct-care staff, the professional staff, the administration, and the architectural environment all have considerable direct or indirect influence over residents.

The *direct-care staff* have the greatest influence over residents and can alter the impact of other components of the system on them. Staff are of especially great concern for the project, in part because of the frequency of their contact with residents and in part because those contacts occur in the principal area of interest, the living environment. These staff have low status on the grounds. They tend to be poorly paid and poorly educated, although the average education has improved somewhat over recent years. A custodial–maintenance attitude is reinforced by high resident/staff ratios (effective, fifteen to thirty residents to each staff member), by training that emphasizes physical care of residents, and by the lack of material and educational support.

The *professional staff* are generally college educated. Although this group is growing in importance, such factors as low salaries, high resident to staff ratios, lack of material support, and poor status attributed to these jobs from outside the state school all decrease this group's effectiveness. Also, the E.L.E.M.R. Project focuses on the immediate living environment. Most professional staff affect residents outside that setting and are therefore less central to the study.

The *administration* holds a great deal of centralized authority, but principally affects residents through other groups, especially the direct-care staff.

The *architectural environment* reflects the treatment model accepted during J.Q.A.'s construction in the 1920s and 1930s. (Note that in this chapter we are principally dealing with the fixed architectural environment as is indicated by the box in Figure 10-1. Although other aspects of the environment such as up-keep, furniture arrangement, and decoration are important, they will be dealt with only peripherally as we focus on more fixed characteristics of the built environment.) Most of the eight hundred residents at J.Q.A. are housed in moderate-sized dormitories that are sited on a rolling campus (a number of residents, however, are now living in nicely designed smaller converted staff cottages). At the outset of the E.L.E.M.R. Project, each dormitory contained six 30' x 40' spaces, three of which slept fifteen to twenty residents in a ward arrangement. The remaining rooms served as day halls, dining rooms, or multipurpose rooms. These rooms were designed in the familiar institutional scheme—that is, asbestos tile floors, ceramic tile walls, and plaster ceilings. Furnishings were sparse, tended to be institutional in design, and were often in poor condition (Figure 10-2 and 10-3).

As of this writing many of these dormitories are undergoing renovations and are being transformed into somewhat more home-like spaces—that is, modular furniture units are being introduced in some buildings and partitions in others. The modular units provide space for individual people, whereas the partitions divide the large rooms into one- to four-person spaces. The modular units have 4.5-foot high walls that are intended to provide privacy while a person is seated or lying down. The walls are joined together in "L" or "T" shapes and have built-in wardrobes, dressers, and work surfaces. The "L"- and

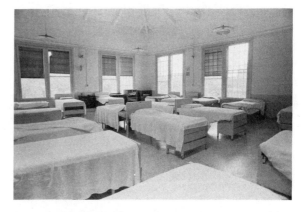

Figure 10-2
A typical sleeping ward for fifteen to twenty persons at J. Q. A. State School prior to renovation.

Figure 10-3
A typical large dayroom at the J. Q. A. State School prior to renovation.

"T"-shaped configurations are the basic units and are arranged to sleep twelve to fourteen people in the large rooms, while they also provide a common lounge space (Figures 10–4 and 10–5). The partition room structures will sleep two to four residents in bedrooms surrounding a central lounge area. The partitions will be 8 feet high and will consist of sheetrock painted in a variety of colors. Also, rugs and draperies will be added. In both arrangements the bathrooms will be modernized with the addition of private toilet stalls and private showers.

The "Person" Level

The systems framework just discussed places designed environments, and any effects that they may have on resident behavior, within the context of a wider community. We are also interested, however, in examining behavior in more specific terms, which might help us to understand and plan physical and social normalization. Several interrelated dimensions of individual behavior that have been discussed in the behavioral science literature may help us to organize this more specific level of analysis. Three of these dimensions are related to our conclusions from the

environmental behavior literature (see our earlier section on Normalization and Environmental Behavior Research) and have been useful in generating and explaining a considerable body of research. They also have special relevance for our understanding of design–behavior relationships and deserve somewhat fuller discussion here. These are: the level of arousal-stimulation, the need for information, and the need for privacy.

Arousal–stimulation[12] theories and empirical findings suggest that we can understand a diverse set of behaviors, such as the ability to concentrate, success on tasks, mood states, and satisfaction, by examining a person's internal physiological level of arousal. A growing body of literature indicates that although optimal, or preferred, levels of arousal depend somewhat on the activity, a moderate level of arousal is facilitative for many tasks. Arousal levels may be affected by personal factors (e.g., individual experience, personality, and needs), and social–situational factors (e.g., social activities, group structures, and norms), as well as environmental factors (e.g., architectural features, noise, and temperature). These theories also suggest that as one source of stimulation, such as noise, is increased and raises the level of arousal, people often try to counterbalance this state by reducing other sources of stimulation or by engaging in arousal-reducing behaviors. In these ways we try to maintain a comfortable level of arousal.

The concept of arousal has been useful in explaining observations in both institutional and everyday settings. Hutt and Hutt have found that autistic children typically exhibit high chronic arousal levels.[13] In an earlier study, the Hutts reported that as the complexity of a room was increased by introducing abstract visual patterns, the amount of stereotypic behavior by autistic children also increased.[14] Stereotypic behavior was seen as an arousal reducing mechanism. Casual observations at J.Q.A. are consistent with these findings. We have observed that the amount of neutral–stereotypic behaviors, such as rocking, seems to increase with increases in surrounding noise and activity. Other kinds of stereotypic behavior such

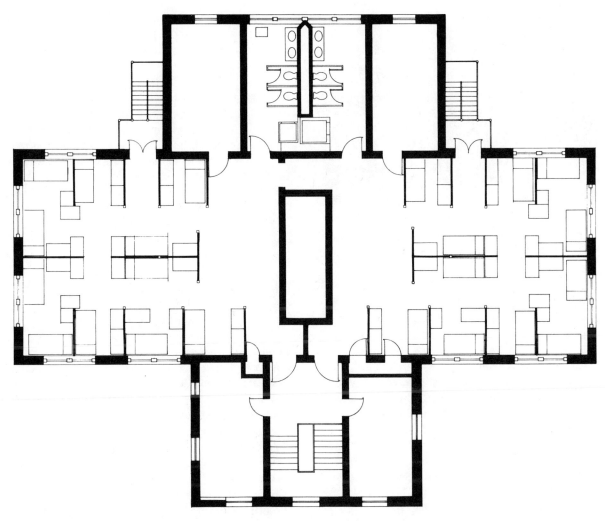

Figure 10–4
A typical layout of the modular sleeping units at J. Q. A. The open areas near the
central utility core function as day halls for ten to fifteen residents.

as masturbation (i.e., more auto-stimulating behaviors) may serve to increase arousal in low stimulating environments.

Coss has proposed that arousal due to interpersonal proximity may be manipulated by design.[15] More specifically, he has suggested that crowding stress may result partially from eye contact. This discomfort may be reduced by providing alternative visual foci such as artwork, posters, or windows. He also suggested that lowering ambient lighting may reduce eye contact and consequently reduce arousal. This link between eye contact and arousal may be pertinent to the common observation that little eye contact occurs in crowded institutional environments.

Figure 10-5
A view of the modular sleeping units that help to divide the renovated large rooms at J. Q. A. into semiprivate spaces.

The need for *information* is a dimension highly related to stimulation. In fact, the importance of novelty as a source of new information in the social and physical environment should be emphasized. Novel situations contain new information, and therefore are arousing and critical to growth. As we would expect from the arousal–stimulation model, different people tend to prefer different amounts of novelty. Most people seem to be comfortable when faced with a moderate amount of new information, although their needs shift over time.

Large residential institutions seem uniquely at odds with these needs for novelty. Because of high noise and activity levels, there may be considerable physical stimulation, but little new information. Residents may live in the same unchanging building for years or decades and may spend days or weeks without leaving the structure. The building interiors are usually very homogeneous, with the same color schemes used throughout. Furnishings tend to be sparse and similar. There are seldom the kinds of physical spaces that offer a range of challenges, and social and educational experiences are often both limited and mundane.

Wolfe, Altman, and others see *privacy* as a central issue in much of social behavior.[16] In this view, the argument is that people have needs for social interaction that vary over time and across individual persons. These needs are, once again, determined by social, physical, and situational factors. Attempting to match these needs with achieved interaction is seen as an important motivator of social behavior. If individual persons have more social interaction than they desire, they tend to feel crowded and withdraw or somehow attempt to reduce the level of interaction. If they have less interaction than they want, they feel isolated and try to increase interaction with others.[17]

Most institutions are not conducive to either the encouragement or discouragement of interaction. Day halls often have furniture that is widely spaced and difficult to move into conversational clusters. Institutions also often lack private bedrooms or even private stalls in bathrooms, which thus makes talking privately or being alone difficult.

The three dimensions just described, *arousal-stimulation*, *information*, and *privacy*, share a common orientation that deserves emphasis and elaboration. In all three cases, designed environments are viewed as influencing individual behavior by first affecting personal experiences or internal states. Needs for arousal-stimulation, information, and privacy are personal phenomenal experiences that are influenced in a variety of ways and in turn may affect various overt behaviors. We can recall from the previous discussion that arousal levels may be raised or lowered through personal, social, or physical factors. Consequently, a given level of arousal may lead to any of a diverse set of behaviors (e.g., moving from one space to another, shifting focus of attention, and altering styles of social interaction). Likewise, needs for information and privacy are also multiply influenced and lead to multiple consequent behaviors. A diagrammed example using "need for privacy" may provide a useful illustration of these relationships (see Figure 10-6). Any or all of the events represented on the left side of the figure may increase the need for privacy. In turn, the need for privacy may be

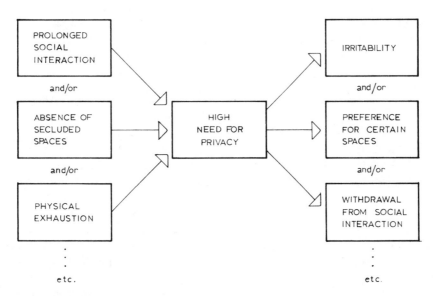

Figure 10-6
A diagram of the environment–behavior relationship relative to need for privacy.

satisfied at least partially by a number of behavioral strategies.

The point is a simple one, but crucial for developing a realistic and useful model of the environment-behavior relationship in general and of normalization in particular. The designed environment must be viewed as one of many influences affecting needs for arousal–stimulation, information, and privacy. The consequences related to the varying levels of these internal states will be varied rather than specific.

THE E.L.E.M.R. MODEL

The three dimensions discussed above may be useful in directing our attention to design factors critical to the environment–behavior relationship. People seem to seek optimal levels of arousal–stimulation, information, and privacy. However, a central issue for designers, planners, and administrators concerns the determination of "optimal." How arousing or stimulating should environments be? How does one design for privacy? What level is appropriate for each group and environment?

Aside from the fact that we are at a rather rudimentary level of scientific knowledge concerning what is arousing, informative, or private, there are other complications for the practitioner wishing to use these concepts. Not only will users vary in their personal needs, but, as we have stated above, the same people will prefer different environments at different times and in varying situations. Moreover, the impact of a given setting is determined not only by its spatial design, but by the activity taking place within it. For example, a space designed to be muted and relaxing, perhaps a small sitting room, may become the hub of raucous social play. This activity will transform the area into a highly arousing and stimulating environment. As we consider the problem of designing for optimal levels of arousal–stimulation, information, and privacy, a paradox becomes apparent. While built environments (both the division of spaces and their design) are fixed or semi-fixed the needs and activities of the users will be varied and will fluctuate over time.

This problem is, of course, not unique to the concern of designing for the developmentally disabled. For all of us, built environments are semi-fixed and our needs are individually dynamic. However, in most instances we have the opportunity to seek spaces appropriate to our needs at a given time and to alter somewhat those spaces. Because there are a variety of spaces available to us, we may gain control through exercising *choice*. The cocktail party chatter and other activities may continue unabated in the living room, but throughout the evening party goers retire, each at their own time, to the porch or kitchen for "fresh air," "a stroll," or "to get away from it all." Our homes are our "castles," and we have at least one room in which we may exert control. The living room is arranged for optimal social interaction—that is, chairs may be placed rather close together and facing each other—but the study or den may serve an equally important need for calm and privacy. If we step back for a moment, the resolution to the paradox is clear. The crucial issues for any person's satisfactory use of the built environment involve *opportunity* and *control*. Normal, well-designed living environments are characterized by a range of opportunities for stimulation, privacy, and so forth. We may satisfy our fluctuating personal needs by exercising freedom to choose among these settings.

Through a single day we may at various times desire social interaction, quiet, aloneness, and intellectual challenge. We may behave in rather "normal" or "healthy" ways by matching out needs to social-physical environments to allow their fulfillment. We can do so by moving to other environments, as in the cocktail party example, or by somehow manipulating the environment. This latter choice can involve constructing a building or fence or simply closing a door for privacy. In the cocktail party example, we can also change the situation by bringing to bear some fairly sophisticated social skills, such as phsyical distancing from others,[18] allowing long lapses in conversation, talking about a busy following day, and otherwise encouraging guests to leave.

The importance of both the physical and the social definition of settings is gaining recognition. In fact, a good deal of research in ecological psychology has demonstrated the central importance of behavioral setting and environment in defining "appropriate" behavior.[19] What is considered appropriate in one setting (e.g., quiet, solitary, uncommunicative behavior while alone in a private area) may be considered very unusual in another (e.g., the same behavior at a social gathering). In fact, any concept of "normal" behavior is meaningless outside the context in which it occurs. Is nudity appropriate? How about screaming, talking, or staring off into space? Of course, what is "normal" depends on the situation.

Normal behavior is supported by providing a variety of spaces and situations that include well-designed public and private spaces. When neither the physical opportunity nor sophisticated social skills are available (e.g., desire for privacy when only crowded social space is available), other less-usual and perhaps less-adequate strategies for control may be used. One means of achieving privacy in a crowded room is social withdrawal, which may become stereotypic behavior at its extreme; in the absence of quiet and calming spaces, the sensory world may be blocked-out by psychologically turning inward. We believe that the physical aspect of normalization may be usefully conceptualized as designing built environments to offer support for a wide range of personal needs. Normal environments contain opportunities to fulfill needs for arousal and quiet, challenge and rest, social contact and aloneness, and excitement and calm. Only environments that offer such a range of opportunity may be considered normal and supportive of normal development.

We have chosen to conceptualize normalization in terms of *opportunity* and *control*. Within this model, there are implications for environmental design in general, but there are also special considerations to be noted in applying these concepts to the developmentally disabled.

Normalizing the living environment of institutions may affect the residents very directly by creating a variety of spaces. Traditionally, institutions consist entirely of public spaces: large open day rooms, unpartitioned dormitories, and bathrooms without stalls. Large "multipurpose" spaces may be dominated by one activity to the exclusion of other incompatible activities. The chosen behavior of one or a few people (e.g., playing ball or dancing) precludes options that may be preferred by others (e.g., sitting quietly, resting, or concentrating on a book). Normalized designs, on the oher hand, must include a range of public, semipublic, semiprivate, and private spaces. Further, this variegated living milieu must allow some segregation of spaces on the dimensions of arousal–stimulation and information. For example, a lounge with a television, a sitting room with comfortable chairs and magazines, and a group activity area serve different and incompatible needs. The ideal design will maximize choice options for the largest number of users by creating multiple spaces that are segregated so as to allow a variety of activities that would be incompatible within a single space.

At J.Q.A. the renovations will represent a limited step on the continuum toward normal environments. The single modular units, with 4.5-foot walls, will offer semiprivate space where there was formerly only public dormitory space. The partitioned rooms will offer shared private spaces. Because each module is designed for one person, and each partitioned space for not more than four, the residents have an increased opportunity to decorate or otherwise affect these spaces to suit their own tastes. In the old buildings, all space was public. The new design will not only create semiprivate modular units, or bedrooms, but semipublic lounge areas for each twelve to fourteen residents. Each lounge could be considered the special area of one group, just as the bedroom is designated as the private space of one resident. As we have described the renovations, residents will have increased opportunity to control stimulation, information, and privacy, but will not enjoy the full range of normal opportunities. There is no truly private space. Moreover, although the stimulation and information in the larger bedroom may be reduced by retiring to the modular unit, ambient noise and visual stimuli may not be escaped completely.

We should also mention that normalized environments also offer the direct-care staff opportunities for personal control unavailable in more homogeneous institutional settings. Personal needs for control of stimulation–arousal, information, and privacy are not suspended simply because the activity is defined as work. Although the staff may have more adaptive and sophisticated social skills with which to achieve personal control, unvariegated environments that do not support the exercise of this control may adversely influence the staff's ability to work effectively. Work satisfaction as well as the amount and even the style of interactions with residents may be less than optimal as staff attempt to fulfill personal needs in a physical setting that offers little opportunity to do so easily. For example, institutions typically offer the staff very little opportunity to lower stimulation or achieve privacy except through refusing to interact or retiring to a staff office that is unavailable to residents. In our belief, these environmental characteristics may partially account for the typically low level of interaction between staff and residents reported in the literature.[20] More normalized environments with opportunities for staff to work with residents in public or semipublic, stimulating or calming spaces may encourage interactions and even affect their style and quality.

A factor of special importance with the developmentally disabled, particularly those with a life history of institutional living, is that the built environment allow opportunity to *learn* normal behavior. Abnormal environments cannot support the learning of appropriate and normal behavior. Where there is no opportunity to regulate stimulation and privacy, residents are not likely to take advantage of those opportunities when they are made available in a newly renovated building. Utilizing the built environment to support internal needs in normal or socially acceptable ways is a learned skill.

Direct-care staff become crucially important in this regard. Both through their actions, as models of normal behavior, and through direct training, the staff may support the resident in learning new ways of using the environment. The meaning of "private" space may be understood by the residents only through staff streatment of that space as "private."

Is the space really under the control of the resident? Does he or she have complete freedom to invite others in or ask them to leave? Can the resident retire to this space and be alone, unseen and undisturbed? Using direct training to assist residents in learning to take full advantage of a normalized environment may be necessary. The staff, for example, may be able to help residents realize their right to privacy and to overcome any timidity or shyness about exercising control over their personal space. Traditional institutions, of course, offer stark and abnormal environments for the direct-care staff as well as the residents. Staff who are used to traditional patterns may need education as well if they are to assume effective roles as models and teachers. The fulfillment of these roles, however, may only occur in normalized environments that offer the opportunity for staff to interact, model, and teach within settings that will support their efforts.

We are not unreasonable to expect that as the developmentally disabled learn to exercise choice and control over built environments, in order to achieve desired levels of arousal–stimulation, infor-mation, and privacy, they may also learn the more general aspects of personal efficacy. Personal efficacy may also foster feelings of adequacy in dealing with other life situations (cf., perceived control.)[21] Learning to attend to the external world and successfully interacting in it to satisfy personal needs may lead to further achievements of autonomy and self-responsibility.

Clearly, then, any opportunity for resident control and learning that is achieved by normalized environments may only be realized through the direct-care staff. The concept of normalization must be viewed in the light of this social-physical system as summarized in Figure 10–7. The designed environment may offer *residents* and *staff* the *opportunity* to seek spaces and settings that fit their need for arousal–stimulation, information, and privacy. There are also other direct effects of normalized environments on the staff. A normal and variegated environment is the only setting that will support staff attempts to teach residents normal and appropriate behavior. In this sense, normalized designs offer the *staff opportunities* not available in traditional institutions.

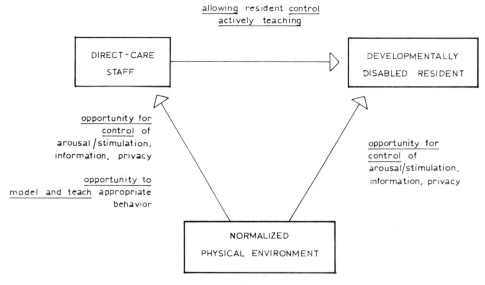

Figure 10–7
Diagram of social–physical system.

However, settings are not only defined by design but by the definitions of those who use them. Opportunity for control and opportunity to teach do not guarantee the achievement of control and learning. Beyond opportunity, *staff* must take an active role in *allowing* resident control of arousal–stimulation, information, and privacy, and even actively *teaching* residents how to achieve this control. The single bedroom may only be private if staff consider it so and demonstrate that it is by asking permission to enter, leaving when requested and encouraging resident control of its decorative arrangements. Areas designed for quiet social interaction must be supported by the staff's assistance in maintaining this special definition of appropriate use. Modeling and teaching become especially important for the developmentally disabled as they acquire new appropriate behaviors within environments that offer a variety of spaces and experiences to meet their fluctuating needs and desires. A community setting, if properly managed and well-integrated into the community, can provide a vast assortment of social–physical spaces.

In summary, the social–physical system that comprises normalization can be viewed in terms of two principles: *opportunity* and *control*. *Opportunity* serves as shorthand for a range of experiences that the environment must offer, which include a gradation of arousal–stimulation, information, and privacy. *Control* is the physical and social act of utilizing these opportunities. Opportunity is a general framework that helps us to focus on issues that are critical to planning and design. The E.L.E.M.R. Project is an attempt to address these specific issues.

THE E.L.E.M.R. PROJECT

The data collection strategy used by the E.L.E.M.R. Project reflects our interest in examining the transactions of the immediate community of residents, staff, and built environment. We have focused our attention on these three key elements in the normalization process as described in our model. Through a variety of observational procedures we have begun to assess the level of normalization (or opportunity) created in the J.Q.A. built environment, the response of residents to these renovations, and the interactive role of the staff in this process. The selection of methods represents an attempt to analyze the model previously described and to generate a wide range of additional exploratory data.

The designed environment is being documented both before and after renovations. This includes photo description of all spaces, floor plans, and narrative descriptions of interior materials. We will also complete an analysis of the acoustical quality of the buildings, including reverberation time and sound pressure homogeneity in various areas of a room.

Residents are observed directly using a forty-item behavior checklist[22] during several periods before and after environments are normalized. Time samples of behavior will allow us to assess the proportion of time spent, for example, in social interaction, solitary behavior, stereotyped actions, or use of manipulatable objects. In addition, each observed behavior is coded for its location in the building (4' x 4' grids) and any physical artifacts involved (e.g., chair, tables, window, pole, TV).

A separate observation scheme is being used to record both frequency and quality of staff–resident interactions.[23] We determine who initiates these interactions, and we also document a variety of qualitative dimensions: command, question, or descriptive initiation, apparent affect, mode of communication (verbal or physical), and context (e.g., social, personal care, formal training). We are following these interactions through three steps: observing initiation, response, and any consequences to the response. As with the resident observations, these interactions are coded for location and physical artifact.

We will be able to tap the ways in which the staff exercise their opportunities to teach by examining context, command-question initiation, and so on. Resident control may be examined through the frequencies of social and solitary behaviors and the distribution of those behaviors in different spaces. In general, we hope to gain insights into environmental influences on behavior by comparing levels and types of resident social interaction, frequency and type of resident–staff interactions, number of aggressive acts, and so forth, both between environments and across time.

The model we have previously presented describes a broad approach within which we have focused on a variety of more specific phenomena. But there are certain limitations to any procedure or method of scientific inquiry, especially within such an embryonic field. Because of this fact, and in the interests of maintaining an exploratory perspective, we have employed a wide range of supplementary observational methods. These include participant observations, staff interviews, and a host of unobtrusive measures (e.g., school records, breakage, building logs, staff employment records, and so forth).[24]

CONCLUSIONS

In summary, we believe the normalization concept to be principally justified on two grounds: morally and by a "behavioral hypothesis." This "behavioral hypothesis" is an empirical question that is being explored in the E.L.E.M.R. Project. It is also partly addressed by "environmental behavior" research. This research seems to suggest three general conclusions: (1) People need to control information and stimulation so as to achieve a moderate level of both; (2) people need to control social interactions in order to attempt to match desired and achieved interaction; and (3) environmental behavior is complex and interactive.

The relationship of the designed environment to the behavior of the residents at John Q. Adams State School can best be understood conceptually if viewed on two levels: (1) at a systems level, which describes the major paths of influence in the state school community system, and (2) at the "person" level, which focuses on somewhat more specific impacts on residents.

A systems approach implies that causality is complex and interrelated and that any effect of change will be equally complex. Most social systems are "open"— that is, sensitive to outside impacts such as funding and policy changes. While we focus on the relationship of residents to the designed environment and the direct-care staff at J.Q.A., we also conceptualize the administration and the professional staff as part of the larger system of influences (see Figure 10-1).

Various theorists have suggested arousal–stimulation, information, and privacy as important dimensions for understanding the environment–behavior relationship. Normalized environments should offer a wide range of spaces to satisfy the residents' and staffs' need along these dimensions.

We propose that normalization implies: (1) *opportunity* for control, learning and modeling, and (2) *achievement of control* over arousal–stimulation, information, and social interaction. We can see that all effects on residents are crucially dependent on the direct-care staff, both because of their direct power and because of their importance for training and modeling. Also, the developmentally disabled should be encouraged to exercise control over spaces through social skills, decoration, arrangement, and maintenance in order to facilitate the satisfaction of their own needs.

The E.L.E.M.R. Project represents one empirical approach for exploring the "behavioral hypothesis" of normalization. The project includes direct observation of resident–staff interaction, direct observation of residents, and other more "global techniques" such as participant observation, critical incidents, unobtrusive measures, and interviews.

The systems perspective we have adopted for our empirical work at J.Q.A. may be viewed as a conceptual map. Like other maps it describes a complex of interconnections. It suggests both specific routes of inquiry and their relationship to the surrounding landscape. As a guide to work with the E.L.E.M.R. Project, this system framework generates a perspective within which to interpret our findings. Our preliminary analysis of the normalization process at J.Q.A., and other literature in environmental behavior, suggests that normalized environments are not likely to encourage normal behavior in developmentally disabled citizens unless *all* elements of the community system are well coordinated. Also, successful planning and administration of normalization programs may be achieved only with multidisciplinary teams that are aware of the system character of the enterprise. This might dictate, for example, a systems expert on administrative staffs and on design teams.

We had mentioned earlier in this chapter our concern that some professionals may have at least partially adopted a naive and limited focus on "environmental determinants" of behavior. By now, that such a focus is inadequate for understanding the relationship of environments to behavior should be clear. Human behavior and social variation are far too rich to yield to such simple deterministic description. The systems approach and the E.L.E.M.R. model were adopted and developed in analyzing environment–behavior relations and normalization at J.Q.A. (cf., Figures 10-1 and 10-2). But at the same time, we believe they offer a broader conceptual scheme that can be usefully applied in other settings. Within any social system, the built environment will play a significant role that may only be understood when viewed as part of the larger context. While the actors and their relative influence in any specific system may vary, every social–physical setting can be seen as having a systems character that may be described and understood. Likewise, built environments may be conceptualized as offering more or less opportunity for users to satisfy human needs. J.Q.A., for example, does not achieve what we consider full physical normalization and indeed may be fairly low on a "continuum of normalization." The developmentally disabled at J.Q.A. are still isolated from the wider community, and despite the renovations, the institution does not offer a full range of public and private space. And, of course, much of the institutional social structure remains intact. While other settings may offer more or less "opportunity," as we have defined it, the basic conceptual issues remain the same.

For the practitioner, the systems approach is a useful framework that can be comprehensively ap-

plied and especially considered in each unique circumstance, thereby providing a structure for professional judgment and creative intuition. It may, if used in this manner, give direction for understanding the complex interaction of persons and physical environments in the normalization process.

We are all affected by the social–physical environments we encounter every day. At home, at work, or at play, people and buildings provide us with opportunities for quiet, social interaction, or activity. We have the opportunity of varied environments and a variety of skills with which to change environments that are unsatisfactory. Subtle social skills allow us to seek aloneness when others are present. Our homes are fashioned and altered to fit our personal desires. The developmentally disabled, while having the same needs for variety and control, often do not have the same social skills to alter situations and hence may be even more affected by the physical environment than are more skilled people. Normalization for the developmentally disabled must offer both opportunity in the built environment and special assistance with social skills, so that they too can learn to use the environment to satisfy their human needs.

NOTES AND REFERENCES

The authors would like to extend sincerest thanks to all those who read this chapter in its earliest stages and whose comments and suggestions were invariably cogent and perceptive.

The E.L.E.M.R. Project described herein is administered by the Institute for Man and Environment, University of Massachusetts at Amherst. This project is wholly supported by DHEW Division of Developmental Disabilities Project Grant #S.R.S. 51-p-05374/01-02. The project staff includes the co-authors as co-directors and Arnold Friedmann, Professor of Art/Design, and Harold Raush, Professor of Psychology, as co-principal investigators. Friedmann and Raush joined the project in the planning stage.

Knight and Zimring were co-equals in the writing of this chapter. The order of these two authors shown on the title page of this chapter is arbitrary. Kent provided invaluable conceptual input, especially for the design issues. The photographs are by Alyce Kaprow of Amherst, Massachusetts.

1. In the interest of confidentiality, the pseudonym is used throughout the chapter.

2. Nirje, B., "The Normalization Principle and Its Human Management Implications," in Kugel, R. B. and W. Wolfensberger (eds.), *Changing Patterns in Residential Services for the Mentally Retarded* (Washington, D.C.: President's Committee on Mental Retardation, 1969), p. 181.

3. We are indebted to Dr. Christopher Hurn, Department of Sociology, University of Massachusetts, for suggesting this distinction.

4. Greg Olley, personal communication, 1976.

5. Variants of the field are referred to as "man–environment relations," "environmental psychology," "architectural psychology," and so forth.

6. Kaplan, S., "An Informal Model for the Prediction of Preference," in E. H. Zube, J. G. Fabos, and R. O. Brush (eds.), *Landscape Assessment: Values, Perceptions and Resources* (Stroudsburg, Pa.: Dowden, Hutchinson & Ross, 1975).

7. Berlyne, D. C., *Confict, Arousal and Curiosity* (New York: McGraw-Hill, 1960); Mehrabian, A., and J. Russell, *An Approach to Environmental Psychology* (Cambridge, Mass.: MIT Press, 1976); and Chapter 9 of this volume by Maxine Wolfe.

8. Altman, I., *The Environment and Social Behavior* (Monterey: California: Brooks/Cole, 1975); Stokols, D., "A Social-Psychological Model of Human Crowding Phenomena," *Journal of the American Institute of Planners*, vol. 38, pp. 72-83; and Wolfe, Chapter 9 of this volume.

9. Holahan, C., "Seating Patterns and Patient Behavior in an Experimental Dayroom," *Journal of Abnormal Psychology*, vol. 802, 1972, pp. 115-24; Mehrabian, A., and S. A. Diamond, "Effects of Furniture Arrangement, Props and Personality on Social Interaction," *Journal of Personality and Social Psychology*, vol. 20, 1971, pp. 18-30; and Sommer, R., *Personal Space: The Behavioral Basis for Design* (Englewood Cliffs, N.J.: Prentice-Hall, 1969). The first two studies found that the amount of conversation among hospitalized geriatric patients was dramatically increased when chairs which had formerly lined the walls were moved closer together and placed in conversational groupings. Mehrabian and Diamond found a similar relationship with college students.

10. DeLong, A., "The Micro-Spatial Structure of the Older Person: Some Implications for Planning the Social and Spatial Environment," in L. A. Pastalan and D. H. Carson (eds.), *Spatial Behavior of Older People* (Ann Arbor: University of Michigan Press, 1970); Proshansky, H. M., W. H. Ittelson, and L. A. Rivlin (eds.), *Environmental Psychology: Man and his Physical Setting* (New York: Holt, Rinehart and Winston, 1970); Wolfe, Chapter 9 of this volume; and Zimring, C., G. Evans, and E. Zube, "Space and Design: The Proxemic Interface," paper presented at the Sixth Annual Meeting of the Environmental Design Research Association, Lawrence, Kan., 1975.

11. Wolfensberger, W., *The Principle of Normalization in Human Services* (Toronto: National Institute on Mental Retardation, 1973).

12. Wolfe, Chapter 9 of this volume, presents a fuller discussion of this position. Other recent reviews are found in Berlyne, *Conflict, Arousal and Curiosity*, and Berlyne, *Aesthetics and Psychobiology* (New York: Appleton-Century-Crofts, 1971); Mehrabian and Russell, *An Approach to Environmental Psychology*; and Zimring et al., "Space and Design."

13. Hutt, C., and S. Hutt, "Effects of Environmental Complexity of Stereotyped Behaviors of Children," *Animal Behavior*, vol. 802, 1965, pp. 115-24.

14. Hutt, C., and S. Hutt, *Behavior Studies in Psychiatry* (New York: Pergamon Press, 1970).

15. Coss, R., "The Cut-off Hypothesis: Its Relevance to the Design of Public Spaces," *Man–Environment Systems*, 1973, pp. 417-40.

16. Wolfe, Chapter 9 of this volume, and Altman, *The Environment and Social Behavior*.

17. Altman, ibid.

18. Hall, E. T. *The Silent Language* (New York: Doubleday, 1959), and Hall, *The Hidden Dimension* (New York: Doubleday, 1966).

19. Barker, R. G., *Ecological Psychology* (Palo Alto, Calif.: Stanford University Press, 1968); and Wright, H. F., *Recording and Analyzing Child Behavior* (New York: Harper & Row, 1967).

20. Allen, G. J., J. M. Chinsky, and S. W. Veit, "Pressures toward Institutionalization within the Aid Culture: A Behavioral-Analytic Case Study," *Journal of Community Psychology*, vol. 2, no. 1, 1974, pp. 67-70. Dailey, W. F., G. J. Allen, J. M. Chinsky, and S. W. Veit, "Attendant Behavior and Attitudes Toward Institutionalized Retarded Children," *American Journal of Mental Deficiency*, vol. 78, no. 5, 1974, pp. 586-91; and Veit, S. W., "A Method for Investigating Interactions Between Institutionalized Retardates and Their Aids, unpublished master's thesis, University of Connecticut, Storrs, 1973.

21. There is a growing body of evidence to indicate that perceived control may alter spatial behaviors, social interactions, and other behaviors. See, for spatial behaviors, Evans, G. W., "Behavioral and Physiological Consequences of Crowding in Humans, unpublished doctoral dissertation, University of Massachusetts at Amherst, 1975; for social interactions, see Altman, *The Environment and Social Behavior*.

22. Adapted from Billings, A. G., J. Simon and S. W. Veit, "Behavior Observation Form," unpublished manuscript, Psychology Department, Mansfield Training School, Mansfield, Conn., 1974.

23. Adapted from Veit, "A Method for Investigating Interactions."

24. Effects of the Living Environment on the Mentally Retarded report series, "Technical Report # 1, Project Description and Experiment Design," and "Technical Report no. 2, Observation Manual," Institute for Man and Environment, University of Massachusetts at Amherst, 1976.

Part IV

Social Barriers: Towards a Barrier-Free Environment

11

Planning and Design for Normalization in Denmark and Sweden

Michael J. Bednar

Michael J. Bednar is Associate Professor of Architecture and Co-Chairman of the Division of Architecture of the University of Virginia. He holds a B. Arch. degree from the University of Michigan and an M. Arch. degree from the University of Pennsylvania, where he studied with the late Louis I. Kahn. Previously, he taught and conducted research at the School of Architecture of Rensselaer Polytechnic Institute. He is a registered architect who has practiced in New York City and Philadelphia, and he currently maintains a practice in Charlottesville, Virginia. In 1972, he received the George G. Booth Travelling Fellowship in Architecture from the University of Michigan. He is a member of the Housing and Environment Steering Committee of the Gerontological Society. His present involvement is in teaching, research, and practice related to special users including children, the physically and mentally handicapped, and the elderly.

INTRODUCTION

The normalization principle originated in Scandinavia where it was first used as the basis for planning and providing services for the mentally handicapped. The Scandinavians are a very socially conscious people and have long been concerned with the welfare of all their citizens. Their methods of planning and providing social, medical, educational, and rehabilitative services are sophisticated and highly developed.

The Scandinavians have also been leaders in the development of contemporary architectural design. Their designers are internationally known for high-quality furniture and interior furnishing. The Scandinavian architects are internationally respected for their sensitivity to the use of natural materials, relationships to site, construction detailing, use of natural light, and spatial proportion.

The combination of these two factors makes Scandinavia a rich place to study planning and design for the mentally handicapped. Guidance resulting from the Scandinavian experience in this field has been sought by many other countries. However, the Scandinavian countries are unique politically, economically, culturally, and geographically, and their experience cannot be directly translated to the United States nor to any other country. Nevertheless, important lessons can be learned from their experience and approach, and it is in this light that this chapter is written.

THE MENTALLY HANDICAPPED IN DENMARK

The Danish National Service for the Mentally Retarded is directly responsible for all services to the mentally retarded in Denmark. It is an administrative unit within the Ministry of Social Affairs. It was created in 1959 by a legislative act that outlined the care and services to be provided for mentally retarded persons. The director of the Service since its inception in 1959 has been N. E. Bank-Mikkelsen.

The Danish National Service is obligated to pro-

vide services to "those who are or appear to be mentally retarded and who also appear to be in need of
special services."[1] Included in the services it is obligated to provide are the following:

Aiding parents in caring for mentally handicapped
children;
Providing education and training from age seven to
twenty-one;
Providing substitute homes if they are needed;
Providing opportunities for work and leisure

The entire costs of these services are paid for by the
Danish National Service even if they are required
from birth to death. Administratively, the mentally
retarded are defined as those requiring care not available through community services.

There are approximately 22,000 registered mentally retarded in Denmark (about .5 percent of the
population). This figure represents the incidence of
care and may not be the incidence of occurrence.
However, little retardation exists in Denmark due to
socioeconomic or cultural deprivation, which is virtually nonexistent. Thus, the incidence rate is much
lower than it is in the United States.

Philosophy

One of the primary reasons for the success of the
Danish National Service for the Mentally Retarded is
the strong philosophy that guides all aspects of its
work. This philosophy, which permeates the organization, is based upon the normalization principle. It
was first articulated by Director Bank-Mikkelsen in
1969, although it had been used as an operational
philosophy for many years before that. As originally
stated, it meant ". . . letting the mentally retarded obtain an existence as close to the normal as possible."[2]
This principle has become the basis of all the laws in
Denmark dealing with the mentally retarded. It also
serves as the philosophical basis for the service delivery systems, the facility planning guidelines, and the
architectural design criteria. It is, on the surface, an
almost obvious and simple principle, which upon
analysis yields profound and pervasive implications.

Implementation of the normalization principle
means according the full rights of citizenship to mentally handicapped persons and providing them with
the opportunities to live normal lives. It does not
mean setting a goal of achieving "normalcy" in behavior or performance. However, it does mean accepting
the individual person with his or her handicap and
providing him or her with the means to live with that
handicap, which includes special treatment, education,
and training, as required. The normalization principle
appears to be revolutionary, but only in contrast to
the attitudes towards the mentally retarded that were
prevalent until recently.

The mentally retarded should be offered the same
conditions of life as are available to all other citizens.
These conditions can be classified into three primary
areas: housing conditions, working conditions, and
leisure.[3]

Mentally retarded children should be given the
opportunity to live with their parents. If this situation is not possible, a substitute home should be
arranged. This home should have the scale and character of a home, not an institution. A normal pattern of
life should be available there, with meals eaten with a
small group and private sleeping accommodations.
Mentally retarded adults should be encouraged to
move away from the parental home. They should be
given the opportunity to live as independently as
possible.

All mentally retarded adults should be given the
opportunity to work and earn money. To this end,
general compulsory education should also apply to
the mentally retarded with special education services
as required for their special needs. As children approach adulthood, vocational training should be provided so that job skills can be developed. All adults
should work whether in normal jobs, sheltered employment, or therapeutic work. Concomitantly, they
should be paid for their work, whatever the product.

Leisure opportunities should be available equally
to all citizens in the community. Games, sports,

vacations, and travel should also be a normal part of the lifestyle of the mentally handicapped.

My purpose here is not to discuss fully the normalization principle nor to analyze its implications for the delivery of human services. This task has been done very convincingly and thoroughly by others.[4] My purpose is to present some relevant aspects of the Danish experience in implementing the normalization principle with regards to facility planning and design. I would like to demonstrate how a strongly articulated philosophy along with the persuasive leadership of Director Bank-Mikkelsen has structured the delivery of services to the mentally handicapped from planning the service systems through detailed architectural design.

Planning Service Systems

The service systems of the Danish National Service are organized such that a "continuum of care" is provided for each client from birth to death, if necessary. (Notice that the term *client* is used, which means a voluntary seeker of service.) This continuum of care is highly differentiated in that appropriate care is provided at all levels at the required time and place.

The initiation of the continuum of care begins with the prevention of mental retardation. The prenatal and postnatal care provided to each mother and child includes early diagnosis and treatment. Research is supported to develop new preventative and diagnostic techniques.

If the child is diagnosed as mentally retarded, before age seven, several forms of care can be provided depending upon the severity of the handicap and the parental circumstances. The child can be placed in a substitute care home, receive treatment at his parental home, or receive periods of treatment at local hospitals or institutions. He will probably attend a nursery school at governmental expense. This nursery school or kindergarten can either be autonomous or integrated with the substitute home.

On reaching the age of seven, the handicapped child must attend school. These schools can take several forms:

> Segregated special schools;
> Integrated school units (within a normal school);
> Boarding school (school and substitute home combined);
> Institutional school (school within a comprehensive institution).

If a substitute home is required, several forms are available:

> School-home (home independent of school but nearby);
> Boarding school (school and home together);
> Residential institution (residence within a comprehensive institution);
> Treatment home (residence at a home where special treatment can be provided).

Additional forms of care can be provided for children, as required. Care can be made available in the parental home. Free-time homes are provided (usually as part of schools) where children can stay after school until parents pick them up. Also, holiday homes are available for children while parents are away. Many children also attend summer camps for recreation and care when school is not in session.

When the child reaches the age of twenty-one, the third phase of the continuum of care is initiated. The adult retarded person is again provided with several options for work, education, and residence. He or she is provided with opportunities for education and training to develop work skills:

> By receiving training at a central institution and working in the sheltered workshop located there;
> By receiving training and working at an autonomous sheltered workshop;
> By receiving training at a training school and working in an independent job in the community;
> By attending a folk high school, or similar schools where vocational courses are offered.

Those persons unable to develop work skills can reside at a long-term care institution where they are engaged in occupational therapy for which they receive "pocket money."

Several forms of residential opportunity are also available for adults:

Long-term care institutions;
Hostel homes, which are autonomous;
Independent housing within the community.

Those persons living independently can rely upon the central institution or day centers for medical care, treatment, or recreational–social programs. Summer camps and holiday homes are also made available for adults.

These differentiated forms of education, training, work, and housing are necessary to maintain flexibility in providing care in accordance with the need of the client. This "continuum of care" is the result of a highly developed system of services that responds to the normalization principle in providing each client with the opportunity for as normal a life as possible.

The service systems in Denmark are organized into twelve regional centers that provide administrative control of services to the mentally handicapped in each region. Each regional center is administered by a four-man interdisciplinary team: an administrator, a chief physician, a director of social work, and a director of education. This team is responsible to the National Board of Directors for all activities in that region. The interdisciplinary nature of the team is in recognition of the multidisciplinary nature of mental retardation and is thus one of the key reasons for the success of the Danish National Service in effectively coping with mental retardation.

Each region has a comprehensive institution that acts as both an administrative and service center for the region. These central institutions contain the full range of diagnostic, educational, and medical services as well as residences for those who require special services on a frequent basis. Specialist personnel such as doctors, physiotherapists, psychologists, and others travel from the central institution to local facilities on a regular basis. In addition, clients at local facilities requiring concentrated testing or

Figure 11–1
The Central Institution for Children in Nyborg, Denmark, has the hospital unit, observation unit, treatment units, school, and houses for spastic children all organized around a large landscaped courtyard. (Architect: Jens Malling Pedersen.)

treatment spend short periods of residence at the central institution. These central institutions are usually located at the center of population concentration for the region.

The Center for Region VIII is located in Nyborg on the island of Funen. It is a dual center with one facility for children and another for adults. Each facility is in a different location. The facility for children was completed in 1972. It contains residential accommodations for 240 children in four disability categories: spastic, profoundly retarded, moderately retarded, and psychotic. There is also an observation ward and a hospital ward. The center contains a school, assembly hall, treatment center, administrative offices, and staff residences (Figure 11–1).

Regional Center I is located in a suburb of Copenhagen. It is also a dual center, with one facility for children and the other for adults. The dual nature of the center is designed to reduce the size of the institution and to separate these client groups on the basis of separate needs. The children's facility, Vangede Children's Hospital, has residential accommodations for three hundred persons. It contains the full range of facilities and services that include an outpatient clinic, acute illness ward, observation ward, physiotherapy unit, kindergarten, school, and adventure playground. The children are grouped into houses according to their disability; for example, cerebral palsy, motor handicap, moderate retardation, profound retardation, and acute illness.

The adult counterpart facility, Lillemosegard, also houses three hundred persons. It is only a half-mile from Vangede, and they share a central kitchen and heating plant. Services and facilities at Lillemosegard include an infirmary, assembly hall, canteen, physical medicine unit, and treatment wards.

One principle maintained in the planning of these central institutions is to separate the place of work from the place of residence, as is the normal situation for most citizens. At Lillemosegard, there are four internal workshops: pottery, sewing, weaving, and woodworking. These are combined with occupational therapy for those who have no work skills. Creative work and handicrafts are emphasized for the personal satisfaction that they produce. All products are sold to the public, and all clients are paid for their efforts.

There is little disagreement in Denmark regarding the validity of the comprehensive service center concept. However, many do think that the residential component of these regional centers can be decentralized and integrated into the community.

In addition to the regional center facility, each region contains a variety of other facilities including homes, schools, treatment centers, sheltered workshops, training centers, hostels, and others. The location, size, and program for each of these decentralized facilities is based upon the particular needs found in each region. The comprehensive facilities plan for each region is developed to serve the unique client population of that region.

Facility Programming and Design Process

The process of facility programming and design in Denmark is a product of a number of special conditions:

The small size of the country (five million, approximate population);
The centralized planning and funding control of the Danish National Service for the Mentally Retarded;
The role of the architect in Denmark.

Briefly, the process that has been used proceeds as follows. The Danish National Service develops the overall national plan for programs and facilities based upon population data and incidence projections. It determines location, size of facility, and programs to be accommodated. It may also choose the site or work with the architect in site selection. In selecting architects, the Danish National Service has decided to work very closely with only four firms for all of its facilities (J. M. Pederson, C. F. Mollers, Ejlers and Graversen, and L. Teschi). In this way, these firms have become specialized in the design of facilities for the mentally handicapped. They have been able to improve upon the design of the facilities through postoccupancy evaluations. The close working relationship with the Danish National Service eases the communication of program objectives and design intentions.

The architect usually writes the facility program. The only criteria provided are in terms of overall area per client and minimum room sizes. No other criteria have been established in order not to impede the rapid evolution of this facility type nor to hinder design innovation. The program is then reviewed and changed in discussions with the Danish National Service and the client body, or a committee representing the client.

The architect then develops a set of preliminary designs. He alone is responsible for determining the environmental design criteria in terms of lighting, acoustics, circulation, colors, and so forth. After design review, design development takes place, working drawings are produced, and construction is undertaken.

An excellent book has been published by the Danish National Service entitled *Ten Years of Planning and Building, 1959-1969,*[5] which effectively describes the evolutionary development of facilities planning and design for the mentally handicapped through the use of case study examples.

Programming guidelines

The normalization principle remains as the most important programmatic guideline. In its full sense, it pervades all programming decisions. However, several other programming guidelines or policies are followed, some of which are corollaries to the normalization principle.

Institutional scale is an area of great concern in Denmark because it is a factor in normalization. The relative economies of operating institutions of different scales are not the primary concern. Rather, the concern is with the depersonalized lifestyles that institutions engender as a result of neglecting the needs of the individual person in order to efficiently serve the needs of the group. The larger the institution, the greater the depersonalization. Thus, the Danes want to reduce institutional scale in order to improve the quality of services rendered. Another concern, is the difficulty of physically, functionally, and socially integrating large institutions into a community.

In the central institutions, where a full range of services is provided for the most handicapped clients, a norm of three hundred persons in residence had been used as the basis for programming. Several of these institutions have been built and evaluated. As a result, a new programming guideline of one hundred persons in residence is being discussed as the optimal size for a full-service institution.

In school-homes and boarding schools for moderately retarded children, a workable norm of thirty resident clients has been in use. However, efforts are being made to make these facilities smaller with only ten to fifteen resident clients. This smaller size would make them closer to the scale of a normal residence and effectuate better community integration.

The level of concern for institutional scale does not seem to be a concern with regards to the optimal size for schools. The Green Schools for mildly retarded children vary in size from 48 to 212 pupils. The three Green Schools that I visited were one hundred pupils in size. This number appears to be a workable norm, although the optimal size for a school is a problem that has not been addressed in Denmark.

Another normalization corollary is the effort to reduce institutionalism, or the lack of alternatives in living patterns. School-homes are a good example of a response to this guideline. They are self contained, independent, substitute homes for twenty-four to thirty children and are usually located in conjunction with a school. At the Hoybo School-Home in Kalundborg (Figure 11–2), thirty children live in nineteen singles, five doubles, and one triple. They are organized into family groups of five that include boys and girls. The children are very proud of their home and participate in decorating it and caring for it (Figure 11–3). The home, originally a residence for the elderly, was built at the turn of the century, but has been completely remodeled. Living in an old house is also consistent with the principle of normalization, since most people in Denmark do live in old houses.

Privacy versus supervision is a programmatic issue that the Danes have effectively addressed by maintaining a careful balance between them. Privacy is achieved by providing each client with his or her own locked room. Each person is responsible for room maintenance and decoration. Staff enter only upon permission, or if there is an emergency. Privacy in toileting is provided by single-fixture bathrooms that have doors and locks. Again, staff intervene only if there is difficulty.

Supervision in the residential facilities is provided through staff presence twenty-four hours per day. Staff accommodations usually include offices, a lounge, service rooms, and sometimes sleeping facilities. These rooms are unobtrusively located within the house.

Decentralization is certainly a strong program guideline in Denmark. The only centralized facility is

Figure 11-2
The Hoybo School-Home in Kalundborg, Denmark, is a handsomely renovated facility housing thirty children. The building, which was formerly a residence for the elderly, is located in a high-quality residential neighborhood. (Architects: Ejlers and Graversen.)

Figure 11-3
One boy at the Hoybo School-Home saved his money to purchase this sophisticated stereo music system, which he installed in this large, handmade cabinet in his room.

the regional center, and its scale and components are being reduced. Residences are being separated from the institutions and placed in the community. External sheltered workshops are being established. Special schools are becoming independent of the residential institution. One of the purposes of this decentralization is integration with the community. Physical integration needs to be achieved first, before functional and social integration can take place.

The criteria used for grouping clients, and therefore services, are an important part of the programmatic guidelines. In general, clients are grouped according to primary disability, with secondary disabilities accepted within that group. Therefore, as an example, those who are both retarded and physically handicapped are grouped with the retarded.

In the residential institutions, there is a clear separation between disability groups. At the Nyborg Central Institution, residents are grouped according to primary disability without regard for sex or age, and the houses are designed accordingly. There are separate houses for the spastic or multiply handicapped, severely retarded, moderately retarded, and

psychotic. These separate groups of children would seldom come together or have contact with each other. At Vangede Children's Hospital in Copenhagen, the situation is similar. There the clients are grouped onto wards for acute illness, cerebral palsy, motor handicaps, severe retardation, and profound retardation. The most seriously handicapped children are living at these central institutions. This grouping by primary disability is justified since very special care is needed for each group.

In the schools, the situation is more open. Children are more likely to be grouped by learning abilities and potential. At the Green School in Hillerod, disabilities are mixed in the same classroom. Children with cerebral palsy are placed with mentally retarded children, if they have the same intellectual ability. When special treatment for the cerebral palsy children is required, they simply leave class. Physically handicapped and brain-injured children are placed in class groups with the mentally retarded if they can work together socially and educationally. In no case is sex or age used as the sole criterion for educational grouping.

In the residences, boys and girls are usually not segregated. In some homes, a range of ages and both

Figure 11-4
Each house unit at the Central Institution in Nyborg, Denmark, has its own well-furnished kitchen and dining areas that look onto adjacent private courtyards through large expanses of glass. (Architect: Jens Malling Pedersen.)

sexes are deliberately placed together in order to create a more normal "family-like" situation. Privacy for different sexes in toiletting is not strictly supervised. For example, in one school-home in Brondbyoster that has two bathrooms for eight children, boys didn't use one and girls the other; they all used both, just as they would in a normal household. When children in these homes become older, sexual relationships do develop. There is general agreement in Scandinavia that the handicapped should enjoy sexual relationships as do normal people. Therefore, these relationships are guided through counselling but are not prohibited.

Environmental design

In terms of environmental design, normalization results in the provision of environments of high quality for the use of the handicapped. It involves the right to use space in a normal way, and the right to experience and to use environments in a normal way. The greatest advancement has taken place in the design of residential facilities. The emphasis has been on providing a more home-like environment—that is, the reduction of institutionalism. All new residential facilities are organized on the basis of houses of twelve as a norm. Most rooms are for single occupancy and have their own wardrobes and furniture. Double rooms are also provided as alternatives. Bathrooms are usually shared amongst two or three persons. The rooms are private and can be locked by the clients, who are also encouraged to express themselves in the decoration of their rooms.

Eating, socializing, and recreating also take place within this house group. Each house has its own living room, dining room, and outdoor recreation courtyard. The staff usually work directly with one house, without rotating from house to house, in order to establish rapport with the clients. The houses are usually one story, and each one has its own exterior entrance. The kitchens are used only for serving food that is prepared in a central kitchen.

This house structure is evident in many facility designs. At the new Central Institution for Children in Nyborg, houses are for twelve children with six single and three double rooms. Each house has its own courtyard, and each has its own dining, living, play, service and lounge rooms (Figure 11-4). The houses for psychotic patients accommodate only six, in four single rooms and one double room. The perceived scale of the institution has been reduced for the client by giving him a relationship to the small identity group that is the house.

In terms of personal scale, most spaces are kept at average standards for their function. Single bedrooms are about one hundred square feet in area. The scale of the rooms is normal adult scale in terms of hardware, switches, door sizes, furniture, and so forth. In some children's facilities, attempts are made to "scale down" the institution through design. At Vangede, the roofs are "pulled-down" close to the ground to make the buildings appear smaller.

The design quality of the interior environment in Denmark is at a very high level of sophistication. The

Danes are internationally known for their unique furniture designs and creative furnishings. This level of design quality is also maintained in the care facilities (Figure 11–5). Much of the furniture is natural wood with woven textile upholstery. Handsome light fixtures and well-chosen wall hangings are in evidence everywhere. Floors in many new facilities are covered with thin, hard-weave carpets. Interior trim is of natural wood with many wall and ceiling surfaces of natural wood slats. These furnishings are durable and easy to maintain. Moreover, the clients are taught to respect and care for fine quality things.

The sophistication in interior design in some facilities seems to be overdone. Some staff have voiced opinions regarding the lack of choice in selecting furniture and graphics, because all was done by the architect. This attitude is an institutional one: Both staff and residents must be able to make a house into a home by individualizing the interiors.

Building exteriors in Denmark are limited by tradition, climate, availability of materials, and building technology. A combination of these factors has caused most building exteriors to be made of brick masonry with wood trim and pitched tile roofs. Most care facilities, schools, and residences are made of these materials with slight variations. The designs are generally contemporary in appearance with large glass areas and plasticity in the walls. Exposed steel frame with glass and asbestos panels were the materials used in building the Green Schools, but this design did not result in any significant economic advantage nor did it meet with the approval of staff, administrators, or the public. The new Regional Center at Nyborg is built of poured-in-place concrete with flat roofs and steel window frames. This building is a very handsome one in terms of architectural design and was also reasonably economical to construct. However, it has a scale and appearance that is appropriate only to an institution. (See Figure 11–1.)

In the interest of normalization, the use of traditional exterior materials and architectural details is justified. It allows buildings to appear familiar, and

Figure 11–5
The interior design of this living-dining room at the Logumgaard Residence for Women in Logumkloster, Denmark, is typical in its use of wood ceilings and trim, large expanses of glass, hanging light fixtures, and Danish-designed wooden furniture. (Architect: Jens Malling Pedersen.)

making them fit into an existing architectural context is easier.

The exterior environment or site is very important to the appearance and use of Danish schools and homes. Despite the harsh climate, exterior sitting areas, courtyards, and play areas are very common. Plants, trees, and flowers are used in creative ways to enhance a building's exterior (Figure 11–6). At the schools, considerable emphasis is placed on physical training for its therapeutic value. Most schools have well-equipped playgrounds. Play houses and large-scale climbing structures are very popular. Parents' associations often aid in constructing playground equipment as do the children themselves, as part of their workshop training.

Denmark is known for its "adventure" or Robinson Crusoe playgrounds. These playgrounds are built by the children from their imaginations out of scraps of materials that are gathered or donated. The Carlsberg and Tuborg breweries are very generous with wooden beer cases, which are used as building blocks to make incredible structures. The largest of these

Figure 11-6
The rose garden at the Logumgaard Residence for Women not only enhances the house's exterior but also provides an activity focus for the residents, who care for the flowers and enjoy their beauty. (Architect: Jens Malling Pedersen.)

playgrounds, which can be found at Vangede, a facility for the mentally retarded, is a labyrinth of trees, playhouses, towers, and climbing structures (Figure 11-7).

The adventure playgrounds often look like rubbish dumps to adults. Their messiness and disorderliness is often contrary to adult attitudes. In appearance they seem dangerous and unsafe, but the experience is to the contrary. Very few, if any, injuries occur there. The children must learn to be safe within them.

They are utopian places to the children, "their own little world." The teachers realize that there is much to be learned in such playgrounds varying from environmental experience to practical hand work training. They are places of high motivation, and therefore encouraged.

The implementation of the normalization principle in building design is not yet fully achieved in Denmark. As yet, no one knows how far it can be developed, but rapid progress is being made. There is still a

Figure 11-7
This "adventure" playground, located at the Vengede Children's Hospital in Copenhagen, was built by the children from scraps of materials. It provides them with an ever changing arena for environmental exploration.

sense of "protectivism" in many of the Danish facilities. They are heavily staffed and luxuriously equipped. Many are still peripherally located. There also remains a "sense of institution" in many of these facilities although progressively this characteristic is being eliminated. The Danes are critical even of their own efforts because they realize how much remains to be done in achieving the fullness of the normalization principle.

Educational Facilities

In 1959, a law was enacted in Denmark that required that all mentally retarded children be granted

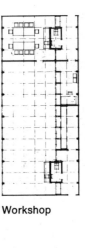
Workshop

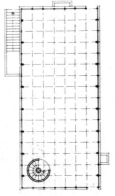
Gymnasium

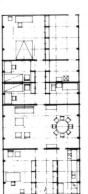
Principal's House

Normal Classes

Administration

Special Classes

education until age twenty-one. The immediate need was for thirty-two new, nonresidential special schools throughout the country. A plan was devised by the archictectural firm of Ejlers and Graversen to build these schools out of steel-framed modular units. Fifteen different functional arrangements were developed all within the same sized module (Figure 11–8). The school program for each site was satisfied by assembling the required unit modules and connecting them together with covered walkways. On many sites the modules were arranged to define abundant play space and courtyards. The ample landscaping in these school plans resulted in the term *Green School* (Figure 11–9).

As a result of the need to build many schools quickly and at low cost, a prefabricated building system was developed and utilized. The system's basic elements consisted of steel frames with folded steel roof panels and cement asbestos wall panels. Steel construction was chosen because concrete prefabrication technology was not yet developed in Denmark in 1959. This experiment in systems building did not result in any cost savings over traditional construction. Moreover, the lack of thermal inertia caused overheating in summer and cold in winter. The teachers and staff have reacted to the school construction as being "too modern looking," "too noisy in the wind," and "too dull and drab." However, the architects believe the simple forms and subdued colors are appropriate in an educational environment for retarded children (Figure 11–10).

Much of Danish special education outside of an institutional setting is focused on the Green Schools. These day schools are attended for the most part by children who live at home with their parents. The schools function well and are well regarded by teachers, parents, and the general public.

There are efforts to integrate special education wtihin the normal school system, but the extent of

Figure 11–8
Represented here are the six most common modular floor plans used in the design of the Green Schools.

Figure 11–9
This typical Green School, Christianslundskolen in Nyborg, Denmark, is an assemblage of classroom, workshop, gymnasium, and administrative modules joined together by covered walkways and sited in a verdant suburban location. (Architects: Ejlers and Graversen.)

these efforts is difficult to ascertain. One example was found in the Ballerup School District, in a suburb of Copenhagen. The plans there were to integrate one special education unit within each of four normal schools. These units would be single disability units of brain-injured, spastic, psychotic, and partially deaf children. The Malov School in this district had eight classes of four to eight children with brain injury. Each class was placed in a different area of the school. No special architectural provisions were made for the classrooms. An old gymnasium had been converted to a free-time facility for special students.

There is little interest in Denmark in open-plan educational facilities. Certain spaces for occupational training or "acts of daily living" training are open plan in the sense of containing several simultaneous activities. Likewise, sheltered workshops are of this form. The design attitude seems to be one of making basic rooms that achieve their flexibility through arrangement of component furniture as opposed to making large, flexible, open-plan spaces.

A unique facility in Copenhagen that needs to be mentioned is a folk high school called Spaniensgade, which is the equivalent of the American community

Figure 11-10
The prefabricated steel construction of the Green Schools is exposed on the interior as seen in this typical classroom view. Large glass areas in the exterior walls bring in natural light, whereas glazing in the interior partitions establishes visual relationships between spaces. (Architects: Ejlers and Graversen.)

college. However, this folk high school is only for the mentally retarded, who attend either full- or part-time in order to improve their educational background or to develop job skills. The subjects range from English to driving, music, drama, photography, and television technology. The folk high school is combined in one building with a hostel and sheltered workshop into a truly unique educational institution.

THE MENTALLY HANDICAPPED IN SWEDEN

The provision of services for the mentally retarded in Sweden is the responsibility of the county, or *lans*. There are now twenty-four such counties and one county borough in the City of Malmo. They vary in population size but average about 25,000 people.

The counties are responsible for all health and medical services to the general population as well as the care, treatment, and education of the mentally retarded. They have an unrestricted right to levy taxes for these purposes, which in 1969 averaged 7 percent of the taxpayer's income.

The responsibility of the county in providing care services is enumerated in the Provisions for Certain Mentally Retarded Persons Act of July 1, 1968. It is a comprehensive act in that it sets forth all mandatory services that must be provided for retardates. The act defines the "mentally retarded" as those who because of retarded mental development require special provisions from the public sector in their education, care, social services, and counselling.[6] The act does not cover all mentally retarded persons; only those in need of special services.

In May 1971, there were a total of 33,824 persons registered as mentally retarded in Sweden. This figure represents an incidence rate of .42 percent of the Swedish population of approximately 8,000,000 people. Some retardates were receiving no provisions other than a pension. However, estimates are that only about half of the total retarded persons are receiving care; the other half are not registered.[7]

The responsibility for implementation of the act lies with the National Board of Education (educational provisions), and the National Board of Health and Welfare (care and residential provisions). Their supervisory duties are exercised in the form of inspection visits to the facilities as well as consultations with the County Council's Board for Provisions and Services to the Mentally Retarded. All activities by the counties in the provision of services must be approved by these National Boards. Karl Grunewald is the Head of the Division for Mental Retardation in the National Board of Health and Welfare, and Lennart Wessman is the Inspector of Special Schools for the National Board of Education.

Philosophy

"In Sweden, the basic aim in all care of the mentally retarded is Normalization," according to Dr. Grunewald.[8] The emphasis is on trying to achieve what is normal without denying the retardate's handicap. As in Denmark, this philosophy underlies the entire approach to the delivery of mental retardation services.

The best way to state the Swedish objectives in terms of normalization is to use Dr. Grunewald's own goal statements:

Retardates should live in as normal a way as possible, with their own room, and in a small group;

They should live in a bisexual world;

Retardates should experience a normal daily rhythm;

They should work in an environment different from that in which they live;

They should eat in a small group, as in a family, with food and drink standing on the tables;

They should be able to choose between different ways of spending their free time;

Their leisure pursuits should be individually designed, and differentiated according to the time of year;

The environment should be adjusted to the age of the retardate;

Retarded young people should be given the opportunity to try out adult activities and forms of life, and be able to detach themselves from their parents.[9]

Although this list contains a comprehensive set of goals, the Swedes have made great progress towards achieving the objectives listed.

The particular emphasis in Sweden on achieving normalization has been through the means of integration. Integration is not viewed as an end in itself, but only a means of organizing services in such a way that the aims of normalization are easier to achieve. Integration has been achieved in Sweden perhaps more completely than anywhere else in the world at this time, and the Swedish experience definitely has important implications for facilities planning and design.

Integration would not be necessary had not segregation previously occurred. In simple terms, integration means an establishment of relationship between the lives of the retarded and those of the rest of society; between the schools for retarded children and normal schools; between the homes of retarded persons and the homes of the community. This establishment of relationship is normal, since all of society is a single unit. To segregate those who are different is a way of denying their equal rights as members of human society. Thus the achieve-

ment of integration is a very important aspect of normalization.

The efforts to achieve integration have been advanced along two separate fronts: (1) Integration in education relative to the public school system, and (2) integration in living relative to housing in the community. Both of these will be discussed in the following sections.

Planning Service Systems

As in Denmark, the guiding principle in the organization of service systems is the continuum of care. The services, facilities, and programs are highly differentiated. They are designed to deliver service appropriate to the level of need at the required time and place. This system is very flexible and the services can be tailored into individualized packages. The continuum of care is available to all retarded citizens regardless of age or economic status.

In broad terms, the care system can be divided into institutional–residential care and educational provisions. The range of residential care varies from day nurseries and short-term homes to residential institutions. In terms of education, it ranges from kindergarten to adult education programs.

The trend in residential care is towards integration within the community in the form of small-scale homes. Accordingly, these homes should fulfill the function of ordinary homes. If they are small in scale, they can be placed in close proximity to the client's hometown, neighborhood, and family. They can be easily integrated into the community both socially and geographically.

Much progress has been made in Sweden to improve the standards of residential care. This improvement is reflected in a survey of all residential institutions conducted in April of 1971 by the National Board of Health and Welfare.[10] There were in total 344 residential facilities with an average of 50 beds each. The total of 17,200 beds were in 9,000 rooms for a mean of 1.9 beds per room. Rooms with a single bed totalled 48 percent whereas rooms with two beds totalled

34 percent. Nearly 20 percent of the clients lived in primary groups or ward units of less than 12 persons. These average conditions are already significant in achieving normalized standards.

As a principle of planning, residential care for children is separated from that for adults. Out of 132 homes for adults, only 22 also house children. Within each county, a central residential home usually provides long-term somatic care for adult retardates. The other homes are considered administrative and functional annexes to this home. However, the absolute number of long-term bed patients has been substantially reduced.

In the future, many more adults who are not able to live alone will be living is hostels. Other persons can be housed in ordinary homes or a group of apartments.

Residential care for children is also following the trends of integration and differentiation. Many children are now living in small-scale homes that are part of the community. Many are placed in homes near hospitals that provide pediatric care. Only those children requiring intensive care will remain living at boarding schools or central institutions.

The newest trend has been to encourage care in the parents' home. To enable retardates to live at home, the county councils are willing to pay a separate sum to their relatives. Regular visits to the home are made by medical staff, therapists and social workers, and when necessary, the retarded person living at home can visit a rehabilitation center.

Special education services are provided in several forms:

Special auxiliary teaching;
Separate special teaching;
Special classes in normal schools;
Special schools.

Special schools in the past have usually been boarding schools. However, the thrust in Swedish special education has been towards integration. The number of boarding schools has not increased in the last fifteen years. The number of retarded children attending special classes or schools in conjunction with normal schools has doubled in the last fifteen years. All new planning for special education is integrated with planning for the normal school system.

The organization of special education begins with kindergarten for children below age seven. Several of these kindergartens are attended by both retarded and normal children.

From age seven to seventeen, education is compulsory. The retarded attend either a basic comprehensive school or a training school, depending upon their abilities. Heretofore, only the "educable" could attend school. With the development of the training school concept, all retarded persons attend school without regard to their intellectual limitations. Much of the emphasis in training school is on learning activities of daily living (ADL).

At age seventeen, all retarded students are given the opportunity to attend vocational school. The training may be in vocational instruction for a particular occupation or actual training for a wider area of work opportunity. Career guidance is also provided.

For certain pupils, regular school attendance may not be possible. In this case, special schools or boarding schools are required. However, the intention is to reduce this form of school to a minimum. In the future, the plan is for almost all retarded students to attend normal schools.

In the Swedish organization of care services, there are three levels of service delivery: local, county, and regional. The local level of responsibility is just beginning to develop. At present, local municipalities are responsible for the education of normal and physically handicapped children. Planning for integration has given them additional responsibilities in educating mentally retarded children.

The county has the primary responsibility for delivering care services. Each county is required to make a five-year plan for the care of the mentally retarded in their area. This plan for the provision of services and the development of new schools and homes must be approved by the two national boards. With this approval, national grants to finance construction of facilities can be awarded. Each county maintains a central home that provides facilities, equipment, and personnel of a more specialized nature than are available at the local homes. Those persons requiring specialized services receive them there. For adult retardates, these central homes also provide wards for long-term care of chronic illnesses.

The third level of the care system is regional. Counties cooperate in organizing regional hospitals and special care units. The regional hospitals provide observation and diagnosis, short-term medical care, intensive treatment, and long-term medical care. They serve as back-up facilities to the local and county homes. In addition, they provide care services for those with physical handicaps, epilepsy, blindness, deafness, and acute illness. The special care units provide similar services although their scope is limited as is the population group served.

Facility Programming and Design Process

The planning, design, and construction of facilities for the mentally retarded in Sweden are the responsibility of each county council. These processes are guided and approved by the National Board of Education (school facilities) and the National Board of Health and Welfare (care and residential facilities). Each county council must prepare a five-year plan that states the location, size, and type of facilities to be provided.

Plans for specific new facilities are developed by the county councils and submitted to the national boards for construction aid approval. These plans are reviewed by SPRI, The Institute for the Planning and Rationalization of Health and Social Welfare Services. SPRI is a semi-independent organization that serves as a consultant to several government agencies including the National Board of Health and Welfare. It bases its recommendations upon criteria that have been developed by the national board. The final approval for the construction of new facilities must come from the Committee for the Construction of Health and

Social Welfare Buildings. SPRI only makes recommendations. Educational facility plans are reviewed by the National Board of Education, Division of Building.

Both national boards have developed criteria and guidelines for the programming and design of new facilities. However, these criteria are quite minimal in their stated forms. Most of the criteria and environmental concepts are communicated directly to the county councils and their architects through meetings and review sessions. The small size of the country (8,000,000 people in an area the size of California) allows this kind of direct communication. The minimal written criteria enable close collaboration to solve facility planning problems in accordance with the specific situation. The following is an example of residential facility programming criteria:

> The typical house shall have eight to ten bedrooms with shared baths, living room, dining room, and kitchen;
> Almost all bedrooms should be singles (100–120 square feet) but one double room per house is suggested (140 square feet);
> Every bedroom shall have a door with a lock, closet, and storage shelves;
> Every two bedrooms should share a toilet and shower.[11]

This list serves to illustrate the generality of the criteria. Specific environmental design criteria are the responsibility of each architect to develop for a particular project.

Programming guidelines

The issue of institutional scale as a programming problem could simply be eliminated by not programming any new institutions. Although the Swedes view this as a desirable goal, they realize that the elimination of institutions is neither practical nor feasible. Special-care institutions will always be needed for persons with serious degrees of handicap and as back-up short-term facilities for others.

Karl Grunewald has provided some guidelines on the scale of an institution:

> That it be organized on the principle of the small group;
> That the physical standard of the institution reduces collective facilities to a minimum i.e., in respect to toilets, basins and showers, bedrooms, etc.;
> That the institution should not be larger than would permit the assimilation of those living there into the community.[12]

The Swedes have been through the arguments regarding small-versus large-scale facilities. They state the advantages of small facilities as the following:

> Greater proximity to residents' own home town and relatives is made possible.
> It is easier to integrate the residences socially and geographically into the community.
> Wider social contacts with the community are made possible.[13]

In the opposing direction, the arguments against small facilities are as follows:

> A small number of clients does not warrant the provision of special facilities such as swimming pools, workshops, gymnasiums.
> A small number does not provide an adequate basis for differentiated care.
> The staff in small facilities feel isolated and there is no opportunity for team work.[14]

In the viewpoint of the Swedish adminstrators, the advantages of the small institutions greatly surpass those of large institutions.

Experience with the rehabilitation of retarded persons demonstrates that one of the most important factors is the size of the interpersonal group. The retarded person needs a small number of interpersonal relationships so that those relationships can be accepted as positive stimulation. This group should be under ten in size, and it should also be heterogeneous, which thus makes the group more interesting and active.

The sizes of group homes for children should be from four to six residents. These should be five-day homes so that the children can return to their parents' homes on weekends. Seven-day hostels of a somewhat larger size should also be available as an alternative.

For adults, the same principles apply. Group homes should house seven to eight persons, but no larger. Adult hostels for twenty-five to forty-eight residents should also be available as an alternative.

In the shift to small-scale homes integrated into the community, staffing patterns will change. In adult group homes, staffing will vary from only a guardian to two or three staff for a home of eight. The children's group homes will require a higher staffing ratio, with four to five staff for each home of five to six children. The provision of these kinds of homes will also require specialists who are not resident at the institutions, but travel from home to home as required.

In an analysis of total cost of services, these small-scale homes are expected to cost less to operate in the long run than traditional institutions. The primary reason is flexibility. Group homes can be established where they are needed, when they are needed. On the other hand, institutions have inertia, and their physical plant must continue to operate and be maintained. Staffing of five-day homes is less expensive than in twenty-four hour institutions. Specialists and equipment can be provided as they are needed in group homes. This flexibility will in the long run result in reduced costs and yet more differentiated service in accordance with client needs.

Decentralization is an important programming guideline in Sweden, primarily because it fosters community integration. The programming objective is to make each of the service components of work, recreation, training, education, treatment, and residence functionally viable. At the same time, these components must be physically integrated within the community and operate as a cohesive system. As an example, an adult hostel cannot function well alone, but requires a day center facility, sheltered workshop, and other facilities to complement it. In like manner, a special school unit cannot function well without available substitute homes and treatment centers.

Privacy versus supervision is less of a programming issue in Sweden because of the fewer number of institutional residential facilities. Each client is given more independence, and thus the need for supervision is reduced, although not the responsibility for care.

In the villa homes and apartment homes, each child has his or her own room with a locked door. The children have the freedom to use the whole residence, since there are no special security provisions. A staff member, who has a small office for his or her use, is always present in these homes.

Many of the adult hostels and villas have even less supervision and more privacy. At an apartment home for young adults in Sodertajle, the staff for six persons consisted of a couple who lived upstairs and one additional part-time staff member. At the adult hostel in Botkyrka, three individually separated apartments were rented as the hostel. A couple lived in one, three men in another, and three girls in the third apartment. A staff member was always present to prepare food (while the residents worked) and to aid in emergencies.

At the Bollmora School and Home for severely physically handicapped, each client was given the opportunity for privacy in the toilet and in his or her own room. However, a sophisticated communication system had been devised so that staff could be summoned when help was needed. In the toilet room, switches had been located in several places around the toilet for use in calling for staff assistance in case of difficulty.

The programming problem of staff accommodation changes when deinstitutionalization occurs. The relationship between staff and clients becomes much closer since there are fewer people responsible for the child's care. The staff become more like substitute parents. Communication between staff is eased, and they share more equally in responsibilities.

In Sweden, criteria used for grouping clients are very similar to those used in Denmark. In general,

children in homes and schools are grouped according to primary disability. Sex and age are not used as criteria except that age is used to separate preschool children from school-age children. In schools, children are grouped on the basis of learning abilities and potential. Grouping into villa and apartment homes is often based on social factors of group dynamics.

Environmental design

In order to achieve normalization, handicapped persons should have the right to live in and use normally designed facilities. Facilities that are specially designed to accommodate specific handicaps are not normal. They remove the challenge and opportunity for each handicapped person to normalize his or her life. These facilities also tend to become segregated by the difference of their design.

The goal of normalized design must be to accommodate the needs of the handicapped without using specialized, conspicuous designs. The facilities should appear to be normal buildings. They should not be defensively designed to protect the handicapped from risks.

There is little defensive design in the new, small scale residential facilities in Sweden, because there is little specialized design. The villas or homes are normal single-family houses in normal neighborhoods that have either been rented or purchased by the county council. They have been furnished with normal residential furniture and equipped with normal residential appliances. Few, if any, physical design changes have been made to these homes (Figure 11–11).

The more prevalent form is the "flat home" or apartment home in a regular apartment building. These homes are established in both low-rise and high-rise buildings. If they are for children, they are located on the first floor of these buildings. In some cases, two or three apartments are joined together to form a larger home. As in the villa homes, there are few design alterations (Figure 11–12).

Figure 11-11
This villa home for five handicapped teenagers in Johannesdal, Sweden, is a normal contemporary house with normal furniture and appliances, but few architectural alterations.

Figure 11-12
Two adjacent apartments on the first floor of this new eight-story building in Norsborg, Sweden, were rented to be used as a group home for children. The apartments were joined together, with no other alterations, so that they can be returned to normal rental when the need for this group home no longer exists.

The primary concern in planning community-based residences is with their location, scale, and function rather than specialized architectural design. The facilities must be planned as part of an overall service delivery system that is integrated within the community and is within easy access to transportation and services.

Another design principle, which is followed in planning residential facilities, is the separation of residence from place of work. Normally, a child goes away from home to school. Likewise, most adults work in places away from their homes. Therefore, in accordance with the normalization principle, residences and places of education and work should be geographically separated. This separation also facilitates effective functional and physical integration in the community, since the units can be located with other similar facilities.

In the design of schools, the use of the exterior environment in education has not been greatly explored. Each of the schools has playgrounds and courtyards, but they are usually unimaginative in design. The equipment is quite standard and generally not innovative or unique. The exception is the

Mockasinen School in Solberga (Stockholm). At this school, the architects had made special efforts to design unique outdoor play equipment for the severely retarded and physically handicapped students. Each courtyard has different therapeutic play equipment that includes crawling mazes, puzzle rails, and a stair-climbing device (Figures 11-13 and 11-14).

The interior environment in Swedish schools and care facilities is of high quality in terms of comfort and appearance. Beautifully designed Scandinavian furniture in bright primary colors is used throughout. There is an abundance of natural wood trim and ceilings. The furnishings in the apartment homes and villa homes are more ordinary since they are usually selected by the staff and clients.

In general, the Swedish architects are quite conservative and unimaginative in their design of schools, care facilities, and residences. There is little evidence of concern with the behavioral and social effects of the designed environment on the lives of the handicapped.

Figure 11–13
This therapeutic play equipment was designed and built at the Mockasinen School for severely retarded and physically handicapped in Solberga, Sweden. The play court shown here has a sand play area with both stand-up and sit-down sand boxes that enable children with different handicaps to play together. (Architects: Britta and Kjell Abramson and Nils Carlson.)

Figure 11–14
This stair-climbing device at the Mockasinen School in Solberga, Sweden, has different riser and tread dimensions and handrail designs to help the handicapped learn how to negotiate stairs.

Educational Facilities

Sweden is currently making great progress in integrating handicapped pupils into the normal school system. Integration is the prevailing basis for the Swedes' educational approach, and they are making great effort to insure its success. This integration movement is in large measure being directed by Lennart Wessman, the Inspector for Special Schools, who has been trying to advance public school integration for the last decade, but is only now receiving wholehearted support.

The opportunity for educational integration is largely dependent upon the attitudes and organization of the public school system. As Wessman says, "If the education in the ordinary school was good enough for the handicapped pupil, there would be no need for special education."[15] A new approach to normal school education was enacted by Parliament in 1962. In principle, it states that the school shall satisfy the demands of the pupil. Education thus became much more individualized with emphasis on specialized instruction. Thus the basis for educational integration was prepared.

In 1972, approximately one-third of the handicapped children were integrated, in some form, with children in the normal schools. By 1975, this ratio was one-half. In the future this ratio will be reduced even further. However, the existence of so many special schools makes the changeover to integrated schools more difficult.

The physical integration of handicapped pupils on the same site and in the same building with normal pupils is a necessary first step toward achieving full integration. Integration of special pupils into normal classes can then take place on an individual basis, either full time or part time, as the pupil's development progresses.

Many of the public school systems in the Stockholm region are at the point of achieving physical integration. A typical example is Solfagraskolan in Huddinge (Stockholm), a one-year-old school for 325 children in first through sixth grades (Figure 11–15), where there

Figure 11-15
This typical special education classroom at Solfagraskolan in Huddinge, Sweden, has been divided by a wood and glass partition into a large group area and two small group areas, which thus allows more flexibility in its usage.

is a special education unit of three classes for mentally retarded (I.Q. 50–70) with six to eleven in each class. This unit consists of three classrooms (each with group room), councilor's room, speech room, free time and rest room, handicrafts shop, and materials room. The full-time staff consists of three teachers, two hostesses, and a speech teacher. The children are integrated with normal children at assemblies and lunchtime and occasionally during gym and handicrafts. Although social integration is voluntary, the fact that all of the children come to school together and live in the same neighborhood eases acceptance and mixing.

In terms of physical facilities, special education should be planned and designed into a school building when it is originally constructed. In this way, special spatial requirements can be accommodated. For example, approximately four normal classrooms of space are required for three special education classrooms. Other facility requirements include a physical therapy room in the gymnasium, special handicraft and shop areas, a speech room and rest room.

If special education is planned from the outset in a

school design, it should not become fixed in its location, because this would be a form of segregation. The goal is to plan new schools in such a way that the building is flexible to accommodate special education classes anywhere. In the new school being designed for Norratajle, flexible space has been left between each normal classroom to be used for special education rooms if they are needed. Therefore, special education classes could be located anywhere in the school. This approach relies more on special equipment and flexible furniture than purpose-built spaces.

Another hopeful integration effort in Sweden is found in the integrated nurseries and kindergartens. The objective is to have normal and handicapped children become socially acquainted before they attend normal school. Storhagen in Akersberga (Stockholm) is a home and nursery school for twenty severely retarded and physically handicapped young children. The facilities consist of five normal courthouses that have been joined together on the inside (Figures 11–16 and 11–17). The nursery school serves the children in residence as well as the normal children from the neighborhood. At Vadervarnen Nursery School in Sodertajle, one of four nursery school suites is used by retarded children. The fifteen retarded children who attend are able to mix with the sixty normal children in the common living, dining, and play areas.

In the educational policy being shaped by Lennart Wessman, there is little future for the special school as a viable institution in Sweden. He believes that almost all special education can be accomplished through special classes that can be placed in normal schools. The exceptions would be for the blind, deaf, seriously physically handicapped and profoundly retarded who, because of special technical arrangements and curricula, would still require special schools. Otherwise, special segregated schools are an anachronism and simply not necessary. Changed public attitudes with regards to acceptance of handicapped children as part of society have made integration in public schools a realistic hope.

Figure 11-16
Storhagen in Akersberga, Sweden, is a combination home and nursery school for both physically and mentally handicapped children located in an existing courthouse development. The courtyard shown here with its added ramps, play equipment, and sun deck is designed to accommodate these children as well as the normal neighborhood children who also attend the school.

SUMMARY AND CONCLUSION

Many similarities as well as considerable differences exist between Denmark and Sweden in terms of services and facilities for the mentally handicapped. Both countries have subscribed to the normalization principle, which they first developed, as the philosophical basis for their work in this area. However, each country has emphasized a different aspect of normalization in its implementation.

Denmark's approach to normalization has been to concentrate on the reduction of the effects of institutionalism. To this end, the primary efforts have been to reduce institutional scale and to humanize institutions functionally, socially, and architecturally. The Danes have tried to normalize institutional living patterns by providing privacy and choice within small indentity groups.

Sweden's primary emphasis has been to achieve physical, functional, and social integration between the mentally handicapped and the rest of society.

Figure 11-17
This puppet theater has been created at the Storhagen nursery school in Akersberga, Sweden, that serves resident mentally and physically handicapped students as well as normal neighborhood children.

Residences, schools, and service facilities have been decentralized and placed under local community control. The residences are located in normal neighborhoods and the children attend normal schools. The objective is to reduce, if not eliminate, those specialized facilities that serve only the mentally handicapped, thereby segregating them from the rest of society.

Both countries have organized their service systems based upon the concept of a "continuum of care." In this way differentiated services are provided in accordance with age level and specific needs. In Denmark, the implementation is based upon an institutional continuum of care through regional administrative control. In Sweden, the continuum of care is decentralized and under local control. The Swedish service systems are more highly differentiated, but not as well organized.

In terms of environmental design, the Danish facilities are more imaginative and creative. They are more sensitive to the environmental needs of the mentally handicapped, and more cognizant of the psychological effects of the environment. Many of them are good architecture, in the fullest sense of the term, by being both well designed and responsive to critical programmatic requirements. Since many of the Swedish facilities were not specifically designed for their purpose, they cannot be easily compared with the Danish design efforts. Nevertheless, the environmental design quality of these normal schools and normal residences is often lacking in sensitivity and imagination.

This chapter is based upon the actual conditions observed in Denmark and Sweden during the summer of 1972. At that time, the level of philosophical and organizational development was in many cases ahead of the concepts represented in the physical facilities. The time required to plan, design, and construct facilities often results in a lag of realization behind philosophy, but with the rapid pace of development in this area, conditions have certainly changed by now in both Denmark and Sweden. This chapter has endeavored to point out these new directions as well as to evaluate past efforts.

NOTES AND REFERENCES

The field research upon which this chapter is based was conducted in Denmark and Sweden during the summer of 1972 and sponsored in part by the George G. Booth Travelling Fellowship in Architecture granted by the College of Architecture & Urban Planning of the University of Michigan and Educational Facilities Laboratories, Inc. *Architecture for the Handicapped in Denmark, Sweden, & Holland* published by the University of Michigan is based upon the same research material.

1. Danish National Service for the Mentally Retarded, "General Survey and Brief History of the Development of Service Systems in Denmark," Copenhagen, 1969.
2. Wolfensberger, Wolf, *The Principle of Normalization in Human Services* (Toronto: National Institute on Mental Retardation, 1972).
3. Bank-Mikkelsen, N. E., "Services for the Mentally Retarded," Danish National Service for the Mentally Retarded, Copenhagen, 1968.
4. Nirje, Bengt, "The Normalization Principle and its Human Management Implications," in R. B. Kugel and Wolf Wolfensberger (eds.), *Changing Patterns in Residential Services for the Mentally Retarded* (Washington, D.C.: President's Committee on Mental Retardation, 1969); Wolfensberger, *The Principle of Normalization in Human Services*; and Grunewald, Karl, "The Mentally Retarded," The Swedish Institute, Stockholm, 1969.
5. Danish National Service for the Mentally Retarded, *Ten Years of Planning and Building, 1959–1969*, Copenhagen, 1969.
6. Grunewald, "The Mentally Retarded."
7. National Board of Health and Welfare, "Provisions and Services for the Mentally Retarded in Sweden," National Board of Health and Welfare, Stockholm, 1971.
8. Grunewald, "The Mentally Retarded."
9. Ibid.
10. National Board of Health and Welfare, "Living Standards in Swedish Facilities for the Mentally Retarded," National Board of Health and Welfare, Stockholm, 1972.
11. Ingrid Gunnas, First Inspector, Division for Mental Retardation, interview, June 20, 1972.
12. Grunewald, "The Mentally Retarded."
13. Ibid.
14. Ibid.
15. Wessman, Lennart, "Organization of Special Education in Sweden," National Board of Education, Stockholm, 1970.

12

Planning Facilities in the Community

H. David Sokoloff

David Sokoloff is an architect and President of Sokoloff, Hamilton, Bennett, AIA Architects and Planners in San Francisco, California. He received his education at Sorbonne University, Cambridge University, and Yale University. As an architectural consultant, he has been involved with over twenty-five state governments, universities, hospitals, and other organizations. His involvement in the affairs of mentally retarded citizens has been deep and long standing. Formerly, he has been Director of the National Association for Retarded Citizens, Chairman of the Residential Services and Facilities Committee, and President of the California Association for the Retarded. Presently, he is Chairman of the State Developmental Disabilities Planning and Advisory Council, Director of the San Francisco Mental Health Association, and Director of the Marin County Workshop.

Knowledge about man's immediate environment, the hollows within his shelters which he calls offices, classrooms, corridors, and hospital wards, is as important as knowledge about outer space and undersea life. For too long we have accepted physical forms and administered the arrangements based on outdated views of human activities.

—Robert Sommer[1]

INTRODUCTION

The "developmental" ideology is now the accepted foundation of service systems for developmentally disabled people. It is widely written into program goals. Its management principle, normalization, is already the dominant influence in future planning in many states, and it is gaining strength in the remainder.

Bengt Nirje's 1969 summary of the normalization principle has become one touchstone for planners:

. . . It means making available to the mentally retarded patterns and conditions of everyday life which are as close as possible to the norms and patterns of the mainstream of society. This principle should be applied to all the retarded regardless of whether mildly or profoundly retarded. . . . An important part of the Normalization principle implies that the standards of physical facilities . . . should be the same as those regularly applied in society to the same kind of facilities for ordinary citizens. Especially should it be kept in mind that a facility for the retarded should never be intended for a larger number of persons than the surrounding neighborhood readily assimilates in its regular everyday community life. It further implies that in planning the location of these facilities they should never be placed in isolated settings merely because they are intended for the mentally retarded.[2]

One implication of normalization, which is an optimistic inference often made by those reading such statements, is that as a result of the increased stimulation from more culturally normative and less restrictive surroundings, the handicapped person will become more "normal" in his or her functioning. But the real meaning of normalization does not depend on the notion that the handicapped person will change substantially, or that the handicap will be-

227

come less severe through the "treatment" of exposure to a less restricted, more normal, environment. Normalization is really concerned with the basic right of a person to have maximum opportunity and experience. In this view, being entitled to as near normal treatment and being able to live in as near normal a setting as is feasible is a matter of basic human dignity. Conversely, the handicapped person has the right *not* to be isolated in a large facility far away from the mainstream activities of the society and has a right *not* to experience the consequences of such isolation.

Community-based, small-to-moderate-scale facilities, with a wide variety of care capabilities, are the key to an implementation of normalization. Their role is recognized by volunteer associations, political leaders, and many other specialists in the field. In 1969, participants from thirteen nations, meeting at a symposium in Frankfurt, defined the general requirements of an environment appropriate to normalization as follows:

The principle of normalization is a sound basis for programming, which, by paralleling the normal patterns of culture and drawing the retarded into the mainstream of society, aims at maximizing his human qualities, as defined by his particular culture. Retarded children and adults therefore should be helped to live as normal a life as possible. The structuring of routines, the "form of life" and the nature of the physical environment should approximate the normal cultural pattern as much as possible. . . . Residential services should be viewed as one segment of a continuum of services available to the mentally retarded. These services should be administered and interrelated to ensure easy transition from service to service based on the unique needs of each resident at any given time. . . . The hospital model is inappropriate for residential services for most of the mentally retarded.[3]

In 1970 the President's Committee on Mental Retardation stated that:

Design and construction of new facilities should adhere to a number of basic principles:

1. The location should be within the community served and provide for normal contacts with the life of the community.

2. The facility should not be isolated from society or community by such factors as difficulty of access, due to distance or lack of public transportation.
3. The facility should be in scale with the community in which it is located.
4. The community in which the facility is located should be capable of meeting the needs of the facility's residents for generic and specialized services.
5. Residents should be integrated to the greatest possible extent with the general population. To this end, generic and specialized community services rather than facility services should be used extensively or, if possible, completely.[4]

There is little doubt that community-based facilities will predominate in service systems for the developmentally disabled at some time in the future; the question is how soon. Community-based facilities have economics on their side (because the costs of large institutions keep escalating and because clients based in communities can make use of general community services). They have logic on their side: We would be unreasonable even to suggest that there can be one answer (the large-scale isolated institution) for all those diverse people with handicaps who need more than extension care in a family setting.

However, achieving a substantial degree of deinstitutionalization in the short-run future (ten years, for instance) is a major challenge. Most of the money available for handicapped people is still tied up in the older, large-scale institutions, and merely keeping them up to or bringing them up to humane standards is very expensive. Conceptualizing and planning community placements for thousands of handicapped people (a conservative one-half of the total institutionalized population of disabled persons as of 1975) is a major task. A state service system composed of highly diverse, dispersed, multi-scaled facilities will present state bureaus and administration with entirely new management tasks. Thus far, too many of the community facilities that do exist are underplanned, underprogrammed, and underfinanced. The quality of many may be adequate for the moderately retarded, partly because location in the community itself constitutes something of a program. Until now few good community-based facilities existed for severely and profoundly retarded people and for those with severe behavior problems.

Clearly, we will overcome these obstacles only if we can create new planning and management processes on the local, state, and national levels—that is, processes that will produce high-quality community facilities for the full range of handicapped people. This chapter is primarily concerned with developing such processes and with the attitudes and ideologies that will support them.

On the local level, parent groups, entrepreneurs, and others will at least see a need for a facility here and there. Part of the chapter is addressed to such people and suggests an ideology and operating principles for a planning process likely to make their efforts successful.

However, in all likelihood local independent efforts will not go far to meet the national need. There must be changed priorities and processes on a larger scale. Most states have only the merest beginnings of a community-based program and even less in the way of comprehensive plans for a transition to community-based facilities. The dominant interests in many states are still oriented toward maintenance of the large hospital-model facility.

Therefore, another part of the chapter is addressed to state service people, planners, legislators, and others whose interest is in changing the macrostructures of the service system. It suggests roles the states can begin to play to facilitate the creation of a community-scale system and describes the roles states now play that not only frustrate local efforts but must obviously be stopped if a different kind of system is to be achieved.

STRUCTURES AND PEOPLE

All the roles involved in planning, both functional and dysfunctional, relate in some way to structures and the human activities that take place in them. We know that people have interacted positively with

carefully considered priorities in mind, when a structure turns out to serve its human purposes. We know that the roles or the process have gone wrong in some way when a structure compounds the problem it was intended to solve.

In facility design, things go wrong when the building is the main focus, when critical elements of its design are set early in the planning process, or when the building is regarded as a simple solution that can be proceeded with in a mechanical way as a matter of arranging and assembling physical materials.

We need to go beyond that conception of a building, particularly a building for people who may be unusually dependent on or involved with it—that is, people with major handicaps. Experience with large institutions should have taught us by now that structures (along with their locations and surroundings) are *investments* and *environments* with powerful effects on a wide range of people. We should have also learned by now that many of the influences of such built environments are not easily anticipated. Hindsight is a much-used tool for assessing these influences, particularly the negative ones, but it doesn't help the people who have to use a misbuilt facility.

Often by hindsight, we have learned about the effects of the scale of a built environment. A large institution, for example, represents permanence and a guarantee of long-term security to the parents of a retarded person. It represents a degree of immortality to donors; their contribution has real permanence when it is manifested as a physical reality. The larger the project the more attractive it is to architects whose fee and visibility increase with size. Contractors and unions have economic incentives in developing larger projects. A large project lures administration with promises of increased "efficiency" and a neat managerial kingdom with clear boundaries. A large facility is a concentrated market—that is, a steady and easily-served account to sellers of food, supplies, and services.

Only for the residents are the rewards in inverse ratio to the size of the facility. They spend the most time in and around it and in the case of a large institution are the most restricted by its typical isolation and its totality as an environment. The massive construction typical of large institutions, boundaries of walls or fences, even atypically neat landscaping and well-serviced lawns send the message, "the people living here are different." (See Wolfensberger's Chapter 8 in this volume for further development of these ideas.—Editor) The message is sent outward to society, but also inward to the residents. The self-image they build from it tends to reinforce the learning of skills required to manage the institutional environment, but these skills for the most part are irrelevant to survival in the community. The large institution thus works in several ways to compound the secondary handicap of the disabled: the stigma of their difference. It helps to fulfill the perception of difference by insuring that the residents do, indeed, become increasingly different from the people in the mainstream of society.

The proponents of normalization can easily read this lesson today; it is well illuminated by hindsight and by the new ideologies. But how well will the lesson be applied to new planning? I am concerned that many people looking ahead to an era of small-scale facilities might think that smaller can't help but be better; that community-based environments will more or less automatically work for more dignity, self-respect, and the increased development of the residents.

Although the scale of large institutions has been a major problem, the essential lesson has less to do with scale than with the care we must use in conceptualizing and designing *any* built environment. Nothing indicates that a small facility, simply because of its reduced scale, interacts with people in any less complex ways or with a greater degree of easy predictability of effect than a large-scale facility. The tone or types of interaction may be considerably different, but the level of complexity is probably not. Further, although careful planning has produced a few outstanding community-scale facilities, few have operated very long. In this country, relatively few are oriented to the more severe handicaps, which thus justifies in part the claim by parents of the profoundly retarded or multiply handicapped that normalization has yet to be proven feasible for their people. (Future community-scale options must take into account the types of services necessary for severely and profoundly handicapped people and the permanence and intensive quality of those services. These considerations almost certainly demand direct operation by the state, and in all likelihood parents will demand such a state role.)

The planning task must still be approached with respect. A good planning effort will have to deal with nearly as many complexities as one focused on a large institutional structure. Financial resources will be fewer, although potential human resources may be greater. And in the short-run future, the developers of a small-scale facility, the architects, staff, parents, and others associated with the effort carry the added burden of being pioneers—pioneers always under the eyes of both boosters and critics.

PLANNING A FACILITY: PERSPECTIVES AND PROCESSES FOR A LOCAL EFFORT

Architects and others primarily involved with physical structures may believe that *facility* is another term for a building, but according to the *American Heritage Dictionary* (Houghton Mifflin, Boston, 1975), a facility is "the means to facilitate an action or a process." In turn, *facilitate* means "to free from obstacles or difficulties, make easier, aid, assist." With these definitions in mind, we can argue that a community-based residential facility is much more than a structure. It is the total means of aiding, assisting, and freeing the process engaged in by the disabled person that, according to the developmental model, includes living, learning, and growing to the fullest extent possible for the particular person.

Therefore when we discuss the planning of a community-based facility, we are concerned not only with a building or buildings (henceforth the singular will be used for the sake of simplicity), but with the spaces around the building, the staff and its activities, and the program that occurs in, around, and often out from that building and its adjacent spaces. We let the structure dominate our thinking only at our peril. Further, our criteria for success must be criteria for the facility, not for the structure. Our structure might be an award-winning expression of spaces flowing into one another; it might be a success as an energy conserver; it might be extremely cost efficient. Yet the facility could be an utter failure because the building was disorienting to a developmentally disabled person, thereby blocking essential program activities. On the other hand, a structure could be ideally suited to clients, conducive to a highly effective program, and free of identifiable frustrations to staff efforts, and still not be a success. Staff members who had worked elsewhere might not respond to the new circumstances, and they might tend to restrict the activities of residents in accordance with their previous experience, or management might simply have an inadequate program philosophy and plan.

A structure functioning well in operation is usually the result of a careful design process that has taken the following points into consideration:

1. The architect (principle decision-maker or leader of decisions on the details of the physical plant) is not likely to be an expert on program, although he may have some general expertise in the field of developmental disabilities. Those who will use the building—resident clients, staff, and management—have or are best positioned to get and develop such information. A fully functional facility is evidence that the architect has gotten the information and that his or her decisions have been verified by those with program knowledge.
2. The success of the building depends in large part upon its acceptance by those who will use it, including staff and residents. Acceptance of the building and the principles and details of the projected program is more likely to take place if those who must live with the design and program decisions are involved in making them.
3. People who have participated in a planning process are more likely to develop a commonness of purpose and a tendency to continue joint discussion and development of goals and strategies. They are thus better equipped to conceptualize and direct later changes and to keep the facility adapted to current needs.

Conversely, there is danger in a nonparticipatory planning process that is either a sole effort by an architect or a limited alliance between the architect and individual developer or group. Staff finding themselves in a new environment and working on a "take-it-or-leave-it" basis will not give the program their most positive energies. Moreover, their attitudes may persist in the behavioral culture of the facility long after the planners have moved on. A pseudo-participatory process can have even worse consequences.

The Facility as "Learning Machine"

More specific requirements for a positive planning process can also be suggested. People find a creative process satisfying, and the process itself is most directly productive when all involved have a clear image of the process and how it relates to its goals; when all involved accept similar criteria for knowing whether they are making progress toward the goals; and when all involved have informed expectations of the different roles to be played. The overarching criterion for all three process dimensions is that each can be communicated and understood in specifics. If people are continually surprised, find themselves disoriented, or suddenly are in disagreement with others in a process group, in all likelihood the criterion of specificity has not been met.

The progress desired in the case of planning for a community-scale residential facility is movement toward increasingly detailed plans for a structure and for the activities that will take place within it. Each of these progressions must remain consistent with the other and with an agreed-on concept, of who the facility is intended for and how it will function. The developmental ideology and the normalization principle imply a very specific concept for a community-based facility, and the author recommends that planning groups adopt and work with it. This concept is "the facility as learning machine."

The typical residence, whether a single-family home or apartment, functions as a learning machine for the people growing up in the normal population. Here, immediately accessible and available for manipulation, are many of the basic living technologies of the culture: faucets in lavatories and showers with their mixing valves, toilets with flush handles, and stoves with heat controls. There are more and different control devices on radios, television sets, and record players. In addition, there are windows to wash, walls that can be painted, carpets that require periodic cleaning, furniture that can be rearranged to thus define or modify spaces. Here, too, is a hierarchy of spaces with territorial values and privacy implications. These spaces represent many of the basic interpersonal values and social relations typical of the culture. There are highly private and personal spaces (bed, dresser drawers, bedroom, clothes-hanging space), spaces shared with one other person, task-related spaces in which cooperation and role definition is the norm, group-shared spaces, and public spaces (the front walk, for example).

Learning to live means in part learning to manipulate this learning machine itself; for example, by switching on lights, shutting off gas, showering, opening doors, locking them, drawing curtains, and so on. It means handling yourself and taking care of yourself in the context of this equipment. It means learning to manage your psychological self in the context of normal groups by starting with small groups and working toward larger and less personal ones.

This particular summary of a residence with its technology and varied spaces reflects my personal involvement with the moderately retarded and the area of learning independent living skills. But the con-

cept of the "facility as learning machine" is not limited to this group, nor is it intrinsically tied to the small-scale residential facility. In fact all facilities, large or small, are learning machines. Facilities are learning machines for management, staff, parents, and families. Even a facility that provides intensive life-support care for a profoundly retarded or multiply handicapped person is a learning machine.

The planning questions that come from this concept are:

1. *Who* will be learning here?
2. *What* can they learn here, given their handicap and level of development?
3. Is the learning thus identified in a culturally normative direction, or of a type that is skewed in some other direction? (I have in mind here a woman in Nevada who moved from an institution into an apartment and one day threw a bucket of water across her small kitchen to clean it. That was the way it was done in the institution and that's the way indeed that large kitchens are cleaned. The institution as a learning machine had taught her how to clean kitchens in institutions.)
4. What features of program and physical plant are likely to facilitate particular desired learnings?
5. What aspects of program and physical plant are likely to inhibit or frustrate desired learnings?

Success in using this scheme depends on extensive and detailed answers to the second question in this list. The specifics within the answer will be considerably different if the facility is oriented to moderately retarded adults or to people with severe behavioral problems or to profoundly retarded children. Multiple-function facilities require answers to the entire serires of questions for each client group.

Working out detailed answers to these questions, with a range of clients in mind, can be an intensive learning exercise for the planning group itself. Conceptions of the program may be deepened and broadened. Ways may be found to increase the amount of learning possible in a number of different spaces. For example, the customary design for a tub shower calls for one type of water-delivery mechanism or at most two (a faucet and a shower head), but the tub shower would be a better learning machine for moderately to profoundly retarded residents if a number of mechanisms were included. Tepid water could be delivered via one faucet. There might also be a set of standard paired faucets, one of which is supplied with 130 degree water. Intermediate in complexity could be a mixing valve supplied on the hot side with 110 degree water. There's some danger that people may hurt themselves, but you've given them the opportunity to use several mechanisms of increasing complexity, and you've given them the dignity of risking and learning for themselves. Kitchen facilities could be designed in a similar way to provide a range of complexity, risks, and opportunities for learning.

The importance of this learning machine concept for program planning is that the planning group using it will make explicit many more of the things that are going to happen in their facility. In turn, the architect has a much fuller idea of the human processes that he will facilitate via the design. The ideology will *not* serve well if it is not followed out in detail, or if it is relegated to a second-place priority, behind criteria that units will be ganged together to reduce costs, that ease of maintenance is crucial, and so forth.

THE PROCESS ITSELF

Clear role and task expectations are as critical to a successful creative process as an agreed-upon ideology. In the planning of a small-scale facility, there are likely to be two levels of involvement. Members of the core planning group are likely to be closely and continually involved throughout most of the planning process, from initial conceptualization to facility start-up and beyond. Within this core group will be the architect, the contracting client (one person or a parent group), senior staff, if they have been contracted (participation in the process might be part of

their employment agreement), parents of known client-residents, some client-residents, and in some cases a representative of the state service system. Another group includes people who will usually be called on only once or twice (the exigencies of the particular location, facility size, state system, and so on will be a basis for deciding how much to try to involve the members of this group and when). Fire and safety officials, local health department officials, neighborhood organization officials, and a representative of the local police department are likely to participate in this way.

The Role of the Architect

The architect wields a heavy influence in a planning process of this sort and will probably, all cautions herein and elsewhere to the contrary, be deferred to as the group's "expert." The architect is often the only person in the group who already possesses a systematic way to think about a complex and lengthy planning process. Clients and others expect the architect to command total knowledge of regulations, jurisdictional authorities, program opportunities, and so on, as well as the mechanics of design and construction. Clients may have ideas about all these things and quite specific ideas about what they want in a facility, but the architect is still the technician who can help them put all their desires together into a neat, buildable package. We have already said that people are likely to load disproportionate expectations on the building, which thus tends to magnify the architect's role as the expert. Usually these expectations should not be pared down too much. The architect probably *is* the person in the group most self-conscious of process. He may be looked to as the major process leader, and this psychological position is a valuable asset for driving the process along when energy dissipates. He may be asked to formalize and state many of the decisions made during the planning process, although they are basically group decisions. However, the architect must remember that whatever his experience with institutional design or design for handicapped people, the environmental needs of mentally handicapped people (particularly from the learning machine point of view) are complex and not easily defined; counterposing requirements are present in a delicate balance. For example, while mentally normal people with physical handicaps need a highly customized environment (and ought to participate in designing it in fact), the facilities for mentally handicapped people ought to be *unspecialized*—that is, as nearly normal as possible. Hopefully the retarded person can learn to handle standard life equipment, but more importantly we do not want the environment to send messages of "difference." A major goal is to reduce the stigma associated with the handicap.

However, the normal-appearing environment must be conceived with the special sensitivities of the handicapped person in mind, and special aids may also need to be hidden within it. A retarded person who is also emotionally disturbed may become easily disoriented by unusual treatments of spaces and unusual spatial definition or a lack thereof. A person handicapped by dyslexia may need a particular definition of the location and nature of control mechanisms—hot and cold water faucets, for example. Cabinet doors in a kitchen used by a dyslexic person probably should have obvious knobs, and the right and left cabinet doors might be painted different colors.

The architect walks a thin line, then, in creating a learning machine for retarded and other mentally handicapped people. The machine must present some challenge to learn and opportunity to learn, yet not raise frustrating challenges. Rare is the facility today that is well-tuned in this respect; residents and staff typically discover many frustrations and missed opportunities after they begin living with a new building. A major reason is that the typical planning process does not provide for extensive contact between the architect, program designers, staff, and the handicapped people themselves.

The hope of a participative process is that the resident clients and a number of others who know them well will be able to communicate an unusual amount of detailed and subtle information about their needs to the architect. It follows that the architect will need to be skillful in using the participative process to get this information, and sensitive to the information as it comes, although it may surface in many forms.

The Role of the Contracting Clients

The architect and the contracting clients share primary responsibility for a full and positive planning process. Clients can rely on the architect for a schedule, and they do not need to learn about the many intricacies of structural design. But they do need to understand the architectural design and construction sequence shown in Figure 12–1 (PERT is an acronym for Program Evaluation and Review Technique—Editor). Throughout the process of development there are opportunities for taking psychological advantage of crucial decision points. One of these points is at the presentation of schematic design drawings. This stage is the first graphic representation of the proposed facility as developed from the architectural guidelines that have been derived from service and program goals. Managed properly, this "coming out" occasion for the facility can produce good attitudes toward it.

Another stage in Figure 12–1 that can be used positively is "beneficial occupancy." This two- or three-week period occurs just before the building is fully finished and legally turned over to the client. The client who has access to the building (minor finishing is still taking place), should use this time to buy furniture, to do decorating, and to conduct walk-through program planning. If the client is well prepared for this period, the full staff will be on board. Furniture purchasing and decorating can be a team effort. Staff training sessions can be interspersed with the work. Some residents might well help decorate. If this kind of use is to be made of the beneficial occupancy period, of course, other actions (staff interviewing and hiring, for instance) will have to

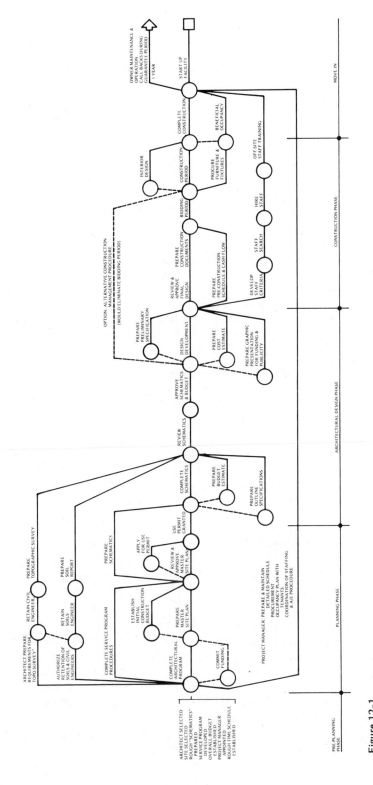

Figure 12-1
Design process PERT Chart.

235

have been scheduled and completed earlier, and staff job specifications will have to have been compiled before that.

The worst enemy of most contracting clients is secondary ignorance—that is, "not knowing what you do not know." For example, the label chosen for a facility often affects what safety codes it must meet. In a borderline case, one label might be preferable to another solely on that basis. Probably the architect will be aware of the problems involved in the use of labels, but as more smaller facilities are built and so more architects without institutional expertise become involved, the client who does not know that the label may affect the design of the facility and fails to ask the architect if that matter has been checked is subject to this major peril of any complex planning process.

The contracting clients together with the management and senior staff (if they are not all the same people) have the primary responsibility within the planning group of keeping the "learning machine" questions in the forefront and of constantly directing the answers to them toward specifics. There must be a framework for deriving such specific plans. A good framework can result from such questions as "What will be happening here and what may Client "X" be learning morning, noon, and night, summer and winter, now and five years from now?" Completely filling in the framework will not always be possible, but the empty spaces are themselves informative insofar as they point to particular needs for flexibility.

Finally, the client should take full advantage of the planning process as an attitude-shaping mechanism. The design development process is in effect the conceptualizing of a future—the constructing of a future. The facility is beginning to exist as increasingly detailed plans for a building, but it is going to be a lot more than a building. Attitudes are also being explored, formed, and reinforced as the planning process goes forward. The image of the facility and its goals are being set and so are the role relationships between the people involved. Individual commitment to the goals is increasing or decreasing. Interaction styles are coalescing to become the behavioral culture of the facility; hopefully they will be characterized by enthusiasm, honesty, and directness of communication, and positive reinforcement. The client should monitor these developments by asking questions like these: Are people feeling involved in the decisions? Are they being listened to? Are people staying with the same image of the facility and its goals? Is there some degree of equality in contributions made, and if not, why not? Is everyone included in the communication?

Roles for State Service System People

Departments of mental health, developmental disabilities, mental hygiene, and others vary so widely from state to state that suggesting the possible variations of their involvement is impossible. Some state departments are so oriented to large institutions that they will be of little assistance, and independent planners of independent facilities will only want to ask them, repeatedly, "What restrictions and requirements must we meet?" Some states now have offices set up to coordinate small-scale facilities programs. Some states may be able to provide consultant specialists in programming. Most states will have someone who can outline basic licensing requirements. A primary area of information-seeking for a client and architect is the nature of the state system itself.

Roles for Fire-Safety, Structural-Safety, Health, and Zoning Officials

These officials are primarily in the business of administering, interpreting, and enforcing laws whose full implications they may not necessarily understand. This fact is particularly true of officials whose interest and jurisdiction relates to the prevention of fires and actions that need to take place after a fire occurs. They cannot be asked to exercise discretion in interpreting laws that might incur liability. However, the laws they administer often run counter to the program goals for facilities designed to improve the quality of life and the capabilities of handicapped people.

Health safety officials, for the most part, administer quantitative codes that relate more to physical health than to psychological health. Quite often the health safety restrictions run counter to program goals, and time spent trying to change codes and regulations to achieve freedoms in the designing of one facility is not usually productive (and the effort required is usually great). Nevertheless, safety officials can be persuaded to be as logical and reasonable as possible, rather than as rigid and legalistic as possible. A process of discussion, explanation, and exploration with these officials will begin to educate them to the new problems and attitudes involved as we bring people into the community who had previously been banished.

The problem with zoning officials is somewhat different in that they deal with the relationship of the resident-clients to the outside world rather than with their relationship to the facility itself. Usually the barriers that are faced come from ignorance and fear within the public.

Since the zoning officials are part of the public, a process of persuading them of the logic and humanity of the proposed facility and programs is in itself a necessary step and one in which they are likely to become allies. During public hearings and at other opportunities, befriending such officials and inviting them personally to contribute information to the planning group is a strategic measure. They can be valuable allies in that they administer a system of detailed rules on a full-time basis and probably know better than anyone else what loopholes or degrees of freedom exist in that system. If a particular requirement is so restrictive that it must be fought, they may know the best arguments to use, or they may have seen design techniques used in other facilities to get around a restriction. These officials usually have a dual function to inform and to force correction (often after a lot of work has been done) of mistakes

that have been made. Obviously consulting them early in the process makes good sense.

The police should not be forgotten. A police representative is not likely to have an extensive input, but he or she is a public safety and community relations specialist, and homes or other facilities are in part refuges in a world of communities, without much "community" left in them. The design group may get a valuable perspective from a policeperson on security, lighting, garage protection, advisable hours for using a street-facing recreation area, and so on.

We should reiterate that the role of the planning process in shaping attitudes is a singular opportunity. A planning group can interact with local officials primarily to get their building constructed properly and to secure the necessary approvals. However, the longer-run goal of having the public and a number of local officials with generally positive attitudes can be an extremely valuable asset as well.

Roles for Resident-Clients

Designing a facility for a group of resident-clients without their being involved in the planning process is perfectly feasible, but if we are to practice what we preach, involving them can be a significant opportunity to learn about their perceptions in order to serve them better. It can also be an opportunity for them to develop a positive feeling about the facility—to increase their sense of ownership of it.

I will not suggest categorical limits on the possibilities of such involvement. We always tend to underestimate the capabilities of handicapped people; we institutionalize this underestimation; and we are constantly amazed to find out we erred!

How are we to find out how residents can communicate their feelings and tastes? How would they like to be involved? Try communicating, and ask, or perhaps find people who can ask on behalf of the planning team. Another handicapped person who communicates better with staff and normally endowed people than the prospective client or a staff member who has worked with clients in a former setting can be helpful. Although judging what impact the experience of participation might have on the handicapped person (determining what another person may be learning in a given experience is always difficult), involving retarded clients in some facility planning activities helps to keep the developmental perspective present in everyone's mind. It focuses emphasis on the similarities of the clients to other people and on their positive abilities rather than on their differences. The planners thereby give them respect, dignity, and encouragement to respond with a positive self-image.

Group Processes

A planning group needs to remain open to a variety of ways of working together, gathering information, and communicating during the planning process. Architects need to remember that they have learned a visual method of communicating and are accustomed to using drawings. But people in general often have difficulty reading and understanding drawings, and they are often threatened by them. Therefore, the architect is wise to experiment with numerous means of communicating and representing conclusions.

There is also a tendency for group members to feel that the full development and translation of the program goals and objectives into architectural guidelines —all in a lengthy interactive process—requires an effort that is not really necessary. Their posture often is, "Why make such a big deal out of this, why don't we just go ahead and do it?" This desire to simplify the process in order to save time and effort is dangerous. The task is complex, and a process for handling that complexity is necessary. We should always remember that the goal is nothing less than the design and creation of a major environment for people who are unusually dependent on that environment and whose participation in it may be the richest and most satisfying part of their lives.

If the facility is to be planned as a learning ma-

chine, then the process leading to it should also be a "learning machine." If we are to take a developmental attitude towards handicapped people, we should take the same attitude toward ourselves. The planning process itself is the single best opportunity for the architect, the program designers, parents, the residents, and the staff to extend their knowledge not only of design and the needs of handicapped people, but of other people's roles and skills.

PUBLIC AGENCIES AND THE PLANNING PROCESS

There are few statewide systems to foster the development of small community-based facilities; each entrepreneurial group has to teach itself how to identify local needs, search for funding, develop programs, and deal with architects, building consultants and contractors, few of whom know how to think creatively about community-based and community-scale facilities for handicapped people. Under such conditions, the work of the local group is difficult, and obviously without a system of assistance from the state level, the development of necessary community facilities is not likely to be fast or efficient.

For many handicapped people to benefit from the kind of creative participatory process we envision at the local level, there may have to be a new kind of state system—an enabling system. The role state bureaus can be equipped to play in such a system is that of taking a planning group through the bureaucratic maze, outlining the processes that have to be followed, insuring that all restrictions are met, and gaining approval from all authorities having jurisdiction in specific problem areas. Such enabling state bureaus would also lend their expertise in professional matters to lay people—expertise, for instance, in how to hire, deal with, and monitor an architect, or how to insure that the total process is laid out in such a way that important considerations are not forgotten. Further, the state could be a gatherer and disseminator of information so that as newcomers decide to embark on this process the state can bring to them the experiences of success and failure of others. The state can put planning groups in touch with others so that each new group can visit, see, and assess other people's solutions. There is no substitute for being able to see the reality—it is like going into a car showroom to look at a car you intend to buy, rather than reading a booklet with no pictures and only a list of specifications and a few sketches.

Typical State Roles

A number of states play roles at present that are specifically *nonenabling* in a variety of ways. The common fault is an inflexibility of attitude and practice quite out of tune with the spirit of a diverse community-facility system.

State design and state construction activities

State architectural and construction bureaus are usually procedurally locked into old program concepts and biased toward low-maintenance, permanent structures. This characteristic is not surprising since their charge has long been to construct "government buildings" and to emphasize initial capital cost considerations. State bureaus may quite successfully design maintenance buildings, steam plants, or office buildings where the delivery of human interaction programs does not take place, but they are ill equipped to design human services facilities. They are in a particularly difficult position—often in a position of conflict of interest—when they try to design the kind of facilities we have discussed. The state bureau designing a small community-based facility and playing the role of the architect will have as its client the department that is the service deliverer (the department of health, for instance); it may have an entrepreneurial group as a second client; and it will certainly have the department of finance as a third. We can see that although the real client is the user, that client is

the least influential of the state's several clients and will be considered last.

This is not to say that state construction bureau personnel are unintelligent or perverse. It is only to say that the rules for community-based facilities are radically different from the rules bureau personnel are used to working with and that a major part of involving state design and construction departments in community facilities is going to be one of educating them toward the new rules and procedures.

State financing processes

The typical funding sequence for a new state facility is long and limiting. A specific request must first develop a high priority within a bureau and then within an agency. When it surfaces in a budget, it must be given specificity so that legislators know what they are appropriating; it is "scoped." The message that always accompanies this process is "When the project really gets going, it can be refined and funding can be adjusted." Such is rarely the case, because detail must be given to the project in order to communicate its nature before any planning money is spent. The detail then becomes solidified in a line-item budget. The adjustment options from such budgets are generally only downward—that is, items may be reduced or eliminated, but not transformed, combined, or shifted. In short, funding controls and often some kind of physical specification, such as a square-foot allotment, are placed on a project before people have really decided what they want to do! Even in final planning stages, in many states, a department of finance will make changes, some of which usually have minor impact on savings but major impact on function (about which the department has little real knowledge or interest). Because of typical state funding practices, then, critical decisions are made too early and are related primarily to money and its allocation. The decisions have major program impact, but program was not a primary consideration. This situation then makes necessary the developing of designs that take into account other efficiencies, such as particular efficiencies of staff utilization, the efficiency of maintenance and repair over the life of the building, and most important the efficiency of successful program outcomes.

State Roles for a Preferable Future

The planning function

A local planning group is likely to consider only an immediate local need, whereas the state has planning capability to assess the entire need for community facilities now and into the long-run future. A long-range plan, logically, is the first obligation of a state moving toward an enabling role. The plan will assess person-units of residential facilities needed within the context of all services, residential and nonresidential. It will project the probable best locations of these services (in all likelihood one primary basis will be family locations and residential density trends), and the range of facilities required in various areas. The state should work with constituency groups to compile all this data, and priorities should be set for facilities within the context of a coordinated comprehensive service continuum.

The state as a process resource

The logic of a transition to community-based facilities as the major component of a service system suggests that a large variety of facilities may evolve. They may be rented or leased as well as owned. They may be programmed, planned, and developed by a variety of people and organizations, including state teams, in areas of special need. They may be funded in a variety of ways. They will be located in a variety of geographic, climatological, and sociological areas. We have suggested throughout this chapter that present federal and state agencies and funding mechanisms are not oriented to creating this kind of diversity, and that local creativity is the major resource to be utilized. With substantial resources committed to an enabling role, the state can teach local planning groups what they need to know about the process and thus reduce the dangers of secondary ignorance. Standards to be met can be simplified, published, and explained by consultants. Program-building specialists can visit local groups when their guidance is most needed. The state could assign some staff as permanent process trainers to serve as specialists in helping local groups communicate, establish, and achieve their own goals. The state might publish general educational materials on principles of program and facilities planning for the use of local groups.

In sum, the state role becomes an explaining, demystifying, and supportive one that moves away from mandating, specifying, and restricting. Some management controls and standards must remain, but these should be transformed into process requirements rather than program or structural requirements whenever possible and should contain options and variations for compliance.

GOVERNMENT ROLES IN AN ERA OF CHANGE

Clearly relationships with government at a variety of levels are a critical part of the development of almost all community-scale facilities. At the minimum, local and state building restrictions and codes and state licensing requirements are significant considerations in planning. In many cases, state and/or federal funding will be involved as well, thus very likely requiring conformance to an additional series of standards and evaluation procedures. At least that is the shape of the future, if we assume a continuation of past trends.

The macroproblem into which any present-day social program or "solution" must fit is the problem of adaptation to rapid change—change that is running more deeply than we usually recognize. The old industrial-mechanical system is giving way to an electronic fast-information system. Cheap raw materials are not so available and nonrenewable fossil energy is becoming more precious and expensive. The nuclear family system is changing, the mass educational system and its purposes are rapidly changing, and high urban concentrations are beginning to spread out again. Employment in the manufacturing sector is giving way to other forms of work, and a great deal of leisure is chosen or enforced. We are moving away from equating progress with economic growth and moving toward something undefined as yet, but relating in some way to the quality of life.

In times of such fundamental change, trying to master past rules better is not a useful goal. A more useful aim would be to keep as many options open for the longest possible time and to develop and agree on general goals. From this viewpoint, a mere continuation of past forms of government assistance and practice may have severe limitations. Consider federal funding practices. Presently, the federal government provides funding to attack a social problem, and the federal bureaucracy writes eligibility and standards regulations for the use of those funds. In line with this approach, a recent proposal was that the Joint Commission on Accreditation of Hospitals, Standards for Residential Facilities for the Mentally Retarded be included in the regulations attached to the Developmental Disabilities Act of 1975. People from various constituency groups fought this proposal, because these Standards are quite specific. Including them as mandatory provisions would have severely limited the creativity and flexibility of state and local organizations in meeting a wide range of needs. Furthermore, once such Standards become part of the law, their real purposes are often only dimly remembered by those applying them. The regulations and rules often counter the original intent of the legislation. (For example, welfare tends to make people go on welfare, and the regulations that were intended to prevent misuse of welfare funds are a major cause.) Working around the standards and looking for loopholes thus become common practices. Something intended to

guard against misuse and insure an efficient direction to the problem-solving effort begins to be perceived as negative and as a major problem in itself.

We may even say that our cultural style has become one of piling restrictions upon restrictions until the overall complexity makes it difficult for those with jurisdictional authority even to take action in their areas of responsibility. In one large eastern state, the combination of codes, regulations, and required agency clearances has made installing toilet seats in seven state institutions literally impossible. So we find people of good heart and competence in positions of authority who are unable to provide even that basic dignity for the retarded residents for whom their jobs were created to serve.

In times of change, then, we ought to seek new strategies for government-originated or government-involved problem solving. We ought to be extremely cautious about creating more bodies of specific regulations that not only tend to produce a uniformity of efforts and solutions, but also require a great deal of effort to make sure the uniformity is maintained.

There are alternatives, if we look for them. In the author's state, California, there is a funding scheme for school districts that have reached the limits of their bonded indebtedness under the law and still require more space to provide for a projected student population. A per-pupil formula gives the district a basis for calculating their eligibility for space (square footage). The district, working with a private architect, may use that space to its own purpose. However, the district must consult with the state bureau during the planning process. Once the plan has been accepted on the basis of educational adequacy, a money formula is applied to it. The allocations board will consider the comments of the state bureau as to the educational adequacy of the projected facilities, but an adverse opinion does not by any means negate the plan. This system has worked well for twenty-five years.

This model substitutes process and evaluation requirements related to a broad goal, educational adequacy, for specific standards and mandatory compliance to detailed specifications. The state bureau is guaranteed an input, and the local designers and district are guaranteed some freedom.

By what principles ought we to judge this variant model of local relationship to a larger governmental entity or any other models that may be suggested? It seems to me that there are three major ones: (1) People ought to be given the greatest range of choice that is manageable; (2) people ought to be given the opportunity to be as free as possible of systems or conditions they cannot influence or control; and (3) people should be involved in the decisions that affect them, regardless of how those who direct or administer, view their worthiness or competence.

Following these principles in human services planning makes particularly good sense because such systems function very badly indeed if they do not have the freely given commitment and enthusiasm of those involved. But wider application of the same ideas has more fundamental benefits as well. A system based on them allows considerable variation and creativity, in problem-solving, with the result that however many surprising problem situations we encounter in a complex future, *somebody* is likely to be ready for each one.

The architect is well-equipped to participate in the creative system of problem solving that these principles imply. He is accustomed to looking at a number of processes interacting with each other and is aware of the need to be sensitive to a number of overlapping issues. The architect is perfectly positioned to lead such participatory processes since society looks to him with respect as a professional involved in the shaping and creation of the future.

The architect, as a generalist, should already be oriented to the view that the development of a human services facility is not solely a task for specialists. It is properly a process of participation, involvement, and discovery on the part of experts and nonexperts together. The chances of success increase as greater involvement enlarges the information base and the motivation of the participants.

Alvin Toffler writes about the model of democracy he thinks will help us adapt to coming worlds and find the lives we truly want. I think he would agree with these statements of human desires in the large-system-dominated last quarter of our century:

More and more of us, expert and non-expert, normal or retarded, rich or poor, want to have what we create belong to us.

More and more we want to know that we can influence the people and processes which touch our lives.

More and more, we want to choose our future.[5]

NOTES AND REFERENCES

1. Sommer, Robert, *Personal Space, The Behavioral Basis of Design* (Englewood-Cliffs, N.J.: Prentice Hall, 1969).
2. Nirje, Bengt, "The Normalization Principle and Its Human Management Implications," in Wolfensberger and Kugel (eds.), *Changing Patterns in Residential Services* (Washington, D.C.: President's Committee on Mental Retardation, 1969).
3. International League of Societies for the Mentally Handicapped, "Report of Symposium in Frankfurt, Germany," Brussels, Belgium, 1969.
4. President's Committee on Mental Retardation, "Residential Services for the Mentally Retarded—An Action Policy Proposal," Washington, D.C., 1970.
5. Toffler, Alvin, "The American Future is Being Bumbled Away," *The Futurist*, April 1976 (The World Future Society, Washington, D.C.).

13

Planning and Designing Group Homes

Arnold G. Gangnes

Arnold Gangnes is principal of Arnold G. Gangnes and Associates, AIA, Architects in Seattle, Washington. He has a B. Arch. degree from the University of Washington and an M. Arch. degree from M.I.T. As an architect, Arnold Gangnes has been involved in the struggle to secure environmental rights for the mentally retarded for twenty-seven years. He has been the architect for many facilities for the handicapped and served as a consultant to federal, state, and local governmental agencies. For a total of nine years, he was a member of the Board of Directors of the National Association for Retarded Citizens. He has also been the Chairman of the N.A.R.C. Architectural Planning Committee and the Chairman of the Committee on Environmental Planning of the International League of Societies for the Mentally Handicapped. In 1975, Arnold Gangnes received the singular distinction of becoming the first architect appointed to the President's Committee on Mental Retardation.

INTRODUCTION

Perhaps the most misinterpreted term to become widely used in recent years has been the term *group home;* Just what is a group home? Is it, as referred to in the laws of one state, a residence for developmentally disabled children, accomodating no more than twenty residents? Is it, as is often the case in Canada and elsewhere, a residential facility accommodating up to sixty or more developmentally disabled persons in accommodations that, though infinitely superior to congregate institutions of the past, are still in reality mini-institutions? Are these mini-institutions capable of dealing with developmentally disabled people on an individual basis, and can they realistically allow them the benefits of a "normal lifestyle"?

Is the group home a small residence, tucked away in a corner of the community, from which the developmentally disabled residents venture forth to a life within the community, even if limited by their disabilities? Is it an eight-bed, four-bedroom house located on the grounds of an existing state institution and thus still engulfed in the institutional system of care and lifestyle? Is it a small boarding house located in the city for fourteen semidependent developmentally disabled persons, some of whom work, some of whom need training, and all of whom need guidance? Is it a farm home for twenty developmentally disabled adult men who work on the farm and who visit the nearby community only rarely?

In current context, a group home can be any or all of these. Yet, in the current concepts of deinstitutionalization, it is most often considered the residential setting in which the average aspects of dehumanized congregate care and living are abandoned. The terminology is most often used for the alternative residential setting within the community where developmentally disabled persons can live with a minimum of dependence and a maximum of normalcy. The term is also, however, quite often used for clusters of residential-sized buildings on the grounds of existing institutions, which are surrounded by service elements in the traditional congregated and segregated societal image.

In the concept of normalization, as related to developmentally disabled individuals and their lifestyles, what should a "group home" be, or better yet, what kind of residential option should the developmentally disabled person have?

As an infant, the developmentally disabled child is best served in a family setting that offers stimulation, interpersonal relations, warmth, and affection. As a child and adolescent, he deserves the same opportunities to grow and learn as his peer group. As an adult, he should be afforded the right to contribute within his capabilities to his own and his community's development. In old age, he deserves the respect, comfort, and security that come from still being a part of a family or small group and of being a member of the community.

In establishing community homes for persons with developmental disabilities, planners should keep in mind that for the retarded, as for others, a home is a place to sleep, a place to eat, a place to find respite, a place to find acceptance and companionships, and a place to regenerate one's strength.

Most formal training and education should take place outside the home. Whatever education, training, and development that must take place at home should be done in a natural, informal fashion. Services that are not normally provided in normal homes should also be performed away from homes for developmentally disabled people.

This chapter will be concerned with those residential settings within the community that allow for the maximum in normalized lifestyles and that are primarily concerned with those design aspects of the living environment that are most supportive of the rights and needs of the developmentally disabled residents. This chapter will further consider that this residence is basically a "home" and therefore the bulk of so-called programming, exclusive of normal parental-type guidance and education that usually takes place in the home, will be conducted elsewhere.

We recognize that the problems of many developmentally disabled persons make living with their parents and families—even at an early age—difficult, inadvisable, and often impossible. This chapter concerns itself with the design of appropriate environments for children as well as adults, with ambulatory as well as nonambulatory persons, and with the additional problems of the profoundly physically handicapped.

Although the problems of codes and standards will not be completely discussed, several points should be made about their effect on the environmental design of facilities for the handicapped.

STANDARDS AND REGULATIONS

Most state design standards, if there are any at all, are usually conceived in haste, often by agencies without the experience that comes from experimentation, and almost invariably with carryover concepts of institutional design and the presumed limits of capabilities of the developmentally disabled occupants. Regulations and standards that have these origins most often fail to recognize the need for adequate space for normal living. They often tend to be overprotective in terms of fire resistivity and durability and are often conceived within the framework of past regulations related to mass-care facilities. These latter regulations often impose needless requirements on small facilities that add to the cost. Often they are not normal to the traditional small setting and can alter the environment beyond reasonable limits. These standards and regulations also often lend support to regulatory officials, such as local building and fire inspectors, who seek to impose needless overly restrictive requirements on the design, because of their lack of understanding of the clients to be served or their fears of legal involvement in the event of accidents. The right to face and be able to cope with reasonable risk is certainly within the context of normalization.

Federal and/or state funding for care and training will continue to be a factor in the provision of services to the developmentally disabled. Gaining or retaining these funds implies adherence to federal and state standards for environmental design. Current federal standards allow use of the Life Safety Code #101, 1975 edition, for design criteria. They also mandate that every facility be totally accessible to and usable by the physically handicapped. Architectural barriers should be eliminated in the initial design, regardless of the mobility of residents, in order to reduce the need to take corrective measures later, should the occupants change and include the physically handicapped.

ZONING AND CODES

Perhaps of greatest concern in the environmental design of community residential alternatives are those restrictions imposed by zoning and building codes. In many parts of the country, particularly in suburban and sparsely populated areas, building codes often have little impact. Even in areas where codes are in force, lack of policing leads to liberal interpretation, which really means *no* code. The same can be said of zoning in suburban areas. In municipalities and/or more heavily populated areas, zoning ordinances and local building codes are however enforced and can have great impact on the total environmental picture.

As an example, the Uniform Building Code, which is in effect in the western United States, defines a *family* as a group of blood-related people or no more than five non-blood–related persons. As a "family," the group can live in a home that is classified for occupancy as "I" and is therefore required to be of certain construction standards. This category is the same as for your house and my house. As a single-family residence, the home comes under zoning ordinances that apply to areas designated for single-family residences only. A "group home" for six or

more nonrelated persons can, however, be built or occupied in these areas only by special permit, following public hearings. Unsympathetic or nonunderstanding citizens can and have prevented this right to "normal" living.

Additionally, certain codes and ordinances use such terms as *child-care homes, institutions for retarded persons,* or other terms that automatically deny certain living areas within the community to the developmentally disabled person and often incite communities to reject the retarded because of unwarranted fears about the developmentally disabled themselves and/or imagined fears for property values.

The Uniform Building Code still classifies all persons as children up to age eighteen and requires that any group of over five "children" reside in houses that have automatic sprinkler systems, regardless of the degree of capability of the occupants.

The Life Safety Code #101, 1973 edition, as published by the National Fire Protection Association seeks to correct and amend these overprotective concerns. However, even those agencies who accept the Life Safety Code can, and often do, elect to impose even more restrictive requirements on facilities for the developmentally disabled.

The effect of these code and regulation mandates is twofold. They invariably increase the cost of construction and/or renovation markedly. This situation invariably forces agencies, entrepreneurs, developers, and so forth to build larger buildings to house more people in order to be able to reasonably finance their projects. This domino effect then forces buildings out of certain living areas and increases the "family" size beyond reasonable and "normal" limits. Secondly, they impose within the structure certain design features and mechanical safeguards that are foreign to the normal, small residence and often destroy the friendliness and warmth of design we enjoy in our own homes. Often these regulations limit the variety of finishes to those of limited flame-spread characteristics. Even ordinary wood finishes, beams, and paneling such as we have in our own homes can be excluded.

A great national movement of reassessment of these regulations and codes should take place. Experiences with "normal" environments for the developmentally disabled should be evaluated so that we may arrive at a reasonable conclusion that stresses adequate fire protection and safety, yet allows for normal construction and normal living patterns. Terminologies must be redefined to allow groups of nonrelated persons up to six or eight to live as a "family," with all the legal rights of other families.

GENERAL REQUIREMENTS

For purposes of covering as much area as possible, this chapter presents design requirements and criteria for basic kinds of residential facilities related to groups of handicapped persons, as well as some additional comments on those for persons with particular problems, such as manifest physical disabilities. These basic kinds of facilities include those designed to serve ambulatory children, ambulatory adults, and physically handicapped (mobile) children or adults; facilities oriented basically toward skills training (i.e., Halfway Houses, Transitional Homes, and so forth); facilities for nonmobile persons.

Note that this writer does not personally opt for nor advocate complete separation of residents into these kinds of programmatic groups. While a great deal of heterogenity may be more advantageous, let us nevertheless assess the design problems of these basic groups.

My firm belief, and the conviction of experts in many areas around the world is that there is *no* person, regardless of handicap, who cannot benefit from placement in a community-oriented facility. World-recognized experts state that early intervention and intense treatment on a personalized basis in small family settings can be conducted and can ultimately allow for full care in the typical residential setting.

This type of treatment is possible for all but those with profound physical handicaps that would relegate them to intense hospital or nursing home care.

It stands to reason that *no* single environment can meet the needs of, nor provide a normal living environment for, *all* types and ages of developmentally disabled persons. This statement is true for *all* people. In our lifetimes, we move through many living experiences and environments. The same should hold true for the developmentally disabled, perhaps even moreso, because many will lose the extended ties to their actual parents. Their moving about will likely be with and through a variety of people with whom they can or can't adjust. Thus, living situations and environments will change because of adaptability, because of age, and because of circumstances.

Any good, thoughtful designer can design good living environments for most developmentally disabled persons. What is a good living environment for normal persons is most often just as acceptable for most developmentally disabled persons. There are, of course, some simple guidelines to follow and some cautions to observe. There are special concerns to learn about and a "feel" about the developmentally disabled that only comes from exposure to them and their problems and from experience.

Persons not experienced with and concerned about the needs of the developmentally disabled usually look upon them as persons with deficiencies and problems requiring that they be protected from their environment. Often we are told that durability and "hardening" of the architecture (i.e., emphasis on durability, resistance to abuse, security, and so forth) are most important because of the damage to be anticipated and the hard wear to be expected. Because of long exposure to institutional lifestyles and environments, many developmentally disabled persons have reacted against their environment and rightly so. However, as Robert Sommer says in his book *Tight Spaces, Hard Architecture and How to Humanize It:* "We must reverse course and make buildings *more*, rather than less responsive to their users." He further states, "Experience has shown that hard architecture isn't working from the standpoint of economics, aesthetics or human dignity. And in the case of 'third party clients' [those persons who will occupy living environments without the opportunity to participate in planning), we cannot continue to assume that 'We know what's best for them, and they don't.'"

A recent example I encountered points up in dramatic fashion the need to humanize the environment. One of the western states has in the past three years completely rebuilt the housing at one of its state institutions. This institution had a population of approximately five hundred residents of all degrees of handicap, including manifest behavioral problems. Residents were housed in large wooden barracks-type buildings, in wards of up to fifty. The replacement buildings were designed to simulate a typical residential community, although still on the grounds of the institution. After some experimentation and testing, two significant decisions were made. The planners concluded that every person had the *right* at some time in life to have his or her own room; therefore rooms are all single rooms. (I think in retrospect the planners now feel that some double rooms would have been advantageous for certain residents who progress better and are happier with a close relationship to another.) The second significant decision was that the "family" group be kept small—they settled at six. Their experimentation revealed that the best degree of management, personal relationship, and progress was with this size group. The buildings were designed as duplex houses and as small apartment buildings. These environments, together with a forward-looking functional program of living that is heavily oriented to use of the community outside the institution (which is in an urban setting), have produced remarkable progress. The staff reports that within six months of the initiation of the new program, virtually all behavioral problems either ceased or were dramatically reduced. Residents behaved like different people because they were treated as people. Staff reports indicate that of four hundred residents, only four had emotional-behavioral problems so gross that

they couldn't adapt. This example is remarkable evidence of the therapeutic effect of environment.

Some of the so-called environmental specialists who have written in recent years of the need to provide "stimulating or restful" settings, or who advocate color as a therapeutic tool, or who suggest that five- or six-sided rooms add to feelings of warmth and security, have served to mislead many designers. Whereas there may be some relevance to these suggested stimuli in the intensive-training setting, they have no real relevance to the family residential setting. Attention to and care about the programmatic size of a group and to the normalized environment in which they live are primary. Reasonable attention must be paid to all aspects of the design: use of varied materials, contrast of surfaces to one another, natural and complementary interrelationship of spaces, good function and convenience, cheerful happy design, warm and varied colors, appropriate indoor-outdoor relationships, architecture indigenous to the area. Designs of this kind, within the normal pattern of everyday living, will produce the kinds of environments needed to support the developmentally disabled and to provide them with the appropriate living setting.

Since we are concerned with the *living* environment as opposed to the educational, training, or work environment, we must not be carried away with concepts about the therapeutic effect of color or graphics on the resident. In design for normal persons, color is restrained and used in fairly conventional ways, and we don't presume to dehumanize through the use of graphics or supergraphics. The same rules should apply to any handicapped group.

Note that as mentioned previously, all formal education and training is assumed and recommended to take place outside the home. The home will of course be a place for the usual informal developmental training that occurs in all growing families.

Much has been written in recent years relative to standards of design for residential facilities for the developmentally disabled. Most of this material, however, has been directed primarily toward the upgrading of the space standards reflected in our overcrowded institutions. Most of it falls short of what can be considered minimally acceptable or minimally cognizant of the needs of individual persons, the rights of individual persons, and the essentials of good, functional design. For the purpose of establishing reasonable design standards for the developmentally disabled, the following minimum standards are recommended:

1. Designs shall comply with the basic requirements of the Uniform Building Code, the Life Safety Code, and the appropriate regulations relative to zoning in the particular locale.
2. All facilities shall be available to and accessible to the physically handicapped.
3. Individual group residences shall be preferably for six residents but in no case more than eight.
4. Individual group residences must be no closer then 600 feet to each other (ASPO recommendation).
5. Residences should be dispersed so as not to impose on any given neighborhood an imbalance of handicapped to normal residents.

HOMES FOR AMBULATORY ADULTS

In the traditional institutional concept of mass housing, among the most criticized, most obvious examples of human degradation have been the sleeping and toileting spaces afforded residents. They are the most talked about spaces and the first to be considered in new design standards. Thus, with normalization of the living process in mind, we can appropriately begin with an analysis of the primary "personal" space—the bedroom— for the ambulatory adult (see also Appendix 13A).

Bedrooms

We can find in the Standards for Residential Facilities for the Mentally Retarded, 1975 printing, published by the Joint Commission on Accreditation of Hospitals, the minimum requirement of 80 square feet per resident in single rooms and 60 square feet per resident in multiple sleeping rooms. These requirements are grossly inadequate, and no doubt we could find even more minimum requirements in other regulations and codes.

The document published by the Public Health Service in 1966, "Design of Facilities for the Mentally Retarded," suggested a minimum of 80 square feet per resident regardless of the number in a room. The Minimum Property Standards for Single or 2-Family Residences (For Normal Persons), as published by HUD, lists a minimum of one bedroom at 120 square feet and all others at a minimum of 80 square feet per resident. HUD, however, in its most recent set of standards (1973 edition) provides a most reasonable rationale on size of rooms that not only is informative reading but seeks to establish a design standard based on comfortable use of the room together with reasonable furniture and circulation space.

Generally speaking, a bedroom for one person should be a minimum of 100 square feet and preferably 120 square feet. This space must be exclusive of wardrobe closets or other clothes closets. This size allows for reasonable room for a single bed, a night stand, a chair, a dresser, a desk, and space for additional small items (i.e., radio, TV, or plants. We should remember that to nonrelated persons, moreso than to related ones, the need for *personal* space for one's own possessions is greater and becomes more important as the degree of transience increases. The increased size allows, in addition, the option to rearrange furniture, which can be highly important in many ways. Certain residents cannot adjust to sleeping in the corner of a room (particularly if they have slept in large groups in institutions), and many need or benefit from the ability to approach the bed from three sides. HUD expects that single rooms for two married persons require larger furniture, hence a minimum of 120 square feet. Thus, allowing space for this option to occur is wise.

For design flexibility, furniture units that contain

drawer and hanging space (similar to those found in college dormitories) and that can be moved about if necessary are desirable. Standards for light and ventilation are ably handled in most codes and need not be repeated here. In bedrooms at the ground floor level, windows are best arranged to allow an alternate escape route in event of emergency (as is mandated in some codes). Vision panels in bedroom and bathroom doors deprive the resident of dignity and privacy and therefore are not acceptable.

The floor plan in Figure 13-1 shows a residence for eight, plus one staff person. This design shows some options in sleeping accommodations and also shows how change can be effected at a later date. The double bedroom can become two singles by placing a wall in the middle of the room. Similarly, the four-bed room may be subdivided to allow for a variety of combinations or even four *single* rooms.

Toilet and Bathing Areas

The modern house of today is not the best example of appropriate bathing and toileting facilities for the developmentally disabled. Designing these facilities requires that a number of good lessons be learned. Remember, however, that this first set of design criteria is for a facility to house adult, ambulatory persons not to exceed eight in number. Other options or revisions for groups of different ages and handicaps will be discussed later.

Traditional institutional bathing and toileting facilities have been totally devoid of concern for human dignity and the rights of personal privacy. Perhaps the traditional concept of mass care made this lack of concern inevitable. Traditional efforts to correct the inhumanity of those concepts have produced various means of improving the degree of personal privacy, but as yet they haven't been totally concerned about the dignity of the person. I am reminded of a comment by a person who had multiple physical handicaps that confined him to a wheelchair and who at the mid-fifties in life said: "I remember just recently when I entered a public building and found a toilet stall which would allow me to close the door behind my wheelchair, that it was the first time in my life that I could enjoy privacy in a toilet in a public place."

The conventional family bathroom can be acceptable for use in a facility for the developmentally disabled. Excluding the need for extra space for mobility for the physically handicapped, the following will make bathing space more functional, more usable, and more acceptable to the developmentally disabled:

1. An overabundance rather than a shortage of separate facilities (see Figure 13-1);
2. A facility convenient to both sleeping and living areas;
3. A shower stall *and* a tub with shower (not all can be trained to use only one or the other);
4. Conventional, rather than different, fixtures, counters, lavatories, medicine chests, and so forth;
5. Adequate space for all adults to be able to prepare for work in the morning without undue wait (which implies more lavatories than are customarily found in a residence);
6. Elimination of institutional-type features (i.e., gang toilets).

In a residence for eight adults, two full baths and one small bath (shower only) are recommended. Each full bath should have two lavatories. Staff and guest toilet facilities may be in addition. These rooms should have conventional finishes.

Living Areas

Living patterns within typical residences differ in various parts of our country and in other countries. For this reason, space patterns can and should be different. One basic thing to remember in trying to follow the "typical family" residential image is that rarely are group homes for the developmentally disabled, or similar residential facilities, the same as

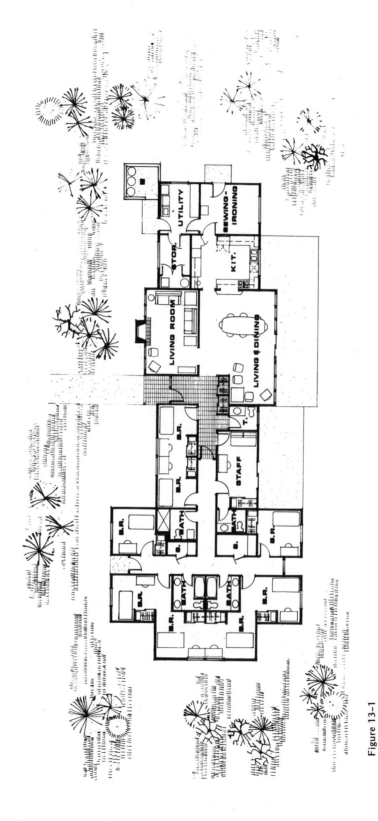

Figure 13–1
An example of a well-designed residence for eight girls and one staff person located in Stanwood, Washington. (Arnold G. Gangnes and Associates, A.I.A. Architects.)

"typical family" homes because the age and size of the occupants tend to be more uniform than in the typical family. This "family" pattern suggests more than the normal amount of space is needed for a residence housing all adults, since all may have use of spaces at the same time (i.e. six to eight adults or more watching TV, using the recreation room or the living room).

The Joint Council on Accreditation of Hospitals Standards suggest 80 square feet per resident, which has usually been inadequate. Size should be based primarily on a study of the anticipated use of each space, the furniture it should have, the amount of space pre-empted by the circulation patterns through the space, the anticipated use by the residents and staff and their guests. Good design can help make better use of many spaces through careful concern for circulation routes. Experience indicates that 100 square feet per resident is more suitable, comfortable, and practicable for "living space" (living room, family room, den). In "Western Design," efficient use can be made of the "open plan concept." (See Figures 13-1 and 13-2). This plan arrangement features one space that is more or less open to another, such as kitchen–dining, or kitchen–family room, or living–dining. In western states, kitchen spaces are commonly open either partially or entirely to the adjacent dining space, whether it be a dining room in the traditional sense or a larger "family room" in which dining as well as other "family" functions take place. In reality we are extending the old-fashioned "family kitchen" concept or, if you prefer, adding the recreation room to the kitchen–dining space.

This open plan concept has great merit for all family groups in that it allows great togetherness and room for the more active and messy family functions to take place, thereby leaving the more formalized "living room" for less active, quiet, and formal activities. Spaces developed with this concept in mind have been unusually successful. One additional advantage of rooms open one to another is the ease of supervision, together with the feeling of always being a "part" of the group. Separated "living rooms" and

adequate personalized sleeping spaces allow for the need for quiet and privacy. Many homes have in addition a "den," or "library," "sewing room," or similar "extra" space for family use. (See Figure 13-1.) Providing such space is useful for adult groups. This space can and often does vary greatly in its use.

Dining-Kitchen Areas

In the conventional sense, any space in a house adjacent to the kitchen, if adequate in size, can appropriately function as a dining space, whether it be a room by itself, a part of a family room or even a part of the kitchen itself. In terms of family groupings, people reasonably and normally sit at one table. Although we have advocated tables for four in the replanning of institutions, mandating that table size in a typical residential setting doesn't make much sense. However, a dining space for six, eight or even ten adults must have more room than that for a conventional family. Use of the dining table and space for other than eating functions serves to add to the spatial variety.

Perhaps the most important concern in food programming is the kitchen. Because of the inability to rationalize kitchens in group homes as similar to those in conventional homes in terms of function, equipment, and use, many states and their fire marshals or regulatory officials have considered them "hazard areas." Therefore, the kitchen is subject to unusual requirements for fire doors, self-closers on doors, and special protection devices. Reducing the number of residents in group homes to six or eight has made possible complying with conventional code requirements and convincing regulatory officials that separation of the kitchen as a "hazard area" is not only unwarranted, but is also restrictive. It interferes with proper management and supervision and defeats the normalization process. Certainly the average residential kitchen, be it all-electric or one with gas-fired appliances, has an acceptable degree of hazard. This degree of hazard is no more for the handicapped than

Figure 13-2
This plan for a group home in Seattle, Washington demonstrates efficient use of the "open plan" concept in which living spaces are more or less open to one another. (Arnold G. Gangnes and Associates, A.I.A. Architects.)

for the normal. Both must learn the rules and limitations. Fortunately, we have been able to demonstrate this rationale and now have kitchens fully open to living–dining and/or family room areas.

The kitchen in a residence for the developmentally disabled is designed to fill the role of a training mechanism to a higher degree than one in a conventional home. For that reason, more adults will be in the kitchen at one time, and it should be large enough to accommodate them. Providing more than the usual amount of electrical outlets is appropriate as is protecting them from overload. Often, cooking can be taught to many at one time through use of small appliances such as electric frypans. This type of training method suggests adequate work counters too, of course, and having space for an additional refrigerator or freezer somewhere in the building is wise. No additional safety requirements other than the usual concern about the safety of inquisitive children from the hazards of stove burners, cutlery drawers, and so forth should be necessary.

Laundry-Utility Areas

Laundry–utility rooms should be adequate in size to accommodate a conventional washer and dryer, space for folding laundry, space for ironing, and a space for a small laundry cart. Additionally, having a deep-well sink for soaking small clothing items, for washing muddy items, and for gardening or other similar uses is advisable. A utility sink for cleaning of mops and so forth may also be desirable. This space can acceptably be placed near or adjacent to the kitchen, to additional storage space, and/or furnace rooms. Unless extensive laundry work will be done (i.e., all the bed linen), the size and location described here should be adequate. There are different schools of thought relative to the normalcy of doing *all* the laundry at the residence. If that function is shared by the residents, it has much more justification than if it requires staff time, which takes staff away from working with the residents.

Supplemental Areas

Just as a typical residence, the group home needs an adequate furnace room, water heater room, entry hall, closet space for off-season clothing, bulk storage space for personal and household use, and storage space for outdoor activity equipment.

HOMES FOR AMBULATORY CHILDREN

Designing facilities for the care of children differs markedly from designing for adults. (See Appendix 13B). Primarily there are code and ordinance considerations. Each local area should be carefully checked for limitations in size of "family" as related to zoning codes. The Uniform Building Code has established categories for children under Chapter 9, Group "D" occupancies. This involves all groups of more than five children. A child is defined as a person under the age of eighteen years. Of particular concern are the mandatory requirements for automatic fire extinguishing systems and for one-hour construction throughout. Architects should check with local agencies early.

Differences in design from adult facilities should reflect the basic size and age differences and the degree of activity of young people. The design of sleeping areas may be virtually identical to those for adults. A variety of bedroom sizes is strongly recommended so that two can share a room. With smaller children, the companionship offers some additional security. We do not recommend that room requirements be totally scaled down to bedrooms only for two. If flexibility is desired, the individual areas can be arrangeable and sized so that a future partition will make the double room into two acceptable singles. As for adults, bedrooms should allow adequate space for suitable furniture. Bedrooms should be as conventional as possible. Windows that allow for easy escape to grade in the event of fire are advisable. Since incontinency can be a factor, the use of throw rugs may be more acceptable than full carpeting. A combination of rooms with and without carpeting is also acceptable. Wall finishes should be readily wash-able: tackboards and pin-up walls are recommended. Doors should not have vision panels.

Bathing and toileting areas for children should be measurably different from those for adults. Adequate counter space should be available for changing of diapers, together with space for adequate control of and storage of soiled clothes.

Counter lavatories should be available for use by children. *All* fixtures should be of standard size and mounting height to assure proper training of the child. Stools or a pull-out step to aid small children should be available or else a lavatory should be lowered. Bathrooms in general should be somewhat larger than conventional to allow for adult assistance of the child in all phases of toileting and bathing. A hand spray in tubs is recommended as a bathing aid. Whether mandated or not, grab bars at tubs are ad-vised. Finishes should be durable, waterproof, and easily cleanable. Floor drains should not be neces-sary. Shower stalls, where individually installed, should have recessed pans so that access by wheel-chairs is possible and easy. This recess will allow some additional protection from overflows. Providing an adequate number of toilets for emergency use is advisable.

Living spaces for children should reflect the same variety as previously stated. Family rooms usually receive heavier use than those for adults, and finishes should reflect this fact. Adequate storage units for toys, games, and other items of play equipment—as well as a paved outdoor space suitable for wheeled toys—should be provided close at hand to the indoor family room.

RESIDENCES FOR PHYSICALLY HANDICAPPED PERSONS

Although current federal and state laws require that all public buildings and those with federal or state funding be accessible to and usable by the physi-cally handicapped, there has been a good deal of con-sternation about what this implies. Existing federal

and state regulations have required use of American National Standard A–117.1, 1961 (revised 1971). This standard, however, is presently being revised and should not be used.

The designer can use either the Handicapped Sec-tion of the North Carolina Building Code or the Handbook on Design of Barrier-Free Facilities, pub-lished as Part 4 of the *Facilities and Construction Manual of the Facilities Engineering & Construction Administration* by DHEW. Designers should also ob-tain a copy of "Into the Mainstream—A Syllabus on Barrier-Free Environment" published by the A.I.A.

One of the debated design standards concerns the mounting height of the toilet seat. Whereas most standards have said 20″ off the floor, there is consid-erable opinion directed toward a more standard height of 16″ or 18″.

Residences for mobile physically handicapped per-sons need not differ greatly from those for ambulatory persons. (See Appendix 13C). Accessibility to and usability by persons in wheelchairs can be readily pro-vided in new design. Of primary importance is access. A one-level plan is optimal with low door thresholds (maximum of 3/4″ is recommended). If more than one person in a wheelchair is to be housed in a given facility, additional space in all functioning spaces should be provided. The scale for design becomes the wheelchair, together with the problems of its ma-neuverability and the additional space needed by the occupant to maneuver in and out of it. Widening of corridors is helpful, and widening of doorways is usually warranted, particularly those to bathrooms. All rooms should, of course, allow for the maneuver-ing of the wheelchair. Maneuvering space becomes critical in bedrooms, bathrooms, and kitchens. Bed-rooms should allow space alongside the bed for trans-fer from chair to bed. Space should also be allowed for storage of the chair when not in use. Bathrooms should allow for use of all fixtures easily by a seated person. Bathrooms should have adequate room to accommodate the chair within the room with the door closed, as well as adequate space to turn the chair and/or make a lateral transfer to the toilet. Lavatories should be lowered, as should be mirrors, medicine cabinets, and so forth. Showers should have recessed pans without curbs to allow for entry of the wheelchair. Appropriately placed grab bars at tubs, showers, and toilets should be provided. Kitchens need to be usable to a degree by the person in a wheelchair. The degree depends on the extent to which the wheelchair occupant will need to assist in the household duties. If this need involves a number of persons and extensive participation, the designer of the residence should refer to a document entitled "Wheelchair Interiors" published by the National Easter Seal Society for Crippled Children and Adults. This publication makes reommendations for space needs and design innovations for all parts of the home.

Additional design features that enhance the use of the residence include:

1. Lever or spade handles on sinks, lavatories, and doors;
2. Electrical outlets 10" above the floor and switches at readily available heights;
3. Flooring materials that can be easily traversed in a wheelchair (deep pile carpeting is often difficult);
4. Doors that can be easily opened and closed;
5. Replaceable, protective "kick strips" along heavily used corridors for protection from the wheelchair footrest.

Generally speaking, facilities for children often require additional space for and consideration of the activities associated with physical therapy.

Allowable construction types are similar to those for ambulatory persons to assure that the nonambulatory can evacuate either by themselves or with assistance. The state fire marshal should be consulted in individual cases.

FACILITIES FOR NONMOBILE PERSONS

This kind of facility has been virtually nonexistent at the community level. Most services to profoundly developmentally disabled and multiply handicapped persons have been provided at state institutions, nursing homes, or hospitals, or they have been limited to parental home care. No facility criteria or standards exist.

There are many, including parents and institutional people, who advocate custodial institutionalization. However, substantial sentiment to the contrary has been expressed by national and international leaders in the care and training of the profoundly handicapped. Their view is that intensive care and treatment administered on a close personal relationship in environments as close to the normal residential setting as possible offers the best hope for improvement and/or an existence at the top-level of capability. The following are thus offered as the governing design criteria:

1. Size of the unit shall not exceed six residents, plus staff.
2. Facilities should be one-story only, or offer a full range of services plus grade access at one or each level.
3. Facilities should meet the criteria for physically handicapped children described previously as a minimum.
4. Facilities shall meet all state fire marshal criteria, the Uniform Building Code, and Life Safety Code Standards for safety of occupants. U.B.C. D–3 occupancy is indicated with special attention to adequate design that will allow rapid evacuation of the building by persons confined to bed. This aspect includes wider doorways and corridors, additional exits, and a minimum of obstacles in the path of evacuation.

Facilities seeking funding for residents under Title XIX, S.S.I., should consult additional federal requirements and Chapter 10, Life Safety Code.

Again, we recommend that facilities for physically handicapped or nonambulatory persons have approximately twenty to twenty-five percent more space in all areas of the residence than is programmed for ambulatory persons.

TRANSITIONAL SHORT-TERM FACILITIES

Facilities designed for skills training—that is, learning basic social skills preparatory to moving into group home placement or semi-independent living—have some special concerns in respect to space for training. Residences should have the same basic program spaces or rooms as a residence for ambulatory adults, with special concern for the following:

1. Residences should have no more then eight trainees.
2. There should be a mixture of single and double bedrooms.
3. Bathroom facilities should be adequate to allow all residents to simultaneously prepare for work in the morning. Lavatories can appropriately be provided in some bedrooms. Bathrooms should remain residential in character rather than for congregate use.
4. Kitchen facilities should provide adequate space and equipment to allow up to six persons to work on simple meal preparation at one time. Electrical wiring should allow for use of more than the usual number of electrical appliances.
5. Zoning of sleeping and living areas to maximize privacy and reduce interference is recommended. Inasmuch as trainees may be expected to come and go at irregular hours, use of the living facilities should be possible at late hours without unduly disturbing others.

This type of facility can be a two-story building, provided that there is accessibility to and usability by the physically handicapped.

STAFF ROOMS

No single, ideal solution exists for the problem of providing adequate and acceptable space for use by staff because of the wide variance in the numbers and types of staff personnel needed. It is one thing to provide staff office space for only one person serving an eight-hour shift and quite another to provide for a married live-in couple. The situation can become more difficult if the live-in couple is not married.

In the interests of normalization, the ideal staff quarters would consist of merely a bedroom, with the remainder of the house conceived of as the "family" home. In reality, however, this plan is in many cases somewhat unrealistic. Providing for all possible contingencies is also somewhat unrealistic.

If staff are to live-in, consideration should be given toward the ability to accommodate a married couple. The design should include consideration for their personal privacy and off-duty ability to entertain in their quarters. (One of the most frequent staff complaints is about the lack of adequate space for minimal off-duty relaxation.) A minimum space for this function would be a bedroom of 120 square feet, a living-sitting room of the same size, and a private bathroom. As much as is possible, staff areas should blend into the overall family residence plan.

If staff are to be shifted and will not live-in, space should be adequate for a small desk, a sofa or hide-a-bed and chair, a file cabinet, and a private bath. (See Figure 13–1.)

DESIGN CONSIDERATION, SITE SELECTION, AND ENVIRONMENTAL CHARACTER

A seemingly obvious and simple way to provide community-oriented residential alternatives to institutionalization would simply be to build typical houses in the community or to remodel existing ones. Groups or "families" of six or eight residents could then move in without fanfare and set up residence.

Unfortunately, the stigmas that have been attached to the developmentally disabled person still remain. The amount of resistance on the part of citizens and even public officials is a result of fear, lack of education, misinformation, and often just simple prejudice. Removing these fears and prejudices to the point where there is acceptance will take time. Adherence to good environmental standards based on the normalization principle, which include reasonable and respected standards for size and quality of space, will aid in the effort to allay the fears, counter the prejudices, and promote acceptance of the developmentally disabled person in society.

Partly for these reasons and also for the reasons associated with the normalization principle, the design of residential facilities should best express the quality and character of the architecture to be found in the specific locale. Designs that are spectacularly unusual, or oversized, or in strong contrast to the indigenous style should be avoided. Use of materials and the organization of exterior as well as interior space, should reflect the normal patterns of everyday life and also stress recognition of the residents' maturity. To do otherwise is to call attention to difference and indirectly attach new stigmas to the occupants.

Sites that have easy access to community facilities and transportation are recommended. Sites that are exposed to unusual community hazard or that require transportation to most community facilities should be avoided. (Appendix 13D presents a complete list of criteria for site selection.)

CONCLUSIONS

Among the major impediments that must be overcome in the process of normalizing the lives of persons who are developmentally disabled are those of fear, prejudice, and misunderstanding. These concerns have presented incredible barriers to those who have been concerned with and who have sought to right the wrongs that society has imposed on the handicapped.

As if physical and mental handicaps were not enough, society has isolated the handicapped person into environments that have and still do contribute to his handicaps, rather than attempt to ameliorate them.

The evidence is increasing in support of the beneficial effect of grouping persons who are developmentally disabled in small groups. Common knowledge today is that many concerns and fears of the past are slowly melting away as a result of society's acceptance of the developmentally disabled person in everyday life.

The effort in this chapter is not to advocate a degree of environmental excellence in excess of what most of us enjoy (although in some cases this might be so). However, because much housing will be in lieu of institutionalization or as a result of deinstitutionalization, the option of group homes will hopefully provide an appropriate environment in which the rehabilitation process can progress. While the environment provides the basis for a good life for the handicapped person, it also contributes to his social adjustment and thereby makes him more acceptable to his fellow men.

Whereas the residential setting is only a part of the rehabilitation process, it is certainly a key one. The intent here is not just to create a better environment than the institution nor merely to upgrade previous standards of housing. The intent is to start with the individual person's needs and then attempt to resolve them as best we know how.

Existing facilities in this image have had remarkable success. However, the failures are also evident. These mostly have been because of inadequate funding and/or inadequate programming. Both are vital to a successful result.

APPENDIX 13A
PROGRAMMING REQUIREMENTS FOR
COMMUNITY RESIDENCES FOR
AMBULATORY ADULTS

Basic residence for six to eight adults
Average gross area for eight adults excluding staff areas = 3200 square feet. (Areas 1, 2, 3, and 4 should provide a minimum of 100 square feet per resident.)

1. Living room with comfortable seating for ten to twelve adults.
2. Family room (or recreation room).
3. Dining room (or area).
4. Supplementary living areas (dens, libraries, sewing rooms).
5. Kitchen (all areas of food preparation), with space to allow resident participation.
6. Utility room for laundry and support services, including space for conventional residential laundry equipment.
7. Sleeping rooms, including singles and doubles for flexibility (minimum 120 square feet for singles, 180 square feet for doubles; doors will not have vision panels).
8. Bathrooms, including a minimum of two full baths, with no gang fixtures and with one bath accessible to the physically handicapped (an additional part bath and/or guest toilet room is recommended; doors will not have vision panels).
9. Staff room or areas (provided as program requires).
10. Entry hall or entrance for coat storage, guest usage and so forth.
11. Mechanical rooms for furnaces, hot water heaters, and so forth.
12. In-House Storage for residents extra gear, household needs; and bulk storage for large items, (i.e., suitcases, skis, bicycles); exterior storage for garden tools, supplies, and so forth.
13. Outdoor spaces, including patios, roofed porches, paved programmed areas, carports, garages (50 square feet per resident is recommended).

APPENDIX 13B
PROGRAMMING REQUIREMENTS FOR
RESIDENCES FOR AMBULATORY
CHILDREN

Basic residence for eight children
Average gross area for eight children excluding staff areas = 3200 square feet. Areas 1, 2, 3, and 4 should provide a minimum of 100 square feet per resident. Area #4 may be included as part of #2.

1. Living room.
2. Family room (adjacent to or part of kitchen–dining area).
3. Dining room (or area).
4. Supplementary living area.
5. Kitchen (all areas of food preparation), including space to allow limited resident participation, depending on age.
6. Utility room, for laundry and support services, including space for conventional residential laundry equipment.
7. Sleeping rooms, including singles and doubles for flexibility (minimum 120 square feet for singles, 180 square feet for doubles).
8. Bathrooms, including a minimum of two full baths, with adequate counter space and special features for children's use (detachable shower spray).
9. Staff room or areas (provided as program requires).
10. Entry hall or entrance for coat storage, guest usage, and so forth.
11. Mechanical rooms for furnaces, hot water heaters, and so forth.
12. In-House Storage for residents' extra gear, household needs; bulk storage for large items (i.e., suitcases, skis, bicycles); and exterior storage for garden tools, supplies, and so forth.
13. Outdoor spaces, including patios, roofed porches, paved programmed areas, carports, garages (50 square feet per resident is recommended).

Recommended specification features

1. Durable wall surfaces (i.e., vinyl fabric in heavy use areas such as corridors and family or play rooms).
2. Rounded corners on counter tops.
3. Use of throw rugs in lieu of full carpet in bedrooms (nonskid backing recommended).
4. Low windows in family room or play area (so that small children can look out).
5. Adequate paved outdoor area convenient to family or play room.
6. Attention to safe design in kitchen areas.
7. Adequate consideration for muddy clothes (i.e., mudroom near rear entry or outdoor play).

APPENDIX 13C
PROGRAMMING REQUIREMENTS FOR
RESIDENCES FOR NONAMBULATORY
PHYSICALLY HANDICAPPED

Basic Residences for physically handicapped (non-ambulatory)

In addition to the requirements for adults and children (Appendixes 13A and 13B), the following features should be incorporated into the residential design.

1. Total accessibility and usability by those in wheelchairs.

2. Grade level entrances and no abnormal thresholds or stairs in single-story residences.

3. Exit routes designed for ease of evacuation for nonambulatory residents.

4. Space for the mobility dimensions of the wheelchair and the occupant's range of reach.

5. Corridors and joint use areas designed for the traffic requirements and mobility of wheelchair users.

6. Personal use spaces (i.e., bathrooms and bedrooms) designed to allow for adequate privacy and room to function for wheelchair users.

7. Durable materials to protect heavy use areas from damage from wheelchairs.

APPENDIX 13D
SITE SELECTION CRITERIA

1. Current zoning laws provide that as long as the number of persons residing in the unit does not exceed eight, each residence can be considered as a single-family residence and therefore acceptable in first residential zones.
2. Siting should provide access to public transportation and be readily available to community services and facilities.
3. Sites should allow adequate land for outdoor activities related to the age and size of the group.
4. Sites should generally be selected where traffic and/or other high hazard conditions are at a minimum.
5. Sites should be within reasonable distance of the specialized services the residents can be expected to use (i.e., schools, training centers, sheltered workshops).
6. Residences located on building sites other than those for single-family residences should maintain a ratio of land to building not less than that prescribed in single-family residential zones (minimum R.S. 7200).
7. Areas on each lot not covered by buildings should be landscaped, seeded in lawn, or otherwise developed in a manner that will support the needs of the residents. Such landscaping and/or lawn areas should be commensurate with those in the average well-maintained residential neighborhood, and these improvements should be maintained in presentable condition.

APPENDIX 13E
SELECTED RESOURCE MATERIALS

The following is a list of recommended publications, including the addresses where they may be obtained, for all persons concerned with housing the developmentally disabled:

Kliment, S. A., "Into the Mainstream—A Syllabus for a Barrier-Free Environment." American Institute of Architects, 1735 New York Avenue, N.W., Washington, D.C. 20036.

Francklin, S., "Mentally Handicapped People Living in Ordinary Houses and Flats." Centre on Environment for the Handicapped, 24 Nutford Place, London, WIH, 6AN, England.

"The Right to Choose—Achieving Residential Alternatives in the Community." National Association for Retarded Citizens, 2709 Avenue "E" East, Arlington, Tex. 76011.

Mace, R. L., "An Illustrated Handbook of the Handicapped Section of the North Carolina State Building Code." North Carolina Department of Insurance, Box 26387, Raleigh, N.C. 27611.

Sommer, R., *Tight Spaces: Hard Architecture and How to Humanize It.* Prentice-Hall, Englewood Cliffs, N.J.

United Nations, Report of United Nations Expert Group on Eliminating Barriers. Rehabilitation International, 122 East 23rd Street, New York, N.Y. 10010.

Kugel, R. B., and W. Wolfensberger (eds.), *Changing Patterns in Residential Services for the Mentally Retarded* (chapters 5, 7, 17). U.S. Government Printing Office, Washington, D.C.

President's Committee on Mental Retardation, "New Environments for Retarded People." U.S. Government Printing Office, Washington, D.C.

——, "New Neighbors—The Retarded Citizen in Search of a Home." U.S. Government Printing Office, Washington, D.C.

——, "People Live in Houses." U.S. Government Printing Office, Washington, D.C.

14

The Center on Environment for the Handicapped

Kenneth Bayes and Janet Levison

Kenneth Bayes, an architect and partner of Design Research Unit of London, has directed his efforts largely towards exploration of environmental considerations in design for mentally handicapped people. He has served as consultant to various governmental and private agencies in Great Britain and abroad (including the National Association of Retarded Citizens in the United States). He was the founder and first Director of the Center on Environment for the Handicapped in London.

Mr. Bayes has authored "The Therapeutic Effect of Environment on Mentally Subnormal and Emotionally Disturbed Children" (1967), "Designing for the Handicapped" (edited with Sandra Francklin in 1972) and "Room for Improvement" (with James Elliot in 1972). He continues his studies and consulting from his home in Southwest France, and he plans futher publications in the near future.

Janet Levison is a former information officer of the Center on Environment for the Handicapped in London. She also served on the editorial staff of Built Environment. *Since March 1976, she has been organizing conferences for high school students on international affairs for the Council for Educational World Citizenship.*

INTRODUCTION

The Center on Environment for the Handicapped (CEH) in London is an advisory and information service for all persons concerned with the physical environment of handicapped people. It is without parallel, as far as is known, in any other country. During the first seven years of its existence, it has shown the sanguine side of its character, by receiving support and giving help in a somewhat informal way. To survive so long as an unstructured body is perhaps only possible in Great Britain—the British nation has, after all, survived even longer without a written constitution.

Admittedly, the story of CEH recounted in this chapter by no means presents a formal blueprint for setting up a service; rather it is a description of the first years of a personal endeavor from which many lessons may be learned. However, CEH is now emerging from this wayward period; it is becoming structured and constitutionalized and more in line with the form of a respectable body others might wish to emulate. This current phase of development is described later in the chapter.

CEH was founded as a result of the personal experience of one of the authors. In 1965 Kenneth Bayes, with the support of a Kaufmann International Design Award, set for himself the task of collecting all the information he could about the therapeutic effect of the environment on emotionally disturbed and mentally handicapped children. He sought three main sources of information:

1. Buildings used for the education or care of emotionally disturbed or mentally handicapped children;
2. Professionals involved with these children, especially those with an awareness of the influence of the environment on behavior and development;
3. Research projects or special studies connected, however remotely, with the subject.

Since environmental concern is primarily an architectural problem, the Royal Institute of British Architects, as the source of all architectural knowledge,

263

was approached first. This staff gave all the help they could, but even the largest architectural library in Europe had very little material about designing for mentally handicapped or disturbed people. On the particular subject of the therapeutic effect of the environment, the ideas of Rudolf Steiner (through which Bayes had entered this field) seemed the most positive, but even these were not easily accessible. Information was sought from all the associations, societies, institutes and other known organizations that represented the concerns and welfare of mentally handicapped and mentally ill people and the groups of professionals caring for them. Centers, schools, and special hospitals were visited; experts in university departments were interviewed; architects, psychiatrists, and pediatricians at the Department of Health and Social Security were consulted.

The responses were usually in the form of kindly interest, sometimes a complete lack of understanding, often offerings of names of other (unlikely) people, and occasionally some mature judgement and opinion. Sixty-five of these sources were visited or contacted in Great Britain, thirty-one in the rest of Europe, eighty-one in the United States, and ten on other continents. A large proportion of these were wholly abortive for the purpose in hand.

An unfortunate waste of time and energy would obviously result if every student in this field during the following years had to suffer the same search and the same frustrations. Ways of systematically recording the found information and of keeping in touch with new sources, new research projects, new buildings as they were completed, and new literature seemed sensible considerations. All such material gathered together in one place thus became a utopian dream. This dream was ultimately realized as an idea through the enthusiasm of Sandra Francklin (whom Bayes met when she was a Churchill Scholar in the United States studying facilities for mentally handicapped people and whose journeys and studies had also produced a considerable number of books, a vast collection of typescripts, and some slides).

THE IDEA FOR AN INFORMATION CENTER

We felt the Bayes–Francklin joint library should be made available to other people, and the idea of forming an information center became more specific. Our first needs were space to house the library and finances to man it. A number of organizations were approached, and the one with which we had had most contact—because of its status both as a national body and as a founder society of the International League of Societies for the Mentally Handicapped—came to our aid. This organization was the National Society for Mentally Handicapped Children. In already over-crowded premises in central London, the Secretary-General, George Lee, persuaded his council to give us some space. It was a very small room in a highly inaccessible part of the building, but we were grateful for this sign of faith in a new enterprise. The National Society also paid the salary of our first assistant—a part-time qualified librarian who established the library classification system (Universal Decimal Classification) that after a lot of consideration seemed the most appropriate for the collection of books and other materials. Sandra Francklin, whose initiative and imagination provided the motive power of the early years, was also retained part-time by the National Society for her valuable advisory services.

An advisory council of friends in various fields who had been helpful during the initial study was formed. The selection was somewhat haphazard—made from the heart rather than by systematically choosing a representative from each relevant discipline or each service. They were people whom we liked and respected and whose names we wanted to have connected with the enterprise. They included pediatricians, child psychiatrists, architects, members of organizations concerning the welfare of handicapped people, representatives of our funding bodies, and later a sociologist and a nursing officer.[1]

The ad hoc nature of this advisory council was perhaps a certain embarrassment in later years to subsequent directors who had a more objective view of management, but it was a good initial choice. However, not enough use was made of the council during this period—or later, for that matter. We kept them informed of progress at too infrequent meetings, perhaps once or twice a year. The early center had no constitution and was run at the discretion of the director. Although it was not modeled as a sensible organization, it worked at that time.

GROWTH OF THE CENTER

In 1967 the first exploratory proposal papers for setting up a center—which at that time was called a therapy and environment information and research center—were written. Another two years passed before the concept was crystallized and the first sponsor found. In the beginning of 1971, CEH, under its new name, was finally launched as a full-fledged service. An inaugural party was held, and reasonable coverage was given in the appropriate press. A statement of aims was issued as follows:

1. To provide a center for the dissemination of information on the design of the physical environment for all types of handicap, but with emphasis in the first instance on mental handicap;
2. To promote among architects and others concerned with the design of the environment, an understanding of human development, the needs of the handicapped, and the programs that meet them;
3. To advise all disciplines of the significance of the environment in relation to the care of the handicapped;
4. To keep under review recent and current research and to encourage and carry out new research projects that need to be undertaken;
5. To maintain an information service and library of books, articles, drawings, photographs, visual aids, films, slides, and so forth for professional

workers and students and to provide a clearing house for inquiries by using other available sources as appropriate;
6. To keep in touch with similar centers in other countries and with the proposed international center (which has not yet materialized) for exchange of material;
7. To arrange multidisciplinary conferences or seminars;
8. To issue regular newsletters, information on recent acquisitions, and reports on activities.

The emphasis on mental handicap was due to our own main interest at the time. The subject was highly topical and it was the concern of our sponsors, but one of our main intentions was eventually to cover all handicaps. The name of the center was carefully chosen with this expansion in mind. The expansion has since taken place (although perhaps it would now be called a center on environment for "handicapped *people*," instead of "*the* handicapped").

In comparison with our first aims, the following statement is from the current CEH brochure:

CEH offers advice and information on the design of the environment of handicapped people. It is concerned with people who are mentally handicapped, mentally ill, blind, deaf or physically handicapped. Environment covers planning, buildings, and equipment—the aim is to help architects and others to understand the needs of handicapped people and how best they can be met.

CEH has a specialized reference library of books, journals, slides, photographs and plans. It publishes a quarterly newsletter, issues reports, information sheets and bibliographies, organizes multidisciplinary seminars, and arranges visits.

CEH has architectural consultants with whom projects can be discussed. Its services are used by health, social services, housing and educational authorities, voluntary agencies, architects, students from a variety of disciplines, and individual disabled people.

From the moment of inauguration the demand for information was considerable. The Ely Hospital scandal, in which inhumane conditions in one of the old institutions for mentally handicapped people were exposed, had drawn attention not only to patterns of staffing and care, but also to obsolete buildings and the effect of a sordid physical environment on behavior. "Normalization" had been practiced in Scandinavia for several years and was becoming a principle of care among progressive practitioners; the precise definition was being argued at midnight sessions in Frankfurt at an International League of Societies for the Mentally Handicapped seminar[2] and elsewhere.

The new attitude toward mentally handicapped people was having its repercussions on the environment. No international conference on mental handicap was complete without a paper on architecture in a plenary session. Students were taking up mental handicap projects for their theses. This group probably constituted the majority of CEH's customers at that time: they consulted and discussed the books and programs in our library, which were usually sadly out-of-date. Other inquiries ensued. This period was the hey-day of the new knowledge in the mental handicap field.

Appointing a full-time secretary became necessary, and for the first time the CEH office was staffed all day every day by at least one person and on occasions by all the staff (within the 70 square feet of space). A young industrial designer also joined us at this time.

Within a short period of time at the National Society, CEH had established itself as a lively and independent body that was perhaps a little precocious. We needed more space, full-time staff, and longer-term financing. A period of frantic searching, finding, cajoling, failing, persuading and applying for grants began and seemed to go on for a long time. The reasons we encountered for any foundation's not financing a worthy project seemed infinite; one wondered what cause could be devised to satisfy all their conditions!

Finally, during 1971, CEH obtained the support of the Department of Health and Social Security (DHSS) with a fabulous grant of £5000 for the first year. This coincided with the publication of the Government White Paper "Better Services for the Mentally Handicapped" (June 1971), which was an important landmark in the development of services in Britain. At the same time as the DHSS grant and through the support of Miles Hardie who was then Director of the Hospital Centre (now the King's Fund Centre), the King Edward VII Hospital Fund for London came up with free office space, lighting, telephone, heating, cleaning, and so forth together with £1500. A grant of £750 per annum from James Loring, Director of the Spastics Society, completed the CEH income. These were riches. Our paid staff now consisted of a part-time director (Bayes), a part-time information officer (Francklin), a full-time librarian, and a secretary. We were a strong team, and we began our new life with great enthusiasm.

A mistake was made at this time that has bugged CEH staff ever since. In the original application to the DHSS for funding, we were too sanguine about the future financing of the center. We suggested that in three year's time we might become self-supporting. We had a rosy, but somewhat vague picture of some kind of membership plan, the subscriptions to which would pay our salaries and overheads. Whether this unrealistic bait influenced the DHSS in acceding to our request for money we do not know, but successive directors of CEH have found it a source of some irritation. The short-sightedness of the suggestion has been brought home to them each year when they have sought the continued support of the DHSS; the Department has in effect said: "Well, what about Mr. Bayes' claim to be self-supporting after three years?" The main reason self-sufficiency turned out to be a vain promise can easily be summed up by saying that the need for our services has proven to be the greatest among those who do not realize that they need them and who certainly would not pay for them.

The basic problem of financing CEH has always been its hand-to-mouth nature—that is, by having to apply for continued support each year, to plead afresh each time, and to make a new case for changing conditions. Not only have successive directors spent too much of their time in fund-raising, but the lack of commitment for more than one year has inhibited long-term planning and deprived staff of security of job tenure. The director's appointment has had to remain part-time. This has been a major weakness. More progress could have been made and the center could have provided more valuable service with a full-time director.

In 1971 CEH organized the Botton symposium, which was another example of CEH activity springing from a personal concern rather than from planned strategy. Bayes had enjoyed a long connection with the Camphill villages for mentally handicapped and disturbed people. The advocates of the normalization principle with whom he aligned himself saw the villages as little different from institutions. This conflict needed resolution, and we wanted these normalization advocates to feel something of the community life of a village and to experience the difference between Botton and an institution based on the medical model.

Attendance at the symposium was by invitation to some of the main figures in the three spheres of care—special hospital, community, and village. The guests were mostly from Great Britain, but some came from abroad. The latter included Karl Grunewald, N. E. Bank-Mikkelsen, Gunnar Dybwad, Tom Mutters, and Jens Malling-Pederson, who were all persuaded to brave both the wilds of Yorkshire in September and the social rigors of "village" life. (One person, unknown to us, but whom Peter Roth from Botton had asked us to invite, was Jean Vanier. We have since regretted that he was unable to come and that the first meeting with him was not on the moors, but in a crowded Montreal conference room.) The symposium seemed mostly to be a rewarding and new experience. We hardly resolved all opposing views, but we did develop increased understanding between those involved in the different kinds of care.

The report of this symposium was one of several documents produced by CEH about this time. Bibliographies were prepared on working environments and training centres and designing for mentally handicapped people; Sandra Francklin had written a lot on educational environments and the importance of play for handicapped children. Articles were written by staff of CEH and were published in many journals, and papers and lectures were given at seminars and conferences.

THE FULL-FLEDGED CEH SERVICE

One of the main issues inherent in CEH and in any similar organization is the extent to which it should have a policy in respect to patterns of care for handicapped people. As a unit set up to provide information on the physical environment, what right have we to have views on types of care? It could be argued that we should be strictly neutral on questions of policy; that it should be our job to do everything we can to encourage the best environment for whatever pattern of care the specialists think is best; and that in the morning we could advise on the color scheme for a group home, in the afternoon discuss the plans for an extension to a 2,000-bed hospital, and in the evening give a lecture on the environmental implications of living at home without any twinge of conscience. To get involved in controversies about how the handicapped should live, work, be educated; whether their problem is medical, social or educational; whether they even have a "problem," could be seen as a dissipation of energies from our real task and an inexcusable interference in the responsibilities of other disciplines. How could we, as architects, enter into arguments with doctors, psychiatrists, psychologists, teachers, nurses, and administrators with a lifetime of experience in mental handicap?

There in fact was no real dilemma because Bayes and Francklin, from the beginning of their interest in mental handicap, had been deeply concerned with mentally handicapped people as people and not as subjects of study. The aim of CEH was to help them to live, work, play, and be educated in buildings that aided their development and made them happy. We were not interested in architecture for its own sake but in design as part of the curative, educational, and supportive process. At a lecture we gave at a conference of teachers, we proudly announced that we should not be called architects any more, but "environmental therapists"!

We believed in the value of the unique contribution of each of the disciplines involved with handicapped people, but in free collaboration and with no rigid barriers dividing them. In any case, avoiding involvement in policy is impossible because policy is indivisible from the buildings in which it is implemented. In settled times an advisory center might be able to give architectural guidance without furthering one policy at the expense of another, but in a time of rapidly changing attitudes, like the last ten years, such action is impossible. Advice either helps a progressive policy to be more effective or shows "how to do the wrong thing better." However, the attitude of CEH has been slightly ambivalent. We have been supporters of community care and have been strongly in favor of normalization, but we have also given advice to special hospitals on how they might improve their buildings or modify their interiors. We have sometimes taken the view that upgrading in hospitals should be done as well as possible because people will continue to live in them for some time and their lives should be made more bearable. Thus we instinctively adopted a British compromise (it is a good thing that we never tried to put it into a written constitution).

The noncompromising—the campaigning—impulse in CEH found another outlet. Francklin, together with Ann Shearer, launched what was soon to be the Campaign for the Mentally Handicapped, a pressure group with strong convictions on community care. The formation of CMH did not change the attitudes of CEH: We continued at CEH to try and act as "practical idealists," to give help where people would benefit, to decline gently in those cases where we thought they would not. The result in practice was that we often spent more time persuading people to change their policies or their briefs than in discussing their plans. If CEH should have been passive in policy, neutral in philosophy, objective in atti-

tude, devoted to architecture with a capital "A", and more respectful of authority and the establishment, it should have been under the control of different people.

Our wish to start a newsletter coincided with a long-felt need of the Architects Planning Committee of the International League of Societies for the Mentally Handicapped to have a regular vehicle for disseminating views and information. We agreed therefore that a joint newsletter edited and distributed in London should be issued. Four issues that appeared between late 1971 and March 1973 dealt with a variety of subjects. As a joint newsletter it was not a great success. Contributions from outside Britain to justify its claim to be international were almost nonexistent, and questions particularly pertinent to Britain did not receive enough attention. In addition, at this time CEH was beginning to find the need to provide information on other handicaps and disabilities.

In 1973 Kenneth Bayes relinquished his position as part-time director. To fill the breach the DHSS seconded George Miles, a senior member of their mental health team, to this post. Prior to this appointment, CEH had been able to secure two additional architects as consultants (also on a part-time basis), Jean Symons to prepare design guidance sheets, and Selwyn Goldsmith (also advisor to the Department of the Environment on housing services for disabled people and author of the classic RIBA publication *Designing for the Disabled*) with a special brief for physical disability.

The design guidance sheets that were initially conceived as providing concise, up-to-date basic design data were turned into two fuller design guides. The first, "Improving Existing Hospital Buildings for Long-Stay Residents," was completed in 1973 and discussed ways of upgrading the institutions that would remain for some time as homes for many people. The second, published in July 1974, was entitled "Residential Accommodation for Disabled People." This guide looked at alternative residential schemes for people who are physically handicapped and do not want or need to live in institutional environments when they can live more independently within the community. Both design guides were well received by the press and widely distributed.

The newsletter continued on a broadly domestic front, but still maintained reasonable support from abroad. It became a quarterly issue containing bibliographies (on designing for mentally handicapped people, designing for the physically handicapped, play and play equipment, and designing for old people), plans of recent new buildings or adaptations to old ones, book reviews and annotations of recent journal articles and books, some commissioned articles, and also reprints of articles from other journals. A constant problem was that of finding enough buildings, or even projects, to illustrate the philosophy towards the handicapped that now represented progressive attitudes and practice. The usual editorial problems of extracting material from contributors made timing of regular issues difficult. In effect, the newsletter became an information kit and also carried other publications by CEH. The design guides were issued to subscribers as part of the contents. Francklin's well-received and important document "Mentally Handicapped People Living in Ordinary Houses and Flats" was also included. Regular broadsheets from other disability organizations were also distributed as part of the issue.

The information service expanded to include a library of architectural plans, a good slide library, and a journal and press cutting service with every subject from designing for blind people to clinical aspects of mental handicap. The collection of books, theses, and other published material grew to around 5,000 items, and a good photographic library of buildings and the people who use them was collected. Visits were made to buildings and notes kept in a diary record file where they could be consulted by staff and visitors. There was not, however, enough close practical involvement with design research groups working at polytechnics, art colleges, or other institutions, although many people involved within this area of work did seek advice and use the reference library. The newsletter tried to keep subscribers

informed as to what research groups were doing, but there was not sufficient feedback either way.

Seminars were established on a regular monthly basis. A series of group seminars on social services and architecture was begun by George Miles, and members of multidisciplinary design teams were invited to bring along plans of buildings either at design stage, on-site, or completed, and about three teams at a time would spend the day in discussion. Such a day would perhaps include plans for a day center for mentally handicapped people, a hostel for physically handicapped children, and a school for disturbed children. Professions attending might include architects, teachers, day center managers, social services directors, and occasionally at this stage handicapped people themselves. As participation by handicapped people became more important, CEH often broke building regulations (and the King's Fund Director shut his eyes) by allowing into the building more than the obligatory maximum number of wheelchairs at any one time. This practice demonstrated how fire restrictions penalized disabled people and often stopped them from being able to join in regular activities without limitations.

Over the next few months the King's Fund Center helped by funding an exhibition entitled "Buildings for Handicapped People." Plans were submitted from all over Great Britain and a final selection was made by the staff of CEH. A wide range of building types was represented, but sadly only one or two examples of adaptations to existing buildings, or of other ways by which disabled or handicapped people could more easily live in their own homes amongst family and friends, were included. Even in mid-summer the exhibition attracted over five-hundred people and a great deal of press coverage. It certainly gave everyone an idea of how the United Kingdom was thinking at this time regarding handicapped people and buldings.

George Miles was recalled full-time to the DHSS in view of his promotion to Superintending Architect on Mental Health and increased workload and responsibilities. Jean Symons was appointed director in October 1974. The publication earlier, by a few months, of the design guide on physical handicap helped pave the way towards CEH's further involvement in physical disability. About this time both the National Health Service and local government were reorganized. The development of the new health authorities along the principle of community-based services meant that contact was made with a range of people. A minister with special responsibility for disabled people was a new government appointment.

Under the direction of Jean Symons and Selwyn Goldsmith, further seminar topics included secure units (following the Butler Committee report on accommodation for mentally handicapped and mentally abnormal offenders); the environment of blind people; the environment of people with spina bifida; community living opportunities for the mentally ill; and a similar one for mentally handicapped people. An old people's home and a home for younger physically handicapped people provided venues for further seminars on these building types, where staff and residents participated. Sometimes visitors to these meetings included guide dogs, people in respirators, friends in wheelchairs, clinicians, nurses, social workers, occupational therapists, designers, social service personnel, and of course architects.

Sometimes the need of building certain schemes and the philosophy behind them was discussed or the specific needs of particular disabilities might be considered, but at all times the seminars were kept small enough so that a very personal involvement and a sense of humor prevailed. The seminars had the added advantage of providing an unofficial meeting place where representatives from central and local government, voluntary organizations, professional workers, and handicapped people themselves could talk freely and uninhibited by bureaucratic restraints, and perhaps learn from each other how best to make life more manageable for handicapped people. There was at all times an excellent rapport with the voluntary organizations.

These meetings provided a wealth of information, especially the ones held at particular buildings. People planning similar schemes were able to meet with others from different parts of the country and to discuss from many points of view various topics with the staff and residents, such as how the building worked and more important what living and working in it was like. Architects working in this field are notoriously very poorly briefed, and many approached CEH without any idea of the kind of people they were designing for, or how the buildings should or would be used, and often with a building already commenced on site. Such elementary questions as, "Do handicapped people drive cars?" left us with an uneasy feeling. Our hope that all design teams be properly briefed became a prayer, and we pressed that anyone concerned with the daily care and welfare of the handicapped person should have a full say in the briefing and that handicapped people themselves, if possible, should participate.

CURRENT PLANS AND PROSPECTS FOR CEH

Inquirers often come to CEH for practical information on details of equipment and finishes—such as whether sluices are required, the most suitable flooring, heating systems, basic gradients for ramps toileting facilities, railing heights, and so forth—rather than basic philosophy. CEH holds much of this information, but when it is not directly available, inquirers are directed to the many organizations and individual contacts made over the years where appropriate advice can be obtained.

The poor economic climate of early 1976 and the consequent appreciable decline in new building has resulted in fewer demands on normal services, but there is still a vital need for CEH to play an educational role for the future. An important recent project undertaken by CEH was a census survey of buildings in the Greater London area that have been adapted or built for handicapped people of all kinds. The survey covered day centers, schools, housing and hostel accommodation, and special care units as well as hospitals. No comprehensive evaluation of the buildings has yet been made, but a register of addresses and accommodations now exists for the basis of future study.

If the director of an organization such as CEH is an architect and therefore competent to give professional advice, restricting his or her activities to the CEH schedule is not always easy. At times it becomes difficult not to trespass on professional preserves. CEH has always tried to be scrupulous in finding the dividing line between the free advice that it can give and the advice subject to a professional fee. The role of CEH is not that of the professional architect, planner, or interior designer. Although to date, the directors of CEH have been architects, members of other disciplines, if sensitive to the environmental needs of handicapped people, would be equally appropriate for this role and in some ways might be preferable.

An important point about CEH is its ability and freedom to criticize government policy (even people in central government departments have found CEH to be invaluable in this respect). The importance of such a center being an autonomous independent body that is free of bureaucracy or commitment to other organizations with a more limited scope—for example, one particular type of handicap—cannot be stressed enough. CEH wishes always to be involved with the crucial issues, needs, and controversies relevant to handicapped people as they develop whether nationally or internationally. Seminars, the newsletter, and personal involvement reflect this concern with current issues such as homes versus hostels, integration in education and in the community, expenditure in upgrading obsolete hospitals, and so forth.

Contact with people and organizations abroad is considered of great importance as is keeping up with all the relevant literature published in other countries. This task is not always easy since few countries have a central body through which communication can be established. CEH always welcomes overseas visitors, and one of its functions is to direct foreign inquirers to sources of information or to buildings relevant to their interests. There are many friends of CEH abroad who willingly reciprocate for British visitors to their

own countries. However, we cannot stress too strongly the value of other groups establishing active CEHs in other countries.

At the present time CEH is going through a transition period—a kind of coming of age—which therefore provides a good moment for us to take stock—that is, to see in which areas CEH in the past has fulfilled its aims and in the future could meet new needs and challenges. This review can be considered from two points of view: the outer form (or structure) of CEH and the creative work of CEH.

Steps are at present being taken to clarify its outer form. Some would say that this measure is desirable for the smooth working of the administration; others would go further and say that it is essential for survival. A written constitution is being prepared with a view to registration as a charitable body, thereby giving an established status to CEH and at the same time enabling it more easily to qualify for grants from foundations and other sources, benefit from tax concessions or subscriptions made "under covenant," and so forth. The constitution will establish a membership structure, the setting up of a policy and general management committee (instead of the present advisory council) under the guidance of a chairman and treasurer, a set procedure for annual general meetings, and so forth—all of which make up the normal framework for any organization of this kind.

This degree of establishment should enable CEH to cope better with two aspects that have been inadequately handled in the past (especially by its founder-director): finance and publicity. Secure financial support for continuity in its work program has already been cited as a CEH problem. Our opinion is that a center of this kind will always need outside funding, but its own capacity to earn some money could be increased to the benefit of its own bank balance and to the encouragement of its backers. For instance, in the year ending March 1975, CEH made a profit of some £500 on the sale of publications and seminar attendance fees. Under more astute business management, these fees and similar sources of income might be substantially increased. Although membership can never support the full activities of CEH, some plan for subscriptions from members or friends of the center could be evolved.

Side by side with increased financial support is the need for CEH to be better known among politicians and high-level civil servants, within local government circles, to professionals concerned with handicapped people, within the media, and in society generally. These dual and interrelated needs of fund-raising and public relations, previously somewhat neglected, may call for a revised staff structure at the top of CEH. The director might more appropriately be more business and publicity orientated than in the past, and the creative work of the center might be better guided by a co-director freed of these responsibilities. There could be an increase in part-time consultant staff, or the policy and general management committee could be more representative of the different handicaps and services and could themselves be called on freely to give advice if necessary. Projects could be given to student or other appointees on a part-time basis.

What about the work that CEH exists to undertake? Has it provided the service set out in its aims? How can it better fulfill its function and provide a more complete service? CEH can reasonably claim that it has given valuable advice and information to people in many varied disciplines concerned with the physical environment of people with many kinds of handicaps. This service has been through personal consultations, seminars and conferences, the newsletters, special publications, and the library. CEH has provided a forum for many different views—that is, it has been a catalyst of ideas to be transformed into action. It has stayed in the forefront of progressive thinking and has remained free of the pressures and restrictions of bureaucracy (it is important that this freedom is retained in spite of a more formal structure).

There will always be needs for CEH to meet. The emphasis and the needs themselves will change in response to such outside conditions as prosperity or economic stringency. At all times there will be both needs of the current time and preparation for the future, but the emphasis between them will vary according to the ouside conditions. The response to economic recession (at the time of writing) must be planning for the future and the formulation of a foward-looking program.

In the past, the activities of CEH have depended largely on the individual interests of the directors and consultants. Fortunately, these have largely coincided with the main issues of national and international concern. But a more specifically planned strategy would ensure concentration of pressure and energy in areas where it is most needed at the time. For instance, the combination of an economic crisis and a disenchantment with professionals could so increase the necessity and demand for public participation and self-help that CEH should turn its attention now to a study of how these aspects of help can be applied to the provision of the right environment for handicapped people.

Ideally the new phase now beginning for CEH in Great Britain should coincide with and be related to the starting of similar centers in other countries. An international network would enormously enhance the service of any national center. The structure and financing of centers in other countries would naturally follow national patterns, but the aims of the services offered would vary little from couuntry to country, even if the methods of collecting, storing, and disseminating information varied in degree of sophistication.

The most valuable and, in some ways, the easiest collaboration would be between CEH in Great Britain and a similar center established in the United States. The importance of such a dual enterprise would lie in its representing in total so large a proportion of the English-speaking world and its ability to cover sources of information in Europe and on the American continent. A joint working out of programs and activities and of exchanging and distributing information could be of great value.

The experience of growing pains from which CEH has benefitted during its seven years have brought it to a mature stage of development. It is now ready not only to begin a new phase in Britain, but also to develop a coordinated strategy for a similar center in the United States, to the benefit of both countries, in a way that would not have been possible earlier.

NOTES AND REFERENCES

The views expressed in this chapter are those of the authors and do not necessarily represent the views of past or present directors, staff, or advisory council members of CEH.

1. Members of the 1969 advisory council are as follows: Lady Allen of Hurtwood, FILA, Handicapped Adventure Playgrounds Association. (resigned 1974); Lady Hamilton, OBE, MA, Chairman, Disabled Living Foundation; Miles Hardie, MA, FHA, Director, King's Fund Centre and present Director, International Hospital Federation; Kenneth Holt, MD, FRCP, DCH, child psychiatrist and Director, Wolfson Centre; Brian Kirman, MD, DPM, child psychiatrist; George Lee, OBE, Secretary-General, National Society for Mentally Handicapped Children. Christopher Ounsted, DM, MRCP, DCH, DPM, child psychiatrist; Mia Kellmer Pringle, BA, PhD, DSc, Director, National Children's Bureau, represented by Dr. Jessie Parfit (resigned 1974); George Stroh, MB, BS, DPM, child psychiatrist; and Jack Tizard, CBE, MA, BLitt, PdD, Institute of Education, University of London. The following members were coopted in 1971: James Elliott, MBE, FHA, Director, Mental Handicap Project, King's Fund Centre; James Loring, Director, Spastics Society; Hugh Freeman, MA, BM, BCh, DPM, FRCPsych, psychiatrist; and Howard Goodman, DiplArch, RIBA, Chief Architect, Department of Health and Social Security. The following were co-opted 1972 or later: David Hobman, Director, Age Concern, (resigned 1974); Edith Morgan, MA, Deputy-Director, National Association for Mental Health; Peter Waugh, BSc(Econ), sociologist, Milton Keynes Development Corporation; Sheila Garrett, SRN, RNT, Senior Nursing Officer, St. Thomas' Hospital and presently with the King's Fund College; and Kenneth Bayes, RIBA, FSIA, architect.
2. International League of Societies for the Mentally Handicapped, "Residential care for the Mentally Retarded," Seminar, Frankfurt, September 1969.

Selected Bibliography

CEH design guides

J. Symons. "Improving Existing Hospital Buildings for Long-Stay Residents." London: CEH, 1973.

J. Symons. "Residential Accommodation for Disabled People." London: CEH, 1974.

CEH bibliographies

CEH. "Introduction to Design for Mentally Handicapped People," revised. London, 1975.
CEH. "Play and Play Equipment for Handicapped Children," Revised. London, 1975.
CEH. "Design of Training Centres and Workshops for Handicapped People. London, 1972.
CEH. "Designing for Old People. London, 1973.
CEH. "Designing for the Physically Handicapped, Revised. London, 1975.

Other CEH publications

CEH. "Designing for Mentally Handicapped People—Residential Care." Full conference text. London, 1971.
CEH. "Patterns of Residential Care—Botton Symposium." London, 1971.
Francklin, S. "Planning for Play for Mentally Handicapped Children," revised. London: CEH.
Francklin, S. "Mentally Handicapped People Living in Ordinary Houses and Flats." London, CEH.
Gardner, R. Appendix to "Buildings for People Who Are Handicapped or Disabled." Updated 1975.
Gardner, R., and J. Symons. "Buildings for People Who Are Handicapped or Disabled: A Pilot Survey in the Greater London Area." London: CEH, 1975.

Non-CEH publications handled by CEH

Bayes, K. *The Therapeutic Effect of Environment on Emotionally Disturbed and Mentally Subnormal Children.* London, 1967. (Presently out of print.)
Bayes, K., and S. Francklin. (eds.). *Designing for the Handicapped.* London: George Godwin, 1971.
Elliott, J., and K. Bayes. *Room for Improvement.* London: King's Fund Centre, 1972.
Note: The address of CEH is 24 Nutford Place, London, W1H, 6AN, England.

Index